THE POETICAL WORKS

OF

MATTHEW ARNOLD

COMPLETE EDITION
WITH BIOGRAPHICAL INTRODUCTION

———o∘⟨∗⟩∘o———

NEW YORK: 46 EAST 14TH STREET
THOMAS Y. CROWELL & COMPANY
BOSTON: 100 PURCHASE STREET

Norwood Press
J. S. Cushing & Co. — Berwick & Smith
Norwood Mass. U.S.A.

CONTENTS.

PAGE

LYRIC AND DRAMATIC POEMS.

ELEGIAC POEMS.

LATER POEMS.

ADDITIONAL EARLY POEMS.

NOTE.

THE present edition of the poetical works of Matthew Arnold is enriched by the addition of all of his earlier and later poems, hitherto uncollected. This includes a reprint of his two prize poems, "Alaric at Rome" and "Cromwell"; the first having been recently discovered in almost unique copies, has attracted much attention and interest not only as the earliest known work of their talented author, but also for its inherent beauty and power.

This edition is therefore most complete in every respect. The brief Biography depends chiefly for its accuracy on the interesting series of letters edited by Mr. George W. C. Russell, and on the friendly criticism of Prof. Charles Eliot Norton, who was one of Mr. Matthew Arnold's most intimate friends.

BIOGRAPHICAL INTRODUCTION.

MATTHEW ARNOLD was born at Laleham, in the valley of the Thames, December 24, 1822. He was the oldest son of "the great and good" Thomas Arnold, so well known as the Head Master of Rugby School. His grandfather Arnold was Collector of Customs at Cowes on the Isle of Wight. His mother was Mary, daughter of the Reverend John Penrose, Vicar of Fledborough Nolls.

When he was eight years old, he became a pupil of his uncle, the Reverend John Buckland, with whom he continued at Laleham until August, 1836, when he entered "Commoners" at Winchester under Dr. Moberly, afterwards Bishop of Salisbury. Matthew Arnold took such high rank in the school that he escaped the "austere system" of fagging then in vogue, and his father, who had desired him to have the full benefit of it, removed him to Rugby at the end of a year. There he had a training for which he rejoiced all his life: it was, to use his own words, "so unworldly, so sound, so pure."

In 1840 he won a school-prize with a poem, "Alaric at Rome," which was published anonymously and has since become very scarce, only four copies being extant. It has been recently republished and commended by able critics for its depth of thought and accuracy of form. Having been elected to an open classical scholarship at Balliol, he went to Oxford the following year. Before he left Rugby he distinguished himself by winning a School-Exhibition. In 1842 he won the Hertford Scholarship; in 1843 his poem on Cromwell brought him the Newdigate Prize. It was not delivered aloud, the students being too uproarious, but it was published in an edition of seven hundred and fifty copies, all of which were sold within a few days. He received ten pounds for the copyright. He was elected Fellow of Oriel in 1845, just thirty years after the election of his father. Arthur Hugh Clough, Dean Church, and other noted men were among his colleagues at the famous college. After teaching the classics for a short time in the Fifth Form at Rugby, he was appointed Private Secretary to the Earl of Lansdowne, Lord President of the Council.

As early as 1848 he began to sound his trumpet against the fictitiousness of English manners and civility and to find in Greek serenity a lesson for all time. He clearly saw what civilization in England lacked, and he felt that he could add to the sum of happiness by stimulating his fellow-men to find in true culture a nobler ideal for their lives. Like other prophets and seers, he was misunderstood and cordially disliked by the very lasses whom he wished to help. In 1849, while the world was in a state of ferment and revolution, he read Homer from beginning to end. He also published "The Strayed Reveller and Other Poems," in an edition of five hundred copies, the title-page having only the initial A. as indication of the authorship. It was withdrawn from circulation before many copies were sold; but all the poems it contained, with one exception, were afterwards reprinted.

In 1851 he found himself withdrawing more and more from society, despising modern literature, which he declared was "only what has been before and what will be again and not bracing or edifying in the least." For months he did not look at a newspaper.

But this same year he was appointed to an Inspectorship of Schools and married Frances Lucy, daughter of Mr. Justice Wightman. For him he often acted in the capacity of Marshal on the Circuits. This gave him an opportunity of seeing some of the most delightful parts of England, together with the most satisfying companionship.

The duties of his school-inspecting kept him constantly on the move. He found the work very oppressive, but his sense of duty was such that he never allowed the feeling to get too strong. His wife frequently accompanied him, and that was "the only thing that made this life anything but positive purgatory."

Such work was necessary, but, in view of Matthew Arnold's genius and his peculiarly lofty qualifications for statesmanship and the higher realms of literature, it makes one's heart bleed to read of his long years of comparatively unremunerative drudgery, of his having to apply that unrivalled mind to the pettiness of examining an average of sixty or more schoolboy compositions a day, of his "being driven furious by seven hundred closely written grammar-papers to be looked over" when he was desirous of doing better things. Oftentimes he mentions, though without complaint, the necessity of examining scores of pupil-teachers in small and inconvenient rooms and going without proper food. Pheidias may make good sandals, but to keep him at it would be a loss to sculpture.

But all the pleasanter were his vacations, which gave him time for employments that he liked, for writing his poems, perhaps taking a few weeks' run upon the Continent, where always, if possible, he sought regions abounding in clear waters. He published in 1852 (semi-anonymously, as before) " Empedocles on Etna," but withdrew it from circulation ere fifty copies were sold; the following year the first series of his " Poems" appeared, with a preface of considerable length. The volume contained nine new titles, among them " Sohrab and Rustum " and " The Scholar Gypsy." In 1854 it went into a second edition with some changes. In 1855 the " second series" of his "Poems" appeared.

In 1856 he wrote his mother of his delight at being elected to the Athenæum Club, and of looking forward with rapture to the use of that Library when he should be in London. He found it a place at which he " enjoyed something like beatitude." The following year he was made Professor of Poetry at Oxford. His first lecture was on the Modern Element in Literature. He afterwards wrote that he almost always had a very fair attendance. " To be sure, it is chiefly composed of ladies," he adds, but he reconciled himself by thinking, as he composed his lectures, ' of the public who would read him, not of the dry bones who would hear him.'

He wrote this year his tragedy of " Merope," as he said, ' to inaugurate his professorship with dignity rather than to move deeply the present race of humans.' He tried to give it " a character of Fixity, that true sign of the law." It was published and had a fair success, though he complained that the British public found it hard to understand his attempted reproduction of the power, grandeur, and dignity of the Greek imagination. He wrote a friend that the poem was reviewed " very expostulatingly."

He would have liked to devote his whole life to poetry, as Wordsworth, Byron, and Shelley were able to do. But he found it no light matter to produce his best — all that was in him — with such a " hampered existence." He felt and resisted the temptation to transfer his poetic operations " to a region where form was everything." It was effort, it was a tearing of himself to pieces to do his best "to attain or approach perfection in the region of thought and to unite this with perfection of form." He found the exhaustion of the best poetical production, coupled with the claims of his serious work, a tremendous strain. Goethe, he reminded himself, was likewise hampered by "the endless matters" that claimed his attention. Indeed, all poets have found fault with their environment: one with his professorship, another with his lectures, another with his very idleness. The birds may very likely say that if it were not for the atmosphere they could fly to the stars!

But Matthew Arnold was not a complaining man. As the editor of his letters says: "Self-denial was the law of his life, yet the word never crossed his lips." What a lovely record that, while always working beyond the limits of his strength, "he never by a word or a sign betrayed a consciousness of the dull indifference to his gifts and services which stirred the fruitless indignation of his friends."

His capacity for work was extraordinary. Occasionally in his letters he hints at the demands upon him. We catch glimpses of him examining half a dozen schools in a day, looking over scores of examination papers, putting his hand to the stores of his well-ordered mind to write reviews or essays for magazines, preparing his Oxford lectures; yet never, amid all the rush of his busy existence, did he neglect the claims of his dearly beloved family, his mother, or his sister, or (if he happened to be away from home) his wife: writing them the fullest, sweetest, happiest letters, giving himself in them as a child gives the typical cup of cold water to a thirsty traveller.

In 1858 he took a house in London, in Chester Square, and, for the first time in the seven years after his marriage, settled down to live.

The following year he was sent abroad as Foreign Assistant Commissioner to report on the Systems of Continental Education. This enabled him not only to see the inner life of France and other countries, but also to travel in a leisurely and satisfactory way. He was fond of beautiful Nature, and his prose descriptions of scenery have a genuinely poetic touch.

On his return he embodied some of his foreign experiences in a pamphlet entitled "England and the Italian Question." He felt that he had inherited from his father his pamphleteering talent. "Even the positive style of statement," he said, "I inherit."

At this time he joined the Queen's Westminster Rifle Volunteers and greatly enjoyed the drilling which he felt "braces one's muscles and does one a world of good."

He was always fond of sport with gun and rod: he keenly enjoyed shooting grouse on a Scotch moor or pulling in a two-pound trout from a clear sparkling mountain stream. His first salmon was a matter of chronicle.

Before he had reached the age of forty he had recognized his special function, already early indicated: it was to tame "the wild beast of Philistinism," using literature as his method. "I have always the risk before me," he said, "of being torn to pieces by him and, even if I succeed to the utmost, of dying in a ditch or a workhouse at the end of it all." He hated with a royal hatred what he called "the vulgarity, the meddlesomeness, and the grossness of the British multitude." They were "Philistines"; but the Aristocracy, so blinded in their confirmed conservatism, were "Barbarians." And the epithets became by-words.

Yet, in spite of his severe criticism on men, manners, and morals, he early determined, and he never failed, "to be scrupulously polite in print," and though he was equally determined to say imperturbably what he thought and to make a great many people uncomfortable, yet he saw that the great thing was "to speak without a particle of vice, malice, or rancor." Time, study, and nature taught him "the precious truth" that everything turns on the way one exercises the power of persuasion and charm, and that without it, all fury, energy, reasoning power, and acquirement were thrown away and rendered their owner more miserable. "Even in one's ridicule," he said, "one must preserve a sweetness and good humor."

Perfectly sweet-tempered himself, he dissociated personality from criticism, and while respecting authors he was often relentless in his judgment of their works. This severity he applied to Thackeray and Ruskin, to Tennyson and Coventry Patmore, to Swinburne and Mrs. Browning. His favorites, after the Greek poets, were Wordsworth and Goethe.

He expressed frankly his own feelings under criticism: at first he felt annoyed; then he cheered himself by remembering how, within a few days, the effect of it upon him would have wholly passed, and then he would begin to think of the openings which he might find to answer back, and so he quickly recovered his gayety and good spirits and was enabled to look on the article as "simply an object of interest" to him.

Under all his serious views of life and the deep sense of responsibility which he felt over his task of inoculating the British public with intelligence, there was hidden largely from common sight but well known to his family and friends a fund of brightness, of radiant wit, of frank, boyish, totally inoffensive self-satisfaction. He liked sympathetic appreciation, especially of his poetry. One feels nearer to his humanity when one reads in a letter to his mother how he walked up Regent Street behind a man with a board on his back announcing his article on Marcus Aurelius. Such hearty acknowledgment of what many men would hypocritically pretend to ignore makes us love him. That it was not conceit is shown by many fearless passages in his home letters: "to be less *personal* in *one's* desires and workings is the great matter . . . for progress in the direction of the 'seeketh not her own' there is always room."

Severely as he attacked the faults of England, he loved her fondly, and it was no idle echo of Gilbert's Admiral when he declared that he would be "sorry to be a Frenchman, German, or American or anything but an Englishman." His respect for America rose higher after the tragic ending of the War of the Rebellion. He was at first inclined to sympathize with the South, not because he sympathized with slavery, but because, judging of the North from the utterances of compromise-seeking politicians, he drew the erroneous conclusion that the North had little character. He was by nature an aristocrat in the best sense of the word and believed in centralization and concentration of government. It was characteristic of him that he found a dramatic interest in the assassination of Lincoln, by reason of the fact that the assassin shouted in Latin as he leapt on the stage.

In 1861 he published three of his Oxford lectures, under the title, "On Translating Homer," in which he severely criticised various versions, — Chapman's, Pope's, Maginn's, Newman's, Wright's, — and showed how they failed — in rapidity, in plainness, directness, and simplicity of style and of ideas, or in nobleness of diction. He himself gave a few examples of what, in his opinion, should be the method of the translator: he chose the hexameter as best reproducing the qualities of Homeric verse, and he conclusively showed that if he had proceeded to translate the whole, it would have approached very near the highest possible ideal. But he left only a few fragments. His lectures gave rise to some controversy, and the following year he issued a fourth essay, entitled "Lost Words on Translating Homer," in which he good-humoredly replied to his critics.

In April, 1865, he was sent abroad for eight months to make further reports on the Continental Schools. He did not like the Italians and believed them incapable of self-government. He thought them "no more civilized by their refinement alone than the English by their energy alone."

Matthew Arnold was a good type of the modern prophet, but his prophecies were not always justified by events: as he thought the new realm of Italy was only a fair-weather kingdom, so he declared that the French would easily defeat the Germans. What he saw in Germany was for the most part unattractive millions inconceivably ugly and speaking a hideous language. His dislike for America and Americans, as standing for the opposite of all his ideals, almost reached contempt. He himself denied that he had contempt for unintellectual people. But his expressions made people think so. He once wrote to his wife : "I am much struck with the utter unfitness of women for teachers or lecturers." These prejudices, which have to be taken into consideration, for the world judged him by them, misjudged him by them, were the defects of his qualities.

They never influenced his warmth of heart, his loyal affection for friends of every race, whether Italians, Germans, or Americans! Few, except his intimates, knew how constantly he went about doing good: looking after the interests of employés and school teachers. Once it was his duty as inspector sharply to criticise a certain school : the school-master, nevertheless, re-marked of him that he was "always gentle and patient with the children."

His tenderness to his own children, his thought for their comfort, his beautiful affection for his dear old mother, to whom he wrote long letters no matter how busy he was, find in his letters their unaffected affecting record. Once he expresses his delight at receiving a box of Manila cheroots, not for himself, for he did not smoke, but to send to his brother, "dear old Tom," who had too few creature comforts. He tells his mother his daily occupations:—

Writing letters before breakfast, working at his Club or at the rooms of the School Society six or seven hours, then at home till midnight, with perhaps an hour's recreation — botanizing in summer, skating in winter — every moment full. It was his ambition to use the years from forty till fifty with poetry, but he did not escape the fatal drudgery.

This year appeared his "Essays in Criticism," eight of the nine being articles reprinted from various reviews. These calm, serene, impartial studies in the highest regions of philosophic and literary thought immediately placed Matthew Arnold on a level with Goethe in Germany, with Saint-Beuve, Taine, and Scherer in France. There had been English critics before, but in his own field Matthew Arnold stood alone and unapproached.

In 1866 he applied for a vacant charity commissionership which would have brought him in £300 more salary, but it was given to a lawyer, as he supposed it would be.

In 1867 he applied for the librarianship of the House of Commons, not really caring much for it, as the residence no longer went with it, but for his wife's sake. He disliked to ask for it, but was almost reconciled to the disagreeableness by the great kindness shown him. He failed to get it. This same year his "New Poems" appeared: they were all "new" except seven, which, at the earnest solicitation of Robert Browning, he reprinted from "Empedocles on Etna." One thousand copies were quickly sold. He brought out, also, his remarks on the Study of Celtic Literature: they were the substance of four lectures delivered at Oxford; for the first time English readers were made to see what a deep and lofty influence the hitherto despised Celt had exercised in helping to develop the most poetic elements of their literature.

Early in 1868 his "dear, dear little man," his youngest son, Basil, died; he himself fell at a railway station and was seriously injured. He moved to Harrow, where he took a comfortable house with ample grounds. Here, in November, his oldest son, Thomas, died at the age of sixteen. Deeply as he felt the loss of these dear ones, and of his brother William, and of his wife's father in the preceding years, his trust that all was well was unbroken. Bereavements and disappointments serve only to strengthen the really noble. In spite of growing older he felt no older, and he attributed his youthfulness of feelings to his "going on reading and thinking." At this time he had been seeing a good deal of high society at Aston Clinton, where the Rothschilds lived. He was very fond of Sir Anthony and Lady Rothschild, and he confessed that he "liked these occasional appearances in the world, — No," he adds, " I do not like them, but they do one good and one learns something from them; but, as a general rule, I agree with all the men of soul from Pythagoras to Byron in thinking that this type of society is the most drying, wasting, depressing, and fatal thing possible."

In 1869 he published his Essay in Political and Social Criticism entitled "Culture and Anarchy," which had previously appeared in successive numbers of the *Cornhill Magazine*, and which attracted great attention, especially through his application of the phrase "Sweetness and Light." He was always most pleased when commendation of his works took this form: "the ideas of it are exactly what papa would have approved." This same year he was asked by the Italian Government to take charge of the young Duke of Genoa, Prince Thomas of Savoy, who was to study at Harrow, and the project greatly pleased him because of the Continental connection which it gave him. He found the Prince "a dear boy" and grew very fond of him. He stayed with the Arnolds until April, 1871, and then the King gave Matthew Arnold the Order of Commander of the Crown of Italy as a token of his good will.

His collected Poems came out in two pretty volumes. He says of them that they represent, on the whole, the main movement of mind of the preceding quarter-century. He thought that it might be fairly urged against them that he had less poetical sentiment than Tennyson and less intellectual vigor and abundance than Browning. But he thought that, as he had "more of a fusion of the two than either of them and had more regularly applied that fusion to the main line of modern development," he was likely to have his turn as they had theirs. He had practically ceased his career as a productive poet as early as 1869; between that date and his death scarcely more than half a dozen titles are added to the succeeding editions of his works. More and more he contented himself with his special function as censor of public morals, as lay preacher to an obdurate generation. He felt that this was his life work, and so sacrificed his predilections to his lofty sense of duty.

He was at this time considering the prospect of one of the three commissionerships under "the Endowed Schools Act," but Gladstone blocked his way, and he was not sorry, because it would have substituted administrative for literary work: literature being, as he felt, his true business. He was greatly pleased the following year by being made Doctor of Civil Law at Oxford. He had doubted if he should ever have that distinction, not having won high honors while there. "The position of a man of letters," he said, " is uncertain, and more uncertain in the eyes of his own University than anywhere else." When he went up to receive it, Lord Salisbury, the Chancellor, told him that some one suggested to him to address him as *vir dulcissime et lucidissime*, so much had his favorite expression "Sweetness and Light" impressed people.

He was shortly afterwards invited with his wife to go, in company with Tennyson, in the Royal Society's expedition to see the eclipse from Etna. But he was unable to accept the tempting offer.

He lets a little light in on his literary profits when he tells his mother of an amusing interview he had in December, 1870, with the Tax Commissioner who had assessed his profits at £1000 a year, on the ground that he was a most distinguished literary man, his works mentioned everywhere. Matthew Arnold said: "You see before you, gentlemen, what you have often heard of, an unpopular author." Whereupon the assessment was cut down to £200 a year.

In February, 1872, Matthew Arnold's second son, Trevenen William, a youth of great promise and universally beloved, died quite suddenly at the age of eighteen. It was a great blow to his parents, but Matthew Arnold's beautiful faith enabled him to write:

> *But him on whom, in the prime*
> *Of life, with vigor undimmed,*
> *With unspent mind, and a soul*
> *Unworn, undebased, undecayed,*
> *Mournfully grating, the gates*
> *Of the city of death have forever closed,—*
> *Him, I count him, well-starred.*

In 1873 the Arnolds, after having enjoyed a trip to Italy, left Harrow and took a house at Pain's Hill, near Cobham in Surrey: this was his home for the rest of his life. In September his mother, Mrs. Thomas Arnold of Fox How, died at the age of eighty-two. Matthew Arnold said of her that she had "a clearness and fairness of mind, an interest in things and a power of appreciating what might not be in her own line, which were very remarkable and which remained with her to the very end of her life." Her character seems to show in the very letters which Matthew Arnold sent her. Her appreciation of her son's work was very dear to him: even his "Literature and Dogma," which went through four editions that year, was not too strong for her advanced thinking.

In 1877 he was invited to stand for the Chair of Poetry at Oxford a second time; but he declined, partly so as to give younger men a chance, partly because he dreaded "the religious row" which he knew would ensue. He also declined to accept the Lord Rectorship of St. Andrews.

In 1882 he announced his intention of retiring from his office as one of her majesty's Lay Inspectors of Schools; he felt that his life was drawing to an end, and as Gladstone, he knew, would never promote the author of "Literature and Dogma," he had "no wish to execute the Dance of Death in an elementary school."

The following year he was asked to give a series of lectures in the United States, and he also received, to his surprise, the offer of a pension of £250 "as a public recognition of service to the poetry and literature of England." But he was inclined to refuse it on the ground that, as the fund available for such purposes was small, it would not look well if a man drawing from the public purse nearly £1000 a year took such a material increase; but his friends were so urgent that at last he yielded, and only the *Echo* sneeringly called him a "a very Bonaparte" for rapacity.

Before he came to America he had to a considerable extent formed his judgment of this country. This is a rather dangerous but quite natural way of doing. It is easy afterwards to make what one sees confirm the prejudice. As early as June, 1883, he wrote to his friend, the Reverend F. B. Zincke: —

"You are very favorable to the Americans, but it is undoubtedly true that the owning and cultivating one's own land as they do is the wholesomest condition for mankind. And you bring out what is most important, that the real America is made up of families and owners and cultivators of this kind. I hope this is true; one hears so much of the cities which do not seem tempting, and of the tendency of every American, farmer or not, to turn into a trader, and a trader of the 'cutest and hardest kind.

"I do not think the bulk of the American nation at present gives one the impression of being made up of fine enough clay to serve the highest purposes of civilization in the way you expect; they are what I call *Philistines*, I suspect, too many of them. But the condition of life of the majority there is the wholesome and good one; there is immense hope for the future in that fact."

In October, after a stormy but "splendid" passage, he landed in New York, "the blatant publicity" of which confirmed his worst fears. But he soon found how well known he was, and it modified his ideas of American philistinism to have hotel barbers and porters reverencing him as a poet and asking for his autograph. Dr. Holmes, whom he called a dear little old man, introduced him to his Boston audience. He was most struck with the buoyancy, enjoyment and freedom from constraint, the universal good nature of the American people. He found much pseudo-culture: few men of note had ever heard of Obermann, and as a knowledge of Obermann was in his eyes a test of civilization, he thought our philistinism extremely depressing, all the more when it was often glossed over with a varnish of pretence. Some individuals even confused him with Sir Edwin Arnold, and supposed that he was the author of "Tom Brown": these confusions naturally disgusted him.

But on the whole he grew more and more interested in the American people, and his lectures were a success from the start. His fee was $150, and, besides what he made, he felt that he was learning much. His delight in some of the *chefs-d'œuvre* of the American table was quite amusing. He was ready to hymn a panegyric to the Yankee Cock-tail! He was delighted with the Richmond schools for negroes and "could have passed hours there." He preferred Philadelphia to Boston. He found nothing picturesque in America except a sledge on a lake with the horses half turned round.

He was greatly amused at the comments of the newspapers. A Chicago paper declared that he had "harsh features, super-cilious manners, parted his hair down the middle, wore a single eye-glass and ill-fitting clothes." A Detroit newspaper com-pared him, as he stooped now and then to look at his manu-script, to "an elderly bird pecking at grapes on a trellis."

After his return from the United States he was sent for the third time to the Continent to report on schools, and was cor-dially received by the most exclusive circles. Most of the time he was in Prussia. His eldest daughter married a gentleman in New York, and he was in this country again in the summer of 1886 lecturing and taking great delight in "nursing" his little granddaughter. He thought the wooden American coun-try-house with its great piazza the prettiest villa in the world.

On his return to England he retired definitely from his inspectorship, the Westminster teachers presenting him with a handsome jug and salver.

Before and during his summer in America he had premoni-tions of heart trouble, — the same malady which had struck down his father and grandfather in active life. He regarded death as a quite natural event and did not look forward to it with dread. In April, 1888, he went to Liverpool, expecting, on the day after his arrival, to meet his elder daughter coming from America. But the meeting never took place. An hour before the steamship was due he started out in the best of spirits to take the tram-car. He may have hurried a little; he had already neglected the physician's injunctions and exerted himself in leaping a low fence near his sister's house. He suddenly fell forward, and never spoke again. He died on the fifteenth at the age of sixty-five years and three months.

"The lives and deaths of the 'pure in heart,'" he himself said, "have perhaps the privilege of touching us more deeply than those of others, partly, no doubt, because with them the disproportion of suffering to desert seems so unusually great."

Matthew Arnold was one of the great intellectual and moral forces of the century. As an essayist he was one of the first to raise criticism to its true significance, placing it on foundations of reason and justice, dissociating from it the elements of personality, making it free, broad, and generous, however severe it might be. And it was never destructive, but always constructive, criticism; he never failed in all that he wrote to reiterate his persuasive assertion of the superiority of the intellectual life. If he failed at all, it was in carrying the virtue of fastidiousness to an extreme.

As a moralist, or perhaps rather as a lay-preacher of theology, he took a position even more radical than that which in his father had so offended the conservative members of the Anglican Church. He never wearied of attacking the narrowness of the English dissenters and showing up the bareness and unlovliness of their cherished creeds. The great middle class of England which he termed materialized, and the lower class which he said was brutalized, cordially detested him for the "artful iteration" by which he called attention to their foibles. His Parthian arrows, in the form of memorable phrases, stuck in their armor and rankled. As they were tipped, not with poison, but with the wholesome bitterness of reason, they ultimately inoculated many unwilling readers with that restlessness and dissatisfaction which bring about a healthier moral state. He was called a Jeremiah, preaching a doctrine of pessimism; but no epithet was unfairer. What he strenuously strove to communicate to the great people which he loved was more abundant life, a more reasonable faith, a sweeter and more luminous view of God's action in the world. As a theological writer Matthew Arnold's influence has so passed into our later thought that he already seems almost trite, but that was inevitable. After prophecy has been fulfilled, the prophet is forgotten. With hammer blows he reiterated his teaching until he compelled the heedless to hear. He had a noble message nobly delivered: he had command of wit, of learning, of persuasion.

As a poet his voice fell silent far too soon. He was not a lyrical poet: composers would not select his verses as perfect in rhythm for setting to music; but they had serene depths of sincerity and a lucidity of thought which marked them out from the wordy beauty of others who perhaps for the time enjoyed greater popularity. He will take his place as one of the greatest poets of this century; beside Wordsworth, with whom he had much in common, to whom he was in some respects — certainly as regard balance and symmetry — immeasurably superior. Lord Beaconsfield once remarked that he was the only living Englishman who had become a classic in his lifetime. "Sohrab," "Balder Dead," "Tristram and Iseult," "The Strayed Reveller," "The Forsaken Merman," "Philomela," "A Summer Night," "Dover Beach," or "Rugby Chapel" are not likely to be forgotten so long as the English tongue is read. As a man, judged by the testimony of his friends and the sincerity of his letters, he was lovable, simple, honest, straightforward, and kind.

NATHAN HASKELL DOLE.

BOSTON, January, 1897.

BIBLIOGRAPHY

OF

MATTHEW ARNOLD'S POETRY.

———◆◇◆———

1840.   ALARIC AT ROME. | A prize poem, | recited in Rugby
School, | June xii, MDCCCXL. | [*Arms of the School.*] |
Rugby: Combe & Crossley. | MDCCCXL.   8vo.   11 pp.

1843.   CROMWELL. | A prize poem, | recited in the Theatre,
Oxford, | June 28, 1843. | By | Matthew Arnold, |
Balliol College. | [*Arms of Oxford.*] | Oxford: |
Printed and published by J. Vincent. | MDCCCXLIII.
12mo.   15 pp.

1846.   OXFORD PRIZE POEMS.   The edition of Oxford Prize
Poems, dated 1846, includes CROMWELL (pp. 393–
404).   It is not stated anywhere in the volume that
the poem is by Matthew Arnold.

OXFORD PRIZE POEMS. | Being | a Collection | of such |
English Poems | as have | at various times obtained
Prizes | in the | University of Oxford. | [*Arms of
Oxford.*] | Printed for J. H. Parker, J. Vincent, |
and H. Slatter. | MDCCCXLVI.   Crown 8vo.   iv + 427
pp.

1849.   THE | STRAYED REVELLER, | and | Other Poems. |
By A. | London: | B. Fellowes, Ludgate Street. |
1849.   Small 8vo.   viii + 128 pp.

1852.   EMPEDOCLES ON ETNA, | and | Other Poems. | By A. |
London: | B. Fellowes, Ludgate Street. | 1852.   Small
8vo.   viii + 236 pp.

1853. POEMS. | By | Matthew Arnold. | A New Edition. | London: | Longman, Brown, Green, and Longmans. | MDCCCLIII. Foolscap 8vo. xxxvi + 248 pp. [Afterwards known as *First Series.*]

1854. POEMS. | Second Edition. | London: | Longman, Brown, Green, and Longmans. | MDCCCLIV. [Preface: v–viii pp. Preface to Ed. I., ix–xxxv.] Five poems omitted: *Thekla's Answer, Richmond Hill, Power of Youth, A Modern Sappho,* and *Sonnet written in Emerson's Essays;* one poem, *A Farewell,* added; also greater part of *Note to Sohrab and Rustum,* pp. 51–59.

1855. POEMS. | By | Matthew Arnold. | Second Series. | London: | Longman, Brown, Green, and Longmans. | MDCCCLV. Foolscap 8vo. viii + 210 pp.

1857. POEMS. | By | Matthew Arnold. | Third Edition. | London: | Longman, Brown, Green, Longmans, & Roberts. | 1857. [One new poem added, *To Marguerite;* the poem thus named in two previous editions under *Switzerland* being charged to *Isolation.*]

1858. MEROPE. | A Tragedy. | By | Matthew Arnold. | London: | Longman, Brown, Green, Longmans, & Roberts. | MDCCCLVIII. Foolscap 8vo. lii + 138 pp. [Preface dated *London: December,* 1857.]

1863. CROMWELL. | Second Edition. | Oxford: | T. & G. Shrimpton, Broad Street. | MDCCCLXIII. Crown 8vo. 15 pp.

1867. SAINT BRANDAN. | By | Matthew Arnold. | London: | E. W. & A. Skipwith. | 1867. Foolscap 8vo. 11 pp. [Appeared first in *Fraser's Magazine,* July, 1860.]

NEW POEMS | by | Matthew Arnold. | London: | Macmillan and Co. | MDCCCLXVII. Foolscap 8vo. viii + 244 pp.

1868. NEW POEMS | by | Matthew Arnold. | Second Edition. | London: | Macmillan and Co. | MDCCCLXVIII. Foolscap 8vo. viii + 246 pp. [The last poem, *Obermann Once More,* has additional stanzas and notes.]

1869. POEMS | by | Matthew Arnold. | The First Volume | Narrative and Elegiac Poems. | London: | Macmillan and Co. | MDCCCLXIX. [*All rights reserved.*] 1869.

1869. POEMS | by | Matthew Arnold. | The Second Volume | Dramatic and Lyric Poems. | (Etc., as above.) Crown 8vo. Vol. I., viii + 276 pp.; Vol. II., viii + 267 pp. [" First Collected Edition."]

1877. POEMS | by | Matthew Arnold. | The First Volume | Early Poems, Narrative Poems, | and Sonnets. | New and Complete Edition. | London : | Macmillan and Co. | MDCCCLXXVII.

POEMS | by | Matthew Arnold. | The Second Volume | Lyric, Dramatic, and Elegiac Poems. | (Etc., as above.) Crown 8vo. Vol. I., viii + 272 pp.; Vol. II., viii + 312 pp.

1878. SELECTED POEMS | of | Matthew Arnold. | [*Illustration.*] | London : | Macmillan and Co. | 1878. Small 8vo. viii + 235 pp. [Golden Treasury Series.] Also large paper, crown 8vo, 250 copies. The selection made by the author.

1881. GEIST'S GRAVE | by | Matthew Arnold. | London : | Printed only for a few Friends. | 1881. Small 8vo. 11 pp. [Appeared first in the *Fortnightly Review*, January, 1881.]

POEMS. New Edition.

This edition of the POEMS agrees in the main, both in contents and in appearance, with its immediate predecessor, dated 1877. The following alterations, however, have to be noted : The date on the title page reads 'MDCCCLXXXI'; the pagination of Vol. I. is viii, 278; of Vol. II., viii, 320; *A Tomb among the Mountains* is omitted ; *The Church of Brou* and *A Dream* are reprinted from earlier volumes; three new poems added : *New Rome, The Lord's Messengers, Geist's Grave.*

1883. THE | MATTHEW ARNOLD BIRTHDAY BOOK. | Arranged by his Daughter | Eleanor Arnold. | With a Portrait. | London : | Smith, Elder, & Co., 15 Waterloo Place. | 1883. Small 4to. [Cabinet photograph of Matthew Arnold seated with his dog in his arms, reproduced by Woodbury type process and subscribed in facsimile *Matthew Arnold, 1883.*]

1885. POEMS. Library Edition. Three volumes.

Vol. I.

Poems | by | Matthew Arnold. | Early Poems, Narrative Poems, | and Sonnets. | London : | Macmillan and Co. | 1885.

Vol. II.

Poems | by | Matthew Arnold. | Lyric and Elegiac Poems. | London : | Macmillan and Co. | 1885.

Vol. III.

Poems | by | Matthew Arnold. | Dramatic and Later Poems. | London : | Macmillan and Co. | 1885.

Crown 8vo. Vol. I., x + 272 pp.; Vol. II., x + 256 pp.; Vol. III., viii + 209 pp.

1888. POEMS | by | Matthew Arnold. | Early Poems, Narrative Poems, | and Sonnets. | [Vol. II., "Lyric and Elegiac Poems"; Vol. III., "Dramatic and Later Poems."] | London | Macmillan and Co. | and New York. | 1888.

1890. POETICAL WORKS | of | Matthew Arnold. | London | Macmillan and Co. | and New York. | 1890. [*All rights reserved.*] Crown 8vo. xiv + 510 pp. Portrait of author from photograph by Sarony, New York.

1891. CROMWELL. | Third Edition. | Oxford : | A. Thomas Shrimpton & Son, Broad Street. | 1891.

Contributions to Periodical Publications, etc.

MEMORIAL VERSES. *Fraser's Magazine*, June, 1850, Vol. XLI., No. 246, p. 630. Signed "A." Dated April 27, 1850. Reprinted in EMPEDOCLES ON ETNA : 1852.

STANZAS FROM THE GRANDE CHARTREUSE. *Fraser's Magazine*, April, 1855, Vol. LI., No. 304, pp. 437–440. Reprinted in NEW POEMS : 1867.

HAWORTH CHURCHYARD. *Fraser's Magazine*, May, 1855, Vol. LI., No. 305, pp. 527–530. Signed "A." Dated April, 1855. Reprinted in POEMS : 1877.

SAINT BRANDAN. *Fraser's Magazine*, July, 1860, Vol. LXII., No. 367, pp. 133, 134. Reprinted in NEW POEMS : 1867.

MEN OF GENIUS. *The Cornhill Magazine*, July, 1860, Vol. II., No. 7, p. 33. Reprinted in POEMS: 1855, under the title of "The Lord's Messengers."

A SOUTHERN NIGHT. *The Victoria Regia* (a volume of original contributions in poetry and prose, edited by Adelaide A. Procter), 1861, pp. 177–183. Reprinted in NEW POEMS: 1867.

THYRSIS. *Macmillan's Magazine*, April, 1866, Vol. XIII., No. 78, pp. 449–454. Reprinted in NEW POEMS: 1867.

NEW ROME. *The Cornhill Magazine*, June, 1873, Vol. XXVII., No. 162, p. 687. Reprinted in POEMS: 1885.

THE NEW SIRENS. A Palinode. (With a Prefatory Note.) *Macmillan's Magazine*, December, 1876, Vol. XXXV., No. 206, pp. 132–138. Previously published in THE STRAYED REVELLER: 1849. Reprinted in POEMS: 1877.

S. S. "LUSITANIA." (A Sonnet.) *The Nineteenth Century*, January, 1879, Vol. V., No. 23, p. 1. Reprinted for the first time in the present edition.

GEIST'S GRAVE. *The Fortnightly Review*, January, 1881, Vol. XXIX., N. S., No. 159, pp. 1–3. Reprinted in POEMS: 1881.

WESTMINSTER ABBEY. *The Nineteenth Century*, January, 1882, Vol. XI., No. 59, pp. 1–8. Reprinted in POEMS: 1885.

POOR MATTHIAS. *Macmillan's Magazine*, December, 1882, Vol. XLVII., No. 278, pp. 81–85. Reprinted in POEMS: 1885.

KAISER DEAD. *The Fortnightly Review*, July, 1887, Vol. XLII., N. S., No. 247, pp. 1–3. Reprinted in POETICAL WORKS: 1890.

HORATIAN ECHO. *The Century Guild Hobby Horse*, July, 1887, No. 7, pp. 81, 82. Reprinted in POETICAL WORKS: 1890.

EARLY POEMS.

SONNETS.

QUIET WORK.

One lesson, Nature, let me learn of thee,
One lesson which in every wind is blown,
One lesson of two duties kept at one
Though the loud world proclaim their enmity, —

Of toil unsevered from tranquillity ;
Of labor, that in lasting fruit outgrows
Far noisier schemes, accomplished in repose,
Too great for haste, too high for rivalry.

Yes, while on earth a thousand discords ring,
Man's senseless uproar mingling with his toil,
Still do thy quiet ministers move on,

Their glorious tasks in silence perfecting ;
Still working, blaming still our vain turmoil,
Laborers that shall not fail, when man is gone.

TO A FRIEND.

Who prop, thou ask'st, in these bad days, my mind?—
He much, the old man, who, clearest-souled of men,
Saw The Wide Prospect, and the Asian Fen,[1]
And Tmolus hill, and Smyrna bay, though blind.

Much he, wnose friendship I not long since won,
That halting slave, who in Nicopolis
Taught Arrian, when Vespasian's brutal son
Cleared Rome of what most shamed him.　But be his

My special thanks, whose even-balanced soul,
From first youth tested up to extreme old age,
Business could not make dull, nor passion wild;

Who saw life steadily, and saw it whole;
The mellow glory of the Attic stage,
Singer of sweet Colonus, and its child.

————

SHAKSPEARE.

Others abide our question.　Thou art free.
We ask and ask.　Thou smilest, and art still,
Out-topping knowledge.　For the loftiest hill,
Who to the stars uncrowns his majesty,

Planting his steadfast footsteps in the sea,
Making the heaven of heavens his dwelling-place,
Spares but the cloudy border of his base
To the foiled searching of mortality;

And thou, who didst the stars and sunbeams know,
Self-schooled, self-scanned, self-honored, self-secure,
Didst tread on earth unguessed at. — Better so !

All pains the immortal spirit must endure,
All weakness which impairs, all griefs which bow,
Find their sole speech in that victorious brow.

WRITTEN IN EMERSON'S ESSAYS.

"O MONSTROUS, dead, unprofitable world,
That thou canst hear, and hearing hold thy way !
A voice oracular hath pealed to-day,
To-day a hero's banner is unfurled ;

Hast thou no lip for welcome?" — So I said.
Man after man, the world smiled and passed by ;
A smile of wistful incredulity,
As though one spake of life unto the dead, —

Scornful, and strange, and sorrowful, and full
Of bitter knowledge.   Yet the will is free ;
Strong is the soul, and wise, and beautiful ;

The seeds of godlike power are in us still ;
Gods are we, bards, saints, heroes, if we will ! —
Dumb judges, answer, truth or mockery?

WRITTEN IN BUTLER'S SERMONS.

AFFECTIONS, Instincts, Principles, and Powers,
Impulse and Reason, Freedom and Control, —
So men, unravelling God's harmonious whole,
Rend in a thousand shreds this life of ours.

Vain labor ! Deep and broad, where none may see,
Spring the foundations of that shadowy throne
Where man's one nature, queen-like, sits alone,
Centred in a majestic unity ;

And rays her powers, like sister-islands seen
Linking their coral arms under the sea,
Or clustered peaks with plunging gulfs between,

Spanned by aërial arches all of gold,
Whereo'er the chariot-wheels of life are rolled
In cloudy circles to eternity.

TO THE DUKE OF WELLINGTON.

ON HEARING HIM MISPRAISED.

BECAUSE thou hast believed, the wheels of life
Stand never idle, but go always round ;
Not by their hands, who vex the patient ground,
Moved only ; but by genius, in the strife

Of all its chafing torrents after thaw,
Urged ; and to feed whose movement, spinning sand,
The feeble sons of pleasure set their hand ;
And, in this vision of the general law,

Hast labored, but with purpose ; hast become
Laborious, persevering, serious, firm, —
For this, thy track across the fretful foam

Of vehement actions without scope or term,
Called history, keeps a splendor ; due to wit,
Which saw one clew to life, and followed it.

IN HARMONY WITH NATURE.

TO A PREACHER.

" In harmony with Nature? "   Restless fool,
Who with such heat dost preach what were to thee,
When true, the last impossibility, —
To be like Nature strong, like Nature cool!

Know, man hath all which Nature hath, but more,
And in that *more* lie all his hopes of good.
Nature is cruel, man is sick of blood;
Nature is stubborn, man would fain adore;

Nature is fickle, man hath need of rest;
Nature forgives no debt, and fears no grave;
Man would be mild, and with safe conscience blest.

Man must begin, know this, where Nature ends;
Nature and man can never be fast friends.
Fool, if thou canst not pass her, rest her slave!

TO GEORGE CRUIKSHANK.

ON SEEING, IN THE COUNTRY, HIS PICTURE OF " THE BOTTLE."

Artist, whose hand, with horror winged, hath torn
From the rank life of towns this leaf! and flung
The prodigy of full-blown crime among
Valleys and men to middle fortune born,

Not innocent, indeed, yet not forlorn, —
Say, what shall calm us when such guests intrude
Like comets on the heavenly solitude?
Shall breathless glades, cheered by shy Dian's horn,

Cold-bubbling springs, or caves? Not so! The soul
Breasts her own griefs; and, urged too fiercely, says,
"Why tremble? True, the nobleness of man

May be by man effaced; man can control
To pain, to death, the bent of his own days.
Know thou the worst! So much, not more, he *can*."

TO A REPUBLICAN FRIEND, 1848.

God knows it, I am with you. If to prize
Those virtues, prized and practised by too few,
But prized, but loved, but eminent in you,
Man's fundamental life; if to despise

The barren optimistic sophistries
Of comfortable moles, whom what they do
Teaches the limit of the just and true
(And for such doing they require not eyes);

If sadness at the long heart-wasting show
Wherein earth's great ones are disquieted;
If thoughts, not idle, while before me flow

The armies of the homeless and unfed, —
If these are yours, if this is what you are,
Then am I yours, and what you feel, I share.

CONTINUED.

YET, when I muse on what life is, I seem
Rather to patience prompted, than that proud
Prospect of hope which France proclaims so loud, —
France, famed in all great arts, in none supreme ;

Seeing this vale, this earth, whereon we dream,
Is on all sides o'ershadowed by the high
Uno'erleaped mountains of necessity,
Sparing us narrower margin than we deem.

Nor will that day dawn at a human nod,
When, bursting through the network superposed
By selfish occupation, — plot and plan,

Lust, avarice, envy, — liberated man,
All difference with his fellow-mortal closed,
Shall be left standing face to face with God.

RELIGIOUS ISOLATION.

TO THE SAME FRIEND.

CHILDREN (as such forgive them) have I known,
Ever in their own eager pastime bent
To make the incurious bystander, intent
On his own swarming thoughts, an interest own, —

Too fearful or too fond to play alone.
Do thou, whom light in thine own inmost soul
(Not less thy boast) illuminates, control
Wishes unworthy of a man full-grown.

What though the holy secret, which moulds thee,
Moulds not the solid earth? though never winds
Have whispered it to the complaining sea,

Nature's great law, and law of all men's minds?
To its own impulse every creature stirs:
Live by thy light, and earth will live by hers!

MYCERINUS.[2]

" Not by the justice that my father spurned,
Not for the thousands whom my father slew,
Altars unfed and temples overturned,
Cold hearts and thankless tongues, where thanks are
          due;
Fell this dread voice from lips that cannot lie,
Stern sentence of the Powers of Destiny.

" I will unfold my sentence and my crime.
My crime, — that, rapt in reverential awe,
I sate obedient, in the fiery prime
Of youth, self-governed, at the feet of Law;
Ennobling this dull pomp, the life of kings,
By contemplation of diviner things.

" My father loved injustice, and lived long;
Crowned with gray hairs he died, and full of sway.
I loved the good he scorned, and hated wrong —
The gods declare my recompense to-day.
I looked for life more lasting, rule more high;
And when six years are measured, lo, I die!

" Yet surely, O my people, did I deem
Man's justice from the all-just gods was given ;
A light that from some upper fount did beam,
Some better archetype, whose seat was heaven ;
A light that, shining from the blest abodes,
Did shadow somewhat of the life of gods.

" Mere phantoms of man's self-tormenting heart,
Which on the sweets that woo it dares not feed !
Vain dreams, which quench our pleasures, then depart,
When the duped soul, self-mastered, claims its meed ·
When, on the strenuous just man, Heaven bestows,
Crown of his struggling life, an unjust close !

" Seems it so light a thing, then, austere powers,
To spurn man's common lure, life's pleasant things?
Seems there no joy in dances crowned with flowers,
Love free to range, and regal banquetings?
Bend ye on these indeed an unmoved eye,
Not gods, but ghosts, in frozen apathy?

" Or is it that some force, too stern, too strong,
Even for yourselves to conquer or beguile,
Bears earth and heaven and men and gods along,
Like the broad volume of the insurgent Nile?
And the great powers we serve, themselves may be
Slaves of a tyrannous necessity?

" Or in mid-heaven, perhaps, your golden cars,
Where earthly voice climbs never, wing their flight,
And in wild hunt, through mazy tracts of stars,
Sweep in the sounding stillness of the night?
Or in deaf ease, on thrones of dazzling sheen,
Drinking deep draughts of joy, ye dwell serene?

" Oh, wherefore cheat our youth, if thus it be,
Of one short joy, one lust, one pleasant dream?
Stringing vain words of powers we cannot see,
Blind divinations of a will supreme ;
Lost labor ! when the circumambient gloom
But hides, if gods, gods careless of our doom?

" The rest I give to joy.   Even while I speak,
My sand runs short ; and as yon star-shot ray,
Hemmed by two banks of cloud, peers pale and weak,
Now, as the barrier closes, dies away, —
Even so do past and future intertwine,
Blotting this six years' space, which yet is mine.

" Six years, — six little years, — six drops of time !
Yet suns shall rise, and many moons shall wane,
And old men die, and young men pass their prime,
And languid pleasure fade and flower again,
And the dull gods behold, ere these are flown,
Revels more deep, joy keener than their own.

" Into the silence of the groves and woods
I will go forth ; though something would I say, —
Something, — yet what, I know not : for the gods
The doom they pass revoke not nor delay ;
And prayers and gifts and tears are fruitless all,
And the night waxes, and the shadows fall.

" Ye men of Egypt, ye have heard your king !
I go, and I return not.   But the will
Of the great gods is plain ; and ye must bring
Ill deeds, ill passions, zealous to fulfil
Their pleasure, to their feet ; and reap their praise, —
The praise of gods, rich boon ! and length of days."

— So spake he, half in anger, half in scorn;
And one loud cry of grief and of amaze
Broke from his sorrowing people; so he spake,
And turning, left them there : and with brief pause,
Girt with a throng of revellers, bent his way
To the cool region of the groves he loved.
There by the river-banks he wandered on,
From palm-grove on to palm-grove, happy trees,
Their smooth tops shining sunward, and beneath
Burying their unsunned stems in grass and flowers;
Where in one dream the feverish time of youth
Might fade in slumber, and the feet of joy
Might wander all day long and never tire.
Here came the king, holding high feast, at morn,
Rose-crowned; and ever, when the sun went down,
A hundred lamps beamed in the tranquil gloom,
From tree to tree all through the twinkling grove,
Revealing all the tumult of the feast, —
Flushed guests, and golden goblets foamed with wine;
While the deep-burnished foliage overhead
Splintered the silver arrows of the moon.

It may be that sometimes his wondering soul
From the loud joyful laughter of his lips
Might shrink half startled, like a guilty man
Who wrestles with his dream; as some pale shape,
Gliding half hidden through the dusky stems,
Would thrust a hand before the lifted bowl,
Whispering, *A little space, and thou art mine!*
It may be, on that joyless feast his eye
Dwelt with mere outward seeming; he, within,
Took measure of his soul, and knew its strength,
And by that silent knowledge, day by day,
Was calmed, ennobled, comforted, sustained.
It may be; but not less his brow was smooth,

And his clear laugh fled ringing through the gloom,
And his mirth quailed not at the mild reproof
Sighed out by winter's sad tranquillity ;
Nor, palled with its own fulness, ebbed and died
In the rich languor of long summer-days ;
Nor withered when the palm-tree plumes, that roofed
With their mild dark his grassy banquet-hall,
Bent to the cold winds of the showerless spring ;
No, nor grew dark when autumn brought the clouds.
　So six long years he revelled, night and day.
And when the mirth waxed loudest, with dull sound
Sometimes from the grove's centre echoes came,
To tell his wondering people of their king ;
In the still night, across the steaming flats,
Mixed with the murmur of the moving Nile.

THE CHURCH OF BROU.

I.

The Castle.

Down the Savoy valleys sounding,
　Echoing round this castle old,
'Mid the distant mountain-chalets
　Hark ! what bell for church is tolled ?

In the bright October morning
　Savoy's Duke had left his bride.
From the castle, past the drawbridge,
　Flowed the hunters' merry tide.

Steeds are neighing, gallants glittering.
  Gay, her smiling lord to greet,
From her mullioned chamber-casement
  Smiles the Duchess Marguerite.

From Vienna, by the Danube,
  Here she came, a bride, in spring.
Now the autumn crisps the forest;
  Hunters gather, bugles ring.

Hounds are pulling, prickers swearing,
  Horses fret, and boar-spears glance.
Off! — They sweep the marshy forests,
  Westward on the side of France.

Hark! the game's on foot; they scatter!
  Down the forest-ridings lone,
Furious, single horsemen gallop.
  Hark! a shout — a crash — a groan!

Pale and breathless, came the hunters —
  On the turf dead lies the boar.
God! the duke lies stretched beside him,
  Senseless, weltering in his gore.

In the dull October evening,
  Down the leaf-strewn forest-road,
To the castle, past the drawbridge,
  Came the hunters with their load.

In the hall, with sconces blazing,
  Ladies waiting round her seat,
Clothed in smiles, beneath the daïs
  Sate the Duchess Marguerite.

Hark ! below the gates unbarring !
   Tramp of men, and quick commands !
" 'Tis my lord come back from hunting ; "
   And the duchess claps her hands.

Slow and tired, came the hunters ;
   Stopped in darkness in the court.
" Ho, this way, ye laggard hunters !
   To the hall !   What sport, what sport ? "

Slow they entered with their master ;
   In the hall they laid him down.
On his coat were leaves and blood-stains,
   On his brow an angry frown.

Dead her princely youthful husband
   Lay before his youthful wife,
Bloody 'neath the flaring sconces —
   And the sight froze all her life.

In Vienna, by the Danube,
   Kings hold revel, gallants meet.
Gay of old amid the gayest
   Was the Duchess Marguerite.

In Vienna, by the Danube,
   Feast and dance her youth beguiled.
Till that hour she never sorrowed ;
   But from then she never smiled.

'Mid the Savoy mountain-valleys,
   Far from town or haunt of man,
Stands a lonely church, unfinished,
   Which the Duchess Maud began.

Old, that duchess stern began it,
   In gray age, with palsied hands;
But she died while it was building,
   And the church unfinished stands, —

Stands as erst the builders left it,
   When she sank into her grave;
Mountain greensward paves the chancel,
   Harebells flower in the nave.

" In my castle all is sorrow,"
   Said the Duchess Marguerite then :
" Guide me, some one, to the mountain;
   We will build the church again."

Sandalled palmers, faring homeward,
   Austrian knights from Syria came.
" Austrian wanderers bring, O warders !
   Homage to your Austrian dame."

From the gate the warders answered, —
   " Gone, O knights, is she you knew !
Dead our duke, and gone his duchess;
   Seek her at the church of Brou."

Austrian knights and march-worn palmers
   Climb the winding mountain-way;
Reach the valley, where the fabric
   Rises higher day by day.

Stones are sawing, hammers ringing;
   On the work the bright sun shines;
In the Savoy mountain-meadows,
   By the stream, below the pines.

On her palfrey white the duchess
    Sate, and watched her working train, —
Flemish carvers, Lombard gilders,
    German masons, smiths from Spain.

Clad in black, on her white palfrey,
    Her old architect beside, —
There they found her in the mountains,
    Morn and noon and eventide.

There she sate, and watched the builders,
    Till the church was roofed and done ;
Last of all, the builders reared her
    In the nave a tomb of stone.

On the tomb two forms they sculptured,
    Lifelike in the marble pale, —
One, the duke in helm and armor ;
    One, the duchess in her veil.

Round the tomb the carved stone fret-work
    Was at Easter-tide put on.
Then the duchess closed her labors ;
    And she died at the St. John.

I.

The Church.

Upon the glistening leaden roof
Of the new pile, the sunlight shines ;
    The stream goes leaping by.
The hills are clothed with pines sun-proof ;

'Mid bright green fields, below the pines,
   Stands the church on high.
What church is this, from men aloof?
'Tis the Church of Brou.

At sunrise, from their dewy lair
Crossing the stream, the kine are seen
   Round the wall to stray, —
The churchyard wall that clips the square
Of open hill-sward fresh and green
   Where last year they lay.
But all things now are ordered fair
Round the Church of Brou.

On Sundays, at the matin-chime,
The Alpine peasants, two and three,
   Climb up here to pray;
Burghers and dames, at summer's prime,
Ride out to church from Chambery,
   Dight with mantles gay.
But else it is a lonely time
Round the Church of Brou.

On Sundays, too, a priest doth come
From the walled town beyond the pass,
   Down the mountain-way;
And then you hear the organ's hum,
You hear the white-robed priest say mass,
   And the people pray.
But else the woods and fields are dumb
Round the Church of Brou.

And after church, when mass is done,
The people to the nave repair
   Round the tomb to stray;
And marvel at the forms of stone,

And praise the chiselled broideries rare —
    Then they drop away.
The princely pair are left alone
In the Church of Brou.

III.

The Tomb.

So rest, forever rest, O princely pair !
In your high church, 'mid the still mountain-air,
Where horn, and hound, and vassals, never come.
Only the blessed saints are smiling dumb
From the rich painted windows of the nave
On aisle, and transept, and your marble grave ;
Where thou, young prince, shalt never more arise
From the fringed mattress where thy duchess lies,
On autumn-mornings, when the bugle sounds,
And ride across the drawbridge with thy hounds
To hunt the boar in the crisp woods till eve ;
And thou, O princess, shalt no more receive,
Thou and thy ladies, in the hall of state,
The jaded hunters with their bloody freight,
Coming benighted to the castle-gate.
    So sleep, forever sleep, O marble pair !
Or, if ye wake, let it be then, when fair
On the carved western front a flood of light
Streams from the setting sun, and colors bright
Prophets, transfigured saints, and martyrs brave,
In the vast western window of the nave ;
And on the pavement round the tomb there glints
A checker-work of glowing sapphire-tints,

And amethyst, and ruby, — then unclose
Your eyelids on the stone where ye repose,
And from your broidered pillows lift your heads,
And rise upon your cold white marble beds ;
And looking down on the warm rosy tints
Which checker, at your feet, the illumined flints,
Say, *What is this ? we are in bliss — forgiven —*
Behold the pavement of the courts of heaven !
Or let it be on autumn-nights, when rain
Doth rustlingly above your heads complain
On the smooth leaden roof, and on the walls
Shedding her pensive light at intervals
The moon through the clere-story windows shines,
And the wind washes through the mountain-pines, —
Then, gazing up 'mid the dim pillars high,
The foliaged marble forest where ye lie,
Hush, ye will say, *it is eternity !*
This is the glimmering verge of heaven, and these
The columns of the heavenly palaces.
And in the sweeping of the wind your ear
The passage of the angels' wings will hear,
And on the lichen-crusted leads above
The rustle of the eternal rain of love.

A MODERN SAPPHO.

THEY are gone — all is still ! Foolish heart, dost thou
    quiver?
  Nothing stirs on the lawn but the quick lilac-
    shade.

Far up shines the house, and beneath flows the
    river :
  Here lean, my head, on this cold balustrade !

Ere he come, — ere the boat by the shining-branched
    border
  Of dark elms shoot round, dropping down the
    proud stream, —
Let me pause, let me strive, in myself make some
    order,
  Ere their boat-music sound, ere their broidered
    flags gleam.

Last night we stood earnestly talking together :
  She entered — that moment his eyes turned from me !
Fastened on her dark hair, and her wreath of white
    heather.
  As yesterday was, so to-morrow will be.

Their love, let me know, must grow strong and yet
    stronger,
  Their passion burn more, ere it ceases to burn.
They must love — while they must ! but the hearts
    that love longer
  Are rare — ah ! most loves but flow once, and return.

I shall suffer — but they will outlive their affection ;
  I shall weep — but their love will be cooling ; and he,
As he drifts to fatigue, discontent, and dejection,
  Will be brought, thou poor heart, how much nearer
    to thee !

For cold is his eye to mere beauty, who, breaking
  The strong band which passion around him hath
    furled,

Disenchanted by habit, and newly awaking,
  Looks languidly round on a gloom-buried world.

Through that gloom he will see but a shadow appearing,
  Perceive but a voice as I come to his side ;
— But deeper their voice grows, and nobler their bearing,
  Whose youth in the fires of anguish hath died.

So, to wait ! But what notes down the wind, hark !
    are driving?
  'Tis he ! 'tis their flag, shooting round by the trees !
— Let my turn, if it *will* come, be swift in arriving !
  Ah ! hope cannot long lighten torments like these.

Hast thou yet dealt him, O life, thy full measure?
  World, have thy children yet bowed at his knee?
Hast thou with myrtle-leaf crowned him, O pleasure?
  — Crown, crown him quickly, and leave him for me.

REQUIESCAT.

STREW on her roses, roses,
  And never a spray of yew :
In quiet she reposes ;
  Ah ! would that I did too !

Her mirth the world required ;
  She bathed it in smiles of glee.
But her heart was tired, tired,
  And now they let her be.

Her life was turning, turning,
    In mazes of heat and sound ;
But for peace her soul was yearning,
    And now peace laps her round.

Her cabined, ample spirit,
    It fluttered and failed for breath ;
To-night it doth inherit
    The vasty hall of death.

YOUTH AND CALM.

'TIS death ! and peace indeed is here,
And ease from shame, and rest from fear.
There's nothing can dismarble now
The smoothness of that limpid brow.
But is a calm like this, in truth,
The crowning end of life and youth?
And when this boon rewards the dead,
Are all debts paid, has all been said?
And is the heart of youth so light,
Its step so firm, its eye so bright,
Because on its hot brow there blows
A wind of promise and repose
From the far grave, to which it goes ;
Because it has the hope to come,
One day, to harbor in the tomb?
Ah, no ! the bliss youth dreams is one
For daylight, for the cheerful sun,
For feeling nerves and living breath ;
Youth dreams a bliss on this side death

It dreams a rest, if not more deep,
More grateful than this marble sleep ;
It hears a voice within it tell, —
Calm's not life's crown, though calm is well
'Tis all, perhaps, which man acquires,
But 'tis not what our youth desires.

———————

A MEMORY–PICTURE.

LAUGH, my friends, and without blame
Lightly quit what lightly came ;
Rich to-morrow as to-day,
Spend as madly as you may !
I, with little land to stir,
Am the exacter laborer.
    Ere the parting hour go by,
    Quick, thy tablets, Memory !

Once I said, " A face is gone
If too hotly mused upon ;
And our best impressions are
Those that do themselves repair."
Many a face I so let flee —
Ah ! — is faded utterly.
    Ere the parting hour go by,
    Quick, thy tablets, Memory !

Marguerite says, " As last year went,
So the coming year'll be spent ;
Some day next year, I shall be,
Entering heedless, kissed by thee."

Ah, I hope ! yet, once away,
What may chain us, who can say?
  Ere the parting hour go by,
  Quick, thy tablets, Memory !

Paint that lilac kerchief, bound
Her soft face, her hair around ;
Tied under the archest chin
Mockery ever ambushed in.
Let the fluttering fringes streak
All her pale, sweet-rounded cheek.
  Ere the parting hour go by,
  Quick, thy tablets, Memory !

Paint that figure's pliant grace
As she toward me leaned her face,
Half refused and half resigned,
Murmuring, " Art thou still unkind?"
Many a broken promise then
Was new made — to break again.
  Ere the parting hour go by,
  Quick, thy tablets, Memory !

Paint those eyes, so blue, so kind,
Eager tell-tales of her mind ;
Paint, with their impetuous stress
Of inquiring tenderness,
Those frank eyes, where deep doth be
An angelic gravity.
  Ere the parting hour go by,
  Quick, thy tablets, Memory !

What ! my friends, these feeble lines
Show, you say, my love declines?

To paint ill as I have done,
Proves forgetfulness begun?
Time's gay minions, pleased you see,
Time, your master, governs me;
    Pleased, you mock the fruitless cry, —
    "Quick, thy tablets, Memory!"

Ah, too true! Time's current strong
Leaves us true to nothing long.
Yet, if little stays with man,
Ah, retain we all we can!
If the clear impression dies,
Ah, the dim remembrance prize!
    Ere the parting hour go by,
    Quick, thy tablets, Memory!

THE NEW SIRENS.

IN the cedar-shadow sleeping,
Where cool grass and fragrant glooms
Late at eve had lured me, creeping
From your darkened palace rooms, —
I, who in your train at morning
Strolled and sang with joyful mind,
Heard, in slumber, sounds of warning;
Saw the hoarse boughs labor in the wind.

Who are they, O pensive Graces,
(For I dreamed they wore your forms)
Who on shores and sea-washed places
Scoop the shelves and fret the storms?

Who, when ships are that way tending,
Troop across the flushing sands,
To all reefs and narrows wending,
With blown tresses, and with beckoning hands?

Yet I see, the howling levels
Of the deep are not your lair;
And your tragic-vaunted revels
Are less lonely than they were.
Like those kings with treasure steering
From the jewelled lands of dawn,
Troops, with gold and gifts, appearing,
Stream all day through your enchanted lawn.

And we too, from upland valleys,
Where some Muse with half-curved frown
Leans her car to your mad sallies
Which the charmed winds never drown;
By faint music guided, ranging
The scared glens, we wandered on,
Left our awful laurels hanging,
And came heaped with myrtles to your throne.

From the dragon-wardered fountains
Where the springs of knowledge are,
From the watchers on the mountains,
And the bright and morning star;
We are exiles, we are falling,
We have lost them at your call —
O ye false ones, at your calling
Seeking ceiled chambers and a palace-hall!

Are the accents of your luring
More melodious than of yore?
Are those frail forms more enduring
Than the charms Ulysses bore?

That we sought you with rejoicings,
    Till at evening we descry
    At a pause of Siren voicings
These vexed branches and this howling sky? . . .

.   .   .   .

    Oh, your pardon !   The uncouthness
    Of that primal age is gone,
    And the skin of dazzling smoothness
    Screens not now a heart of stone.
    Love has flushed those cruel faces ;
    And those slackened arms forego
    The delight of death-embraces,
And yon whitening bone-mounds do not grow.

    "Ah !" you say ; "the large appearance
    Of man's labor is but vain,
    And we plead as stanch adherence
    Due to pleasure as to pain."
    Pointing to earth's careworn creatures,
    "Come," you murmur with a sigh :
    "Ah ! we own diviner features,
Loftier bearing, and a prouder eye.

    "Come," you say, "the hours were dreary ;
    Life without love does not fade ;
    Vain it wastes, and we grew weary
    In the slumbrous cedarn shade.
    Round our hearts with long caresses,
    With low sighings, Silence stole,
    And her load of steaming tresses
Weighed, like Ossa, on the aery soul.

"Come," you say, "the soul is fainting
Till she search and learn her own,
And the wisdom of man's painting
Leaves her riddle half unknown.
Come," you say, "the brain is seeking,
While the princely heart is dead ;
Yet this gleaned, when gods were speaking,
Rarer secrets than the toiling head.

"Come," you say, "opinion trembles,
Judgment shifts, convictions go ;
Life dries up, the heart dissembles :
Only, what we feel, we know.
Hath your wisdom known emotions ?
Will it weep our burning tears ?
Hath it drunk of our love-potions
Crowning moments with the weight of years ? '

I am dumb.   Alas ! too soon all
Man's grave reasons disappear !
Yet, I think, at God's tribunal
Some large answer you shall hear.
But for me, my thoughts are straying
Where at sunrise, through your vines,
On these lawns I saw you playing,
Hanging garlands on your odorous pines ;

When your showering locks inwound you,
And your heavenly eyes shone through ;
When the pine-boughs yielded round you,
And your brows were starred with dew ;
And immortal forms, to meet you,
Down the statued alleys came,
And through golden horns, to greet you,
Blew such music as a god may frame.

Yes, I muse ! And if the dawning
Into daylight never grew,
If the glistering wings of morning
On the dry noon shook their dew,
If the fits of joy were longer,
Or the day were sooner done,
Or, perhaps, if hope were stronger,
No weak nursling of an earthly sun . . .
    Pluck, pluck cypress, O pale maidens,
      Dusk the hall with yew !

  .   .   .   .

For a bound was set to meetings,
And the sombre day dragged on ;
And the burst of joyful greetings,
And the joyful dawn, were gone.
For the eye grows filled with gazing,
And on raptures follow calms ;
And those warm locks men were praising
Drooped, unbraided, on your listless arms.

Storms unsmoothed your folded valleys,
And made all your cedars frown ;
Leaves were whirling in the alleys
Which your lovers wandered down.
— Sitting cheerless in your bowers,
The hands propping the sunk head,
Do they gall you, the long hours,
And the hungry thought that must be fed ?

Is the pleasure that is tasted
Patient of a long review ?

Will the fire joy hath wasted,
Mused on, warm the heart anew?
— Or, are those old thoughts returning,
Guests the dull sense never knew,
Stars, set deep, yet inly burning,
Germs, your untrimmed passion overgrew?

Once, like us, you took your station,
Watchers for a purer fire ;
But you drooped in expectation,
And you wearied in desire.
When the first rose flush was steeping
All the frore peak's awful crown,
Shepherds say, they found you sleeping
In some windless valley, farther down.

Then you wept, and slowly raising
Your dozed eyelids, sought again,
Half in doubt, they say, and gazing
Sadly back, the seats of men ;
Snatched a turbid inspiration
From some transient earthly sun,
And proclaimed your vain ovation
For those mimic raptures you had won. . . .

.   .   .   .

With a sad, majestic motion,
With a stately, slow surprise,
From their earthward-bound devotion
Lifting up your languid eyes —
Would you freeze my louder boldness,
Dumbly smiling as you go,
One faint frown of distant coldness
Flitting fast across each marble brow?

Do I brighten at your sorrow,
O sweet pleaders? doth my lot
Find assurance in to-morrow
Of one joy which you have not?
Oh, speak once, and shame my sadness!
Let this sobbing, Phrygian strain,
Mocked and baffled by your gladness,
Mar the music of your feasts in vain!

. . . .

Scent, and song, and light, and flowers!
Gust on gust, the harsh winds blow —
Come, bind up those ringlet showers!
Roses for that dreaming brow!
Come, once more that ancient lightness,
Glancing feet, and eager eyes!
Let your broad lamps flash the brightness
Which the sorrow-stricken day denies.

Through black depths of serried shadows,
Up cold aisles of buried glade;
In the mist of river-meadows
Where the looming deer are laid;
From your dazzled windows streaming,
From your humming festal room,
Deep and far, a broken gleaming
Reels and shivers on the ruffled gloom.

Where I stand, the grass is glowing:
Doubtless you are passing fair!
But I hear the north wind blowing,
And I feel the cold night-air.

Can I look on your sweet faces,
   And your proud heads backward thrown,
   From this dusk of leaf-strewn places
With the dumb woods and the night alone?

Yet, indeed, this flux of guesses, —
   Mad delight, and frozen calms, —
   Mirth to-day, and vine-bound tresses,
   And to-morrow — folded palms ;
   Is this all? this balanced measure?
   Could life run no happier way?
   Joyous at the height of pleasure,
Passive at the nadir of dismay?

But, indeed, this proud possession,
   This far-reaching, magic chain,
   Linking in a mad succession
   Fits of joy and fits of pain, —
   Have you seen it at the closing?
   Have you tracked its clouded ways?
   Can your eyes, while fools are dozing,
Drop, with mine, adown life's latter days?

When a dreary light is wading
   Through this waste of sunless greens,
   When the flashing lights are fading
   On the peerless cheek of queens,
   When the mean shall no more sorrow,
   And the proudest no more smile ;
   While the dawning of the morrow
Widens slowly westward all that while?

Then, when change itself is over,
   When the slow tide sets one way,
   Shall you find the radiant lover,
   Even by moments, of to-day?

The eye wanders, faith is failing:
Oh, loose hands, and let it be!
Proudly, like a king bewailing,
Oh, let fall one tear, and set us free!

All true speech and large avowal
Which the jealous soul concedes;
All man's heart which brooks bestowal,
All frank faith which passion breeds,—
These we had, and we gave truly;
Doubt not, what we had, we gave!
False we were not, nor unruly;
Lodgers in the forest and the cave.

Long we wandered with you, feeding
Our rapt souls on your replies,
In a wistful silence reading
All the meaning of your eyes.
By moss-bordered statues sitting,
By well-heads, in summer days.
But we turn, our eyes are flitting—
See, the white east, and the morning-rays!

And you too, O worshipped Graces,
Sylvan gods of this fair shade!
Is there doubt on divine faces?
Are the blessed gods dismayed?
Can men worship the wan features,
The sunk eyes, the wailing tone,
Of unsphered, discrownèd creatures,
Souls as little godlike as their own?

Come, loose hands! The wingèd fleetness
Of immortal feet is gone;
And your scents have shed their sweetness,
And your flowers are overblown.

And your jewelled gauds surrender
Half their glories to the day ;
Freely did they flash their splendor,
Freely gave it — but it dies away.

In the pines, the thrush is waking ;
Lo, yon orient hill in flames !
Scores of true-love-knots are breaking
At divorce which it proclaims.
When the lamps are paled at morning,
Heart quits heart, and hand quits hand.
Cold in that unlovely dawning,
Loveless, rayless, joyless, you shall stand !

Pluck no more red roses, maidens,
Leave the lilies in their dew ;
Pluck, pluck cypress, O pale maidens,
Dusk, oh, dusk the hall with yew !
— Shall I seek, that I may scorn her,
Her I loved at eventide ?
Shall I ask, what faded mourner
Stands, at daybreak, weeping by my side ? . . .
Pluck, pluck cypress, O pale maidens !
Dusk the hall with yew !

THE VOICE.

As the kindling glances,
Queen-like and clear,
Which the bright moon lances
From her tranquil sphere
At the sleepless waters
Of a lonely mere,
On the wild whirling waves, mournfully, mournfully,
Shiver and die ;

As the tears of sorrow
    Mothers have shed —
Prayers that to-morrow
    Shall in vain be sped
When the flower they flow for
    Lies frozen and dead —
Fall on the throbbing brow, fall on the burning breast,
        Bringing no rest;

    Like bright waves that fall
    With a lifelike motion
On the lifeless margin of the sparkling ocean;
A wild rose climbing up a mouldering wall;
A gush of sunbeams through a ruined hall;
Strains of glad music at a funeral, —
    So sad, and with so wild a start
    To this deep-sobered heart,
    So anxiously and painfully,
    So drearily and doubtfully,
And, oh! with such intolerable change
    Of thought, such contrast strange,
O unforgotten voice, thy accents come,
Like wanderers from the world's extremity,
    · Unto their ancient home!

In vain, all, all in vain,
They beat upon mine ear again, —
Those melancholy tones so sweet and still;
Those lute-like tones which in the bygone year
    Did steal into mine ear;
Blew such a thrilling summons to my will,
    Yet could not shake it;
Made my tost heart its very life-blood spill,
    Yet could not break it.

YOUTH'S AGITATIONS.

WHEN I shall be divorced, some ten years hence,
From this poor present self which I am now;
When youth has done its tedious vain expense
Of passions that forever ebb and flow:

Shall I not joy youth's heats are left behind,
And breathe more happy in an even clime?
Ah, no! for then I shall begin to find
A thousand virtues in this hated time!

Then I shall wish its agitations back,
And all its thwarting currents of desire;
Then I shall praise the heat which then I lack,
And call this hurrying fever, generous fire;

And sigh that one thing only has been lent
To youth and age in common, — discontent.

THE WORLD'S TRIUMPHS.

So far as I conceive the world's rebuke
To him addressed who would recast her new,
Not from herself her fame of strength she took,
But from their weakness who would work her rue.

"Behold," she cries, "so many rages lulled,
So many fiery spirits quite cooled down;
Look how so many valors, long undulled,
After short commerce with me, fear my frown!

Thou too, when thou against my crimes wouldst cry,
Let thy foreboded homage check thy tongue ! " —
The world speaks well ; yet might her foe reply,
" Are wills so weak ? then let not mine wait long !

Hast thou so rare a poison ? let me be
Keener to slay thee, lest thou poison me ! "

STAGIRIUS.[3]

THOU, who dost dwell alone ;
Thou, who dost know thine own ;
Thou, to whom all are known
From the cradle to the grave, —
    Save, oh ! save.
From the world's temptations,
From tribulations,
From that fierce anguish
Wherein we languish,
From that torpor deep
Wherein we lie asleep,
Heavy as death, cold as the grave,
    Save, oh ! save.

When the soul, growing clearer,
  Sees God no nearer ;
When the soul, mounting higher,
  To God comes no nigher ;
But the arch-fiend Pride
Mounts at her side,
Foiling her high emprise,
Sealing her eagle eyes,
And, when she fain would soar,
Makes idols to adore,

Changing the pure emotion
Of her high devotion,
To a skin-deep sense
Of her own éloquence ;
Strong to deceive, strong to enslave, —
Save, oh ! save.

· From the ingrained fashion
Of this earthly nature
That mars thy creature ;
From grief that is but passion,
From mirth that is but feigning,
From tears that bring no healing,
From wild and weak complaining.
Thine old strength revealing,
Save, oh ! save.
From doubt, where all is double ;
Where wise men are not strong,
Where comfort turns to trouble,
Where just men suffer wrong ;
Where sorrow treads on joy,
Where sweet things soonest cloy,
Where faiths are built on dust,
Where love is half mistrust,
Hungry, and barren, and sharp as the sea, —
Oh ! set us free.
Oh, let the false dream fly,
Where our sick souls do lie
Tossing continually !
Oh, where thy voice doth come,
Let all doubts be dumb,
Let all words be mild,
All strifes be reconciled,
All pains beguiled !

Light bring no blindness,
Love no unkindness,
Knowledge no ruin,
Fear no undoing !
From the cradle to the grave,
   Save, oh ! save.

HUMAN LIFE.

WHAT mortal, when he saw,
Life's voyage done, his heavenly Friend,
Could ever yet dare tell him fearlessly, —
" I have kept uninfringed my nature's law ;
The inly-written chart thou gavest me,
To guide me, I have steered by to the end " ?

Ah ! let us make no claim,
On life's incognizable sea,
To too exact a steering of our way ;
Let us not fret and fear to miss our aim,
If some fair coast has lured us to make stay,
Or some friend hailed us to keep company.

Ay ! we would each fain drive
At random, and not steer by rule.
Weakness ! and worse, weakness bestowed in vain !
Winds from our side the unsuiting consort rive ;
We rush by coasts where we had lief remain :
Man cannot, though he would, live chance's fool.

No ! as the foaming swath
Of torn-up water, on the main,
Falls heavily away with long-drawn roar

On either side the black deep-furrowed path
Cut by an onward-laboring vessel's prore,
And never touches the ship-side again ;

Even so we leave behind,
As, chartered by some unknown Powers,
We stem across the sea of life by night,
The joys which were not for our use designed, —
The friends to whom we had no natural right,
The homes that were not destined to be ours.

TO A GYPSY CHILD BY THE SEA-SHORE;

DOUGLAS, ISLE OF MAN.

WHO taught this pleading to unpractised eyes?
Who hid such import in an infant's gloom?
Who lent thee, child, this meditative guise?
Who massed, round that slight brow, these clouds of
          doom?

Lo ! sails that gleam a moment, and are gone ;
The swinging waters, and the clustered pier.
Not idly earth and ocean labor on,
Nor idly do these sea-birds hover near.

But thou, whom superfluity of joy
Wafts not from thine own thoughts, nor longings vain,
Nor weariness, the full-fed soul's annoy,
Remaining in thy hunger and in thy pain ;

Thou, drugging pain by patience ; half averse
From thine own mother's breast, that knows not thee ;
With eyes which sought thine eyes thou didst con-
    verse,
And that soul-searching vision fell on me.

Glooms that go deep as thine, I have not known ;
Moods of fantastic sadness, nothing worth.
Thy sorrow and thy calmness are thine own ;
Glooms that enhance and glorify this earth.

What mood wears like complexion to thy woe ?
His, who in mountain glens, at noon of day,
Sits rapt, and hears the battle break below ?
— Ah ! thine was not the shelter, but the fray.

Some exile's, mindful how the past was glad ?
Some angel's, in an alien planet born ?
— No exile's dream was ever half so sad,
Nor any angel's sorrow so forlorn.

Is the calm thine of stoic souls, who weigh
Life well, and find it wanting, nor deplore ;
But in disdainful silence turn away,
Stand mute, self-centred, stern, and dream no more ?

Or do I wait, to hear some gray-haired king
Unravel all his many-colored lore ;
Whose mind hath known all arts of governing,
Mused much, loved life a little, loathed it more ?

Down the pale cheek, long lines of shadow slope,
Which years, and curious thought, and suffering give.
— Thou hast foreknown the vanity of hope,
Foreseen thy harvest, yet proceed'st to live.

O meek anticipant of that sure pain
Whose sureness gray-haired scholars hardly learn !
What wonder shall time breed, to swell thy strain?
What heavens, what earth, what suns, shalt thou dis-
     cern?

Ere the long night, whose stillness brooks no star,
Match that funereal aspect with her pall,
I think thou wilt have fathomed life too far,
Have known too much — or else forgotten all.

The Guide of our dark steps, a triple veil
Betwixt our senses and our sorrow keeps ;
Hath sown with cloudless passages the tale
Of grief, and eased us with a thousand sleeps.

Ah ! not the nectarous poppy lovers use,
Not daily labor's dull, Lethæan spring,
Oblivion in lost angels can infuse
Of the soiled glory, and the trailing wing ;

And though thou glean, what strenuous gleaners may,
In the thronged fields where winning comes by strife ;
And though the just sun gild, as mortals pray,
Some reaches of thy storm-vexed stream of life ;

Though that blank sunshine blind thee ; though the
     cloud
That severed the world's march and thine, be gone ;
Though ease dulls grace, and wisdom be too proud
To halve a lodging that was all her own, —

Once, ere thy day go down, thou shalt discern,
Oh, once, ere night, in thy success, thy chain !
Ere the long evening close, thou shalt return,
And wear this majesty of grief again.

A QUESTION.

TO FAUSTA.

Joy comes and goes, hope ebbs and flows
  Like the wave ;
Change doth unknit the tranquil strength of men.
  Love lends life a little grace,
  A few sad smiles ; and then
  Both are laid in one cold place, —
   In the grave.

Dreams dawn and fly, friends smile and die
  Like spring flowers ;
Our vaunted life is one long funeral.
  Men dig graves with bitter tears
  For their dead hopes ; and all,
  Mazed with doubts and sick with fears,
   Count the hours.

We count the hours ! These dreams of ours,
  False and hollow,
Do we go hence, and find they are not dead?
  Joys we dimly apprehend
  Faces that smiled and fled,
  Hopes born here, and born to end,
   Shall we follow?

IN UTRUMQUE PARATUS.

If, in the silent mind of One all-pure,
  At first imagined lay
The sacred world ; and by procession sure

From those still deeps, in form and color drest,
Seasons alternating, and night and day,
The long-mused thought to north, south, east, and west,
      Took then its all-seen way ;

Oh, waking on a world which thus-wise springs !
      Whether it needs thee count
Betwixt thy waking and the birth of things
Ages or hours — oh, waking on life's stream !
By lonely pureness to the all-pure fount
(Only by this thou canst) the colored dream
      Of life remount !

Thin, thin the pleasant human noises grow,
      And faint the city gleams ;
Rare the lone pastoral huts — marvel not thou !
The solemn peaks but to the stars are known, —
But to the stars, and the cold lunar beams ;
Alone the sun arises, and alone
      Spring the great streams.

But, if the wild unfathered mass no birth
      In divine seats hath known ;
In the blank, echoing solitude, if Earth,
Rocking her obscure body to and fro,
Ceases not from all time to heave and groan,
Unfruitful oft, and at her happiest throe
      Forms, what she forms, alone ;

Oh, seeming sole to awake, thy sun-bathed head
      Piercing the solemn cloud
Round thy still dreaming brother-world outspread !
O man, whom Earth, thy long-vexed mother, bare
Not without joy, — so radiant, so endowed
(Such happy issue crowned her painful care), —
      Be not too proud !

Oh, when most self-exalted most alone,
    Chief dreamer, own thy dream !
Thy brother-world stirs at thy feet unknown ;
Who hath a monarch's hath no brother's part —
Yet doth thine inmost soul with yearning teem.
Oh, what a spasm shakes the dreamer's heart !
    " I, too, but seem."

THE WORLD AND THE QUIETIST.

TO CRITIAS.

"WHY, when the world's great mind
    Hath finally inclined,
Why," you say, Critias, " be debating still ?
    Why, with these mournful rhymes
    Learned in more languid climes,
    Blame our activity
    Who, with such passionate will,
    Are what we mean to be ? "

Critias, long since, I know
    (For Fate decreed it so),
Long since the world hath set its heart to live ;
    Long since, with credulous zeal
    It turns life's mighty wheel,
    Still doth for laborers send
    Who still their labor give,
    And still expects an end.

Yet, as the wheel flies round,
    With no ungrateful sound
Do adverse voices fall on the world's ear.
    Deafened by his own stir,
    The rugged laborer

Caught not till then a sense
So glowing and so near
   Of his omnipotence.

So, when the feast grew loud
In Susa's palace proud,
A white-robed slave stole to the great king's side.
   He spake — the great king heard ;
   Felt the slow-rolling word
   Swell his attentive soul ;
   Breathed deeply as it died,
      And drained his mighty bowl.

THE SECOND BEST.

MODERATE tasks and moderate leisure,
Quiet living, strict-kept measure
Both in suffering and in pleasure, —
   'Tis for this thy nature yearns.

But so many books thou readest,
But so many schemes thou breedest,
But so many wishes feedest,
   That thy poor head almost turns.

And (the world's so madly jangled,
Human things so fast entangled)
Nature's wish must now be strangled
   For that best which she discerns.

So it *must* be ! yet, while leading
A strained life, while over-feeding,
Like the rest, his wit with reading,
   No small profit that man earns, —

Who through all he meets can steer him,
Can reject what cannot clear him,
Cling to what can truly cheer him ;
   Who each day more surely learns

That an impulse, from the distance
Of his deepest, best existence,
To the words, " Hope, Light, Persistence,"
   Strongly sets and truly burns.

CONSOLATION.

MIST clogs the sunshine.
Smoky dwarf houses
Hem me round everywhere ;
A vague dejection
Weighs down my soul.

Yet, while I languish,
Everywhere countless
Prospects unroll themselves,
And countless beings
Pass countless moods.

Far hence, in Asia,
On the smooth convent-roofs,
On the gold terraces,
Of holy Lassa,
Bright shines the sun.

Gray time-worn marbles
Hold the pure Muses ;
In their cool gallery,
By yellow Tiber,
They still look fair.

Strange unloved uproar [1]
Shrills round their portal;
Yet not on Helicon
Kept they more cloudless
Their noble calm.

Through sun-proof alleys
In a lone, sand-hemmed
City of Africa,
A blind, led beggar,
Age-bowed, asks alms.

No bolder robber
Erst abode ambushed
Deep in the sandy waste;
No clearer eyesight
Spied prey afar.

Saharan sand-winds
Seared his keen eyeballs;
Spent is the spoil he won.
For him the present
Holds only pain.

Two young, fair lovers,
Where the warm June-wind,
Fresh from the summer fields
Plays fondly round them,
Stand, tranced in joy.

With sweet, joined voices,
And with eyes brimming,
" Ah ! " they cry, " Destiny,
Prolong the present !
Time, stand still here ! "

---

[1] Written during the siege of Rome by the French, 1849.

The prompt stern goddess
Shakes her head, frowning:
Time gives his hour-glass
Its due reversal;
Their hour is gone.

With weak indulgence
Did the just goddess
Lengthen their happiness,
She lengthened also
Distress elsewhere.

The hour whose happy
Unalloyed moments
I would eternalize,
Ten thousand mourners
Well pleased see end.

The bleak, stern hour,
Whose severe moments
I would annihilate,
Is passed by others
In warmth, light, joy.

Time, so complained of,
Who to no one man
Shows partiality,
Brings round to all men
Some undimmed hours.

RESIGNATION.

TO FAUSTA.

To die be given us, or attain!
Fierce work it were, to do again.

So pilgrims, bound for Mecca, prayed
At burning noon ; so warriors said,
Scarfed with the cross, who watched the miles
Of dust which wreathed their struggling files
Down Lydian mountains ; so, when snows
Round Alpine summits, eddying, rose,
The Goth, bound Rome-wards; so the Hun,
Crouched on his saddle, while the sun
Went lurid down o'er flooded plains
Through which the groaning Danube strains
To the drear Euxine : so pray all,
Whom labors, self-ordained, inthrall ;
Because they to themselves propose
On this side the all-common close
A goal which, gained, may give repose.
So pray they ; and to stand again
Where they stood once, to them were pain ;
Pain to thread back and to renew
Past straits, and currents long steered through.

But milder natures, and more free, —
Whom an unblamed serenity
Hath freed from passions, and the state
Of struggle these necessitate ;
Whom schooling of the stubborn mind
Hath made, or birth hath found, resigned, —
These mourn not, that their goings pay
Obedience to the passing day.
These claim not every laughing hour
For handmaid to their striding power ;
Each in her turn, with torch upreared,
To await their march ; and when appeared,
Through the cold gloom, with measured race,
To usher for a destined space

(Her own sweet errands all foregone)
The too imperious traveller on.
These, Fausta, ask not this ; nor thou,
Time's chafing prisoner, ask it now !

We left just ten years since, you say,
That wayside inn we left to-day.[4]
Our jovial host, as forth we fare,
Shouts greeting from his easy-chair.
High on a bank our leader stands,
Reviews and ranks his motley bands,
Makes clear our goal to every eye, —
The valley's western boundary.
A gate swings to ! our tide hath flowed
Already from the silent road.
The valley-pastures, one by one,
Are threaded, quiet in the sun ;
And now, beyond the rude stone bridge,
Slopes gracious up the western ridge.
Its woody border, and the last
Of its dark upland farms, is past ;
Cool farms, with open-lying stores,
Under their burnished sycamores, —
All past ! and through the trees we glide
Emerging on the green hillside.
There climbing hangs, a far-seen sign,
Our wavering, many-colored line ;
There winds, up-streaming slowly still
Over the summit of the hill.
And now, in front, behold outspread
Those upper regions we must tread, —
Mild hollows, and clear heathy swells,
The cheerful silence of the fells.

Some two hours' march, with serious air,
Through the deep noontide heats we fare ;
The red-grouse, springing at our sound,
Skims, now and then, the shining ground ;
No life, save his and ours, intrudes
Upon these breathless solitudes.
Oh, joy ! again the farms appear.
Cool shade is there, and rustic cheer ;
There springs the brook will guide us down,
Bright comrade, to the noisy town.
Lingering, we follow down ; we gain
The town, the highway, and the plain.
And many a mile of dusty way,
Parched and road-worn, we made that day ;
But, Fausta, I remember well,
That as the balmy darkness fell,
We bathed our hands with speechless glee,
That night, in the wide-glimmering sea.

Once more we tread this self-same road,
Fausta, which ten years since we trod ;
Alone we tread it, you and I,
Ghosts of that boisterous company.
Here, where the brook shines, near its head,
In its clear, shallow, turf-fringed bed ;
Here, whence the eye first sees, far down,
Capped with faint smoke, the noisy town, —
Here sit we, and again unroll,
Though slowly, the familiar whole.
The solemn wastes of heathy hill
Sleep in the July sunshine still ;
The self-same shadows now, as then,
Play through this grassy upland glen ;

The loose dark stones on the green way
Lie strewn, it seems, where then they lay ;
On this mild bank above the stream,
(You crush them !) the blue gentians gleam.
Still this wild brook, the rushes cool,
The sailing foam, the shining pool !
These are not changed ; and we, you say,
Are scarce more changed, in truth, than they.

The gypsies, whom we met below,
They too have long roamed to and fro ;
They ramble, leaving, where they pass,
Their fragments on the cumbered grass.
And often to some kindly place
Chance guides the migratory race,
Where, though long wanderings intervene,
They recognize a former scene.
The dingy tents are pitched ; the fires
Give to the wind their wavering spires ;
In dark knots crouch round the wild flame
Their children, as when first they came ;
They see their shackled beasts again
Move, browsing, up the gray-walled lane.
Signs are not wanting, which might raise
The ghost in them of former days, —
Signs are not wanting, if they would ;
Suggestions to disquietude.
For them, for all, time's busy touch,
While it mends little, troubles much.
Their joints grow stiffer — but the year
Runs his old round of dubious cheer ;
Chilly they grow — yet winds in March,
Still, sharp as ever, freeze and parch ;

They must live still — and yet, God knows,
Crowded and keen the country grows ;
It seems as if, in their decay,
The law grew stronger every day.
So might they reason, so compare,
Fausta, times past with times that are ;
But no ! they rubbed through yesterday
In their hereditary way,
And they will rub through, if they can,
To-morrow on the self-same plan,
Till death arrive to supersede,
For them, vicissitude and need.

The poet, to whose mighty heart
Heaven doth a quicker pulse impart,
Subdues that energy to scan
Not his own course, but that of man.
Though he move mountains, though his day
Be passed on the proud heights of sway,
Though he hath loosed a thousand chains,
Though he hath borne immortal pains,
Action and suffering though he know, —
He hath not lived, if he lives so.
He sees, in some great-historied land,
A ruler of the people stand,
Sees his strong thought in fiery flood
Roll through the heaving multitude,
Exults — yet for no moment's space
Envies the all-regarded place.
Beautiful eyes meet his, and he
Bears to admire uncravingly ;
They pass : he, mingled with the crowd,
Is in their far-off triumphs proud.

From some high station he looks down,
At sunset, on a populous town ;
Surveys each happy group which fleets,
Toil ended, through the shining streets, —
Each with some errand of its own, —
And does not say, *I am alone.*
He sees the gentle stir of birth
When morning purifies the earth ;
He leans upon a gate, and sees
The pastures, and the quiet trees.
Low, woody hill, with gracious bound,
Folds the still valley almost round ;
The cuckoo, loud on some high lawn,
Is answered from the depth of dawn ;
In the hedge straggling to the stream,
Pale, dew-drenched, half-shut roses gleam.
But, where the farther side slopes down,
He sees the drowsy new-waked clown
In his white quaint-embroidered frock
Make, whistling, toward his mist-wreathed
        flock,
Slowly, behind his heavy tread,
The wet, flowered grass heaves up its head.
Leaned on his gate, he gazes : tears
Are in his eyes, and in his ears
The murmur of a thousand years.
Before him he sees life unroll,
A placid and continuous whole, —
That general life, which does not cease,
Whose secret is not joy, but peace ;
That life, whose dumb wish is not missed
If birth proceeds, if things subsist ;
The life of plants, and stones, and rain,
The life he craves — if not in vain

Fate gave, what chance shall not control,
His sad lucidity of soul.

You listen ; but that wandering smile,
Fausta, betrays you cold the while !
Your eyes pursue the bells of foam
Washed, eddying, from this bank, their home.
Those gypsies — so your thoughts I scan —
Are less, the poet more, than man.
They feel not, though they move and see.
Deeper the poet feels ; but he
Breathes, when he will, immortal air,
Where Orpheus and where Homer are.
In the day's life, whose iron round
Hems us all in, he is not bound ;
He leaves his kind, o'erleaps their pen,
And flees the common life of men.
He escapes thence, but we abide.
Not deep the poet sees, but wide.

The world in which we live and move
Outlasts aversion, outlasts love,
Outlasts each effort, interest, hope,
Remorse, grief, joy ; and, were the scope
Of these affections wider made,
Man still would see, and see dismayed,
Beyond his passion's widest range,
Far regions of eternal change.
Nay, and since death, which wipes out man,
Finds him with many an unsolved plan,
With much unknown, and much untried,
Wonder not dead, and thirst not dried,
Still gazing on the ever full
Eternal mundane spectacle, —

This world in which we draw our breath,
In some sense, Fausta, outlasts death.

   Blame thou not, therefore, him who dares
Judge vain beforehand human cares ;
Whose natural insight can discern
What through experience others learn ;
Who needs not love and power, to know
Love transient, power an unreal show ;
Who treads at ease life's uncheered ways :
Him blame not, Fausta, rather praise !
Rather thyself for some aim pray,
Nobler than this, to fill the day ;
Rather that heart, which burns in thee,
Ask, not to amuse, but to set free ;
Be passionate hopes not ill resigned
For quiet, and a fearless mind.
And though fate grudge to thee and me
The poet's rapt security,
Yet they, believe me, who await
No gifts from chance, have conquered fate.
They, winning room to see and hear,
And to men's business not too near,
Through clouds of individual strife
Draw homeward to the general life.
Like leaves by suns not yet uncurled ;
To the wise, foolish ; to the world,
Weak : yet not weak, I might reply,
Not foolish, Fausta, in His eye,
To whom each moment in its race,
Crowd as we will its neutral space,
Is but a quiet watershed
Whence, equally, the seas of life and death are
      fed.

Enough, we live ! and if a life
With large results so little rife,
Though bearable, seem hardly worth
This pomp of worlds, this pain of birth ;
Yet, Fausta, the mute turf we tread,
The solemn hills around us spread,
This stream which falls incessantly,
The strange-scrawled rocks, the lonely sky,
If I might lend their life a voice,
Seem to bear rather than rejoice.
And even could the intemperate prayer
Man iterates, while these forbear,
For movement, for an ampler sphere,
Pierce Fate's impenetrable ear ;
Not milder is the general lot
Because our spirits have forgot,
In action's dizzying eddy whirled,
The something that infects the world.

A DREAM.

Was it a dream? We sail'd, I thought we sail'd,
Martin and I, down a green Alpine stream,
Border'd, each bank, with pines ; the morning sun,
On the wet umbrage of their glossy tops,
On the red pinings of their forest-floor,
Drew a warm scent abroad ; behind the pines
The mountain-skirts, with all their sylvan change
Of bright-leaf'd chestnuts and moss'd walnut-trees
And the frail scarlet-berried ash, began.
Swiss chalets glitter'd on the dewy slopes,
And from some swarded shelf, high up, there came
Notes of wild pastoral music — over all
Ranged, diamond-bright, the eternal wall of snow.
Upon the mossy rocks at the stream's edge,

Back'd by the pines, a plank-built cottage stood,
Bright in the sun; the climbing gourd-plant's leaves
Muffled its walls, and on the stone-strewn roof
Lay the warm golden gourds; golden, within,
Under the eaves, peer'd rows of Indian corn.
We shot beneath the cottage with the stream.
On the brown, rude-carved balcony, two forms
Came forth — Olivia's, Marguerite! and thine.
Clad were they both in white, flowers in their breast;
Straw hats bedeck'd their heads, with ribbons blue,
Which danced, and on their shoulders, fluttering, play'd.
They saw us, they conferr'd; their bosoms heaved,
And more than mortal impulse fill'd their eyes.
Their lips moved; their white arms, waved eagerly,
Flash'd once, like falling streams; we rose, we gazed.
One moment, on the rapid's top, our boat
Hung poised — and then the darting river of Life
(Such now, methought, it was), the river of Life,
Loud thundering, bore us by; swift, swift it foam'd,
Black under cliffs it raced, round headlands shone.
Soon the plank'd cottage by the sun-warm'd pines
Faded — the moss — the rocks; us burning plains,
Bristled with cities, us the sea received.

HORATIAN ECHO.

TO AN AMBITIOUS FRIEND.

Written in 1847. Printed by permission of Mr. Arthur Galton, to whom the Poem was given in 1886 for publication in *The Hobby Horse.*

OMIT, omit, my simple friend,
Still to inquire how parties tend,
Or what we fix with foreign powers.
If France and we are really friends,
And what the Russian czar intends,
Is no concern of ours.

Us not the daily quickening race
Of the invading populace
Shall draw to swell that shouldering herd.
Mourn will we not your closing hour,
Ye imbeciles in present power,
  Doom'd, pompous, and absurd !

And let us bear, that they debate
Of all the engine-work of state,
Of commerce, laws, and policy,
The secrets of the world's machine,
And what the rights of man may mean,
  With readier tongue than we.

Only, that with no finer art
They cloak the troubles of the heart
With pleasant smile, let us take care ;
Nor with a lighter hand dispose
Fresh garlands of this dewy rose,
  To crown Eugenia's hair.

Of little threads our life is spun,
And he spins ill, who misses one.
But is thy fair Eugenia cold ?
Yet Helen had an equal grace,
And Juliet's was as fair a face,
  And now their years are told.

The day approaches, when we must
Be crumbling bones and windy dust ;
And scorn us as our mistress may,
Her beauty will no better be
Than the poor face she slights in thee,
  When dawns that day, that day.

NARRATIVE POEMS.

SOHRAB AND RUSTUM.[5]

AN EPISODE.

AND the first gray of morning filled the east,
And the fog rose out of the Oxus stream.
But all the Tartar camp along the stream
Was hushed, and still the men were plunged in sleep.
Sohrab alone, he slept not; all night long
He had lain wakeful, tossing on his bed:
But when the gray dawn stole into his tent,
He rose, and clad himself, and girt his sword,
And took his horseman's cloak, and left his tent,
And went abroad into the cold wet fog,
Through the dim camp to Peran-Wisa's tent.
 Through the black Tartar tents he passed, which stood
Clustering like bee-hives on the low flat strand
Of Oxus, where the summer-floods o'erflow
When the sun melts the snows in high Pamere;
Through the black tents he passed, o'er that low strand,
And to a hillock came, a little back
From the stream's brink, — the spot where first a boat,
Crossing the stream in summer, scrapes the land.
The men of former times had crowned the top
With a clay fort; but that was fallen, and now

The Tartars built there Peran-Wisa's tent,
A dome of laths, and o'er it felts were spread.
And Sohrab came there, and went in, and stood
Upon the thick piled carpets in the tent,
And found the old man sleeping on his bed
Of rugs and felts, and near him lay his arms.
And Peran-Wisa heard him, though the step
Was dulled ; for he slept light, an old man's sleep ;
And he rose quickly on one arm, and said, —
    "Who art thou? for it is not yet clear dawn.
Speak ! is there news, or any night alarm?"
    But Sohrab came to the bedside, and said, —
"Thou know'st me, Peran-Wisa ! it is I.
The sun has not yet risen, and the foe
Sleep : but I sleep not ; all night long I lie
Tossing and wakeful, and I come to thee.
For so did King Afrasiab bid me seek
Thy counsel, and to heed thee as thy son,
In Samarcand, before the army marched ;
And I will tell thee what my heart desires.
Thou know'st if, since from Ader-baijan first
I came among the Tartars, and bore arms,
I have still served Afrasiab well, and shown,
At my boy's years, the courage of a man.
This too thou know'st, that while I still bear on
The conquering Tartar ensigns through the world,
And beat the Persians back on every field,
I seek one man, one man, and one alone, —
Rustum, my father ; who I hoped should greet,
Should one day greet, upon some well-fought field,
His not unworthy, not inglorious son.
So I long hoped, but him I never find.
Come then, hear now, and grant me what I ask.
Let the two armies rest to-day ; but I

Will challenge forth the bravest Persian lords
To meet me, man to man : if I prevail,
Rustum will surely hear it ; if I fall —
Old man, the dead need no one, claim no kin.
Dim is the rumor of a common fight,
Where host meets host, and many names are sunk ;
But of a single combat fame speaks clear."
   He spoke ; and Peran-Wisa took the hand
Of the young man in his, and sighed, and said, —
   " O Sohrab, an unquiet heart is thine !
Canst thou not rest among the Tartar chiefs,
And share the battle's common chance with us
Who love thee, but must press forever first,
In single fight incurring single risk,
To find a father thou hast never seen ?
That were far best, my son, to stay with us
Unmurmuring ; in our tents, while it is war,
And when 'tis truce, then in Afrasiab's towns.
But if this one desire indeed rules all,
To seek out Rustum — seek him not through fight !
Seek him in peace, and carry to his arms,
O Sohrab, carry an unwounded son !
But far hence seek him, for he is not here.
For now it is not as when I was young,
When Rustum was in front of every fray :
But now he keeps apart, and sits at home,
In Seistan, with Zal, his father old ;
Whether that his own mighty strength at last
Feels the abhorred approaches of old age ;
Or in some quarrel with the Persian king.
There go ! — Thou wilt not ? Yet my heart forebodes
Danger or death awaits thee on this field.
Fain would I know thee safe and well, though lost
To us ; fain therefore send thee hence in peace

To seek thy father, not seek single fights
In vain.   But who can keep the lion's cub
From ravening, and who govern Rustum's son?
Go, I will grant thee what thy heart desires."
　　So said he, and dropped Sohrab's hand, and left
His bed, and the warm rugs whereon he lay;
And o'er his chilly limbs his woollen coat
He passed, and tied his sandals on his feet,
And threw a white cloak round him, and he took
In his right hand a ruler's staff, no sword;
And on his head he set his sheep-skin cap,
Black, glossy, curled, the fleece of Kara-Kul;
And raised the curtain of his tent, and called
His herald to his side, and went abroad.
　　The sun by this had risen, and cleared the fog
From the broad Oxus and the glittering sands.
And from their tents the Tartar horsemen filed
Into the open plain : so Haman bade, —
Haman, who next to Peran-Wisa ruled
The host, and still was in his lusty prime.
From their black tents, long files of horse, they
　　　　streamed;
As when some gray November morn the files,
In marching order spread, of long-necked cranes
Stream over Casbin and the southern slopes
Of Elburz, from the Aralian estuaries,
Or some frore Caspian reed-bed, southward bound
For the warm Persian seaboard, — so they streamed.
The Tartars of the Oxus, the king's guard,
First, with black sheep-skin caps and with long spears;
Large men, large steeds, who from Bokhara come
And Khiva, and ferment the milk of mares.
Next, the more temperate Toorkmuns of the south,
The Tukas, and the lances of Salore,

And those from Attruck and the Caspian sands ;
Light men and on light steeds, who only drink
The acrid milk of camels, and their wells.
And then a swarm of wandering horse, who came
From far, and a more doubtful service owned, —
The Tartars of Ferghana, from the banks
Of the Jaxartes, men with scanty beards
And close-set skull-caps ; and those wilder hordes
Who roam o'er Kipchak and the northern waste,
Kalmucks and unkempt Kuzzaks, tribes who stray
Nearest the Pole, and wandering Kirghizzes,
Who come on shaggy ponies from Pamere, —
These all filed out from camp into the plain.
And on the other side the Persians formed, —
First a light cloud of horse, Tartars they seemed,
The Ilyats of Khorassan ; and behind,
The royal troops of Persia, horse and foot,
Marshalled battalions bright in burnished steel.
But Peran-Wisa with his herald came,
Threading the Tartar squadrons to the front,
And with his staff kept back the foremost ranks.
And when Ferood, who led the Persians, saw
That Peran-Wisa kept the Tartars back,
He took his spear, and to the front he came,
And checked his ranks, and fixed them where they
        stood.
And the old Tartar came upon the sand
Betwixt the silent hosts, and spake, and said, —
    " Ferood, and ye, Persians and Tartars, hear !
Let there be truce between the hosts to-day.
But choose a champion from the Persian lords
To fight our champion Sohrab, man to man."
    As in the country, on a morn in June,
When the dew glistens on the pearled ears,

A shiver runs through the deep corn for joy, —
So, when they heard what Peran-Wisa said,
A thrill through all the Tartar squadrons ran
Of pride and hope for Sohrab, whom they loved.

But as a troop of pedlers from Cabool
Cross underneath the Indian Caucasus,
That vast sky-neighboring mountain of milk snow ;
Crossing so high, that, as they mount, they pass
Long flocks of travelling birds dead on the snow,
Choked by the air, and scarce can they themselves
Slake their parched throats with sugared mulberries ;
In single file they move, and stop their breath,
For fear they should dislodge the o'erhanging snows, —
So the pale Persians held their breath with fear.

And to Ferood his brother chiefs came up
To counsel ; Gudurz and Zoarrah came,
And Feraburz, who ruled the Persian host
Second, and was the uncle of the king ;
These came and counselled, and then Gudurz said, —

"Ferood, shame bids us take their challenge up,
Yet champion have we none to match this youth.
He has the wild stag's foot, the lion's heart.
But Rustum came last night ; aloof he sits
And sullen, and has pitched his tents apart.
Him will I seek, and carry to his ear
The Tartar challenge, and this young man's name ;
Haply he will forget his wrath, and fight.
Stand forth the while, and take their challenge up."

So spake he ; and Ferood stood forth and cried, —
"Old man, be it agreed as thou hast said !
Let Sohrab arm, and we will find a man."

He spake ; and Peran-Wisa turned, and strode
Back through the opening squadrons to his tent.
But through the anxious Persians Gudurz ran,

And crossed the camp which lay behind, and reached,
Out on the sands beyond it, Rustum's tents.
Of scarlet cloth they were, and glittering gay,
Just pitched ; the high pavilion in the midst
Was Rustum's, and his men lay camped around.
And Gudurz entered Rustum's tent, and found
Rustum ; his morning meal was done, but still
The table stood before him, charged with food, —
A side of roasted sheep, and cakes of bread,
And dark-green melons ; and there Rustum sate
Listless, and held a falcon on his wrist,
And played with it ; but Gudurz came and stood
Before him ; and he looked, and saw him stand,
And with a cry sprang up, and dropped the bird,
And greeted Gudurz with both hands, and said, —

"Welcome ! these eyes could see no better sight.
What news ? but sit down first, and eat and drink."

But Gudurz stood in the tent-door, and said, —
"Not now.   A time will come to eat and drink,
But not to-day : to-day has other needs.
The armies are drawn out, and stand at gaze ;
For, from the Tartars is a challenge brought
To pick a champion from the Persian lords
To fight their champion — and thou know'st his name :
Sohrab men call him, but his birth is hid.
O Rustum, like thy might is this young man's !
He has the wild stag's foot, the lion's heart ;
And he is young, and Iran's chiefs are old,
Or else too weak ; and all eyes turn to thee.
Come down and help us, Rustum, or we lose !"

He spoke ; but Rustum answered with a smile, —
"Go to ! if Iran's chiefs are old, then I
Am older.   If the young are weak, the king
Errs strangely ; for the king, for Kai Khosroo,

Himself is young, and honors younger men,
And lets the aged moulder to their graves.
Rustum he loves no more, but loves the young:
The young may rise at Sohrab's vaunts, not I.
For what care I, though all speak Sohrab's fame?
For would that I myself had such a son,
And not that one slight helpless girl I have!—
A son so famed, so brave, to send to war,
And I to tarry with the snow-haired Zal,
My father, whom the robber Afghans vex,
And clip his borders short, and drive his herds,
And he has none to guard his weak old age.
There would I go, and hang my armor up,
And with my great name fence that weak old man,
And spend the goodly treasures I have got,
And rest my age, and hear of Sohrab's fame,
And leave to death the hosts of thankless kings,
And with these slaughterous hands draw sword no
    more."
    He spoke, and smiled; and Gudurz made reply, —
"What then, O Rustum, will men say to this,
When Sohrab dares our bravest forth, and seeks
Thee most of all, and thou, whom most he seeks,
Hidest thy face?   Take heed lest men should say, —
*Like some old miser, Rustum hoards his fame,
And shuns to peril it with younger men.*"
    And, greatly moved, then Rustum made reply, —
"O Gudurz, wherefore dost thou say such word?
Thou knowest better words than this to say.
What is one more, one less, obscure or famed,
Valiant or craven, young or old, to me?
Are not they mortal? am not I myself?
But who for men of naught would do great deeds?
Come, thou shalt see how Rustum hoards his fame!

But I will fight unknown, and in plain arms :
Let not men say of Rustum, he was matched
In single fight with any mortal man."
 He spoke, and frowned ; and Gudurz turned, and ran
Back quickly through the camp in fear and joy, —
Fear at his wrath, but joy that Rustum came.
But Rustum strode to his tent-door, and called
His followers in, and bade them bring his arms,
And clad himself in steel.   The arms he chose
Were plain, and on his shield was no device ;
Only his helm was rich, inlaid with gold,
And, from the fluted spine a-top, a plume
Of horse-hair waved, a scarlet horse-hair plume.
So armed, he issued forth ; and Ruksh, his horse,
Followed him like a faithful hound at heel, —
Ruksh, whose renown was noised through all the earth,
The horse whom Rustum on a foray once
Did in Bokhara by the river find
A colt beneath its dam, and drove him home,
And reared him ; a bright bay, with lofty crest,
Dight with a saddle-cloth of broidered green
Crusted with gold, and on the ground were worked
All beasts of chase, all beasts which hunters know.
So followed, Rustum left his tents, and crossed
The camp, and to the Persian host appeared.
And all the Persians knew him, and with shouts
Hailed ; but the Tartars knew not who he was.
And dear as the wet diver to the eyes
Of his pale wife who waits and weeps on shore,
By sandy Bahrein, in the Persian Gulf,
Plunging all day in the blue waves, at night,
Having made up his tale of precious pearls,
Rejoins her in their hut upon the sands, —
So dear to the pale Persians Rustum came.

And Rustum to the Persian front advanced;
And Sohrab armed in Haman's tent, and came.
And as a-field the reapers cut a swath
Down through the middle of a rich man's corn,
And on each side are squares of standing corn,
And in the midst a stubble short and bare, —
So on each side were squares of men, with spears
Bristling, and in the midst the open sand.
And Rustum came upon the sand, and cast
His eyes toward the Tartar tents, and saw
Sohrab come forth, and eyed him as he came.

As some rich woman, on a winter's morn,
Eyes through her silken curtains the poor drudge
Who with numb blackened fingers makes her fire, —
At cock-crow, on a starlit winter's morn,
When the frost flowers the whitened window-panes, —
And wonders how she lives, and what the thoughts
Of that poor drudge may be; so Rustum eyed
The unknown adventurous youth, who from afar
Came seeking Rustum, and defying forth
All the most valiant chiefs; long he perused
His spirited air, and wondered who he was.
For very young he seemed, tenderly reared;
Like some young cypress, tall and dark and straight,
Which in a queen's secluded garden throws
Its slight dark shadow on the moonlit turf,
By midnight, to a bubbling fountain's sound, —
So slender Sohrab seemed, so softly reared.
And a deep pity entered Rustum's soul
As he beheld him coming; and he stood,
And beckoned to him with his hand, and said, —

"O thou young man, the air of heaven is soft,
And warm, and pleasant; but the grave is cold!
Heaven's air is better than the cold dead grave.

Behold me ! I am vast, and clad in iron,
And tried ; and I have stood on many a field
Of blood, and I have fought with many a foe :
Never was that field lost, or that foe saved.
O Sohrab, wherefore wilt thou rush on death?
Be governed : quit the Tartar host, and come
To Iran, and be as my son to me,
And fight beneath my banner till I die !
There are no youths in Iran brave as thou."
　　So he spake, mildly.　Sohrab heard his voice,
The mighty voice of Rustum, and he saw
His giant figure planted on the sand,
Sole, like some single tower, which a chief
Hath builded on the waste in former years
Against the robbers ; and he saw that head,
Streaked with its first gray hairs ; hope filled his soul,
And he ran forward, and embraced his knees,
And clasped his hand within his own, and said, —
　　"Oh, by thy father's head ! by thine own soul !
Art thou not Rustum?　Speak ! art thou not he?"
　　But Rustum eyed askance the kneeling youth,
And turned away, and spake to his own soul, —
　　"Ah me ! I muse what this young fox may mean !
False, wily, boastful, are these Tartar boys.
For if I now confess this thing he asks,
And hide it not, but say, *Rustum is here !*
He will not yield indeed, nor quit our foes ;
But he will find some pretext not to fight,
And praise my fame, and proffer courteous gifts,
A belt or sword perhaps, and go his way.
And on a feast-tide, in Afrasiab's hall
In Samarcand, he will arise and cry, —
　　'I challenged once, when the two armies camped
Beside the Oxus, all the Persian lords

To cope with me in single fight; but they
Shrank, only Rustum dared; then he and I
Changed gifts, and went on equal terms away.'
So will he speak, perhaps, while men applaud;
Then were the chiefs of Iran shamed through me."

And then he turned, and sternly spake aloud, —
"Rise! wherefore dost thou vainly question thus
Of Rustum? I am here, whom thou hast called
By challenge forth; make good thy vaunt, or yield!
Is it with Rustum only thou wouldst fight?
Rash boy, men look on Rustum's face, and flee!
For well I know, that did great Rustum stand
Before thy face this day, and were revealed,
There would be then no talk of fighting more.
But being what I am, I tell thee this, —
Do thou record it in thine inmost soul:
Either thou shalt renounce thy vaunt, and yield,
Or else thy bones shall strew this sand, till winds
Bleach them, or Oxus with his summer-floods,
Oxus in summer wash them all away."

He spoke; and Sohrab answered, on his feet, —
"Art thou so fierce? Thou wilt not fight me so!
I am no girl, to be made pale by words.
Yet this thou hast said well, did Rustum stand
Here on this field, there were no fighting then.
But Rustum is far hence, and we stand here.
Begin! thou art more vast, more dread than I;
And thou art proved, I know, and I am young —
But yet success sways with the breath of Heaven.
And though thou thinkest that thou knowest sure
Thy victory, yet thou canst not surely know.
For we are all, like swimmers in the sea,
Poised on the top of a huge wave of fate,
Which hangs uncertain to which side to fall;

And whether it will heave us up to land,
Or whether it will roll us out to sea, —
Back out to sea, to the deep waves of death, —
We know not, and no search will make us know :
Only the event will teach us in its hour."

He spoke ; and Rustum answered not, but hurled
His spear: down from the shoulder, down it came,
As on some partridge in the corn a hawk,
That long has towered in the airy clouds,
Drops like a plummet ; Sohrab saw it come,
And sprang aside, quick as a flash ; the spear
Hissed, and went quivering down into the sand,
Which it sent flying wide.   Then Sohrab threw
In turn, and full struck Rustum's shield ; sharp rang,
The iron plates rang sharp, but turned the spear.
And Rustum seized his club, which none but he
Could wield ; an unlopped trunk it was, and huge,
Still rough, — like those which men in treeless plains
To build them boats fish from the flooded rivers,
Hyphasis or Hydaspes, when, high up
By their dark springs, the wind in winter-time
Hath made in Himalayan forests wrack,
And strewn the channels with torn boughs, — so huge
The club which Rustum lifted now, and struck
One stroke ; but again Sohrab sprang aside,
Lithe as the glancing snake, and the club came
Thundering to earth, and leapt from Rustum's hand.
And Rustum followed his own blow, and fell
To his knees, and with his fingers clutched the sand.
And now might Sohrab have unsheathed his sword,
And pierced the mighty Rustum while he lay
Dizzy, and on his knees, and choked with sand ;
But he looked on, and smiled, nor bared his sword,
But courteously drew back, and spoke, and said, —

"Thou strik'st too hard! that club of thine will float
Upon the summer-floods, and not my bones.
But rise, and be not wroth! not wroth am I;
No, when I see thee, wrath forsakes my soul.
Thou say'st thou art not Rustum; be it so!
Who art thou, then, that canst so touch my soul?
Boy as I am, I have seen battles too,—
Have waded foremost in their bloody waves,
And heard their hollow roar of dying men;
But never was my heart thus touched before.
Are they from Heaven, these softenings of the heart?
O thou old warrior, let us yield to Heaven!
Come, plant we here in earth our angry spears,
And make a truce, and sit upon this sand,
And pledge each other in red wine, like friends,
And thou shalt talk to me of Rustum's deeds.
There are enough foes in the Persian host,
Whom I may meet, and strike, and feel no pang;
Champions enough Afrasiab has, whom thou
Mayst fight; fight *them*, when they confront thy spear!
But oh, let there be peace 'twixt thee and me!"

He ceased; but while he spake, Rustum had risen,
And stood erect, trembling with rage; his club
He left to lie, but had regained his spear,
Whose fiery point now in his mailed right hand
Blazed bright and baleful, like that autumn-star,
The baleful sign of fevers; dust had soiled
His stately crest, and dimmed his glittering arms.
His breast heaved, his lips foamed, and twice his voice
Was choked with rage; at last these words broke
        way:—

"Girl! nimble with thy feet, not with thy hands!
Curled minion, dancer, coiner of sweet words!
Fight, let me hear thy hateful voice no more!

Thou art not in Afrasiab's gardens now
With Tartar girls, with whom thou art wont to dance;
But on the Oxus-sands, and in the dance
Of battle, and with me, who make no play
Of war: I fight it out, and hand to hand.
Speak not to me of truce, and pledge, and wine!
Remember all thy valor; try thy feints
And cunning! all the pity I had is gone,
Because thou hast shamed me before both the hosts
With thy light skipping tricks and thy girl's wiles."
    He spoke; and Sohrab kindled at his taunts,
And he too drew his sword; at once they rushed
Together, as two eagles on one prey
Come rushing down together from the clouds,
One from the east, one from the west; their shields
Dashed with a clang together, and a din
Rose, such as that the sinewy woodcutters
Make often in the forest's heart at morn,
Of hewing axes, crashing trees, — such blows
Rustum and Sohrab on each other hailed.
And you would say that sun and stars took part
In that unnatural conflict: for a cloud
Grew suddenly in heaven, and darked the sun
Over the fighters' heads; and a wind rose
Under their feet, and moaning swept the plain,
And in a sandy whirlwind wrapped the pair.
In gloom they twain were wrapped, and they alone;
For both the on-looking hosts on either hand
Stood in broad daylight, and the sky was pure,
And the sun sparkled on the Oxus stream.
But in the gloom they fought, with bloodshot eyes
And laboring breath. First Rustum struck the shield
Which Sohrab held stiff out; the steel-spiked spear
Rent the tough plates, but failed to reach the skin,

And Rustum plucked it back with angry groan.
Then Sohrab with his sword smote Rustum's helm,
Nor clove its steel quite through ; but all the crest
He shore away, and that proud horse-hair plume,
Never till now defiled, sank to the dust ;
And Rustum bowed his head.   But then the gloom
Grew blacker, thunder rumbled in the air,
And lightnings rent the cloud ; and Ruksh the horse,
Who stood at hand, uttered a dreadful cry :
No horse's cry was that, most like the roar
Of some pained desert-lion, who all day
Has trailed the hunter's javelin in his side,
And comes at night to die upon the sand ;
The two hosts heard that cry, and quaked for fear,
And Oxus curdled as it crossed his stream.
But Sohrab heard, and quailed not, but rushed on,
And struck again ; and again Rustum bowed
His head ; but this time all the blade, like glass,
Sprang in a thousand shivers on the helm,
And in the hand the hilt remained alone.
Then Rustum raised his head ; his dreadful eyes
Glared, and he shook on high his menacing spear,
And shouted, *Rustum !*   Sohrab heard that shout,
And shrank amazed : back he recoiled one step,
And scanned with blinking eyes the advancing form ;
And then he stood bewildered, and he dropped
His covering shield, and the spear pierced his side.
He reeled, and staggering back sank to the ground.
And then the gloom dispersed, and the wind fell,
And the bright sun broke forth, and melted all
The cloud ; and the two armies saw the pair, —
Saw Rustum standing safe upon his feet,
And Sohrab wounded on the bloody sand.
  Then, with a bitter smile, Rustum began, —

"Sohrab, thou thoughtest in thy mind to kill
A Persian lord this day, and strip his corpse,
And bear thy trophies to Afrasiab's tent ;
Or else that the great Rustum would come down
Himself to fight, and that thy wiles would move
His heart to take a gift, and let thee go.
And then that all the Tartar host would praise
Thy courage or thy craft, and spread thy fame,
To glad thy father in his weak old age.
Fool, thou art slain, and by an unknown man !
Dearer to the red jackals shalt thou be
Than to thy friends, and to thy father old."

   And, with a fearless mien, Sohrab replied, —
"Unknown thou art, yet thy fierce vaunt is vain.
Thou dost not slay me, proud and boastful man !
No ! Rustum slays me, and this filial heart.
For, were I matched with ten such men as thee,
And I were that which till to-day I was,
They should be lying here, I standing there.
But that belovèd name unnerved my arm, —
That name, and something, I confess, in thee,
Which troubles all my heart, and made my shield
Fall ; and thy spear transfixed an unarmed foe.
And now thou boastest, and insult'st my fate.
But hear thou this, fierce man, tremble to hear :
The mighty Rustum shall avenge my death !
My father, whom I seek through all the world,
He shall avenge my death, and punish thee !"

   As when some hunter in the spring hath found
A breeding eagle sitting on her nest,
Upon the craggy isle of a hill-lake,
And pierced her with an arrow as she rose,
And followed her to find her where she fell
Far off ; anon her mate comes winging back

From hunting, and a great way off descries
His huddling young left sole ; at that, he checks
His pinion, and with short uneasy sweeps
Circles above his eyry, with loud screams
Chiding his mate back to her nest ; but she
Lies dying, with the arrow in her side,
In some far stony gorge out of his ken,
A heap of fluttering feathers, — never more
Shall the lake glass her, flying over it ;
Never the black and dripping precipices
Echo her stormy scream as she sails by, —
As that poor bird flies home, nor knows his loss,
So Rustum knew not his own loss, but stood
Over his dying son, and knew him not.

And with a cold, incredulous voice, he said, —
" What prate is this of fathers and revenge?
The mighty Rustum never had a son."

And, with a failing voice, Sohrab replied, —
" Ah, yes, he had ! and that lost son am I.
Surely the news will one day reach his ear, —
Reach Rustum, where he sits, and tarries long,
Somewhere, I know not where, but far from here ;
And pierce him like a stab, and make him leap
To arms, and cry for vengeance upon thee.
Fierce man, bethink thee, for an only son !
What will that grief, what will that vengeance, be?
Oh, could I live till I that grief had seen !
Yet him I pity not so much, but her,
My mother, who in Ader-baijan dwells
With that old king, her father, who grows gray
With age, and rules over the valiant Koords.
Her most I pity, who no more will see
Sohrab returning from the Tartar camp,
With spoils and honor, when the war is done.

But a dark rumor will be bruited up,
From tribe to tribe, until it reach her ear ;
And then will that defenceless woman learn
That Sohrab will rejoice her sight no more ;
But that in battle with a nameless foe,
By the far-distant Oxus, he is slain."
　He spoke ; and as he ceased, he wept aloud,
Thinking of her he left, and his own death.
He spoke ; but Rustum listened, plunged in thought.
Nor did he yet believe it was his son
Who spoke, although he called back names he knew ;
For he had had sure tidings that the babe
Which was in Ader-baijan born to him
Had been a puny girl, no boy at all —
So that sad mother sent him word, for fear
Rustum should seek the boy, to train in arms.
And so he deemed that either Sohrab took,
By a false boast, the style of Rustum's son ;
Or that men gave it him, to swell his fame.
So deemed he : yet he listened, plunged in thought ;
And his soul set to grief, as the vast tide
Of the bright rocking ocean sets to shore
At the full moon ; tears gathered in his eyes ;
For he remembered his own early youth,
And all its bounding rapture ; as, at dawn,
The shepherd from his mountain-lodge descries
A far, bright city, smitten by the sun,
Through many rolling clouds, — so Rustum saw
His youth ; saw Sohrab's mother in her bloom ;
And that old king, her father, who loved well
His wandering guest, and gave him his fair child
With joy ; and all the pleasant life they led,
They three, in that long-distant summer-time, —
The castle, and the dewy woods, and hunt

And hound, and morn on those delightful hills
In Ader-baijan.   And he saw that youth,
Of age and looks to be his own dear son,
Piteous and lovely, lying on the sand ;
Like some rich hyacinth which by the scythe
Of an unskilful gardener has been cut,
Mowing the garden grass-plots near its bed,
And lies, a fragrant tower of purple bloom,
On the mown, dying grass, — so Sohrab lay,
Lovely in death, upon the common sand.
And Rustum gazed on him with grief, and said, —

  "O Sohrab, thou indeed art such a son
Whom Rustum, wert thou his, might well have loved !
Yet here thou errest, Sohrab, or else men
Have told thee false : thou art not Rustum's son.
For Rustum had no son : one child he had, —
But one, — a girl ; who with her mother now
Plies some light female task, nor dreams of us, —
Of us she dreams not, nor of wounds, nor war."

  But Sohrab answered him in wrath ; for now
The anguish of the deep-fixed spear grew fierce,
And he desired to draw forth the steel,
And let the blood flow free, and so to die.
But first he would convince his stubborn foe ;
And, rising sternly on one arm, he said, —

  "Man, who art thou who dost deny my words?
Truth sits upon the lips of dying men ;
And falsehood, while I lived, was far from mine.
I tell thee, pricked upon this arm I bear
That seal which Rustum to my mother gave,
That she might prick it on the babe she bore."

  He spoke ; and all the blood left Rustum's cheeks,
And his knees tottered, and he smote his hand
Against his breast, his heavy mailèd hand,

That the hard iron corslet clanked aloud;
And to his heart he pressed the other hand,
And in a hollow voice he spake, and said, —
  "Sohrab, that were a proof which could not lie!
If thou show this, then art thou Rustum's son."
  Then, with weak hasty fingers, Sohrab loosed
His belt, and near the shoulder bared his arm,
And showed a sign in faint vermilion points
Pricked; as a cunning workman, in Pekin,
Pricks with vermilion some clear porcelain vase,
An emperor's gift, — at early morn he paints,
And all day long, and, when night comes, the lamp
Lights up his studious forehead and thin hands, —
So delicately pricked the sign appeared
On Sohrab's arm, the sign of Rustum's seal.
It was that griffin which of old reared Zal,
Rustum's great father, whom they left to die,
A helpless babe, among the mountain rocks;
Him that kind creature found, and reared, and loved;
Then Rustum took it for his glorious sign.
And Sohrab bared that image on his arm,
And himself scanned it long with mournful eyes,
And then he touched it with his hand, and said, —
  "How say'st thou? Is that sign the proper sign
Of Rustum's son, or of some other man's?"
  He spoke; but Rustum gazed, and gazed, and stood
Speechless; and then he uttered one sharp cry, —
O boy — thy father! and his voice choked there.
And then a dark cloud passed before his eyes,
And his head swam, and he sank down to earth.
But Sohrab crawled to where he lay, and cast
His arms about his neck, and kissed his lips,
And with fond faltering fingers stroked his cheeks,
Trying to call him back to life; and life

Came back to Rustum, and he oped his eyes,
And they stood wide with horror ; and he seized
In both his hands the dust which lay around,
And threw it on his head, and smirched his hair, —
His hair, and face, and beard, and glittering arms ;
And strong convulsive groanings shook his breast,
And his sobs choked him ; and he clutched his sword,
To draw it, and forever let life out.
But Sohrab saw his thought, and held his hands,
And with a soothing voice he spake, and said, —
　　 "Father, forbear ! for I but meet to-day
The doom which at my birth was written down
In Heaven, and thou art Heaven's unconscious hand.
Surely my heart cried out that it was thou,
When first I saw thee ; and thy heart spoke too,
I know it ! But fate trod those promptings down
Under its iron heel ; fate, fate engaged
The strife, and hurled me on my father's spear.
But let us speak no more of this. I find
My father, let me feel that I have found !
Come, sit beside me on this sand, and take
My head betwixt thy hands, and kiss my cheeks,
And wash them with thy tears, and say, *My son !*
Quick, quick ! for numbered are my sands of life,
And swift ; for like the lightning to this field
I came, and like the wind I go away, —
Sudden, and swift, and like a passing wind ;
But it was writ in Heaven that this should be."
　　 So said he ; and his voice released the heart
Of Rustum, and his tears broke forth ; he cast
His arms round his son's neck, and wept aloud,
And kissed him. And awe fell on both the hosts,
When they saw Rustum's grief ; and Ruksh, the horse,
With his head bowing to the ground, and mane

Sweeping the dust, came near, and in mute woe
First to the one, then to the other, moved
His head, as if inquiring what their grief
Might mean ; and from his dark, compassionate eyes,
The big warm tears rolled down, and caked the sand.
But Rustum chid him with stern voice, and said, —

    "Ruksh, now thou grievest ; but, O Ruksh, thy feet
Should then have rotted on their nimble joints,
When first they bore thy master to this field ! "

    But Sohrab looked upon the horse, and said, —
" Is this, then, Ruksh? How often, in past days,
My mother told me of thee, thou brave steed,
My terrible father's terrible horse ! and said,
That I should one day find thy lord and thee.
Come, let me lay my hand upon thy mane !
O Ruksh, thou art more fortunate than I !
For thou hast gone where I shall never go,
And snuffed the breezes of my father's home.
And thou hast trod the sands of Seistan,
And seen the River of Helmund, and the Lake
Of Zirrah ; and the aged Zal himself
Has often stroked thy neck, and given thee food,
Corn in a golden platter, soaked with wine,
And said, *O Ruksh ! bear Rustum well !* But I
Have never known my grandsire's furrowed face,
Nor seen his lofty house in Seistan,
Nor slaked my thirst at the clear Helmund stream ;
But lodged among my father's foes, and seen
Afrasiab's cities only, Samarcand,
Bokhara, and lone Khiva in the waste,
And the black Toorkmun tents ; and only drunk
The desert rivers, Moorghab and Tejend,
Kohik, and where the Kalmuks feed their sheep,
The northern Sir ; and this great Oxus stream,
The yellow Oxus, by whose brink I die."

Then, with a heavy groan, Rustum bewailed, —
" Oh that its waves were flowing over me !
Oh that I saw its grains of yellow silt
Roll tumbling in the current o'er my head !"
    But, with a grave mild voice, Sohrab replied, —
" Desire not that, my father ! thou must live.
For some are born to do great deeds, and live
As some are born to be obscured, and die.
Do thou the deeds I die too young to do,
And reap a second glory in thine age ;
Thou art my father, and thy gain is mine.
But come ! thou seest this great host of men
Which follow me ; I pray thee, slay not these !
Let me entreat for them : what have they done ?
They followed me, my hope, my fame, my star.
Let them all cross the Oxus back in peace.
But me thou must bear hence, not send with them,
But carry me with thee to Seistan,
And place me on a bed, and mourn for me, —
Thou, and the snow-haired Zal, and all thy friends.
And thou must lay me in that lovely earth,
And heap a stately mound above my bones,
And plant a far-seen pillar over all ;
That so the passing horseman on the waste
May see my tomb a great way off, and cry, —
Sohrab, the mighty Rustum's son, lies there,
Whom his great father did in ignorance kill !
And I be not forgotten in my grave."
    And, with a mournful voice, Rustum replied, —
" Fear not ! as thou hast said, Sohrab my son,
So shall it be ; for I will burn my tents,
And quit the host, and bear thee hence with me,
And carry thee away to Seistan,
And place thee on a bed, and mourn for thee,

With the snow-headed Zal, and all my friends.
And I will lay thee in that lovely earth,
And heap a stately mound above thy bones,
And plant a far-seen pillar over all,
And men shall not forget thee in thy grave.
And I will spare thy host; yea, let them go!
Let them all cross the Oxus back in peace!
What should I do with slaying any more?
For would that all whom I have ever slain
Might be once more alive, — my bitterest foes,
And they who were called champions in their time,
And through whose death I won that fame I have, —
And I were nothing but a common man,
A poor, mean soldier, and without renown,
So thou mightest live too, my son, my son!
Or rather would that I, even I myself,
Might now be lying on this bloody sand,
Near death, and by an ignorant stroke of thine,
Not thou of mine! and I might die, not thou;
And I, not thou, be borne to Seistan;
And Zal might weep above my grave, not thine;
And say, *O son, I weep thee not too sore,*
For willingly, I know, thou met'st thine end!
But now in blood and battles was my youth,
And full of blood and battles is my age,
And I shall never end this life of blood."

Then, at the point of death, Sohrab replied, —
" A life of blood indeed, thou dreadful man!
But thou shalt yet have peace; only not now,
Not yet! but thou shalt have it on that day,
When thou shalt sail in a high-masted ship,
Thou and the other peers of Kai Khosroo,
Returning home over the salt blue sea,
From laying thy dear master in his grave."

And Rustum gazed in Sohrab's face, and said,—
"Soon be that day, my son, and deep that sea!
Till then, if fate so wills, let me endure."

He spoke; and Sohrab smiled on him, and took
The spear, and drew it from his side, and eased
His wound's imperious anguish; but the blood
Came welling from the open gash, and life
Flowed with the stream; all down his cold white side
The crimson torrent ran, dim now and soiled,
Like the soiled tissue of white violets
Left, freshly gathered, on their native bank,
By children whom their nurses call with haste
In-doors from the sun's eye; his head drooped low,
His limbs grew slack; motionless, white, he lay,—
White, with eyes closed; only when heavy gasps,
Deep heavy gasps quivering through all his frame,
Convulsed him back to life, he opened them,
And fixed them feebly on his father's face;
Till now all strength was ebbed, and from his limbs
Unwillingly the spirit fled away,
Regretting the warm mansion which it left,
And youth, and bloom, and this delightful world.

So, on the bloody sand, Sohrab lay dead;
And the great Rustum drew his horseman's cloak
Down o'er his face, and sate by his dead son.
As those black granite pillars, once high-reared
By Jemshid in Persepolis, to bear
His house, now 'mid their broken flights of steps
Lie prone, enormous, down the mountain side,—
So in the sand lay Rustum by his son.

And night came down over the solemn waste,
And the two gazing hosts, and that sole pair,
And darkened all; and a cold fog, with night,
Crept from the Oxus. Soon a hum arose,

As of a great assembly loosed, and fires
Began to twinkle through the fog ; for now
Both armies moved to camp, and took their meal ;
The Persians took it on the open sands
Southward, the Tartars by the river-marge ;
And Rustum and his son were left alone.

   But the majestic river floated on,
Out of the mist and hum of that low land,
Into the frosty starlight, and there moved,
Rejoicing, through the hushed Chorasmian waste,
Under the solitary moon ; he flowed
Right for the polar star, past Orgunjè,
Brimming, and bright, and large ; then sands begin
To hem his watery march, and dam his streams,
And split his currents ; that for many a league
The shorn and parcelled Oxus strains along
Through beds of sand and matted rushy isles, —
Oxus, forgetting the bright speed he had
In his high mountain cradle in Pamere,
A foiled circuitous wanderer, — till at last
The longed-for dash of waves is heard, and wide
His luminous home of waters opens, bright
And tranquil, from whose floor the new-bathed stars
Emerge, and shine upon the Aral Sea.

THE SICK KING IN BOKHARA.

HUSSEIN.

O MOST just vizier, send away
The cloth-merchants, and let them be,
Them and their dues, this day ! the king
Is ill at ease, and calls for thee.

THE VIZIER.

O merchants, tarry yet a day
Here in Bokhara ! but at noon
To-morrow come, and ye shall pay
Each fortieth web of cloth to me,
As the law is, and go your way.

O Hussein, lead me to the king !
Thou teller of sweet tales, thine own,
Ferdousi's, and the others', lead !
How is it with my lord?

HUSSEIN.

Alone,
Ever since prayer-time, he doth wait,
O vizier ! without lying down,
In the great window of the gate,
Looking into the Registàn,
Where through the sellers' booths the slaves
Are this way bringing the dead man
O vizier, here is the king's door !

THE KING.

O vizier, I may bury him?

THE VIZIER.

O king, thou know'st, I have been sick
These many days, and heard no thing
(For Allah shut my ears and mind),
Not even what thou dost, O king!
Wherefore, that I may counsel thee,
Let Hussein, if thou wilt, make haste
To speak in order what hath chanced.

THE KING.

O vizier, be it as thou say'st!

HUSSEIN.

Three days since, at the time of prayer,
A certain Moollah, with his robe
All rent, and dust upon his hair,
Watched my lord's coming forth, and pushed
The golden mace-bearers aside,
And fell at the king's feet, and cried,—

"Justice, O king, and on myself!
On this great sinner, who did break
The law, and by the law must die!
Vengeance, O king!"

But the king spake:
"What fool is this, that hurts our ears
With folly? or what drunken slave?
My guards, what! prick him with your spears!
Prick me the fellow from the path!"

As the king said, so was it done,
And to the mosque my lord passed on.

But on the morrow, when the king
Went forth again, the holy book
Carried before him, as is right,
And through the square his way he took;

My man comes running, flecked with blood
From yesterday, and falling down
Cries out most earnestly, " O king,
My lord, O king, do right, I pray!

" How canst thou, ere thou hear, discern
If I speak folly? but a king,
Whether a thing be great or small,
Like Allah, hears and judges all.

" Wherefore hear thou! Thou know'st, how fierce
In these last days the sun hath burned;
That the green water in the tanks
Is to a putrid puddle turned;
And the canal, that from the stream
Of Samarcand is brought this way,
Wastes and runs thinner every day.

' Now I at nightfall had gone forth
Alone, and in a darksome place
Under some mulberry-trees I found
A little pool; and in short space
With all the water that was there
I filled my pitcher, and stole home
Unseen; and having drink to spare,
I hid the can behind the door,
And went up on the roof to sleep.

"But in the night, which was with wind
And burning dust, again I creep
Down, having fever, for a drink.

"Now, meanwhile had my brethren found
The water-pitcher, where it stood
Behind the door upon the ground,
And called my mother ; and they all,
As they were thirsty, and the night
Most sultry, drained the pitcher there ;
That they sate with it, in my sight,
Their lips still wet, when I came down.

"Now mark !   I, being fevered, sick,
(Most unblest also), at that sight
Brake forth, and cursed them — dost thou hear ? —
One was my mother. —— Now do right ! "

But my lord mused a space, and said, —
"Send him away, sirs, and make on !
It is some madman," the king said.
As the king bade, so was it done.

The morrow, at the self-same hour,
In the king's path, behold, the man,
Not kneeling, sternly fixed !   He stood
Right opposite, and thus began,
Frowning grim down : "Thou wicked king,
Most deaf where thou shouldst most give ear !
What ! must I howl in the next world,
Because thou wilt not listen here ?

"What ! wilt thou pray, and get thee grace,
And all grace shall to me be grudged ?
Nay, but I swear, from this thy path
I will not stir till I be judged ! "

Then they who stood about the king
Drew close together, and conferred;
Till that the king stood forth, and said,
"Before the priests thou shalt be heard."

But when the Ulemas were met,
And the thing heard, they doubted not;
But sentenced him, as the law is,
To die by stoning on the spot.

Now the king charged us secretly:
"Stoned must he be, the law stands so.
Yet, if he seek to fly, give way:
Hinder him not, but let him go."

So saying, the king took a stone,
And cast it softly; but the man,
With a great joy upon his face,
Kneeled down, and cried not, neither ran.

So they, whose lot it was, cast stones,
That they flew thick, and bruised him sore.
But he praised Allah with loud voice,
And remained kneeling as before.

My lord had covered up his face;
But when one told him, "He is dead,"
Turning him quickly to go in,
"Bring thou to me his corpse," he said.

And truly, while I speak, O king,
I hear the bearers on the stair:
Wilt thou they straightway bring him in?
— Ho! enter ye who tarry there!

THE VIZIER.

O king, in this I praise thee not !
Now must I call thy grief not wise.
Is he thy friend, or of thy blood,
To find such favor in thine eyes?

Nay, were he thine own mother's son,
Still thou art king, and the law stands.
It were not meet the balance swerved,
The sword were broken in thy hands.

But being nothing, as he is,
Why for no cause make sad thy face?
Lo, I am old ! three kings ere thee
Have I seen reigning in this place.

But who, through all this length of time,
Could bear the burden of his years,
If he for strangers pained his heart
Not less than those who merit tears?

Fathers we *must* have, wife and child,
And grievous is the grief for these ;
This pain alone, which *must* be borne,
Makes the head white, and bows the knees.

But other loads than this his own,
One man is not well made to bear.
Besides, to each are his own friends,
To mourn with him, and show him care.

Look, this is but one single place,
Though it be great ; all the earth round,
If a man bear to have it so,
Things which might vex him shall be found.

Upon the Russian frontier, where
The watchers of two armies stand
Near one another, many a man,
Seeking a prey unto his hand,

Hath snatched a little fair-haired slave ;
They snatch also, towards Mervè,
The Shiah dogs, who pasture sheep,
And up from thence to Orgunjè.

And these all, laboring for a lord,
  Eat not the fruit of their own hands ;
Which is the heaviest of all plagues,
To that man's mind who understands.

The kaffirs also (whom God curse !)
Vex one another, night and day ;
There are the lepers, and all sick ;
There are the poor, who faint alway.

All these have sorrow, and keep still,
Whilst other men make cheer, and sing.
Wilt thou have pity on all these ?
No, nor on this dead dog, O king !

THE KING.

O vizier, thou art old, I young !
Clear in these things I cannot see.
My head is burning, and a heat
Is in my skin which angers me.

But hear ye this, ye sons of men !
They that bear rule, and are obeyed,
Unto a rule more strong than theirs
Are in their turn obedient made.

In vain therefore, with wistful eyes
Gazing up hither, the poor man,
Who loiters by the high-heaped booths,
Below there, in the Registàn, —

Says, "Happy he who lodges there!
With silken raiment, store of rice,
And for this drought, all kinds of fruits,
Grape-sirup, squares of colored ice, —

"With cherries served in drifts of snow."
In vain hath a king power to build
Houses, arcades, enamelled mosques;
And to make orchard-closes, filled

With curious fruit-trees brought from far,
With cisterns for the winter-rain,
And, in the desert, spacious inns
In divers places, — if that pain

Is not more lightened, which he feels,
If his will be not satisfied;
And that it be not, from all time
The law is planted, to abide.

Thou wast a sinner, thou poor man!
Thou wast athirst; and didst not see,
That, though we take what we desire, ·
We must not snatch it eagerly.

And I have meat and drink at will,
And rooms of treasures, not a few.
But I am sick, nor heed I these;
And what I would, I cannot do.

Even the great honor which I have,
When I am dead, will soon grow still;
So have I neither joy, nor fame.
But what I can do, that I will.

I have a fretted brick-work tomb
Upon a hill on the right hand,
Hard by a close of apricots,
Upon the road of Samarcand;

Thither, O vizier, will I bear
This man my pity could not save,
And, plucking up the marble flags,
There lay his body in my grave.

Bring water, nard, and linen-rolls!
Wash off all blood, set smooth each limb!
Then say, " He was not wholly vile,
Because a king shall bury him."

BALDER DEAD.[6]

I. SENDING.

So on the floor lay Balder dead; and round
Lay thickly strewn swords, axes, darts, and spears,
Which all the gods in sport had idly thrown
At Balder, whom no weapon pierced or clove;
But in his breast stood fixed the fatal bough
Of mistletoe, which Lok the Accuser gave
To Hoder, and unwitting Hoder threw —
'Gainst that alone had Balder's life no charm.

And all the gods and all the heroes came,
And stood round Balder on the bloody floor,
Weeping and wailing; and Valhalla rang
Up to its golden roof with sobs and cries;
And on the tables stood the untasted meats,
And in the horns and gold-rimmed sculls the wine.
And now would night have fallen, and found them yet
Wailing; but otherwise was Odin's will.
And thus the Father of the ages spake:—

"Enough of tears, ye gods, enough of wail!
Not to lament in was Valhalla made.
If any here might weep for Balder's death,
I most might weep, his father; such a son
I lose to-day, so bright, so loved a god.
But he has met that doom which long ago
The Nornies, when his mother bare him, spun,
And fate set seal, that so his end must be.
Balder has met his death, and ye survive.
Weep him an hour, but what can grief avail?
For ye yourselves, ye gods, shall meet your doom,—
All ye who hear me, and inhabit heaven,
And I too, Odin too, the lord of all.
But ours we shall not meet, when that day comes,
With women's tears and weak complaining cries:
Why should we meet another's portion so?
Rather it fits you, having wept your hour,
With cold dry eyes, and hearts composed and stern,
To live, as erst, your daily life in heaven.
By me shall vengeance on the murderer Lok,
The foe, the accuser, whom, though gods, we hate,
Be strictly cared for, in the appointed day.
Meanwhile, to-morrow, when the morning dawns,
Bring wood to the seashore to Balder's ship,
And on the deck build high a funeral pile,

And on the top lay Balder's corpse, and put
Fire to the wood, and send him out to sea
To burn ; for that is what the dead desire."

So spake the king of gods, and straightway rose,
And mounted his horse Sleipner, whom he rode ;
And from the hall of heaven he rode away
To Lidskialf, and sate upon his throne,
The mount, from whence his eye surveys the world.
And far from heaven he turned his shining orbs
To look on Midgard, and the earth, and men.
And on the conjuring Lapps he bent his gaze,
Whom antlered reindeer pull over the snow ;
And on the Finns, the gentlest of mankind,
Fair men, who live in holes under the ground ;
Nor did he look once more to Ida's plain,
Nor toward Valhalla and the sorrowing gods ;
For well he knew the gods would heed his word,
And cease to mourn, and think of Balder's pyre.

But in Valhalla all the gods went back
From around Balder, all the heroes went ;
And left his body stretched upon the floor.
And on their golden chairs they sate again,
Beside the tables, in the hall of heaven ;
And before each the cooks who served them placed
New messes of the boar Serimner's flesh,
And the Valkyries crowned their horns with mead.
So they, with pent-up hearts and tearless eyes,
Wailing no more, in silence ate and drank,
While twilight fell, and sacred night came on.

But the blind Hoder left the feasting gods
In Odin's hall, and went through Asgard streets,
And past the haven where the gods have moored
Their ships, and through the gate, beyond the wall ;
Though sightless, yet his own mind led the god.

Down to the margin of the roaring sea
He came, and sadly went along the sand,
Between the waves and black o'erhanging cliffs
Where in and out the screaming seafowl fly;
Until he came to where a gully breaks
Through the cliff-wall, and a fresh stream runs down
From the high moors behind, and meets the sea.
There, in the glen, Fensaler stands, the house
Of Frea, honored mother of the gods,
And shows its lighted windows to the main.
There he went up, and passed the open doors;
And in the hall he found those women old,
The prophetesses, who by rite eterne
On Frea's hearth feed high the sacred fire
Both night and day; and by the inner wall
Upon her golden chair the mother sate,
With folded hands, revolving things to come.
To her drew Hoder near, and spake, and said, —

  "Mother, a child of bale thou bar'st in me!
For, first, thou barest me with blinded eyes,
Sightless and helpless, wandering weak in heaven;
And, after that, of ignorant witless mind
Thou barest me, and unforeseeing soul;
That I alone must take the branch from Lok,
The foe, the accuser, whom, though gods, we hate,
And cast it at the dear-loved Balder's breast,
At whom the gods in sport their weapons threw.
'Gainst that alone had Balder's life no charm.
Now therefore what to attempt, or whither fly,
For who will bear my hateful sight in heaven?
Can I, O mother, bring them Balder back?
Or — for thou know'st the fates, and things allowed —
Can I with Hela's power a compact strike,
And make exchange, and give my life for his?"

He spoke : the mother of the gods replied, —
" Hoder, ill-fated, child of bale, my son,
Sightless in soul and eye, what words are these ?
That one, long portioned with his doom of death,
Should change his lot, and fill another's life,
And Hela yield to this, and let him go !
On Balder, Death hath laid her hand, not thee ;
Nor doth she count this life a price for that.
For many gods in heaven, not thou alone,
Would freely die to purchase Balder back,
And wend themselves to Hela's gloomy realm.
For not so gladsome is that life in heaven
Which gods and heroes lead, in feast and fray,
Waiting the darkness of the final times,
That one should grudge its loss for Balder's sake, —
Balder their joy, so bright, so loved a god.
But fate withstands, and laws forbid this way.
Yet in my secret mind one way I know,
Nor do I judge if it shall win or fail ;
But much must still be tried, which shall but fail."

     And the blind Hoder answered her, and said, —
" What way is this, O mother, that thou show'st ?
Is it a matter which a god might try ? "

     And straight the mother of the gods replied, —
" There is a way which leads to Hela's realm,
Untrodden, lonely, far from light and heaven.
Who goes that way must take no other horse
To ride, but Sleipner, Odin's horse, alone.
Nor must he choose that common path of gods
Which every day they come and go in heaven,
O'er the bridge Bifrost, where is Heimdall's watch,
Past Midgard fortress, down to earth and men.
But he must tread a dark untravelled road
Which branches from the north of heaven, and ride

Nine days, nine nights, toward the northern ice,
Through valleys deep-ingulfed with roaring streams.
And he will reach on the tenth morn a bridge
Which spans with golden arches Giall's stream,
Not Bifrost, but that bridge a damsel keeps,
Who tells the passing troops of dead their way
To the low shore of ghosts, and Hela's realm.
And she will bid him northward steer his course.
Then he will journey through no lighted land,
Nor see the sun arise, nor see it set ;
But he must ever watch the northern Bear,
Who from her frozen height with jealous eye
Confronts the Dog and Hunter in the south,
And is alone not dipt in ocean's stream ;
And straight he will come down to ocean's strand, --
Ocean, whose watery ring infolds the world,
And on whose marge the ancient giants dwell.
But he will reach its unknown northern shore,
Far, far beyond the outmost giant's home,
At the chinked fields of ice, the wastes of snow.
And he must fare across the dismal ice
Northward, until he meets a stretching wall
Barring his way, and in the wall a grate.
But then he must dismount, and on the ice
Tighten the girths of Sleipner, Odin's horse,
And make him leap the grate, and come within.
And he will see stretch round him Hela's realm,
The plains of Niflheim, where dwell the dead,
And hear the roaring of the streams of hell.
And he will see the feeble, shadowy tribes,
And Balder sitting crowned, and Hela's throne.
Then must he not regard the wailful ghosts
Who all will flit, like eddying leaves, around ;
But he must straight accost their solemn queen,

And pay her homage, and entreat with prayers,
Telling her all that grief they have in heaven
For Balder, whom she holds by right below;
If haply he may melt her heart with words,
And make her yield, and give him Balder back."

She spoke; but Hoder answered her and said, --
"Mother, a dreadful way is this thou show'st;
No journey for a sightless god to go!"

And straight the mother of the gods replied, —
"Therefore thyself thou shalt not go, my son.
But he whom first thou meetest when thou com'st
To Asgard, and declar'st this hidden way,
Shall go; and I will be his guide unseen."
She spoke, and on her face let fall her veil,
And bowed her head, and sate with folded hands.
But at the central hearth those women old,
Who while the mother spake had ceased their toil,
Began again to heap the sacred fire.
And Hoder turned, and left his mother's house,
Fensaler, whose lit windows look to sea;
And came again down to the roaring waves,
And back along the beach to Asgard went,
Pondering on that which Frea said should be.

But night came down, and darkened Asgard streets.
Then from their loathèd feast the gods arose,
And lighted torches, and took up the corpse
Of Balder from the floor of Odin's hall,
And laid it on a bier, and bare him home
Through the fast-darkening streets to his own house
Breidablik, on whose columns Balder graved
The enchantments that recall the dead to life.
For wise he was, and many curious arts,
Postures of runes, and healing herbs he knew;
Unhappy! but that art he did not know,

To keep his own life safe, and see the sun.
There to his hall the gods brought Balder home,
And each bespake him as he laid him down, —

    "Would that ourselves, O Balder, we were borne
Home to our halls, with torchlight, by our kin,
So thou might'st live, and still delight the gods!"

    They spake, and each went home to his own house.
But there was one, the first of all the gods
For speed, and Hermod was his name in heaven;
Most fleet he was, but now he went the last,
Heavy in heart for Balder, to his house
Which he in Asgard built him, there to dwell,
Against the harbor, by the city-wall.
Him the blind Hoder met, as he came up
From the sea cityward, and knew his step;
Nor yet could Hermod see his brother's face,
For it grew dark; but Hoder touched his arm.
And as a spray of honeysuckle-flowers
Brushes across a tired traveller's face
Who shuffles through the deep dew-moistened dust,
On a May evening, in the darkened lanes,
And starts him, that he thinks a ghost went by, —
So Hoder brushed by Hermod's side, and said, —

    "Take Sleipner, Hermod, and set forth with dawn
To Hela's kingdom, to ask Balder back;
And they shall be thy guides, who have the power."

    He spake, and brushed soft by, and disappeared.
And Hermod gazed into the night, and said, —

    "Who is it utters through the dark his hest
So quickly, and will wait for no reply?
The voice was like the unhappy Hoder's voice.
Howbeit I will see, and do his hest;
For there rang note divine in that command."

    So speaking, the fleet-footed Hermod came

Home, and lay down to sleep in his own house;
And all the gods lay down in their own homes.
And Hoder too came home, distraught with grief,
Loathing to meet, at dawn, the other gods;
And he went in, and shut the door, and fixed
His sword upright, and fell on it, and died.

But from the hill of Lidskialf Odin rose, —
The throne from which his eye surveys the world, —
And mounted Sleipner, and in darkness rode
To Asgard.   And the stars came out in heaven,
High over Asgard, to light home the king.
But fiercely Odin galloped, moved in heart;
And swift to Asgard, to the gate, he came;
And terribly the hoofs of Sleipner rang
Along the flinty floor of Asgard streets;
And the gods trembled on their golden beds
Hearing the wrathful Father coming home, —
For dread, for like a whirlwind, Odin came.
And to Valhalla's gate he rode, and left
Sleipner; and Sleipner went to his own stall;
And in Valhalla Odin laid him down.

But in Breidablik Nanna, Balder's wife,
Came with the goddesses who wrought her will,
And stood by Balder lying on his bier.
And at his head and feet she stationed scalds
Who in their lives were famous for their song;
These o'er the corpse intoned a plaintive strain,
A dirge, — and Nanna and her train replied.
And far into the night they wailed their dirge;
But when their souls were satisfied with wail,
They went, and laid them down, and Nanna went
Into an upper chamber, and lay down;
And Frea sealed her tired lids with sleep.

And 'twas when night is bordering hard on dawn,

When air is chilliest, and the stars sunk low;
Then Balder's spirit through the gloom drew near,
In garb, in form, in feature, as he was,
Alive; and still the rays were round his head
Which were his glorious mark in heaven; he stood
Over against the curtain of the bed,
And gazed on Nanna as she slept, and spake, —

"Poor lamb, thou sleepest, and forgett'st thy woe!
Tears stand upon the lashes of thine eyes,
Tears wet the pillow by thy cheek; but thou,
Like a young child, hast cried thyself to sleep.
Sleep on; I watch thee, and am here to aid.
Alive I kept not far from thee, dear soul!
Neither do I neglect thee now, though dead.
For with to-morrow's dawn the gods prepare
To gather wood, and build a funeral-pile
Upon my ship, and burn my corpse with fire,
That sad, sole honor of the dead; and thee
They think to burn, and all my choicest wealth,
With me, for thus ordains the common rite.
But it shall not be so; but mild, but swift,
But painless, shall a stroke from Frea come,
To cut thy thread of life, and free thy soul,
And they shall burn thy corpse with mine, not thee.
And well I know that by no stroke of death,
Tardy or swift, wouldst thou be loath to die,
So it restored thee, Nanna, to my side,
Whom thou so well hast loved; but I can smooth
Thy way, and this, at least, my prayers avail.
Yes, and I fain would altogether ward
Death from thy head, and with the gods in heaven
Prolong thy life, though not by thee desired;
But right bars this, not only thy desire.
Yet dreary, Nanna, is the life they lead

In that dim world, in Hela's mouldering realm;
And doleful are the ghosts, the troops of dead,
Whom Hela with austere control presides.
For of the race of gods is no one there,
Save me alone, and Hela, solemn queen.
For all the nobler souls of mortal men
On battle-field have met their death, and now
Feast in Valhalla, in my father's hall:
Only the inglorious sort are there below;
The old, the cowards, and the weak are there,—
Men spent by sickness, or obscure decay.
But even there, O Nanna, we might find
Some solace in each other's look and speech,
Wandering together through that gloomy world,
And talking of the life we led in heaven,
While we yet lived, among the other gods."

　　He spake, and straight his lineaments began
To fade; and Nanna in her sleep stretched out
Her arms towards him with a cry; but he
Mournfully shook his head, and disappeared.
And as the woodman sees a little smoke
Hang in the air afield, and disappear,
So Balder faded in the night away.
And Nanna on her bed sank back; but then
Frea, the mother of the gods, with stroke
Painless and swift, set free her airy soul,
Which took, on Balder's track, the way below;
And instantly the sacred morn appeared.

II. JOURNEY TO THE DEAD.

FORTH from the east, up the ascent of heaven,
Day drove his courser with the shining mane;

And in Valhalla, from his gable-perch,
The golden-crested cock began to crow.
Hereafter, in the blackest dead of night,
With shrill and dismal cries that bird shall crow,
Warning the gods that foes draw nigh to heaven ;
But now he crew at dawn, a cheerful note,
To wake the gods and heroes to their tasks.
And all the gods and all the heroes woke.
And from their beds the heroes rose, and donned
Their arms, and led their horses from the stall,
And mounted them, and in Valhalla's court
Were ranged ; and then the daily fray began.
And all day long they there are hacked and hewn
'Mid dust, and groans, and limbs lopped off, and
        blood ;
But all at night return to Odin's hall
Woundless and fresh : such lot is theirs in heaven.
And the Valkyries on their steeds went forth
Toward earth and fights of men ; and at their side
Skulda, the youngest of the Nornies, rode ;
And over Bifrost, where is Heimdall's watch,
Past Midgard fortress, down to earth they came ;
There through some battle-field, where men fall fast,
Their horses fetlock-deep in blood, they ride,
And pick the bravest warriors out for death,
Whom they bring back with them at night to heaven,
To glad the gods, and feast in Odin's hall.
    But the gods went not now, as otherwhile,
Into the tilt-yard, where the heroes fought,
To feast their eyes with looking on the fray ;
Nor did they to their judgment-place repair
By the ash Igdrasil, in Ida's plain,
Where they hold council, and give laws for men.
But they went, Odin first, the rest behind,

To the hall Gladheim, which is built of gold;
Where are in circle ranged twelve golden chairs,
And in the midst one higher, Odin's throne.
There all the gods in silence sate them down;
And thus the Father of the ages spake: —
    "Go quickly, gods, bring wood to the seashore,
With all which it beseems the dead to have,
And make a funeral-pile on Balder's ship;
On the twelfth day the gods shall burn his corpse.
But, Hermod, thou take Sleipner, and ride down
To Hela's kingdom, to ask Balder back."
    So said he; and the gods arose, and took
Axes and ropes, and at their head came Thor,
Shouldering his hammer, which the giants know.
Forth wended they, and drave their steeds before.
And up the dewy mountain tracks they fared
To the dark forests, in the early dawn;
And up and down, and side and slant they roamed.
And from the glens all day an echo came
Of crashing falls; for with his hammer Thor
Smote 'mid the rocks the lichen-bearded pines,
And burst their roots, while to their tops the gods
Made fast the woven ropes, and haled them down,
And lopped their boughs, and clove them on the sward,
And bound the logs behind their steeds to draw,
And drave them homeward; and the snorting steeds
Went straining through the crackling brushwood down,
And by the darkling forest-paths the gods
Followed, and on their shoulders carried boughs.
And they came out upon the plain, and passed
Asgard, and led their horses to the beach,
And loosed them of their loads on the seashore,
And ranged the wood in stacks by Balder's ship;
And every god went home to his own house.

But when the gods were to the forest gone,
Hermod led Sleipner from Valhalla forth,
And saddled him : before that, Sleipner brooked
No meaner hand than Odin's on his mane,
On his broad back no lesser rider bore ;
Yet docile now he stood at Hermod's side,
Arching his neck, and glad to be bestrode,
Knowing the god they went to seek, how dear.
But Hermod mounted him, and sadly fared
In silence up the dark untravelled road
Which branches from the north of heaven, and went
All day ; and daylight waned, and night came on.
And all that night he rode, and journeyed so,
Nine days, nine nights, toward the northern ice,
Through valleys deep-ingulfed, by roaring streams.
And on the tenth morn he beheld the bridge
Which spans with golden arches Giall's stream,
And on the bridge a damsel watching armed,
In the strait passage, at the farther end,
Where the road issues between walling rocks.
Scant space that warder left for passers-by ;
But as when cowherds in October drive
Their kine across a snowy mountain pass
To winter pasture on the southern side,
And on the ridge a wagon chokes the way,
Wedged in the snow ; then painfully the hinds
With goad and shouting urge their cattle past,
Plunging through deep untrodden banks of snow
To right and left, and warm steam fills the air, —
So on the bridge that damsel blocked the way,
And questioned Hermod as he came, and said, —

  "Who art thou on thy black and fiery horse,
Under whose hoofs the bridge o'er Giall's stream
Rumbles and shakes? Tell me thy race and home.

But yester-morn, five troops of dead passed by,
Bound on their way below to Hela's realm,
Nor shook the bridge so much as thou alone.
And thou hast flesh and color on thy cheeks,
Like men who live, and draw the vital air;
Nor look'st thou pale and wan, like men deceased,
Souls bound below, my daily passers here."

And the fleet-footed Hermod answered her, —
"O damsel, Hermod am I called, the son
Of Odin; and my high-roofed house is built
Far hence, in Asgard, in the city of gods;
And Sleipner, Odin's horse, is this I ride.
And I come, sent this road on Balder's track:
Say, then, if he hath crossed thy bridge or no?"

He spake; the warder of the bridge replied, —
"O Hermod, rarely do the feet of gods
Or of the horses of the gods resound
Upon my bridge; and, when they cross, I know.
Balder hath gone this way, and ta'en the road
Below there, to the north, toward Hela's realm.
From here the cold white mist can be discerned,
Not lit with sun, but through the darksome air
By the dim vapor-blotted light of stars,
Which hangs over the ice where lies the road.
For in that ice are lost those northern streams,
Freezing and ridging in their onward flow,
Which from the fountain of Vergelmer run,
The spring that bubbles up by Hela's throne.
There are the joyless seats, the haunt of ghosts,
Hela's pale swarms; and there was Balder bound.
Ride on! pass free! but he by this is there."

She spake, and stepped aside, and left him room.
And Hermod greeted her, and galloped by
Across the bridge; then she took post again.

But northward Hermod rode, the way below;
And o'er a darksome tract, which knows no sun,
But by the blotted light of stars, he fared.
And he came down to ocean's northern strand,
At the drear ice, beyond the giants' home.
Thence on he journeyed o'er the fields of ice
Still north, until he met a stretching wall
Barring his way, and in the wall a grate.
Then he dismounted, and drew tight the girths,
On the smooth ice, of Sleipner, Odin's horse,
And made him leap the grate, and came within.
And he beheld spread round him Hela's realm,
The plains of Niflheim, where dwell the dead,
And heard the thunder of the streams of hell.
For near the wall the river of Roaring flows,
Outmost; the others near the centre run, —
The Storm, the Abyss, the Howling, and the Pain;
These flow by Hela's throne, and near their spring.
And from the dark flocked up the shadowy tribes;
And as the swallows crowd. the bulrush-beds
Of some clear river, issuing from a lake,
On autumn-days, before they cross the sea;
And to each bulrush-crest a swallow hangs
Swinging, and others skim the river-streams,
And their quick twittering fills the banks and shores, —
So around Hermod swarmed the twittering ghosts.
Women, and infants, and young men who died
Too soon for fame, with white ungraven shields;
And old men, known to glory, but their star
Betrayed them, and of wasting age they died,
Not wounds; yet, dying, they their armor wore,
And now have chief regard in Hela's realm.
Behind flocked wrangling up a piteous crew,
Greeted of none. disfeatured and forlorn, —

Cowards, who were in sloughs interred alive;
And round them still the wattled hurdles hung
Wherewith they stamped them down, and trod them
          deep,
To hide their shameful memory from men.
But all he passed unhailed, and reached the throne
Of Hela, and saw, near it, Balder crowned,
And Hela set thereon, with countenance stern;
And thus bespake him first the solemn queen : —
     " Unhappy, how hast thou endured to leave
The light, and journey to the cheerless land
Where idly flit about the feeble shades?
How didst thou cross the bridge o'er Giall's stream,
Being alive, and come to ocean's shore?
Or how o'erleap the grate that bars the wall?"
     She spake; but down off Sleipner Hermod sprang,
And fell before her feet, and clasped her knees;
And spake, and mild entreated her, and said, —
     " O Hela, wherefore should the gods declare
Their errands to each other, or the ways
They go? the errand and the way is known.
Thou know'st, thou know'st, what grief we have in
          heaven
For Balder, whom thou hold'st by right below.
Restore him! for what part fulfils he here?
Shall he shed cheer over the cheerless seats,
And touch the apathetic ghosts with joy?
Not for such end, O queen, thou hold'st thy realm.
For heaven was Balder born, the city of gods
And heroes, where they live in light and joy.
Thither restore him, for his place is there!"
     He spoke; and grave replied the solemn queen, —
" Hermod, for he thou art, thou son of heaven!
A strange unlikely errand, sure, is thine.

Do the gods send to me to make them blest?
Small bliss my race hath of the gods obtained.
Three mighty children to my father Lok
Did Angerbode, the giantess, bring forth, —
Fenris the wolf, the serpent huge, and me.
Of these the serpent in the sea ye cast,
Who since in your despite hath waxed amain,
And now with gleaming ring infolds the world;
Me on this cheerless nether world ye threw,
And gave me nine unlighted realms to rule;
While on his island in the lake afar,
Made fast to the bored crag, by wile not strength
Subdued, with limber chains lives Fenris bound.
Lok still subsists in heaven, our father wise,
Your mate, though loathed, and feasts in Odin's hall;
But him too foes await, and netted snares,
And in a cave a bed of needle-rocks,
And o'er his visage serpents dropping gall.
Yet he shall one day rise, and burst his bonds,
And with himself set us his offspring free,
When he guides Muspel's children to their bourne.
Till then in peril or in pain we live,
Wrought by the gods — and ask the gods our aid?
Howbeit, we abide our day: till then,
We do not as some feebler haters do, —
Seek to afflict our foes with petty pangs,
Helpless to better us, or ruin them.
Come, then! if Balder was so dear beloved,
And this is true, and such a loss is heaven's, —
Hear how to heaven may Balder be restored.
Show me through all the world the signs of grief!
Fails but one thing to grieve, here Balder stops!
Let all that lives and moves upon the earth
Weep him, and all that is without life weep;

Let gods, men, brutes, beweep him ; plants and stones.
So shall I know the lost was dear indeed,
And bend my heart, and give him back to heaven."

    She spake ; and Hermod answered her, and said, —
" Hela, such as thou say'st, the terms shall be.
But come, declare me this, and truly tell :
May I, ere I depart, bid Balder hail,
Or is it here withheld to greet the dead ? "

    He spake ; and straightway Hela answered him, —
" Hermod, greet Balder if thou wilt, and hold
Converse ; his speech remains, though he be dead."

    And straight to Balder Hermod turned, and spake :
" Even in the abode of death, O Balder, hail !
Thou hear'st, if hearing, like as speech, is thine,
The terms of thy releasement hence to heaven ;
Fear nothing but that all shall be fulfilled.
For not unmindful of thee are the gods,
Who see the light, and blest in Asgard dwell ;
Even here they seek thee out, in Hela's realm.
And, sure, of all the happiest far art thou
Who ever have been known in earth or heaven :
Alive, thou wast of gods the most beloved ;
And now thou sittest crowned by Hela's side,
Here, and hast honor among all the dead."

    He spake ; and Balder uttered him reply,
But feebly, as a voice far off ; he said, —

    " Hermod the nimble, gild me not my death !
Better to live a serf, a captured man,
Who scatters rushes in a master's hall,
Than be a crowned king here, and rule the dead.
And now I count not of these terms as safe
To be fulfilled, nor my return as sure,
Though I be loved, and many mourn my death ;
For double-minded ever was the seed

Of Lok, and double are the gifts they give.
Howbeit, report thy message ; and therewith,
To Odin, to my father, take this ring,
Memorial of me, whether saved or no ;
And tell the heaven-born gods how thou hast seen
Me sitting here below by Hela's side,
Crowned, having honor among all the dead."
   He spake, and raised his hand, and gave the ring.
And with inscrutable regard the queen
Of hell beheld them, and the ghosts stood dumb.
But Hermod took the ring, and yet once more
Kneeled and did homage to the solemn queen ;
Then mounted Sleipner, and set forth to ride
Back, through the astonished tribes of dead, to heaven.
And to the wall he came, and found the grate
Lifted, and issued on the fields of ice.
And o'er the ice he fared to ocean's strand,
And up from thence, a wet and misty road,
To the armed damsel's bridge, and Giall's stream.
Worse was that way to go than to return,
For him : for others, all return is barred.
Nine days he took to go, two to return,
And on the twelfth morn saw the light of heaven.
And as a traveller in the early dawn
To the steep edge of some great valley comes,
Through which a river flows, and sees, beneath,
Clouds of white rolling vapors fill the vale,
But o'er them, on the farther slope, descries
Vineyards, and crofts, and pastures, bright with sun, —
So Hermod, o'er the fog between, saw heaven.
And Sleipner snorted, for he smelt the air
Of heaven ; and mightily, as winged, he flew.
And Hermod saw the towers of Asgard rise ;
And he drew near, and heard no living voice

In Asgard; and the golden halls were dumb.
Then Hermod knew what labor held the gods;
And through the empty streets he rode, and passed
Under the gate-house to the sands, and found
The gods on the seashore by Balder's ship.

III. FUNERAL.

THE gods held talk together, grouped in knots,
Round Balder's corpse, which they had thither borne;
And Hermod came down towards them from the gate.
And Lok, the father of the serpent, first
Beheld him come, and to his neighbor spake, —
   "See, here is Hermod, who comes single back
From hell; and shall I tell thee how he seems?
Like as a farmer, who hath lost his dog,
Some morn, at market, in a crowded town, —
Through many streets the poor beast runs in vain,
And follows this man after that, for hours;
And late at evening, spent and panting, falls
Before a stranger's threshold, not his home,
With flanks a-tremble, and his slender tongue
Hangs quivering out between his dust-smeared jaws,
And piteously he eyes the passers-by;
But home his master comes to his own farm,
Far in the country, wondering where he is, —
So Hermod comes to-day unfollowed home."
   And straight his neighbor, moved with wrath, re-
      plied, —
" Deceiver! fair in form, but false in heart!
Enemy, mocker, whom, though gods, we hate, —
Peace, lest our father Odin hear thee gibe!
Would I might see him snatch thee in his hand,

And bind thy carcass, like a bale, with cords,
And hurl thee in a lake, to sink or swim !
If clear from plotting Balder's death, to swim ;
But deep, if thou devisedst it, to drown,
And perish, against fate, before thy day."
  So they two soft to one another spake.
But Odin looked toward the land, and saw
His messenger ; and he stood forth, and cried.
And Hermod came, and leapt from Sleipner down,
And in his father's hand put Sleipner's rein,
And greeted Odin and the gods, and said, —
  " Odin, my father, and ye, gods of heaven !
Lo, home, having performed your will, I come.
Into the joyless kingdom have I been,
Below, and looked upon the shadowy tribes
Of ghosts, and communed with their solemn queen ;
And to your prayer she sends you this reply : —
Show her through all the world the signs of grief !
Fails but one thing to grieve, there Balder stops !
Let gods, men, brutes, beweep him; plants and stones.
So shall she know your loss was dear indeed,
And bend her heart, and give you Balder back."
  He spoke, and all the gods to Odin looked ;
And straight the Father of the ages said, —
  " Ye gods, these terms may keep another day.
But now put on your arms, and mount your steeds,
And in procession all come near, and weep
Balder ; for that is what the dead desire.
When ye enough have wept, then build a pile
Of the heaped wood, and burn his corpse with fire
Out of our sight ; that we may turn from grief,
And lead, as erst, our daily life in heaven."
  He spoke, and the gods armed ; and Odin donned
His dazzling corslet and his helm of gold,

And led the way on Sleipner; and the rest
Followed, in tears, their father and their king.
And thrice in arms around the dead they rode,
Weeping; the sands were wetted, and their arms,
With their thick-falling tears, — so good a friend
They mourned that day, so bright, so loved a god.
And Odin came, and laid his kingly hands
On Balder's breast, and thus began the wail: —

" Farewell, O Balder, bright and loved, my son !
In that great day, the twilight of the gods,
When Muspel's children shall beleaguer heaven,
Then we shall miss thy counsel and thy arm."

Thou camest near the next, O warrior Thor !
Shouldering thy hammer, in thy chariot drawn,
Swaying the long-haired goats with silvered rein ;
And over Balder's corpse these words didst say : —

" Brother, thou dwellest in the darksome land,
And talkest with the feeble tribes of ghosts,
Now, and I know not how they prize thee there —
But here, I know, thou wilt be missed and mourned.
For haughty spirits and high wraths are rife
Among the gods and heroes here in heaven,
As among those whose joy and work is war ;
And daily strifes arise, and angry words.
But from thy lips, O Balder, night or day,
Heard no one ever an injurious word
To god or hero, but thou keptest back
The others, laboring to compose their brawls.
Be ye then kind, as Balder too was kind !
For we lose him, who smoothed all strife in heaven."

He spake, and all the gods assenting wailed.
And Freya next came nigh, with golden tears ;
The loveliest goddess she in heaven, by all
Most honored after Frea, Odin's wife.

Her long ago the wandering Oder took
To mate, but left her to roam distant lands;
Since then she seeks him, and weeps tears of gold.
Names hath she many; Vanadis on earth
They call her, Freya is her name in heaven;
She in her hands took Balder's head, and spake, —
  "Balder, my brother, thou art gone a road
Unknown and long, and haply on that way
My long-lost wandering Oder thou hast met,
For in the paths of heaven he is not found.
Oh! if it be so, tell him what thou wast
To his neglected wife, and what he is,
And wring his heart with shame, to hear thy word!
For he, my husband, left me here to pine,
Not long a wife, when his unquiet heart
First drove him from me into distant lands;
Since then I vainly seek him through the world,
And weep from shore to shore my golden tears,
But neither god nor mortal heeds my pain.
Thou only, Balder, wast forever kind,
To take my hand, and wipe my tears, and say, —
Weep not, O Freya, weep no golden tears!
One day the wandering Oder will return,
Or thou wilt find him in thy faithful search,
On some great road, or resting in an inn,
Or at a ford, or sleeping by a tree.
So Balder said; but Oder, well I know,
My truant Oder I shall see no more
To the world's end; and Balder now is gone,
And I am left uncomforted in heaven."
  She spake, and all the goddesses bewailed.
Last from among the heroes one came near,
No god, but of the hero-troop the chief, —
Regner, who swept the northern sea with fleets,

And ruled o'er Denmark and the heathy isles,
Living ; but Ella captured him and slew, —
A king, whose fame then filled the vast of heaven :
Now time obscures it, and men's later deeds.
He last approached the corpse, and spake and said, —
    " Balder, there yet are many scalds in heaven
Still left, and that chief scald, thy brother Brage,
Whom we may bid to sing, though thou art gone.
And all these gladly, while we drink, we hear,
After the feast is done, in Odin's hall ;
But they harp ever on one string, and wake
Remembrance in our soul of wars alone,
Such as on earth we valiantly have waged,
And blood, and ringing blows, and violent death.
But when thou sangest, Balder, thou didst strike
Another note, and, like a bird in spring,
Thy voice of joyance minded us, and youth,
And wife, and children, and our ancient home.
Yes, and I too remembered then no more
My dungeon, where the serpents stung me dead,
Nor Ella's victory on the English coast ;
But I heard Thora laugh in Gothland Isle,
And saw my shepherdess, Aslauga, tend
Her flock along the white Norwegian beach.
Tears started to mine eyes with yearning joy.
Therefore with grateful heart I mourn thee dead."
    So Regner spake, and all the heroes groaned.
But now the sun had passed the height of heaven,
And soon had all that day been spent in wail ;
But then the Father of the ages said, —
    " Ye gods, there well may be too much of wail !
Bring now the gathered wood to Balder's ship ;
Heap on the deck the logs, and build the pyre."
    But when the gods and heroes heard, they brought

The wood to Balder's ship, and built a pile,
Full the deck's breadth, and lofty ; then the corpse
Of Balder on the highest top they laid,
With Nanna on his right, and on his left
Hoder, his brother, whom his own hand slew.
And they set jars of wine and oil to lean
Against the bodies, and stuck torches near,
Splinters of pine-wood, soaked with turpentine ;
And brought his arms and gold, and all his stuff,
And slew the dogs who at his table fed,
And his horse, Balder's horse, whom most he loved,
And threw them on the pyre ; and Odin threw
A last choice gift thereon, his golden ring.
The mast they fixed, and hoisted up the sails ;
Then they put fire to the wood ; and Thor
Set his stout shoulder hard against the stern
To push the ship through the thick sand ; sparks flew
From the deep trench she ploughed, so strong a god
Furrowed it ; and the water gurgled in.
And the ship floated on the waves, and rocked.
But in the hills a strong east-wind arose,
And came down moaning to the sea ; first squalls
Ran black o'er the sea's face, then steady rushed
The breeze, and filled the sails, and blew the fire.
And wreathed in smoke the ship stood out to sea.
Soon with a roaring rose the mighty fire,
And the pile crackled ; and between the logs
Sharp quivering tongues of flame shot out, and leapt.
Curling and darting, higher, until they licked
The summit of the pile, the dead, the mast,
And ate the shrivelling sails ; but still the ship
Drove on, ablaze above her hull with fire.
And the gods stood upon the beach, and gazed.
And while they gazed, the sun went lurid down

Into the smoke-wrapt sea, and night came on.
Then the wind fell, with night, and there was calm;
But through the dark they watched the burning ship
Still carried o'er the distant waters on,
Farther and farther, like an eye of fire.
And long, in the far dark, blazed Balder's pile;
But fainter, as the stars rose high, it flared;
The bodies were consumed, ash choked the pile.
And as, in a decaying winter-fire,
A charred log, falling, makes a shower of sparks, —
So with a shower of sparks the pile fell in,
Reddening the sea around; and all was dark.

But the gods went by starlight up the shore
To Asgard, and sate down in Odin's hall
At table, and the funeral-feast began.
All night they ate the boar Serimner's flesh,
And from their horns, with silver rimmed, drank mead,
Silent, and waited for the sacred morn.

And morning over all the world was spread.
Then from their loathèd feast the gods arose,
And took their horses, and set forth to ride
O'er the bridge Bifrost, where is Heimdall's watch,
To the ash Igdrasil, and Ida's plain.
Thor came on foot, the rest on horseback rode.
And they found Mimir sitting by his fount
Of wisdom, which beneath the ash-tree springs;
And saw the Nornies watering the roots
Of that world-shadowing tree with honey-dew.
There came the gods, and sate them down on stones;
And thus the Father of the ages said: —

        "Ye gods, the terms ye know, which Hermod
            brought.
Accept them or reject them! both have grounds.
Accept them, and they bind us, unfulfilled,

To leave forever Balder in the grave,
An unrecovered prisoner, shade with shades.
But how, ye say, should the fulfilment fail? —
Smooth sound the terms, and light to be fulfilled;
For dear-beloved was Balder while he lived
In heaven and earth, and who would grudge him tears?
But from the traitorous seed of Lok they come,
These terms, and I suspect some hidden fraud.
Bethink ye, gods, is there no other way?
Speak, were not this a way, the way for gods, —
If I, if Odin, clad in radiant arms,
Mounted on Sleipner, with the warrior Thor
Drawn in his car beside me, and my sons,
All the strong brood of heaven, to swell my train,
Should make irruption into Hela's realm,
And set the fields of gloom ablaze with light,
And bring in triumph Balder back to heaven?"
    He spake, and his fierce sons applauded loud.
But Frea, mother of the gods, arose,
Daughter and wife of Odin; thus she said: —
    "Odin, thou whirlwind, what a threat is this!
Thou threatenest what transcends thy might, even thine.
For of all powers the mightiest far art thou,
Lord over men on earth, and gods in heaven;
Yet even from thee thyself hath been withheld
One thing, — to undo what thou thyself hast ruled.
For all which hath been fixed was fixed by thee.
In the beginning, ere the gods were born,
Before the heavens were builded, thou didst slay
The giant Ymir, whom the abyss brought forth, —
Thou and thy brethren fierce, the sons of Bor, —
And cast his trunk to choke the abysmal void.
But of his flesh and members thou didst build
The earth and ocean, and above them heaven.

And from the flaming world, where Muspel reigns,
Thou sent'st and fetchedst fire, and madest lights,
Sun, moon, and stars, which thou hast hung in
    heaven,
Dividing clear the paths of night and day.
And Asgard thou didst build, and Midgard fort ;
Then me thou mad'st ; of us the gods were born.
Last, walking by the sea, thou foundest spars
Of wood, and framedst men, who till the earth,
Or on the sea, the field of pirates, sail.
And all the race of Ymir thou didst drown,
Save one, Bergelmer : he on shipboard fled
Thy deluge, and from him the giants sprang.
But all that brood thou hast removed far off,
And set by ocean's utmost marge to dwell.
But Hela into Niflheim thou threw'st,
And gav'st her nine unlighted worlds to rule,
A queen, and empire over all the dead.
That empire wilt thou now invade, light up
Her darkness, from her grasp a subject tear?
Try it ; but I, for one, will not applaud.
Nor do I merit, Odin, thou shouldst slight
Me and my words, though thou be first in heaven ;
For I too am a goddess, born of thee,
Thine eldest, and of me the gods are sprung ;
And all that is to come I know, but lock
In mine own breast, and have to none revealed.
Come, then ! since Hela holds by right her prey,
But offers terms for his release to heaven,
Accept the chance : thou canst no more obtain.
Send through the world thy messengers ; entreat
All living and unliving things to weep
For Balder : if thou haply thus may'st melt
Hela, and win the loved one back to heaven."

She spake, and on her face let fall her veil,
And bowed her head, and sate with folded hands.
Nor did the all-ruling Odin slight her word;
Straightway he spake, and thus addressed the gods : —
  "Go quickly forth through all the world, and pray
All living and unliving things to weep
Balder, if haply he may thus be won."
  When the gods heard, they straight arose, and
    took
Their horses, and rode forth through all the world.
North, south, east, west, they struck, and roamed the
    world,
Entreating all things to weep Balder's death ;
And all that lived, and all without life, wept.
And as in winter, when the frost breaks up,
At winter's end, before the spring begins,
And a warm west-wind blows, and thaw sets in,
After an hour a dripping sound is heard
In all the forests, and the soft-strewn snow
Under the trees is dibbled thick with holes,
And from the boughs the snow-loads shuffle down ;
And, in fields sloping to the south, dark plots
Of grass peep out amid surrounding snow,
And widen, and the peasant's heart is glad, —
So through the world was heard a dripping noise
Of all things weeping to bring Balder back ;
And there fell joy upon the gods to hear.
  But Hermod rode with Niord, whom he took
To show him spits and beaches of the sea
Far off, where some unwarned might fail to weep, —
Niord, the god of storms, whom fishers know ;
Not born in heaven, he was in Vanheim reared,
With men, but lives a hostage with the gods ;
He knows each frith, and every rocky creek

Fringed with dark pines, and sands where seafowl
        scream, —
They two scoured every coast, and all things wept.
And they rode home together, through the wood
Of Jarnvid, which to east of Midgard lies
Bordering the giants, where the trees are iron ;
There in the wood before a cave they came,
Where sate, in the cave's mouth, a skinny hag,
Toothless and old ; she gibes the passers-by.
Thok is she called, but now Lok wore her shape.
She greeted them the first, and laughed, and said, —

  "Ye gods, good lack, is it so dull in heaven,
That ye come pleasuring to Thok's iron wood?
Lovers of change ye are, fastidious sprites.
Look, as in some boor's yard a sweet-breathed cow,
Whose manger is stuffed full of good fresh hay,
Snuffs at it daintily, and stoops her head
To chew the straw, her litter, at her feet, —
So ye grow squeamish, gods, and sniff at heaven !"

  She spake ; but Hermod answered her, and said, —
"Thok, not for gibes we come, we come for tears.
Balder is dead, and Hela holds her prey,
But will restore if all things give him tears.
Begrudge not thine ! to all was Balder dear."

  Then, with a louder laugh, the hag replied, —
" Is Balder dead? and do ye come for tears?
Thok with dry eyes will weep o'er Balder's pyre.
Weep him all other things, if weep they will :
I weep him not ! let Hela keep her prey."

  She spake, and to the cavern's depth she fled,
Mocking ; and Hermod knew their toil was vain.
And as seafaring men, who long have wrought
In the great deep for gain, at last come home,
And towards evening see the headlands rise

Of their dear country, and can plain descry
A fire of withered furze which boys have lit
Upon the cliffs, or smoke of burning weeds
Out of a tilled field inland : then the wind
Catches them, and drives out again to sea;
And they go long days tossing up and down
Over the gray sea-ridges, and the glimpse
Of port they had makes bitterer far their toil, —
So the gods' cross was bitterer for their joy.

Then, sad at heart, to Niord Hermod spake, —
"It is the accuser Lok, who flouts us all!
Ride back, and tell in heaven this heavy news;
I must again below, to Hela's realm."

He spoke, and Niord set forth back to heaven.
But northward Hermod rode, the way below,
The way he knew; and traversed Giall's stream,
And down to ocean groped, and crossed the ice,
And came beneath the wall, and found the grate
Still lifted : well was his return foreknown.
And once more Hermod saw around him spread
The joyless plains, and heard the streams of hell.
But as he entered, on the extremest bound
Of Niflheim, he saw one ghost come near,
Hovering, and stopping oft, as if afraid, —
Hoder, the unhappy, whom his own hand slew.
And Hermod looked, and knew his brother's ghost,
And called him by his name, and sternly said, —

"Hoder, ill-fated, blind in heart and eyes!
Why tarriest thou to plunge thee in the gulf
Of the deep inner gloom, but flittest here,
In twilight, on the lonely verge of hell,
Far from the other ghosts, and Hela's throne?
Doubtless thou fearest to meet Balder's voice,
Thy brother, whom through folly thou didst slay."

He spoke ; but Hoder answered him, and said, —
" Hermod the nimble, dost thou still pursue
The unhappy with reproach, even in the grave ?
For this I died, and fled beneath the gloom,
Not daily to endure abhorring gods,
Nor with a hateful presence cumber heaven ;
And canst thou not, even here, pass pitying by ?
No less than Balder have I lost the light
Of heaven, and communion with my kin ;
I too had once a wife, and once a child,
And substance, and a golden house in heaven ·
But all I left of my own act, and fled
Below ; and dost thou hate me even here ?
Balder upbraids me not, nor hates at all,
Though he has cause, have any cause ; but he,
When that with downcast looks I hither came,
Stretched forth his hand, and with benignant voice,
Welcome, he said, *if there be welcome here,*
Brother and fellow-sport of Lok with me !
And not to offend thee, Hermod, nor to force
My hated converse on thee, came I up
From the deep gloom, where I will now return ;
But earnestly I longed to hover near,
Not too far off, when that thou camest by ;
To feel the presence of a brother god,
And hear the passage of a horse of heaven,
For the last time — for here thou com'st no more."

He spake, and turned to go to the inner gloom.
But Hermod stayed him with mild words, and said, —
" Thou doest well to chide me, Hoder blind !
Truly thou say'st, the planning guilty mind
Was Lok's : the unwitting hand alone was thine.
But gods are like the sons of men in this :
When they have woe, they blame the nearest cause.

Howbeit stay, and be appeased ; and tell,
Sits Balder still in pomp by Hela's side,
Or is he mingled with the unnumbered dead ? "

And the blind Hoder answered him and spake, —
" His place of state remains by Hela's side,
But empty ; for his wife, for Nanna, came
Lately below, and joined him ; and the pair
Frequent the still recesses of the realm
Of Hela, and hold converse undisturbed.
But they too, doubtless, will have breathed the balm
Which floats before a visitant from heaven,
And have drawn upward to this verge of hell."

He spake ; and, as he ceased, a puff of wind
Rolled heavily the leaden mist aside
Round where they stood, and they beheld two forms
Make toward them o'er the stretching cloudy plain.
And Hermod straight perceived them, who they were, —
Balder and Nanna ; and to Balder said, —

" Balder, too truly thou foresaw'st a snare !
Lok triumphs still, and Hela keeps her prey.
No more to Asgard shalt thou come, nor lodge
In thy own house Breidablik, nor enjoy
The love all bear toward thee, nor train up
Forset, thy son, to be beloved like thee.
Here must thou lie, and wait an endless age.
Therefore for the last time, O Balder, hail ! "

He spake ; and Balder answered him, and said, —
" Hail and farewell ! for here thou com'st no more.
Yet mourn not for me, Hermod, when thou sitt'st
In heaven, nor let the other gods lament,
As wholly to be pitied, quite forlorn.
For Nanna hath rejoined me, who of old,
In heaven, was seldom parted from my side ;
And still the acceptance follows me, which crowned

My former life, and cheers me even here.
The iron frown of Hela is relaxed
When I draw nigh, and the wan tribes of dead
Love me, and gladly bring for my award
Their ineffectual feuds and feeble hates, —
Shadows of hates, but they distress them still."

  And the fleet-footed Hermod made reply, —
"Thou hast, then, all the solace death allows, —
Esteem and function; and so far is well.
Yet here thou liest, Balder, underground,
Rusting forever; and the years roll on,
The generations pass, the ages grow,
And bring us nearer to the final day
When from the south shall march the fiery band,
And cross the bridge of heaven, with Lok for guide,
And Fenris at his heel with broken chain;
While from the east the giant Rymer steers
His ship, and the great serpent makes to land;
And all are marshalled in one flaming square
Against the gods, upon the plains of heaven.
I mourn thee, that thou canst not help us then."

  He spake; but Balder answered him, and said, —
"Mourn not for me! Mourn, Hermod, for the gods
Mourn for the men on earth, the gods in heaven,
Who live, and with their eyes shall see that day!
The day will come, when fall shall Asgard's towers,
And Odin, and his sons, the seed of heaven;
But what were I, to save them in that hour?
If strength might save them, could not Odin save,
My father, and his pride, the warrior Thor,
Vidar the silent, the impetuous Tyr?
I, what were I, when these can naught avail?
Yet, doubtless, when the day of battle comes,
And the two hosts are marshalled, and in heaven

The golden-crested cock shall sound alarm,
And his black brother-bird from hence reply,
And bucklers clash, and spears begin to pour, —
Longing will stir within my breast, though vain.
But not to me so grievous as, I know,
To other gods it were, is my enforced
Absence from fields where I could nothing aid ;
For I am long since weary of your storm
Of carnage, and find, Hermod, in your life
Something too much of war and broils, which make
Life one perpetual fight, a bath of blood.
Mine eyes are dizzy with the arrowy hail ;
Mine ears are stunned with blows, and sick for calm.
Inactive therefore let me lie, in gloom,
Unarmed, inglorious : I attend the course
Of ages, and my late return to light,
In times less alien to a spirit mild,
In new-recovered seats, the happier day."

He spake, and the fleet Hermod thus replied : —
" Brother, what seats are these, what happier day ?
Tell me, that I may ponder it when gone."

And the ray-crownèd Balder answered him, —
" Far to the south, beyond the blue, there spreads
Another heaven, the boundless. No one yet
Hath reached it. There hereafter shall arise
The second Asgard, with another name.
Thither, when o'er this present earth and heavens
The tempest of the latter days hath swept,
And they from sight have disappeared and sunk,
Shall a small remnant of the gods repair ;
Hoder and I shall join them from the grave.
There re-assembling we shall see emerge
From the bright ocean at our feet an earth
More fresh, more verdant than the last, with fruits

Self-springing, and a seed of man preserved,
Who then shall live in peace, as now in war.
But we in heaven shall find again with joy
The ruined palaces of Odin, seats
Familiar, halls where we have supped of old;
Re-enter them with wonder, never fill
Our eyes with gazing, and rebuild with tears.
And we shall tread once more the well-known plain
Of Ida, and among the grass shall find
The golden dice wherewith we played of yore;
And that will bring to mind the former life
And pastime of the gods, the wise discourse
Of Odin, the delights of other days.
O Hermod, pray that thou may'st join us then!
Such for the future is my hope; meanwhile,
I rest the thrall of Hela, and endure
Death, and the gloom which round me even now
Thickens, and to its inner gulf recalls.
Farewell, for longer speech is not allowed!"

   He spoke, and waved farewell, and gave his hand
To Nanna; and she gave their brother blind
Her hand, in turn, for guidance; and the three
Departed o'er the cloudy plain, and soon
Faded from sight into the interior gloom.
But Hermod stood beside his drooping horse,
Mute, gazing after them in tears; and fain,
Fain had he followed their receding steps,
Though they to death were bound, and he to heaven,
Then: but a power he could not break withheld.
And as a stork which idle boys have trapped,
And tied him in a yard, at autumn sees
Flocks of his kind pass flying o'er his head
To warmer lands, and coasts that keep the sun;
He strains to join their flight, and from his shed

Follows them with a long complaining cry, —
So Hermod gazed, and yearned to join his kin.

At last he sighed, and set forth back to heaven.

TRISTRAM AND ISEULT.[1]

I.

Tristram.

TRISTRAM.

Is she not come? The messenger was sure.
Prop me upon the pillows once again.
Raise me, my page! this cannot long endure.
— Christ, what a night! how the sleet whips the pane!
What lights will those out to the northward be?

THE PAGE.

The lanterns of the fishing-boats at sea.

TRISTRAM.

Soft — who is that, stands by the dying fire?

THE PAGE.

Iseult.

TRISTRAM.

Ah! not the Iseult I desire.

· · · · · · · ·

What knight is this so weak and pale,
Though the locks are yet brown on his noble head,
Propped on pillows in his bed,
Gazing seaward for the light
Of some ship that fights the gale
On this wild December night?

Over the sick man's feet is spread
A dark green forest-dress ;
A gold harp leans against the bed,
Ruddy in the fire's light.
I know him by his harp of gold,
Famous in Arthur's court of old ;
I know him by his forest-dress,—
The peerless hunter, harper, knight,
Tristram of Lyoness.

What lady is this, whose silk attire
Gleams so rich in the light of the fire?
The ringlets on her shoulders lying
In their flitting lustre vying
With the clasp of burnished gold
Which her heavy robe doth hold.
Her looks are mild, her fingers slight
As the driven snow are white ;
But her cheeks are sunk and pale.
Is it that the bleak sea-gale
Beating from the Atlantic sea
On this coast of Brittany,
Nips too keenly the sweet flower?
Is it that a deep fatigue
Hath come on her, a chilly fear,
Passing all her youthful hour
Spinning with her maidens here,
Listlessly through the window-bars
Gazing seawards many a league
From her lonely shore-built tower,
While the knights are at the wars?
Or, perhaps, has her young heart
Felt already some deeper smart,
Of those that in secret the heart-strings rive,

Leaving her sunk and pale, though fair?
Who is this snowdrop by the sea? —
I know her by her mildness rare,
Her snow-white hands, her golden hair;
I know her by her rich silk dress,
And her fragile loveliness, —
The sweetest Christian soul alive,
Iseult of Brittany.

Iseult of Brittany? but where
Is that other Iseult fair,
That proud, first Iseult, Cornwall's queen?
She, whom Tristram's ship of yore
From Ireland to Cornwall bore,
To Tyntagel, to the side
Of King Marc, to be his bride?
She who, as they voyaged, quaffed
With Tristram that spiced magic draught
Which since then forever rolls
Through their blood, and binds their souls,
Working love, but working teen?
There were two Iseults who did sway
Each her hour of Tristram's day;
But one possessed his waning time,
The other his resplendent prime.
Behold her here, the patient flower,
Who possessed his darker hour!
Iseult of the snow-white hand
Watches pale by Tristram's bed.
She is here who had his gloom:
Where art thou who hadst his bloom?
One such kiss as those of yore
Might thy dying knight restore!
Does the love-draught work no more?

Art thou cold, or false, or dead,
Iseult of Ireland?

. . . .

Loud howls the wind, sharp patters the rain,
And the knight sinks back on his pillows again;
He is weak with fever and pain,
And his spirit is not clear.
Hark! he mutters in his sleep,
As he wanders far from here,
Changes place and time of year,
And his closèd eye doth sweep
O'er some fair unwintry sea,
Not this fierce Atlantic deep,
While he mutters brokenly, —

TRISTRAM.

The calm sea shines, loose hang the vessel's sails;
Before us are the sweet green fields of Wales,
And overhead the cloudless sky of May.
"Ah! would I were in those green fields at play,
Not pent on shipboard this delicious day!
Tristram, I pray thee, of thy courtesy,
Reach me my golden cup that stands by thee,
But pledge me in it first for courtesy."
Ha! dost thou start? are thy lips blanched like mine?
Child, 'tis no water this, 'tis poisoned wine!
Iseult! . . .

. . . .

Ah, sweet angels, let him dream!
Keep his eyelids; let him seem
Not this fever-wasted wight
Thinned and paled before his time,
But the brilliant youthful knight
In the glory of his prime,

Sitting in the gilded barge,
At thy side, thou lovely charge,
Bending gayly o'er thy hand,
Iseult of Ireland!
And she too, that princess fair,
If her bloom be now less rare,
Let her have her youth again,
Let her be as she was then!
Let her have her proud dark eyes,
And her petulant quick replies;
Let her sweep her dazzling hand
With its gesture of command,
And shake back her raven hair
With the old imperious air!
As of old, so let her be,
That first Iseult, princess bright,
Chatting with her youthful knight
As he steers her o'er the sea,
Quitting at her father's will
The green isle where she was bred,
And her bower in Ireland,
For the surge-beat Cornish strand;
Where the prince whom she must wed
Dwells on loud Tyntagel's hill,
High above the sounding sea.
And that golden cup her mother
Gave her, that her future lord,
Gave her, that King Marc and she,
Might drink it on their marriage-day,
And forever love each other, —
Let her, as she sits on board,
— Ah! sweet saints, unwittingly! —
See it shine, and take it up,
And to Tristram laughing say, —

"Sir Tristram, of thy courtesy,
Pledge me in my golden cup."
Let them drink it; let their hands
Tremble, and their cheeks be flame,
As they feel the fatal bands
Of a love they dare not name,
With a wild delicious pain,
Twine about their hearts again!
Let the early summer be
Once more round them, and the sea
Blue, and o'er its mirror kind
Let the breath of the May-wind,
Wandering through their drooping sails,
Die on the green fields of Wales;
Let a dream like this restore
What his eye must see no more.

TRISTRAM.

Chill blows the wind, the pleasaunce-walks are drear:
Madcap, what jest was this, to meet me here?
Were feet like those made for so wild a way?
The southern winter-parlor, by my fay,
Had been the likeliest trysting-place to-day! —
"*Tristram!*—*nay, nay*—*thou must not take my
     hand!* —
Tristram! — *sweet love!* — *we are betrayed* — *out-
     planned.*
Fly — *save thyself* — *save me!   I dare not stay.*"
One last kiss first! — "'*Tis vain* — *to horse* — *away!*"
     .   .   .   .

Ah! sweet saints, his dream doth move
Faster surely than it should,
From the fever in his blood!
All the spring-time of his love

Is already gone and past,
And instead thereof is seen
Its winter, which endureth still, —
Tyntagel on its surge-beat hill,
The pleasaunce-walks, the weeping queen,
The flying leaves, the straining blast,
And that long, wild kiss, — their last.
And this rough December-night,
And his burning fever-pain,
Mingle with his hurrying dream,
Till they rule it ; till he seem
The pressed fugitive again,
The love-desperate, banished knight,
With a fire in his brain,
Flying o'er the stormy main.
— Whither does he wander now?
Haply in his dreams the wind
Wafts him here, and lets him find
The lovely orphan child again
In her castle by the coast ;
The youngest, fairest chatelaine,
That this realm of France can boast,
Our snowdrop by the Atlantic sea, —
Iseult of Brittany.
And — for through the haggard air,
The stained arms, the matted hair,
Of that stranger-knight ill-starred,
There gleamed something which recalled
The Tristram who in better days
Was Launcelot's guest at Joyous Gard —
Welcomed here, and here installed,
Tended of his fever here,
Haply he seems again to move
His young guardian's heart with love,

In his exiled loneliness,
In his stately, deep distress,
Without a word, without a tear.
— Ah ! 'tis well he should retrace
His tranquil life in this lone place ;
His gentle bearing at the side
Of his timid youthful bride ;
His long rambles by the shore
On winter-evenings, when the roar
Of the near waves came, sadly grand,
Through the dark, up the drowned sand ;
Or his endless reveries
In the woods, where the gleams play
On the grass under the trees,
Passing the long summer's day
Idle as a mossy stone
In the forest-depths alone,
The chase neglected, and his hound
Couched beside him on the ground.
— Ah ! what trouble's on his brow?
Hither let him wander now ;
Hither, to the quiet hours
Passed among these heaths of ours
By the gray Atlantic sea, —
Hours, if not of ecstasy,
From violent anguish surely free !

TRISTRAM.

All red with blood the whirling river flows,
The wide plain rings, the dazed air throbs with
    blows.
Upon us are the chivalry of Rome ;
Their spears are down, their steeds are bathed in
    foam.

"Up, Tristram, up!" men cry, "thou moonstruck
     knight!
What foul fiend rides thee? On into the fight!"
— Above the din, her voice is in my ears;
I see her form glide through the crossing spears. —
Iseult! . . .

    .   .   .   .

    Ah! he wanders forth again;
    We cannot keep him: now, as then,
    There's a secret in his breast
    Which will never let him rest.
    These musing fits in the green wood,
    They cloud the brain, they dull the blood!
    — His sword is sharp, his horse is good;
    Beyond the mountains will he see
    The famous towns of Italy,
    And label with the blessed sign
    The heathen Saxons on the Rhine.
    At Arthur's side he fights once more
    With the Roman Emperor.
    There's many a gay knight where he goes
    Will help him to forget his care;
    The march, the leaguer, heaven's blithe air,
    The neighing steeds, the ringing blows, —
    Sick pining comes not where these are.
    — Ah! what boots it, that the jest
    Lightens every other brow,
    What, that every other breast
    Dances as the trumpets blow,
    If one's own heart beats not light
    On the waves of the tossed fight,
    If one's self cannot get free
    From the clog of misery?

Thy lovely youthful wife grows pale
Watching by the salt sea-tide,
With her children at her side,
For the gleam of thy white sail.
Home, Tristram, to thy halls again!
To our lonely sea complain,
To our forests tell thy pain.

TRISTRAM.

All round the forest sweeps off, black in shade,
But it is moonlight in the open glade;
And in the bottom of the glade shine clear
The forest-chapel and the fountain near.
— I think I have a fever in my blood;
Come, let me leave the shadow of this wood,
Ride down, and bathe my hot brow in the flood.
— Mild shines the cold spring in the moon's clear
    light.
God! 'tis *her* face plays in the waters bright!
" Fair love," she says, " canst thou forget so soon,
At this soft hour, under this sweet moon?"—
Iseult! . . .

.   .   .   .

Ah, poor soul! if this be so,
Only death can balm thy woe.
The solitudes of the green wood
Had no medicine for thy mood;
The rushing battle cleared thy blood
As little as did solitude.
— Ah! his eyelids slowly break
Their hot seals, and let him wake;
What new change shall we now see?
A happier?   Worse it cannot be.

TRISTRAM.

Is my page here? Come, turn me to the fire!
Upon the window-panes the moon shines bright;
The wind is down; but she'll not come to-night.
Ah, no! she is asleep in Cornwall now,
Far hence; her dreams are fair, smooth is her brow.
Of me she recks not, nor my vain desire.
— I have had dreams, I have had dreams, my page,
Would take a score years from a strong man's age;
And with a blood like mine, will leave, I fear,
Scant leisure for a second messenger.
— My princess, art thou there? Sweet, 'tis too late!
To bed, and sleep! my fever is gone by;
To-night my page shall keep me company.
Where do the children sleep? kiss them for me!
Poor child, thou art almost as pale as I:
This comes of nursing long and watching late.
To bed — good night!

.   .   .   .

She left the gleam-lit fireplace,
She came to the bedside;
She took his hands in hers, her tears
Down on her slender fingers rained.
She raised her eyes upon his face,
Not with a look of wounded pride,
A look as if the heart complained;
Her look was like a sad embrace, —
The gaze of one who can divine
A grief, and sympathize.
Sweet flower! thy children's eyes
Are not more innocent than thine.

But they sleep in sheltered rest,
Like helpless birds in the warm nest,
On the castle's southern side;

Where feebly comes the mournful roar
Of buffeting wind and surging tide
Through many a room and corridor.
— Full on their window the moon's ray
Makes their chamber as bright as day.
It shines upon the blank white walls,
And on the snowy pillow falls,
And on two angel-heads doth play
Turned to each other ; the eyes closed,
The lashes on the cheeks reposed.
Round each sweet brow the cap close-set
Hardly lets peep the golden hair ;
Through the soft-opened lips, the air
Scarcely moves the coverlet.
One little wandering arm is thrown
At random on the counterpane,
And often the fingers close in haste
As if their baby-owner chased
The butterflies again.
This stir they have, and this alone ;
But else they are so still !
— Ah, tired madcaps ! you lie still ;
But were you at the window now,
To look forth on the fairy sight
Of your illumined haunts by night,
To see the park-glades where you play
Far lovelier than they are by day,
To see the sparkle on the eaves,
And upon every giant-bough
Of those old oaks, whose wet red leaves
Are jewelled with bright drops of rain, —
How would your voices run again !
And far beyond the sparkling trees
Of the castle-park, one sees

The bare heaths spreading, clear as day,
Moor behind moor, far, far away,
Into the heart of Brittany.
And here and there, locked by the land,
Long inlets of smooth glittering sea,
And many a stretch of watery sand
All shining in the white moonbeams.
But you see fairer in your dreams !
What voices are these on the clear night air?
What lights in the court, what steps on the stair?

TRISTRAM AND ISEULT.

II.

Iseult of Ireland.

TRISTRAM.

RAISE the light, my page ! that I may see her. —
 Thou art come at last, then, haughty queen !
Long I've waited, long I've fought my fever ;
 Late thou comest, cruel thou hast been.

ISEULT.

Blame me not, poor sufferer ! that I tarried :
 Bound I was, I could not break the band.
Chide not with the past, but feel the present ;
 I am here, we meet, I hold thy hand.

TRISTRAM.

Thou art come, indeed ; thou hast rejoined me ;
 Thou hast dared it — but too late to save.
Fear not now that men should tax thine honor !
 I am dying ; build (thou may'st) my grave.

ISEULT.

Tristram, ah ! for love of heaven, speak kindly !
    What ! I hear these bitter words from thee ?
Sick with grief I am, and faint with travel ;
    Take my hand — dear Tristram, look on me !

TRISTRAM.

I forgot, thou comest from thy voyage ;
    Yes, the spray is on thy cloak and hair.
But thy dark eyes are not dimmed, proud Iseult !
    And thy beauty never was more fair.

ISEULT.

Ah, harsh flatterer ! let alone my beauty !
    I, like thee, have left my youth afar.
Take my hand, and touch these wasted fingers ;
    See my cheek and lips, how white they are !

TRISTRAM.

Thou art paler ; but thy sweet charm, Iseult,
    Would not fade with the dull years away.
Ah, how fair thou standest in the moonlight !
    I forgive thee, Iseult ! thou wilt stay ?

ISEULT.

Fear me not, I will be always with thee ;
    I will watch thee, tend thee, soothe thy pain ;
Sing thee tales of true, long-parted lovers,
    Joined at evening of their days again.

TRISTRAM.

No, thou shalt not speak ! I should be finding
    Something altered in thy courtly tone.
Sit — sit by me ! I will think, we've lived so
    In the green wood, all our lives, alone.

ISEULT.

Altered, Tristram? Not in courts, believe me,
  Love like mine is altered in the breast :
Courtly life is light, and cannot reach it ;
  Ah ! it lives, because so deep-suppressed !

What ! thou think'st men speak in courtly chambers
  Words by which the wretched are consoled ?
What ! thou think'st this aching brow was cooler,
  Circled, Tristram, by a band of gold ?

Royal state with Marc, my deep-wronged husband, —
  That was bliss to make my sorrows flee !
Silken courtiers whispering honeyed nothings, —
  Those were friends to make me false to thee !

Ah ! on which, if both our lots were balanced,
  Was indeed the heaviest burden thrown, —
Thee, a pining exile in thy forest,
  Me, a smiling queen upon my throne ?

Vain and strange debate, where both have suffered,
  Both have passed a youth repressed and sad,
Both have brought their anxious day to evening,
  And have now short space for being glad !

Joined we are henceforth ; nor will thy people
  Nor thy younger Iseult take it ill,
That a former rival shares her office,
  When she sees her humbled, pale, and still.

I, a faded watcher by thy pillow,
  I, a statue on thy chapel-floor,
Poured in prayer before the Virgin-Mother,
  Rouse no anger, make no rivals more.

She will cry, " Is this the foe I dreaded?
    This his idol, this that royal bride?
Ah! an hour of health would purge his eyesight!
    Stay, pale queen, forever by my side."

Hush, no words! that smile, I see, forgives me.
    I am now thy nurse, I bid thee sleep.
Close thine eyes: this flooding moonlight blinds them.
    Nay, all's well again! thou must not weep.

TRISTRAM.

I am happy! yet I feel there's something
    Swells my heart, and takes my breath away.
Through a mist I see thee; near — come nearer!
    Bend — bend down! I yet have much to say.

ISEULT.

Heaven! his head sinks back upon the pillow. —
    Tristram! Tristram! let thy heart not fail!
Call on God and on the holy angels!
    What, love, courage! — Christ! he is so pale.

TRISTRAM.

Hush, 'tis vain: I feel my end approaching.
    This is what my mother said should be,
When the fierce pains took her in the forest,
    The deep draughts of death, in bearing me.

" Son," she said, " thy name shall be of sorrow;
    Tristram art thou called for my death's sake."
So she said, and died in the drear forest.
    Grief since then his home with me doth make.

I am dying.   Start not, nor look wildly !
  Me, thy living friend, thou canst not save.
But, since living we were ununited,
    Go not far, O Iseult ! from my grave.

Close mine eyes, then seek the princess Iseult ;
  Speak her fair, she is of royal blood.
Say, I charged her, that thou stay beside me :
  She will grant it ; she is kind and good.

Now to sail the seas of death I leave thee —
  One last kiss upon the living shore !

ISEULT.

Tristram ! Tristram ! stay — receive me with thee !
  Iseult leaves thee, Tristram ! nevermore.

        .   .   .   .

You see them clear — the moon shines bright.
Slow, slow and softly, where she stood,
She sinks upon the ground ; her hood
Had fallen back, her arms outspread
Still hold her lover's hands ; her head
Is bowed, half-buried, on the bed.
O'er the blanched sheet, her raven hair
Lies in disordered streams ; and there,
Strung like white stars, the pearls still are ;
And the golden bracelets, heavy and rare,
Flash on her white arms still, —
The very same which yesternight
Flashed in the silver sconces' light,
When the feast was gay and the laughter loud
In Tyntagel's palace proud.
But then they decked a restless ghost

With hot-flushed cheeks and brilliant eyes,
And quivering lips on which the tide
Of courtly speech abruptly died,
And a glance which over the crowded floor,
The dancers, and the festive host,
Flew ever to the door ;
That the knights eyed her in surprise,
And the dames whispered scoffingly, —
" Her moods, good lack, they pass like showers !
But yesternight and she would be
As pale and still as withered flowers ;
And now to-night she laughs and speaks,
And has a color in her cheeks.
Christ keep us from such fantasy ! " —

Yes, now the longing is o'erpast,
Which, dogged by fear and fought by shame
Shook her weak bosom day and night,
Consumed her beauty like a flame,
And dimmed it like the desert-blast.
And though the curtains hide her face,
Yet, were it lifted to the light,
The sweet expression of her brow
Would charm the gazer, till his thought
Erased the ravages of time,
Filled up the hollow cheek, and brought
A freshness back as of her prime, —
So healing is her quiet now ;
So perfectly the lines express
A tranquil, settled loveliness,
Her younger rival's purest grace.

The air of the December-night
Steals coldly around the chamber bright,

Where those lifeless lovers be.
Swinging with it, in the light
Flaps the ghost-like tapestry.
And on the arras wrought you see
A stately huntsman, clad in green,
And round him a fresh forest-scene.
On that clear forest-knoll he stays,
With his pack round him, and delays.
He stares and stares, with troubled face,
At this huge, gleam-lit fireplace,
At that bright, iron-figured door,
And those blown rushes on the floor.
He gazes down into the room
With heated cheeks and flurried air,
And to himself he seems to say, —
" *What place is this, and who are they?*
Who is that kneeling lady fair?
And on his pillows that pale knight
Who seems of marble on a tomb?
How comes it here, this chamber bright,
Through whose mullioned windows clear
The castle-court all wet with rain,
The drawbridge and the moat appear,
And then the beach, and, marked with spray,
The sunken reefs, and far away
The unquiet bright Atlantic plain?
— What! has some glamour made me sleep,
And sent me with my dogs to sweep,
By night, with boisterous bugle-peal,
Through some old, sea-side, knightly hall,
Not in the free green wood at all?
That knight's asleep, and at her prayer
That lady by the bed doth kneel —
Then hush, thou boisterous bugle-peal!

— The wild boar rustles in his lair ;
The fierce hounds snuff the tainted air ;
But lord and hounds keep rooted there.

Cheer, cheer thy dogs into the brake,
O hunter ! and without a fear
Thy golden-tasselled bugle blow,
And through the glades thy pastime take —
For thou wilt rouse no sleepers here !
For these thou seest are unmoved ;
Cold, cold as those who lived and loved
A thousand years ago.

TRISTRAM AND ISEULT.

III.

Iseult of Brittany.

A YEAR had flown, and o'er the sea away,
In Cornwall, Tristram and Queen Iseult lay ;
In King Marc's chapel, in Tyntagel old :
There in a ship they bore those lovers cold.

The young surviving Iseult, one bright day,
Had wandered forth.   Her children were at play
In a green circular hollow in the heath
Which borders the seashore ; a country path
Creeps over it from the tilled fields behind.
The hollow's grassy banks are soft-inclined ;
And to one standing on them, far and near
The lone unbroken view spreads bright and clear
Over the waste.   This cirque of open ground
Is light and green ; the heather, which all round

Creeps thickly, grows not here ; but the pale grass
Is strewn with rocks and many a shivered mass
Of veined white-gleaming quartz, and here and there
Dotted with holly-trees and juniper.
In the smooth centre of the opening stood
Three hollies side by side, and made a screen,
Warm with the winter-sun, of burnished green
With scarlet berries gemmed, the fell-fare's food.
Under the glittering hollies Iseult stands,
Watching her children play : their little hands
Are busy gathering spars of quartz, and streams
Of stagshorn for their hats ; anon, with screams
Of mad delight they drop their spoils, and bound
Among the holly-clumps and broken ground,
Racing full speed, and startling in their rush
The fell-fares and the speckled missel-thrush
Out of their glossy coverts ; but when now
Their cheeks were flushed, and over each hot brow,
Under the feathered hats of the sweet pair,
In blinding masses showered the golden hair,
Then Iseult called them to her, and the three
Clustered under the holly-screen, and she
Told them an old-world Breton history.

Warm in their mantles wrapped, the three stood there,
Under the hollies, in the clear still air, —
Mantles with those rich furs deep glistering
Which Venice ships do from swart Egypt bring.
Long they stayed still, then, pacing at their ease,
Moved up and down under the glossy trees ;
But still, as they pursued their warm dry road,
From Iseult's lips the unbroken story flowed,
And still the children listened, their blue eyes
Fixed on their mother's face in wide surprise.

Nor did their looks stray once to the sea-side,
Nor to the brown heaths round them, bright and wide,
Nor to the snow, which, though 'twas all away
From the open heath, still by the hedgerows lay,
Nor to the shining sea-fowl, that with screams
Bore up from where the bright Atlantic gleams,
Swooping to landward ; nor to where, quite clear,
The fell-fares settled on the thickets near.
And they would still have listened, till dark night
Came keen and chill down on the heather bright ;
But when the red glow on the sea grew cold,
And the gray turrets of the castle old
Looked sternly through the frosty evening-air,
Then Iseult took by the hand those children fair,
And brought her tale to an end, and found the path,
And led them home over the darkening heath.

    And is she happy? Does she see unmoved
The days in which she might have lived and loved
Slip without bringing bliss slowly away,
One after one, to-morrow like to-day?
Joy has not found her yet, nor ever will :
Is it this thought which makes her mien so still,
Her features so fatigued, her eyes, though sweet,
So sunk, so rarely lifted save to meet
Her children's? She moves slow ; her voice alone
Hath yet an infantine and silver tone,
But even that comes languidly ; in truth,
She seems one dying in a mask of youth.
And now she will go home, and softly lay
Her laughing children in their beds, and play
A while with them before they sleep ; and then
She'll light her silver lamp, — which fishermen
Dragging their nets through the rough waves afar,
Along this iron coast, know like a star, —

And take her broidery-frame, and there she'll sit
Hour after hour, her gold curls sweeping it;
Lifting her soft-bent head only to mind
Her children, or to listen to the wind.
And when the clock peals midnight, she will move
Her work away, and let her fingers rove
Across the shaggy brows of Tristram's hound,
Who lies, guarding her feet, along the ground;
Or else she will fall musing, her blue eyes
Fixed, her slight hands clasped on her lap; then
    rise,
And at her prie-dieu kneel, until she have told
Her rosary-beads of ebony tipped with gold;
Then to her soft sleep — and to-morrow'll be
To-day's exact repeated effigy.
Yes, it is lonely for her in her hall.
The children, and the gray-haired seneschal,
Her women, and Sir Tristram's aged hound,
Are there the sole companions to be found.
But these she loves; and noisier life than this
She would find ill to bear, weak as she is.
She has her children, too, and night and day
Is with them; and the wide heaths where they play,
The hollies, and the cliff, and the sea-shore,
The sand, the sea-birds, and the distant sails,
These are to her dear as to them; the tales
With which this day the children she beguiled
She gleaned from Breton grandames, when a child,
In every hut along this sea-coast wild;
She herself loves them still, and, when they are told,
Can forget all to hear them, as of old.

Dear saints, it is not sorrow, as I hear,
Not suffering, which shuts up eye and ear

To all that has delighted them before,
And lets us be what we were once no more.
No : we may suffer deeply, yet retain
Power to be moved and soothed, for all our pain,
By what of old pleased us, and will again.
No : 'tis the gradual furnace of the world,
In whose hot air our spirits are upcurled
Until they crumble, or else grow like steel,
Which kills in us the bloom, the youth, the spring ;
Which leaves the fierce necessity to feel,
But takes away the power : this can avail,
By drying up our joy in every thing,
To make our former pleasures all seem stale.
This, or some tyrannous single thought, some fit
Of passion, which subdues our souls to it,
Till for its sake alone we live and move, —
Call it ambition, or remorse, or love, —
This too can change us wholly, and make seem
All which we did before, shadow and dream.

　　And yet, I swear, it angers me to see
How this fool passion gulls men potently ;
Being, in truth, but a diseased unrest,
And an unnatural overheat at best.
How they are full of languor and distress
Not having it ; which when they do possess,
They straightway are burnt up with fume and care,
And spend their lives in posting here and there
Where this plague drives them ; and have little ease.
Are furious with themselves, and hard to please.
Like that bald Cæsar, the famed Roman wight,
Who wept at reading of a Grecian knight
Who made a name at younger years than he ;
Or that renowned mirror of chivalry,
Prince Alexander, Philip's peerless son,

Who carried the great war from Macedon
Into the Soudan's realm, and thundered on
To die at thirty-five in Babylon.

What tale did Iseult to the children say,
Under the hollies, that bright winter's day?

She told them of the fairy-haunted land
Away the other side of Brittany,
Beyond the heaths, edged by the lonely sea;
Of the deep forest-glades of Broce-liande,
Through whose green boughs the golden sunshine
        creeps,
Where Merlin by the enchanted thorn-tree sleeps.
For here he came with the fay Vivian,
One April, when the warm days first began.
He was on foot, and that false fay, his friend,
On her white palfrey; here he met his end,
In these lone sylvan glades, that April-day.
This tale of Merlin and the lovely fay
Was the one Iseult chose, and she brought clear
Before the children's fancy him and her.

Blowing between the stems, the forest-air
Had loosened the brown locks of Vivian's hair,
Which played on her flushed cheek, and her blue eyes
Sparkled with mocking glee and exercise.
Her palfrey's flanks were mired and bathed in sweat,
For they had travelled far and not stopped yet.
A brier in that tangled wilderness
Had scored her white right hand, which she allows
To rest ungloved on her green riding-dress;
The other warded off the drooping boughs.
But still she chatted on, with her blue eyes
Fixed full on Merlin's face, her stately prize.

Her 'havior had the morning's fresh clear grace,
The spirit of the woods was in her face ;
She looked so witching fair, that learned wight
Forgot his craft, and his best wits took flight,
And he grew fond, and eager to obey
His mistress, use her empire as she may.

They came to where the brushwood ceased, and day
Peered 'twixt the stems ; and the ground broke away
In a sloped sward down to a brawling brook.
And up as high as where they stood to look
On the brook's farther side was clear ; but then
The underwood and trees began again.
This open glen was studded thick with thorns
Then white with blossom ; and you saw the horns,
Through last year's fern, of the shy fallow-deer
Who come at noon down to the water here.
You saw the bright-eyed squirrels dart along
Under the thorns on the green sward ; and strong
The blackbird whistled from the dingles near,
And the weird chipping of the woodpecker
Rang lonelily and sharp ; the sky was fair,
And a fresh breath of spring stirred everywhere.
Merlin and Vivian stopped on the slope's brow,
To gaze on the light sea of leaf and bough
Which glistering plays all round them, lone and mild,
As if to itself the quiet forest smiled.
Upon the brow-top grew a thorn, and here
The grass was dry and mossed, and you saw clear
Across the hollow ; white anemones
Starred the cool turf, and clumps of primroses
Ran out from the dark underwood behind.
No fairer resting-place a man could find.

" Here let us halt," said Merlin then ; and she
Nodded, and tied her palfrey to a tree.

They sate them down together, and a sleep
Fell upon Merlin, more like death, so deep.
Her finger on her lips, then Vivian rose,
And from her brown-locked head the wimple throws,
And takes it in her hand, and waves it over
The blossomed thorn-tree and her sleeping lover.
Nine times she waved the fluttering wimple round,
And made a little plot of magic ground.
And in that daisied circle, as men say,
Is Merlin prisoner till the judgment-day ;
But she herself whither she will can rove —
For she was passing weary of his love.

SAINT BRANDAN.

Saint Brandan sails the northern main ;
The brotherhoods of saints are glad.
He greets them once, he sails again ;
So late ! such storms ! The saint is mad !

He heard, across the howling seas,
Chime convent-bells on wintry nights;
He saw, on spray-swept Hebrides,
Twinkle the monastery-lights ;

But north, still north, Saint Brandan steered ;
And now no bells, no convents more !
The hurtling Polar lights are neared,
The sea without a human shore.

At last (it was the Christmas-night;
Stars shone after a day of storm)
He sees float past an iceberg white,
And on it — Christ ! — a living form.

That furtive mien, that scowling eye,
Of hair that red and tufted fell,
It is — oh, where shall Brandan fly ? —
The traitor Judas, out of hell !

Palsied with terror, Brandan sate ;
The moon was bright, the iceberg near.
He hears a voice sigh humbly, " Wait !
By high permission I am here.

" One moment wait, thou holy man !
On earth my crime, my death, they knew ;
My name is under all men's ban :
Ah ! tell them of my respite too.

" Tell them, one blessed Christmas-night
(It was the first after I came,
Breathing self-murder, frenzy, spite,
To rue my guilt in endless flame), —

" I felt, as I in torment lay
'Mid the souls plagued by heavenly power,
An angel touch mine arm, and say, —
Go hence, and cool thyself an hour !

" ' Ah ! whence this mercy, Lord ? ' I said.
The leper recollect, said he,
Who asked the passers-by for aid,
In Joppa, and thy charity.

" Then I remembered how I went,
In Joppa, through the public street,
One morn when the sirocco spent
Its storms of dust with burning heat ;

" And in the street a leper sate,
Shivering with fever, naked, old ;
Sand raked his sores from heel to pate,
The hot wind fevered him fivefold.

" He gazed upon me as I passed,
And murmured, *Help me, or I die !*
To the poor wretch my cloak I cast,
Saw him look eased, and hurried by.

" O Brandan ! think what grace divine,
What blessing must full goodness shower,
When fragment of it small, like mine,
Hath such inestimable power !

" Well-fed, well-clothed, well-friended, I
Did that chance act of good, that one !
Then went my way to kill and lie,
Forgot my good as soon as done.

" That germ of kindness, in the womb
Of mercy caught, did not expire ;
Outlives my guilt, outlives my doom,
And friends me in the pit of fire.

" Once every year, when carols wake,
On earth, the Christmas-night's repose,
Arising from the sinner's lake,
I journey to these healing snows.

" I stanch with ice my burning breast,
With silence balm my whirling brain.
O Brandan ! to this hour of rest,
That Joppan leper's ease was pain."

Tears started to Saint Brandan's eyes ;
He bowed his head, he breathed a prayer,
Then looked — and lo, the frosty skies !
The iceberg, and no Judas there !

THE NECKAN.

In summer, on the headlands,
　The Baltic Sea along,
Sits Neckan with his harp of gold,
　And sings his plaintive song.

Green rolls, beneath the headlands,
　Green rolls the Baltic Sea ;
And there, below the Neckan's feet,
　His wife and children be.

He sings not of the ocean,
　Its shells and roses pale :
Of earth, of earth, the Neckan sings,
　He hath no other tale.

He sits upon the headlands,
　And sings a mournful stave
Of all he saw and felt on earth,
　Far from the kind sea-wave.

Sings how, a knight, he wandered
　By castle, field, and town ;
But earthly knights have harder hearts
　Than the sea-children own.

Sings of his earthly bridal,
　Priest, knights, and ladies gay.
"And who art thou," the priest began,
　"Sir Knight, who wedd'st to-day?"

"I am no knight," he answered ;
　"From the sea-waves I come."
The knights drew sword, the ladies screamed,
　The surpliced priest stood dumb.

He sings how from the chapel
    He vanished with his bride,
And bore her down to the sea-halls,
    Beneath the salt sea-tide.

He sings how she sits weeping
    'Mid shells that round her lie.
" False Neckan shares my bed," she weeps ;
    "No Christian mate have I."

He sings how through the billows
    He rose to earth again,
And sought a priest to sign the cross,
    That Neckan heaven might gain.

He sings how, on an evening,
    Beneath the birch-trees cool,
He sate and played his harp of gold,
    Beside the river-pool.

Beside the pool sate Neckan,
    Tears filled his mild blue eye.
On his white mule, across the bridge,
    A cassocked priest rode by.

" Why sitt'st thou there, O Neckan,
    And play'st thy harp of gold?
Sooner shall this my staff bear leaves,
    Than thou shalt heaven behold."

But, lo ! the staff, it budded ;
    It greened, it branched, it waved.
" O ruth of God !" the priest cried out,
    "This lost sea-creature saved !"

The cassocked priest rode onwards,
    And vanished with his mule ;
And Neckan in the twilight gray
    Wept by the river-pool.

He wept, " The earth hath kindness,
    The sea, the starry poles ;
Earth, sea, and sky, and God above, —
    But, ah ! not human souls ! "

In summer, on the headlands,
    The Baltic Sea along,
Sits Neckan with his harp of gold,
    And sings this plaintive song.

THE FORSAKEN MERMAN.

COME, dear children, let us away ;
Down and away below !
Now my brothers call from the bay,
Now the great winds shoreward blow,
Now the salt tides seaward flow ;
Now the wild white horses play,
Champ and chafe and toss in the spray.
Children dear, let us away !
This way, this way !

Call her once before you go, —
Call once yet !
In a voice that she will know, —
" Margaret ! Margaret ! "
Children's voices should be dear
(Call once more) to a mother's ear ;
Children's voices, wild with pain, —
Surely she will come again !
Call her once, and come away ;
This way, this way !
" Mother dear, we cannot stay !

The wild white horses foam and fret."
Margaret ! Margaret !

Come, dear children, come away down :
Call no more !
One last look at the white-walled town,
And the little gray church on the windy shore ;
Then come down !
She will not come, though you call all day ;
Come away, come away !

Children dear, was it yesterday
We heard the sweet bells over the bay, —
In the caverns where we lay,
Through the surf and through the swell,
The far-off sound of a silver bell?
Sand-strewn caverns, cool and deep,
Where the winds are all asleep ;
Where the spent lights quiver and gleam,
Where the salt weed sways in the stream,
Where the sea-beasts, ranged all round,
Feed in the ooze of their pasture-ground ;
Where the sea-snakes coil and twine,
Dry their mail and bask in the brine ;
Where great whales come sailing by,
Sail and sail, with unshut eye,
Round the world for ever and aye?
When did music come this way?
Children dear, was it yesterday?

Children dear, was it yesterday
(Call yet once) that she went away?
Once she sate with you and me,
On a red gold throne in the heart of the sea,
And the youngest sate on her knee.

She combed its bright hair, and she tended it well,
When down swung the sound of a far-off bell.
She sighed, she looked up through the clear green sea ;
She said, " I must go, for my kinsfolk pray
In the little gray church on the shore to-day.
'Twill be Easter-time in the world — ah me !
And I lose my poor soul, merman ! here with thee."
I said, " Go up, dear heart, through the waves ;
Say thy prayer, and come back to the kind sea-caves ! "
She smiled, she went up through the surf in the bay.

Children dear, was it yesterday?
Children dear, were we long alone?
" The sea grows stormy, the little ones moan ;
Long prayers," I said, " in the world they say ;
Come !" I said ; and we rose through the surf in the
    bay.
We went up the beach, by the sandy down
Where the sea-stocks bloom, to the white-walled town ;
Through the narrow paved streets, where all was still,
To the little gray church on the windy hill.
From the church came a murmur of folk at their
    prayers,
But we stood without in the cold blowing airs.
We climbed on the graves, on the stones worn with
    rains,
And we gazed up the aisle through the small leaded
    panes.
She sate by the pillar ; we saw her clear :
" Margaret, hist ! come quick, we are here !
Dear heart," I said, " we are long alone ;
The sea grows stormy, the little ones moan."
But, ah ! she gave me never a look,
For her eyes were sealed to the holy book.

Loud prays the priest ; shut stands the door.
Come away, children, call no more !
Come away, come down, call no more !

Down, down, down !
Down to the depths of the sea !
She sits at her wheel in the humming town,
Singing most joyfully.
Hark what she sings : " O joy, O joy,
For the humming street, and the child with its toy !
For the priest, and the bell, and the holy well ;
For the wheel where I spun,
And the blessed light of the sun ! "
And so she sings her fill,
Singing most joyfully,
Till the spindle drops from her hand,
And the whizzing wheel stands still.
She steals to the window, and looks at the sand,
And over the sand at the sea ;
And her eyes are set in a stare ;
And anon there breaks a sigh,
And anon there drops a tear,
From a sorrow-clouded eye,
And a heart sorrow-laden,
A long, long sigh,
For the cold strange eyes of a little mermaiden,
And the gleam of her golden hair.

Come away, away, children ;
Come, children, come down !
The hoarse wind blows colder ;
Lights shine in the town.
She will start from her slumber
When gusts shake the door :

She will hear the winds howling,
Will hear the waves roar.
We shall see, while above us
The waves roar and whirl,
A ceiling of amber,
A pavement of pearl.
Singing, " Here came a mortal,
But faithless was she !
And alone dwell forever
The kings of the sea."

But, children, at midnight,
When soft the winds blow,
When clear falls the moonlight,
When spring-tides are low ;
When sweet airs come seaward
From heaths starred with broom,
And high rocks throw mildly
On the blanched sands a gloom ;
Up the still, glistening beaches,
Up the creeks we will hie,
Over banks of bright seaweed
The ebb-tide leaves dry.
We will gaze, from the sand-hills,
At the white sleeping town ;
At the church on the hill-side,
And then come back down,
Singing, " There dwells a loved one,
But cruel is she !
She left lonely forever
The kings of the sea."

SONNETS.

AUSTERITY OF POETRY.

That son of Italy who tried to blow,[8]
Ere Dante came, the trump of sacred song,
In his light youth amid a festal throng
Sate with his bride to see a public show.

Fair was the bride, and on her front did glow
Youth like a star ; and what to youth belong, —
Gay raiment, sparkling gauds, elation strong.
A prop gave way ! crash fell a platform ! Lo,

Mid struggling sufferers, hurt to death, she lay !
Shuddering, they drew her garments off — and found
A robe of sackcloth next the smooth, white skin.

Such, poets, is your bride, the Muse ! young, gay,
Radiant, adorned outside ; a hidden ground
Of thought and of austerity within.

A PICTURE AT NEWSTEAD.

What made my heart, at Newstead, fullest swell? —
'Twas not the thought of Byron, of his cry
Stormily sweet, his Titan-agony ;
It was the sight of that Lord Arundel

Who struck, in heat, his child he loved so well,
And his child's reason flickered, and did die.
Painted (he willed it) in the gallery
They hang ; the picture doth the story tell.

Behold the stern, mailed father, staff in hand !
The little fair-haired son, with vacant gaze,
Where no more lights of sense or knowledge are !

Methinks the woe, which made that father stand
Baring his dumb remorse to future days,
Was woe than Byron's woe more tragic far.

RACHEL.

I.

In Paris all looked hot and like to fade ;
Sere, in the garden of the Tuileries,
Sere with September, drooped the chestnut-trees ;
'Twas dawn, a brougham rolled through the streets,
     and made

Halt at the white and silent colonnade
Of the French Theatre.   Worn with disease,
Rachel, with eyes no gazing can appease,
Sate in the brougham, and those blank walls surveyed.

She follows the gay world, whose swarms have fled
To Switzerland, to Baden, to the Rhine ;
Why stops she by this empty playhouse drear ?

Ah ! where the spirit its highest life hath led,
All spots, matched with that spot, are less divine ;
And Rachel's Switzerland, her Rhine, is here !

II.

Unto a lonely villa, in a dell
Above the fragrant warm Provençal shore,
The dying Rachel in a chair they bore
Up the steep pine-plumed paths of the Estrelle,

And laid her in a stately room, where fell
The shadow of a marble Muse of yore, —
The rose-crowned queen of legendary lore,
Polymnia, — full on her death-bed. 'Twas well!

The fret and misery of our northern towns,
In this her life's last day, our poor, our pain,
Our jangle of false wits, our climate's frowns,

Do for this radiant Greek-souled artist cease:
Sole object of her dying eyes remain
The beauty and the glorious art of Greece.

III.

Sprung from the blood of Israel's scattered race,
At a mean inn in German Aarau born,
To forms from antique Greece and Rome uptorn,
Tricked out with a Parisian speech and face,

Imparting life renewed, old classic grace;
Then soothing with thy Christian strain forlorn,
A-Kempis! her departing soul outworn,
While by her bedside Hebrew rites have place, —

Ah! not the radiant spirit of Greece alone
She had — one power, which made her breast its home.
In her, like us, there clashed, contending powers,

Germany, France, Christ, Moses, Athens, Rome.
The strife, the mixture in her soul, are ours;
Her genius and her glory are her own.

WORLDLY PLACE.

Even in a palace, life may be led well!
So spake the imperial sage, purest of men,
Marcus Aurelius. But the stifling den
Of common life, where, crowded up pell-mell,

Our freedom for a little bread we sell,
And drudge under some foolish master's ken
Who rates us if we peer outside our pen, —
Matched with a palace, is not this a hell?

Even in a palace! On his truth sincere,
Who spoke these words, no shadow ever came;
And when my ill schooled spirit is aflame

Some nobler, ampler stage of life to win,
I'll stop, and say, "There were no succor here!
The aids to noble life are all within."

EAST LONDON.

'Twas August, and the fierce sun overhead
Smote on the squalid streets of Bethnal Green,
And the pale weaver, through his windows seen
In Spitalfields, looked thrice dispirited.

I met a preacher there I knew, and said, —
"Ill and o'erworked, how fare you in this scene?"
"Bravely!" said he; "for I of late have been
Much cheered with thoughts of Christ, *the living bread.*"

O human soul! as long as thou canst so
Set up a mark of everlasting light,
Above the howling senses' ebb and flow,

To cheer thee, and to right thee if thou roam, —
Not with lost toil thou laborest through the night!
Thou mak'st the heaven thou hop'st indeed thy home.

WEST LONDON.

CROUCHED on the pavement, close by Belgrave Square,
A tramp I saw, ill, moody, and tongue-tied ;
A babe was in her arms, and at her side
A girl ; their clothes were rags, their feet were bare.

Some laboring-men, whose work lay somewhere there,
Passed opposite ; she touched her girl, who hied
Across, and begged, and came back satisfied.
The rich she had let pass with frozen stare.

Thought I, " Above her state this spirit towers ;
She will not ask of aliens, but of friends,
Of sharers in a common human fate.

She turns from that cold succor, which attends
The unknown little from the unknowing great,
And points us to a better time than ours."

EAST AND WEST.

IN the bare midst of Anglesey they show
Two springs which close by one another play ;
And, " Thirteen hundred years agone," they say,
" Two saints met often where those waters flow.

One came from Penmon westward, and a glow
Whitened his face from the sun's fronting ray ;
Eastward the other, from the dying day,
And he with unsunned face did always go."

Seiriol the Bright, Kybi the Dark ! men said.
The seer from the East was then in light,
The seer from the West was then in shade.

Ah ! now 'tis changed.   In conquering sunshine bright
The man of the bold West now comes arrayed :
He of the mystic East is touched with night.

THE BETTER PART.

LONG fed on boundless hopes, O race of man,
How angrily thou spurn'st all simpler fare !
" Christ," some one says, " was human as we are ;
No judge eyes us from heaven, our sin to scan ;

We live no more, when we have done our span."
" Well, then, for Christ," thou answerest, " who can care ?
From sin which Heaven records not, why forbear ?
Live we like brutes our life without a plan ! "

So answerest thou ; but why not rather say, —
" Hath man no second life ?   *Pitch this one high !*
Sits there no judge in heaven, our sin to see ?

More strictly, then, the inward judge obey !
Was Christ a man like us ?   *Ah ! let us try*
If we then, too, can be such men as he ! "

THE DIVINITY.

" YES, write it in the rock," Saint Bernard said,
" Grave it on brass with adamantine pen !
'Tis God himself becomes apparent, when
God's wisdom and God's goodness are displayed ;

For God of these his attributes is made." —
Well spake the impetuous saint, and bore of men
The suffrage captive : now not one in ten
Recalls the obscure opposer he outweighed.[9]

God's wisdom and God's goodness! Ay, but fools
Mis-define these till God knows them no more.
Wisdom and goodness, they are God! — what schools

Have yet so much as heard this simpler lore?
This no saint preaches, and this no Church rules;
'Tis in the desert, now and heretofore.

IMMORTALITY.

FOILED by our fellow-men, depressed, outworn,
We leave the brutal world to take its way,
And, *Patience! in another life,* we say,
The world shall be thrust down, and we upborne.

And will not, then, the immortal armies scorn
The world's poor, routed leavings? or will they
Who failed under the heat of this life's day
Support the fervors of the heavenly morn?

No, no! the energy of life may be
Kept on after the grave, but not begun;
And he who flagged not in the earthly strife,

From strength to strength advancing, — only he,
His soul well-knit, and all his battles won,
Mounts, and that hardly, to eternal life.

THE GOOD SHEPHERD WITH THE KID.

HE saves the sheep, the goats he doth not save.
So rang Tertullian's sentence, on the side
Of that unpitying Phrygian sect which cried, [10]
" Him can no fount of fresh forgiveness lave,

Who sins, once washed by the baptismal wave."
So spake the fierce Tertullian.   But she sighed,
The infant Church ! of love she felt the tide
Stream on her from her Lord's yet recent grave.

And then she smiled ; and in the Catacombs,
With eye suffused but heart inspired true,
On those walls subterranean, where she hid

Her head 'mid ignominy, death, and tombs,
She her Good Shepherd's hasty image drew —
And on his shoulders, not a lamb, a kid.

MONICA'S LAST PRAYER.[1]

" Ah ! could thy grave at home, at Carthage, be ! "
Care not for that, and lay me where I fall !
Everywhere heard will be the judgment-call ;
But at God's altar, oh ! remember me.

Thus Monica, and died in Italy.
Yet fervent had her longing been, through all
Her course, for home at last, and burial
With her own husband, by the Libyan sea.

Had been ! but at the end, to her pure soul
All tie with all beside seemed vain and cheap,
And union before God the only care.

Creeds pass, rites change, no altar standeth whole.
Yet we her memory, as she prayed, will keep,
Keep by this : *Life in God, and union there !*

LYRIC AND DRAMATIC POEMS.

SWITZERLAND.

I. MEETING.

AGAIN I see my bliss at hand,
  The town, the lake, are here;
My Marguerite smiles upon the strand,[12]
  Unaltered with the year.

I know that graceful figure fair,
  That cheek of languid hue;
I know that soft, enkerchiefed hair,
  And those sweet eyes of blue.

Again I spring to make my choice;
  Again in tones of ire
I hear a God's tremendous voice, —
  "Be counselled, and retire."

Ye guiding Powers who join and part,
  What would ye have with me?
Ah, warn some more ambitious heart,
  And let the peaceful be!

II. PARTING.

YE storm-winds of autumn !
Who rush by, who shake
The window, and ruffle
The gleam-lighted lake ;
Who cross to the hillside
Thin-sprinkled with farms,
Where the high woods strip sadly
Their yellowing arms, —
Ye are bound for the mountains !
Ah ! with you let me go
Where your cold, distant barrier,
The vast range of snow,
Through the loose clouds lifts dimly
Its white peaks in air.
How deep is their stillness !
Ah ! would I were there !

But on the stairs what voice is this I hear,
Buoyant as morning, and as morning clear?
Say, has some wet bird-haunted English lawn
Lent it the music of its trees at dawn?
Or was it from some sun-flecked mountain brook
That the sweet voice its upland clearness took?
        Ah ! it comes nearer —
        Sweet notes, this way !

Hark ! fast by the window
The rushing winds go,
To the ice-cumbered gorges,
The vast seas of snow !
There the torrents drive upward
    Their rock-strangled hum ;

There the avalanche thunders
The hoarse torrent dumb.
— I come, O ye mountains !
Ye torrents, I come !

But who is this, by the half-opened door,
Whose figure casts a shadow on the floor?
The sweet blue eyes — the soft, ash-colored hair —
The cheeks that still their gentle paleness wear —
The lovely lips, with their arched smile that tells
The unconquered joy in which her spirit dwells —
       Ah ! they bend nearer —
       Sweet lips, this way !

   Hark ! the wind rushes past us !
   Ah ! with that let me go
   To the clear, waning hill-side,
   Unspotted by snow,
   There to watch, o'er the sunk vale,
   The frore mountain wall,
   Where the niched snow-bed sprays down
   Its powdery fall.
   There its dusky blue clusters
   The aconite spreads ;
   There the pines slope, the cloud-strips
   Hung soft in their heads.
   No life but, at moments,
   The mountain bee's hum.
   — I come, O ye mountains !
   Ye pine-woods, I come !

   Forgive me ! forgive me !
     Ah, Marguerite, fain
   Would these arms reach to clasp thee !
     But see ! 'tis in vain.

In the void air, towards thee,
　My stretched arms are cast;
But a sea rolls between us, —
　Our different past!

To the lips, ah! of others
　Those lips have been prest,
And others, ere I was,
　Were strained to that breast.

Far, far from each other
　Our spirits have grown.
And what heart knows another?
　Ah! who knows his own?

Blow, ye winds! lift me with you!
　I come to the wild.
Fold closely, O Nature!
　Thine arms round thy child.

To thee only God granted
　A heart ever new, —
To all always open,
　To all always true.

Ah! calm me, restore me;
　And dry up my tears
On thy high mountain platforms,
　Where morn first appears;

Where the white mists, forever,
　Are spread and upfurled, —
In the stir of the forces
　Whence issued the world.

III. A FAREWELL.

My horse's feet beside the lake,
Where sweet the unbroken moonbeams lay,
Sent echoes through the night to wake
Each glistening strand, each heath-fringed bay.

The poplar avenue was passed,
And the roofed bridge that spans the stream;
Up the steep street I hurried fast,
Led by thy taper's starlike beam.

I came ! I saw thee rise ! the blood
Poured flushing to thy languid cheek.
Locked in each other's arms we stood,
In tears, with hearts too full to speak.

Days flew ; ah, soon I could discern
A trouble in thine altered air !
Thy hand lay languidly in mine,
Thy cheek was grave, thy speech grew rare.

I blame thee not !   This heart, I know,
To be long loved was never framed ;
For something in its depths doth glow
Too strange, too restless, too untamed.

And women, — things that live and move
Mined by the fever of the soul, —
They seek to find in those they love
Stern strength, and promise of control.

They ask not kindness, gentle ways ;
These they themselves have tried and known :
They ask a soul which never sways
With the blind gusts that shake their own.

I too have felt the load I bore
In a too strong emotion's sway;
I too have wished, no woman more,
This starting, feverish heart away.

I too have longed for trenchant force,
And will like a dividing spear;
Have praised the keen, unscrupulous course,
Which knows no doubt, which feels no fear.

But in the world I learnt, what there
Thou too wilt surely one day prove, —
That will, that energy, though rare,
Are yet far, far less rare than love.

Go, then! till time and fate impress
This truth on thee, be mine no more!
They will! for thou, I feel, not less
Than I, wast destined to this lore.

We school our manners, act our parts;
But He, who sees us through and through,
Knows that the bent of both our hearts
Was to be gentle, tranquil, true.

And though we wear out life, alas!
Distracted as a homeless wind,
In beating where we must not pass,
In seeking what we shall not find;

Yet we shall one day gain, life past,
Clear prospect o'er our being's whole;
Shall see ourselves, and learn at last
Our true affinities of soul.

We shall not then deny a course
To every thought the mass ignore;
We shall not then call hardness force,
Nor lightness wisdom any more.

Then, in the eternal Father's smile,
Our soothed, encouraged souls will dare
To seem as free from pride and guile,
As good, as generous, as they are.

Then we shall know our friends!   Though much
Will have been lost, — the help in strife,
The thousand sweet, still joys of such
As hand in hand face earthly life, —

Though these be lost, there will be yet
A sympathy august and pure;
Ennobled by a vast regret,
And by contrition sealed thrice sure.

And we, whose ways were unlike here,
May then more neighboring courses ply;
May to each other be brought near,
And greet across infinity.

How sweet, unreached by earthly jars,
My sister! to maintain with thee
The hush among the shining stars,
The calm upon the moonlit sea!

How sweet to feel, on the boon air,
All our unquiet pulses cease!
To feel that nothing can impair
The gentleness, the thirst for peace, —

The gentleness too rudely hurled
On this wild earth of hate and fear ;
The thirst for peace, a raving world
Would never let us satiate here.

IV. ISOLATION. TO MARGUERITE.

WE were apart : yet, day by day,
I bade my heart more constant be.
I bade it keep the world away,
And grow a home for only thee ;
Nor feared but thy love likewise grew,
Like mine, each day, more tried, more true.

The fault was grave ! I might have known,
What far too soon, alas ! I learned, —
The heart can bind itself alone,
And faith may oft be unreturned.
Self-swayed our feelings ebb and swell.
Thou lov'st no more.   Farewell ! Farewell !

Farewell ! — And thou, thou lonely heart,
Which never yet without remorse
Even for a moment didst depart
From thy remote and spherèd course
To haunt the place where passions reign, —
Back to thy solitude again !

Back ! with the conscious thrill of shame
Which Luna felt, that summer-night,
Flash through her pure immortal frame,
When she forsook the starry height
To hang o'er Endymion's sleep
Upon the pine-grown Latmian steep.

Yet she, chaste queen, had never proved
How vain a thing is mortal love,
Wandering in heaven, far removed;
But thou hast long had place to prove
This truth, — to prove, and make thine own:
"Thou hast been, shalt be, art, alone."

Or, if not quite alone, yet they
Which touch thee are unmating things, —
Ocean and clouds and night and day;
Lorn autumns and triumphant springs;
And life, and others' joy and pain,
And love, if love, of happier men.

Of happier men; for they, at least,
Have *dreamed* two human hearts might blend
In one, and were through faith released
From isolation without end
Prolonged; nor knew, although not less
Alone than thou, their loneliness.

V. TO MARGUERITE. CONTINUED.

YES! in the sea of life enisled,
With echoing straits between us thrown,
Dotting the shoreless watery wild,
We mortal millions live *alone*.
The islands feel the enclasping flow,
And then their endless bounds they know.

But when the moon their hollows lights,
And they are swept by balms of spring,
And in their glens, on starry nights,
The nightingales divinely sing;
And lovely notes, from shore to shore,
Across the sounds and channels pour, —

Oh ! then a longing like despair
Is to their farthest caverns sent ;
For surely once, they feel, we were
Parts of a single continent !
Now round us spreads the watery plain :
Oh, might our marges meet again !

Who ordered that their longing's fire
Should be, as soon as kindled, cooled?
Who renders vain their deep desire? —
A God, a God their severance ruled !
And bade betwixt their shores to be
The unplumbed, salt, estranging sea.

VI. ABSENCE.

In this fair stranger's eyes of gray,
    Thine eyes, my love ! I see.
I shiver ; for the passing day
    Had borne me far from thee.

This is the curse of life ! that not
    A nobler, calmer train
Of wiser thoughts and feelings blot
    Our passions from our brain ;

But each day brings its petty dust,
    Our soon-choked souls to fill ;
And we forget because we must,
    And not because we will.

I struggle towards the light ; and ye,
    Once-longed-for storms of love !
If with the light ye cannot be,
    I bear that ye remove.

I struggle towards the light; but oh,
    While yet the night is chill,
Upon time's barren, stormy flow,
    Stay with me, Marguerite, still!

VII. THE TERRACE AT BERNE.

(COMPOSED TEN YEARS AFTER THE PRECEDING.)

TEN years! and to my waking eye
Once more the roofs of Berne appear;
The rocky banks, the terrace high,
The stream! and do I linger here?

The clouds are on the Oberland,
The Jungfrau snows look faint and far;
But bright are those green fields at hand,
And through those fields comes down the Aar,

And from the blue twin lakes it comes,
Flows by the town, the churchyard fair;
And 'neath the garden-walk it hums,
The house! and is my Marguerite there?

Ah! shall I see thee, while a flush
Of startled pleasure floods thy brow,
Quick through the oleanders brush,
And clap thy hands, and cry, *'Tis thou!*

Or hast thou long since wandered back,
Daughter of France! to France, thy home;
And flitted down the flowery track
Where feet like thine too lightly come?

Doth riotous laughter now replace
Thy smile, and rouge, with stony glare,
Thy cheek's soft hue, and fluttering lace
The kerchief that inwound thy hair?

Or is it over? art thou dead? —
Dead ! — and no warning shiver ran
Across my heart, to say thy thread
Of life was cut, and closed thy span !

Could from earth's ways that figure slight
Be lost, and I not feel 'twas so?
Of that fresh voice the gay delight
Fail from earth's air, and I not know?

Or shall I find thee still, but changed,
But not the Marguerite of thy prime?
With all thy being re-arranged, —
Passed through the crucible of time ;

With spirit vanished, beauty waned,
And hardly yet a glance, a tone,
A gesture — any thing — retained
Of all that was my Marguerite's own?

I will not know !   For wherefore try,
To things by mortal course that live,
A shadowy durability,
For which they were not meant, to give?

Like driftwood spars, which meet and pass
Upon the boundless ocean-plain,
So on the sea of life, alas !
Man meets man, — meets, and quits again.

I knew it when my life was young ;
I feel it still now youth is o'er.
— The mists are on the mountain hung,
And Marguerite I shall see no more.

THE STRAYED REVELLER.

THE PORTICO OF CIRCE'S PALACE. EVENING.

A YOUTH.   CIRCE.

THE YOUTH.

FASTER, faster,
O Circe, goddess,
Let the wild, thronging train,
The bright procession
Of eddying forms,
Sweep through my soul !

Thou standest, smiling
Down on me ! thy right arm,
Leaned up against the column there,
Props thy soft cheek ;
Thy left holds, hanging loosely,
The deep cup, ivy-cinctured,
I held but now.

Is it then evening
So soon ?   I see, the night-dews,
Clustered in thick beads, dim
The agate brooch-stones
On thy white shoulder ;
The cool night-wind, too,
Blows through the portico,
Stirs thy hair, goddess,
Waves thy white robe !

CIRCE.

Whence art thou, sleeper?

THE YOUTH.

When the white dawn first
Through the rough fir-planks
Of my hut, by the chestnuts,
Up at the valley-head,
Came breaking, goddess !
I sprang up, I threw round me
My dappled fawn-skin ;
Passing out, from the wet turf,
Where they lay, by the hut door,
I snatched up my vine-crown, my fir-staff,
All drenched in dew, —
Came swift down to join
The rout early gathered
In the town, round the temple,
Iacchus' white fane
On yonder hill.

Quick I passed, following
The woodcutters' cart-track
Down the dark valley.   I saw
On my left, through the beeches,
Thy palace, goddess,
Smokeless, empty !
Trembling, I entered ; beheld
The court all silent,
The lions sleeping,
On the altar this bowl.
I drank, goddess !
And sank down here, sleeping,
On the steps of thy portico.

CIRCE.

Foolish boy !   Why tremblest thou ?
Thou lovest it, then, my wine ?
Wouldst more of it ?   See how glows,
Through the delicate, flushed marble,
The red creaming liquor,
Strewn with dark seeds !
Drink, then ! I chide thee not,
Deny thee not my bowl.
Come, stretch forth thy hand, then — so !
Drink — drink again !

THE YOUTH.

Thanks, gracious one !
Ah, the sweet fumes again !
More soft, ah me !
More subtle-winding,
Than Pan's flute-music !
Faint — faint !   Ah me,
Again the sweet sleep !

CIRCE.

Hist !   Thou — within there !
Come forth, Ulysses !
Art tired with hunting ?
While we range the woodland,
See what the day brings.

ULYSSES.

Ever new magic !
Hast thou then lured hither,
Wonderful goddess, by thy art,
The young, languid-eyed Ampelus,

Iacchus' darling,
Or some youth beloved of Pan,
Of Pan and the nymphs;
That he sits, bending downward
His white, delicate neck
To the ivy-wreathed marge
Of thy cup; the bright, glancing vine-leaves
That crown his hair,
Falling forward, mingling
With the dark ivy-plants;
His fawn-skin, half untied,
Smeared with red wine-stains?   Who is he,
That he sits, overweighed
By fumes of wine and sleep,
So late, in thy portico?
What youth, goddess, — what guest
Of gods or mortals?

CIRCE.

Hist! he wakes!
I lured him not hither, Ulysses.
Nay, ask him!

THE YOUTH.

Who speaks?   Ah! who comes forth
To thy side, goddess, from within?
How shall I name him, —
This spare, dark-featured,
Quick-eyed stranger?
Ah! and I see too
His sailor's bonnet,
His short coat, travel-tarnished,
With one arm bare! —
Art thou not he, whom fame

This long time rumors
The favored guest of Circe, brought by the waves?
Art thou he, stranger, —
The wise Ulysses,
Laertes' son?

ULYSSES.

I am Ulysses.
And thou too, sleeper?
Thy voice is sweet.
It may be thou hast followed
Through the islands some divine bard,
By age taught many things, —
Age, and the Muses;
And heard him delighting
The chiefs and people
In the banquet, and learned his songs,
Of gods and heroes,
Of war and arts,
And peopled cities,
Inland, or built
By the gray sea.   If so, then hail!
I honor and welcome thee.

THE YOUTH.

The gods are happy.
They turn on all sides
Their shining eyes,
And see below them
The earth and men.

They see Tiresias
Sitting, staff in hand,
On the warm, grassy
Asopus bank,

His robe drawn over
His old sightless head,
Revolving inly
The doom of Thebes.

They see the centaurs
In the upper glens
Of Pelion, in the streams
Where red-berried ashes fringe
The clear-brown shallow pools,
With streaming flanks, and heads
Reared proudly, snuffing
The mountain wind.

They see the Indian
Drifting, knife in hand,
His frail boat moored to
A floating isle thick-matted
With large-leaved, low-creeping melon-plants,
And the dark cucumber.
He reaps and stows them,
Drifting — drifting; round him,
Round his green harvest-plot,
Flow the cool lake-waves,
The mountains ring them.

They see the Scythian
On the wide steppe, unharnessing
His wheeled house at noon.
He tethers his beast down, and makes his meal, —
Mares' milk, and bread
Baked on the embers.   All around,
The boundless, waving grass-plains stretch, thick-starred
With saffron and the yellow hollyhock
And flag-leaved iris-flowers.

Sitting in his cart
He makes his meal; before him, for long miles,
Alive with bright green lizards,
And the springing bustard-fowl,
The track, a straight black line,
Furrows the rich soil; here and there
Clusters of lonely mounds
Topped with rough-hewn,
Gray, rain-bleared statues, overpeer
The sunny waste.

They see the ferry
On the broad, clay-laden
Lone Chorasmian stream; thereon,
With snort and strain,
Two horses, strongly swimming, tow
The ferry-boat, with woven ropes
To either bow
Firm-harnessed by the mane; a chief,
With shout and shaken spear,
Stands at the prow, and guides them; but astern
The cowering merchants in long robes
Sit pale beside their wealth
Of silk-bales and of balsam-drops,
Of gold and ivory,
Of turquoise-earth, and amethyst,
Jasper and chalcedony,
And milk-barred onyx-stones.
The loaded boat swings groaning
In the yellow eddies;
The gods behold them.

They see the heroes
Sitting in the dark ship

On the foamless, long-heaving,
Violet sea,
At sunset nearing
The Happy Islands.

These things, Ulysses,
The wise bards also
Behold, and sing.
But oh, what labor !
O prince, what pain !

They too can see
Tiresias ; but the gods,
Who gave them vision,
Added this law :
That they should bear too
His groping blindness,
His dark foreboding,
His scorned white hairs ;
Bear Hera's anger
Through a life lengthened
To seven ages.

They see the centaurs
On Pelion : then they feel,
They too, the maddening wine
Swell their large veins to bursting ; in wild pain
They feel the biting spears
Of the grim Lapithæ, and Theseus, drive,
Drive crashing through their bones ; they feel,
High on a jutting rock in the red stream,
Alcmena's dreadful son
Ply his bow.   Such a price
The gods exact for song :
To become what we sing.

They see the Indian
On his mountain lake ; but squalls
Make their skiff reel, and worms
In the unkind spring have gnawn
Their melon-harvest to the heart.   They see
The Scythian ; but long frosts
Parch them in winter-time on the bare steppe,
Till they too fade like grass ; they crawl
Like shadows forth in spring.

They see the merchants
On the Oxus-stream ; but care
Must visit first them too, and make them pale :
Whether, through whirling sand,
A cloud of desert robber-horse have burst
Upon their caravan ; or greedy kings,
In the walled cities the way passes through,
Crushed them with tolls ; or fever-airs,
On some great river's marge,
Mown them down, far from home.

They see the heroes
Near harbor ; but they share
Their lives, and former violent toil in Thebes, —
Seven-gated Thebes, or Troy ;
Or where the echoing oars
Of Argo first
Startled the unknown sea.

The old Silenus
Came, lolling in the sunshine,
From the dewy forest-coverts,
This way, at noon.
Sitting by me, while his fauns

Down at the water-side
Sprinkled and smoothed
His drooping garland,
He told me these things.

But I, Ulysses,
Sitting on the warm steps,
Looking over the valley,
All day long, have seen,
Without pain, without labor,
Sometimes a wild-haired mænad,
Sometimes a faun with torches,
And sometimes, for a moment,
Passing through the dark stems
Flowing-robed, the beloved,
The desired, the divine,
 Beloved Iacchus.

Ah, cool night-wind, tremulous stars !
Ah, glimmering water,
Fitful earth-murmur,
Dreaming woods !
Ah, golden-haired, strangely smiling goddess
And thou, proved, much-enduring,
Wave-tossed wanderer !
Who can stand still?
Ye fade, ye swim, ye waver before me —
The cup again !

Faster, faster,
O Circe, goddess,
Let the wild, thronging train,
The bright procession
Of eddying forms,
Sweep through my soul !

FRAGMENT OF AN "ANTIGONE."

THE CHORUS.

WELL hath he done who hath seized happiness !
For little do the all-containing hours,
    Though opulent, freely give, —
    Who, weighing that life well
    Fortune presents unprayed,
Declines her ministry, and carves his own ;
    And, justice not infringed,
Makes his own welfare his unswerved-from law.

He does well too, who keeps that clew the mild
Birth-goddess and the austere Fates first gave.
    For, from the day when these
    Bring him, a weeping child,
    First to the light, and mark
A country for him, kinsfolk, and a home,
    Unguided he remains,
Till the Fates come again, this time with death.

    In little companies,
    And, our own place once left,
Ignorant where to stand, or whom to avoid,
By city and household grouped, we live ; and many
    shocks
    Our order heaven-ordained
    Must every day endure, —
Voyages, exiles, hates, dissensions, wars.
    Besides what waste *he* makes,
    The all-hated, order-breaking,

Without friend, city, or home, —
Death, who dissevers all.

Him then I praise, who dares
To self-selected good
Prefer obedience to the primal law
Which consecrates the ties of blood; for these,
    indeed,
Are to the gods a care :
That touches but himself.
For every day man may be linked and loosed
With strangers ; but the bond
Original, deep-inwound,
Of blood, can he not bind,
Nor, if fate binds, not bear.

But hush ! Hæmon, whom Antigone,
Robbing herself of life in burying,
Against Creon's law, Polynices,
Robs of a loved bride, — pale, imploring,
    Waiting her passage,
Forth from the palace hitherward comes.

HÆMON.

No, no, old men, Creon I curse not !
    I weep, Thebans,
    One than Creon crueller far !
For he, he, at least, by slaying her,
August laws doth mightily vindicate ;
But thou, too bold, headstrong, pitiless !—
Ah me ! — honorest more than thy lover,
        O Antigone !
A dead, ignorant, thankless corpse.

THE CHORUS.

Nor was the love untrue
Which the Dawn-Goddess bore
To that fair youth she erst,
Leaving the salt sea-beds,
And coming flushed over the stormy frith
Of loud Euripus, saw, —
Saw and snatched, wild with love,
From the pine-dotted spurs
Of Parnes, where thy waves,
Asopus ! gleam rock-hemmed, —
The Hunter of the Tanagræan Field.[13]

But him, in his sweet prime,
By severance immature,
By Artemis' soft shafts,
She, though a goddess born,
Saw in the rocky isle of Delos die.
Such end o'ertook that love.
For she desired to make
Immortal mortal man,
And blend his happy life,
Far from the gods, with hers ;
To him postponing an eternal law.

HÆMON.

But like me, she, wroth, complaining,
Succumbed to the envy of unkind gods ;
And, her beautiful arms unclasping,
Her fair youth unwillingly gave.

THE CHORUS.

Nor, though enthroned too high
To fear assault of envious gods,

His beloved Argive seer would Zeus retain
    From his appointed end

     In this our Thebes ; but when
     His flying steeds came near
     To cross the steep Ismenian glen,
The broad earth opened, and whelmed them and him,
      And through the void air sang
      At large his enemy's spear.

And fain would Zeus have saved his tired son,
Beholding him where the Two Pillars stand
    O'er the sun-reddened western straits,[14]
Or at his work in that dim lower world.
     Fain would he have recalled
     The fraudulent oath which bound
To a much feebler wight the heroic man.

But he preferred fate to his strong desire.
Nor did there need less than the burning pile
    Under the towering Trachis crags,
And the Spercheios vale, shaken with groans,
     And the roused Maliac gulf,
     And scared Œtæan snows,
To achieve his son's deliverance, O my child !

FRAGMENT OF CHORUS OF A
"DEJANEIRA."

O FRIVOLOUS mind of man,
Light ignorance, and hurrying, unsure thoughts!
Though man bewails you not,
How *I* bewail you!

Little in your prosperity
Do you seek counsel of the gods.
Proud, ignorant, self-adored, you live alone.
In profound silence stern,
Among their savage gorges and cold springs,
Unvisited remain
The great oracular shrines.

Thither in your adversity
Do you betake yourselves for light,
But strangely misinterpret all you hear.
For you will not put on
New hearts with the inquirer's holy robe,
And purged, considerate minds.

And him on whom, at the end
Of toil and dolour untold,
The gods have said that repose
At last shall descend undisturbed, —
Him you expect to behold
In an easy old age, in a happy home:
No end but this you praise.

But him on whom, in the prime
Of life, with vigor undimmed,
With unspent mind, and a soul

Unworn, undebased, undecayed,
Mournfully grating, the gates
Of the city of death have forever closed, —
Him, I count *him*, well-starred.

EARLY DEATH AND FAME.

For him who must see many years,
I praise the life which slips away
Out of the light, and mutely; which avoids
Fame, and her less fair followers, envy, strife,
Stupid detraction, jealousy, cabal,
Insincere praises; which descends
The quiet mossy track to age.

But when immature death
Beckons too early the guest
From the half-tried banquet of life,
Young, in the bloom of his days;
Leaves no leisure to press,
Slow and surely, the sweets
Of a tranquil life in the shade, —
Fuller for him be the hours!
Give him emotion, though pain!
Let him live, let him feel, *I have lived.*
Heap up his moments with life!
Triple his pulses with fame!

PHILOMELA.

Hark! ah, the nightingale —
The tawny-throated!

Hark ! from that moonlit cedar what a burst !
What triumph ! hark ! what pain !

O wanderer from a Grecian shore,
Still, after many years, in distant lands,
Still nourishing in thy bewildered brain
That wild, unquenched, deep-sunken, old-world pain.
Say, will it never heal?
And can this fragrant lawn
With its cool trees, and night,
And the sweet, tranquil Thames,
And moonshine, and the dew,
To thy racked heart and brain
Afford no balm?

Dost thou to-night behold,
Here, through the moonlight on this English grass,
The unfriendly palace in the Thracian wild?
Dost thou again peruse
With hot cheeks and seared eyes
The too clear web, and thy dumb sister's shame?
Dost thou once more assay
Thy flight, and feel come over thee,
Poor fugitive, the feathery change
Once more, and once more seem to make resound
With love and hate, triumph and agony,
Lone Daulis, and the high Cephissian vale?
Listen, Eugenia, —
How thick the bursts come crowding through the
  leaves !
Again — thou hearest?
Eternal passion !
Eternal pain !

URANIA.

SHE smiles and smiles, and will not sigh,
While we for hopeless passion die ;
Yet she could love, those eyes declare,
Were but men nobler than they are.

Eagerly once her gracious ken
Was turned upon the sons of men ;
But light the serious visage grew —
She looked, and smiled, and saw them through.

Our petty souls, our strutting wits,
Our labored, puny passion fits, —
Ah, may she scorn them still, till we
Scorn them as bitterly as she !

Yet show her once, ye heavenly Powers,
One of some worthier race than ours !
One for whose sake she once might prove
How deeply she who scorns can love.

His eyes be like the starry lights,
His voice like sounds of summer nights ;
In all his lovely mien let pierce
The magic of the universe !

And she to him will reach her hand,
And gazing in his eyes will stand,
And know her friend, and weep for glee,
And cry, *Long, long I've looked for thee.*

Then will she weep : with smiles, till then,
Coldly she mocks the sons of men ;
Till then, her lovely eyes maintain
Their pure, unwavering, deep disdain.

EUPHROSYNE.

I MUST not say that she was true,
Yet let me say that she was fair;
And they, that lovely face who view,
They should not ask if truth be'there.

Truth — what is truth? Two bleeding hearts,
Wounded by men, by fortune tried,
Outwearied with their lonely parts,
Vow to beat henceforth side by side.

The world to them was stern and drear,
Their lot was but to weep and moan;
Ah! let them keep their faith sincere,
For neither could subsist alone.

But souls whom some benignant breath
Hath charmed at birth from gloom and care, —
These ask no love, these plight no faith,
For they are happy as they are.

The world to them may homage make,
And garlands for their forehead weave;
And what the world can give, they take —
But they bring more than they receive.

They shine upon the world; their ears
To one demand alone are coy:
They will not give us love and tears,
They bring us light and warmth and joy.

On one she smiled, and he was blest;
She smiles elsewhere — we make a din!
But 'twas not love which heaved her breast,
Fair child! it was the bliss within.

CALAIS SANDS.

A THOUSAND knights have reined their steeds
To watch this line of sand-hills run,
Along the never-silent strait,
To Calais glittering in the sun ;

To look toward Ardres' Golden Field
Across this wide aërial plain,
Which glows as if the Middle Age
Were gorgeous upon earth again.

Oh, that to share this famous scene,
I saw, upon the open sand,
Thy lovely presence at my side, —
Thy shawl, thy look, thy smile, thy hand !

How exquisite thy voice would come,
My darling, on this lonely air !
How sweetly would the fresh sea-breeze
Shake loose some band of soft brown hair !

Yet now my glance but once hath roved
O'er Calais and its famous plain ;
To England's cliffs my gaze is turned,
O'er the blue strait mine eyes I strain.

Thou comest !　Yes ! the vessel's cloud
Hangs dark upon the rolling sea.
Oh that yon sea-bird's wings were mine,
To win one instant's glimpse of thee !

I must not spring to grasp thy hand,
To woo thy smile, to seek thine eye ;
But I may stand far off, and gaze,
And watch thee pass unconscious by, —

And spell thy looks, and guess thy thoughts,
Mixed with the idlers on the pier.
Ah ! might I always rest unseen,
So I might have thee always near !

To-morrow hurry through the fields
Of Flanders to the storied Rhine !
To-night those soft-fringed eyes shall close
Beneath one roof, my queen ! with mine.

FADED LEAVES.

I. THE RIVER.

STILL glides the stream, slow drops the boat
Under the rustling poplars' shade ;
Silent the swans beside us float :
None speaks, none heeds ; ah, turn thy head !

Let those arch eyes now softly shine,
That mocking mouth grow sweetly bland ;
Ah ! let them rest, those eyes, on mine !
On mine let rest that lovely hand !

My pent-up tears oppress my brain,
My heart is swoln with love unsaid.
Ah ! let me weep, and tell my pain,
And on thy shoulder rest my head !

Before I die, — before the soul,
Which now is mine, must re-attain
Immunity from my control,
And wander round the world again ;

Before this teased, o'er-labored heart
Forever leaves its vain employ,
Dead to its deep habitual smart,
And dead to hopes of future joy.

II. TOO LATE.

EACH on his own strict line we move,
And some find death ere they find love;
So far apart their lives are thrown
From the twin soul that halves their own.

And sometimes, by still harder fate,
The lovers meet, but meet too late.
 Thy heart is mine ! *True, true! ah, true!*
— Then, love, thy hand ! *Ah, no! adieu!*

III. SEPARATION.

STOP ! not to me, at this bitter departing,
 Speak of the sure consolations of time !
Fresh be the wound, still-renewed be its smarting,
 So but thy image endure in its prime !

But if the steadfast commandment of Nature
 Wills that remembrance should always decay;
If the loved form and the deep-cherished feature
 Must, when unseen, from the soul fade away, —

Me let no half-effaced memories cumber;
 Fled, fled at once, be all vestige of thee !
Deep be the darkness, and still be the slumber;
 Dead be the past and its phantoms to me !

Then, when we meet, and thy look strays toward me,
 Scanning my face and the changes wrought there;
Who, let me say, *is this stranger regards me,*
 With the gray eyes, and the lovely brown hair?

IV. ON THE RHINE.

Vain is the effort to forget.
Some day I shall be cold, I know,
As is the eternal moon-lit snow
Of the high Alps, to which I go ;
But ah ! not yet, not yet !

Vain is the agony of grief.
'Tis true, indeed, an iron knot
Ties straitly up from mine thy lot ;
And, were it snapped — thou lov'st me not !
But is despair relief?

A while let me with thought have done.
And as this brimmed unwrinkled Rhine,
And that far purple mountain line,
Lie sweetly in the look divine
Of the slow-sinking sun ;

So let me lie, and, calm as they,
Let beam upon my inward view
Those eyes of deep, soft, lucent hue, —
Eyes too expressive to be blue,
Too lovely to be gray.

Ah, quiet, all things feel thy balm !
Those blue hills too, this river's flow,
Were restless once, but long ago.
Tamed is their turbulent youthful glow ;
Their joy is in their calm.

V. LONGING.

Come to me in my dreams, and then
By day I shall be well again !
For then the night will more than pay
The hopeless longing of the day.

Come, as thou cam'st a thousand times,
A messenger from radiant climes,
And smile on thy new world, and be
As kind to others as to me !

Or, as thou never cam'st in sooth,
Come now, and let me dream it truth ;
And part my hair, and kiss my brow,
And say, *My love ! why sufferest thou ?*

Come to me in my dreams, and then
By day I shall be well again !
For then the night will more than pay
The hopeless longing of the day.

DESPONDENCY.

THE thoughts that rain their steady glow
Like stars on life's cold sea,
Which others know, or say they know, —
They never shone for me.

Thoughts light, like gleams, my spirit's sky,
But they will not remain.
They light me once, they hurry by,
And never come again.

SELF–DECEPTION.

SAY, what blinds us, that we claim the glory
Of possessing powers not our share ?
— Since man woke on earth, he knows his story ;
But, before we woke on earth, we were.

Long, long since, undowered yet, our spirit
Roamed, ere birth, the treasuries of God ;
Saw the gifts, the powers it might inherit,
Asked an outfit for its earthly road.

Then, as now, this tremulous, eager being
Strained and longed, and grasped each gift it saw ;
Then, as now, a Power beyond our seeing
Staved us back, and gave our choice the law.

Ah ! whose hand that day through heaven guided
Man's new spirit, since it was not we?
Ah ! who swayed our choice, and who decided
What our gifts and what our wants should be?

For, alas ! he left us each retaining
Shreds of gifts which he refused in full ;
Still these waste us with their hopeless straining,
Still the attempt to use them proves them null.

And on earth we wander, groping, reeling ;
Powers stir in us, stir and disappear.
Ah ! and he, who placed our master-feeling,
Failed to place that master-feeling clear.

We but dream we have our wished-for powers ;
Ends we seek, we never shall attain.
Ah ! *some* power exists there, which is ours?
Some end is there, we indeed may gain?

DOVER BEACH.

THE sea is calm to-night.
The tide is full, the moon lies fair
Upon the straits ; on the French coast, the light
Gleams and is gone ; the cliffs of England stand,
Glimmering and vast, out in the tranquil bay.

Come to the window, sweet is the night-air !
Only, from the long line of spray
Where the sea meets the moon-blanched sand,
Listen ! you hear the grating roar
Of pebbles which the waves draw back, and fling,
At their return, up the high strand,
Begin and cease, and then again begin,
With tremulous cadence slow, and bring
The eternal note of sadness in.

Sophocles long ago
Heard it on the Ægean, and it brought
Into his mind the turbid ebb and flow
Of human misery : we
Find also in the sound a thought,
Hearing it by this distant northern sea.

The sea of faith
Was once, too, at the full, and round earth's shore
Lay like the folds of a bright girdle furled.
But now I only hear
Its melancholy, long, withdrawing roar,
Retreating, to the breath
Of the night-wind, down the vast edges drear
And naked shingles of the world.

Ah, love, let us be true
To one another ! for the world, which seems
To lie before us like a land of dreams,
So various, so beautiful, so new,
Hath really neither joy, nor love, nor light,
Nor certitude, nor peace, nor help for pain ;
And we are here as on a darkling plain
Swept with confused alarms of struggle and flight,
Where ignorant armies clash by night.

GROWING OLD.

WHAT is it to grow old?
Is it to lose the glory of the form,
The lustre of the eye?
Is it for beauty to forego her wreath?
— Yes, but not this alone.

Is it to feel our strength —
Not our bloom only, but our strength — decay?
Is it to feel each limb
Grow stiffer, every function less exact,
Each nerve more loosely strung?

Yes, this, and more; but not,
Ah! 'tis not what in youth we dreamed 'twould be.
'Tis not to have our life
Mellowed and softened as with sunset-glow, —
A golden day's decline.

'Tis not to see the world
As from a height, with rapt prophetic eyes,
And heart profoundly stirred;
And weep, and feel the fulness of the past,
The years that are no more.

It is to spend long days,
And not once feel that we were ever young;
It is to add, immured
In the hot prison of the present, month
To month with weary pain.

It is to suffer this,
And feel but half, and feebly, what we feel.
Deep in our hidden heart
Festers the dull remembrance of a change,
But no emotion, — none.

It is — last stage of all —
When we are frozen up within, and quite
The phantom of ourselves,
To hear the world applaud the hollow ghost,
Which blamed the living man.

THE PROGRESS OF POESY.

A VARIATION.

YOUTH rambles on life's arid mount,
And strikes the rock, and finds the vein,
And brings the water from the fount, —
The fount which shall not flow again.

The man mature with labor chops
For the bright stream a channel grand,
And sees not that the sacred drops
Ran off and vanished out of hand.

And then the old man totters nigh,
And feebly rakes among the stones.
The mount is mute, the channel dry ;
And down he lays his weary bones.

PIS ALLER.

" MAN is blind because of sin ;
Revelation makes him sure :
Without that, who looks within
Looks in vain, for all's obscure."

Nay, look closer into man !
Tell me, can you find indeed
Nothing sure, no moral plan
Clear prescribed, without your creed?

"No, I nothing can perceive !
Without that, all's dark for men.
That, or nothing, I believe." —
For God's sake, believe it, then !

THE LAST WORD.

CREEP into thy narrow bed, —
Creep, and let no more be said.
Vain thy onset ! all stands fast.
Thou thyself must break at last.

Let the long contention cease !
Geese are swans, and swans are geese.
Let them have it how they will !
Thou art tired : best be still.

They out-talked thee, hissed thee, tore thee ?
Better men fared thus before thee ;
Fired their ringing shot, and passed,
Hotly charged — and sank at last.

Charge once more, then, and be dumb !
Let the victors, when they come,
When the forts of folly fall,
Find thy body by the wall !

A NAMELESS EPITAPH.

ASK not my name, O friend !
That Being only, which hath known each man
From the beginning, can
Remember each unto the end.

EMPEDOCLES ON ETNA.

A DRAMATIC POEM.

PERSONS.

EMPEDOCLES.
PAUSANIAS, *a Physician*
CALLICLES, a *young Harp-player.*

The Scene of the Poem is on Mount Etna; at first in the forest region,
afterwards on the summit of the mountain.

ACT I.

SCENE I. — *Morning. A Pass in the forest region of*
Etna.

CALLICLES (*alone, resting on a rock by the path*).

The mules, I think, will not be here this hour :
They feel the cool wet turf under their feet
By the stream-side, after the dusty lanes
In which they have toiled all night from Catana,
And scarcely will they budge a yard.   O Pan,
How gracious is the mountain at this hour !
A thousand times have I been here alone,
Or with the revellers from the mountain towns,
But never on so fair a morn.   The sun
Is shining on the brilliant mountain crests,
And on the highest pines ; but farther down,
Here in the valley, is in shade ; the sward
Is dark, and on the stream the mist still hangs ;
One sees one's footprints crushed in the wet grass,

One's breath curls in the air ; and on these pines
That climb from the stream's edge, the long gray tufts,
Which the goats love, are jewelled thick with dew.
Here will I stay till the slow litter comes.
I have my harp too : that is well. — Apollo !
What mortal could be sick or sorry here?
I know not in what mind Empedocles,
Whose mules I followed, may be coming up ;
But if, as most men say, he is half mad
With exile, and with brooding on his wrongs,
Pausanias, his sage friend, who mounts with him,
Could scarce have lighted on a lovelier cure.
The mules must be below, far down.   I hear
Their tinkling bells, mixed with the song of birds,
Rise faintly to me : now it stops ! — Who's here?
Pausanias ! and on foot? alone?

PAUSANIAS.

And thou, then?
I left thee supping with Peisianax,
With thy head full of wine, and thy hair crowned,
Touching thy harp as the whim came on thee,
And praised and spoiled by master and by guests
Almost as much as the new dancing-girl.
Why hast thou followed us?

CALLICLES.

The night was hot,
And the feast past its prime : so we slipped out,
Some of us, to the portico to breathe, —
Peisianax, thou know'st, drinks late, — and then,
As I was lifting my soiled garland off,
I saw the mules and litter in the court,
And in the litter sate Empedocles ;
Thou too wast with him.   Straightway I sped home ;

I saddled my white mule, and all night long
Through the cool lovely country followed you,
Passed you a little since as morning dawned,
And have this hour sate by the torrent here,
Till the slow mules should climb in sight again.
And now?

PAUSANIAS.

                    And now, back to the town with speed!
Crouch in the wood first, till the mules have passed;
They do but halt, they will be here anon.
Thou must be viewless to Empedocles;
Save mine, he must not meet a human eye.
One of his moods is on him that thou know'st;
I think, thou wouldst not vex him.

CALLICLES.   No; and yet
I would fain stay, and help thee tend him.   Once
He knew me well, and would oft notice me;
And still, I know not how, he draws me to him,
And I could watch him with his proud sad face,
His flowing locks and gold-encircled brow
And kingly gait, forever; such a spell
In his severe looks, such a majesty
As drew of old the people after him,
In Agrigentum and Olympia,
When his star reigned, before his banishment,
Is potent still on me in his decline.
But, O Pausanias, he is changed of late:
There is a settled trouble in his air
Admits no momentary brightening now;
And when he comes among his friends at feasts,
'Tis as an orphan among prosperous boys.
Thou know'st of old he loved this harp of mine,
When first he sojourned with Peisianax;

He is now always moody, and I fear him ;
But I would serve him, soothe him, if I could,
Dared one but try.

PAUSANIAS.

Thou wast a kind child ever.
He loves thee, but he must not see thee now.
Thou hast indeed a rare touch on thy harp ;
He loves that in thee, too ; there was a time
(But that is past), he would have paid thy strain
With music to have drawn the stars from heaven.
He has his harp and laurel with him still ;
But he has laid the use of music by,
And all which might relax his settled gloom.
Yet thou may'st try thy playing, if thou wilt,
But thou must keep unseen : follow us on,
But at a distance ! in these solitudes,
In this clear mountain air, a voice will rise,
Though from afar, distinctly ; it may soothe him.
Play when we halt ; and when the evening comes,
And I must leave him (for his pleasure is
To be left musing these soft nights alone
In the high unfrequented mountain spots),
Then watch him, for he ranges swift and far,
Sometimes to Etna's top, and to the cone ;
But hide thee in the rocks a great way down,
And try thy noblest strains, my Callicles,
With the sweet night to help thy harmony !
Thou wilt earn my thanks sure, and perhaps his.

CALLICLES.

More than a day and night, Pausanias,
Of this fair summer-weather, on these hills,
Would I bestow to help Empedocles.
That needs no thanks : one is far better here
Than in the broiling city in these heats.

But tell me, how hast thou persuaded him
In this his present fierce, man-hating mood,
To bring thee out with him alone on Etna?

PAUSANIAS.

Thou hast heard all men speaking of Pantheia,
The woman who at Agrigentum lay
Thirty long days in a cold trance of death,
And whom Empedocles called back to life.
Thou art too young to note it, but his power
Swells with the swelling evil of this time,
And holds men mute to see where it will rise.
He could stay swift diseases in old days,
Chain madmen by the music of his lyre,
Cleanse to sweet airs the breath of poisonous streams,
And in the mountain chinks inter the winds.
This he could do of old; but now, since all
Clouds and grows daily worse in Sicily,
Since broils tear us in twain, since this new swarm
Of sophists has got empire in our schools
Where he was paramount, since he is banished,
And lives a lonely man in triple gloom, —
He grasps the very reins of life and death.
I asked him of Pantheia yesterday,
When we were gathered with Peisianax;
And he made answer, I should come at night
On Etna here, and be alone with him,
And he would tell me, as his old, tried friend,
Who still was faithful, what might profit me, —
That is, the secret of this miracle.

CALLICLES.

Bah! Thou a doctor! Thou art superstitious.
Simple Pausanias, 'twas no miracle!
Pantheia, for I know her kinsmen well,

Was subject to these trances from a girl.
Empedocles would say so, did he deign;
But he still lets the people, whom he scorns,
Gape and cry *wizard* at him, if they list.
But thou, thou art no company for him:
Thou art as cross, as soured as himself.
Thou hast some wrong from thine own citizens,
And then thy friend is banished; and on that,
Straightway thou fallest to arraign the times,
As if the sky was impious not to fall.
The sophists are no enemies of his;
I hear, Gorgias, their chief, speaks nobly of him,
As of his gifted master, and once friend.
He is too scornful, too high-wrought, too bitter.
'Tis not the times, 'tis not the sophists, vex him:
There is some root of suffering in himself,
Some secret and unfollowed vein of woe,
Which makes the time look black and sad to him.
Pester him not, in this his sombre mood,
With questionings about an idle tale,
But lead him through the lovely mountain paths,
And keep his mind from preying on itself,
And talk to him of things at hand and common,
Not miracles! thou art a learned man,
But credulous of fables as a girl.

PAUSANIAS.

And thou, a boy whose tongue outruns his knowledge,
And on whose lightness blame is thrown away.
Enough of this! I see the litter wind
Up by the torrent-side, under the pines.
I must rejoin Empedocles. Do thou
Crouch in the brushwood till the mules have passed;
Then play thy kind part well. Farewell till night!

SCENE II. — *Noon.   A Glen on the highest skirts of the woody region of Etna.*

EMPEDOCLES.   PAUSANIAS.

PAUSANIAS.

The noon is hot.   When we have crossed the stream,
We shall have left the woody tract, and come
Upon the open shoulder of the hill.
See how the giant spires of yellow bloom
Of the sun-loving gentian, in the heat,[15]
Are shining on those naked slopes like flame !
Let us rest here ;   and now, Empedocles,
Pantheia's history !

> [*A harp-note below is heard.*

EMPEDOCLES.

        Hark ! what sound was that
Rose from below?   If it were possible,
And we were not so far from human haunt,
I should have said that some one touched a harp.
Hark ! there again !

PAUSANIAS.

        'Tis the boy Callicles,
The sweetest harp-player in Catana.
He is forever coming on these hills,
In summer, to all country-festivals,
With a gay revelling band ; he breaks from them
Sometimes, and wanders far among the glens.
But heed him not, he will not mount to us ;
I spoke with him this morning.   Once more, therefore,
Instruct me of Pantheia's story, master,
As I have prayed thee.

EMPEDOCLES.

That? and to what end?

PAUSANIAS.

It is enough that all men speak of it.
But I will also say, that when the gods
Visit us as they do with sign and plague,
To know those spells of thine which stay their hand
Were to live free from terror.

EMPEDOCLES.

Spells? Mistrust them!
Mind is the spell which governs earth and heaven;
Man has a mind with which to plan his safety,—
Know that, and help thyself!

PAUSANIAS.

But thine own words?
"The wit and counsel of man was never clear;
Troubles confound the little wit he has."
Mind is a light which the gods mock us with,
To lead those false who trust it.

[*The harp sounds again*

EMPEDOCLES.

Hist! once more!
Listen, Pausanias!—Ay, 'tis Callicles;
I know those notes among a thousand. Hark!

CALLICLES (*sings unseen, from below*).

The track winds down to the clear stream,
To cross the sparkling shallows; there
The cattle love to gather, on their way
To the high mountain pastures, and to stay,

Till the rough cow-herds drive them past,
Knee-deep in the cool ford; for 'tis the last
Of all the woody, high, well-watered dells
On Etna; and the beam
Of noon is broken there by chestnut-boughs
Down its steep verdant sides; the air
Is freshened by the leaping stream, which throws
Eternal showers of spray on the mossed roots
Of trees, and veins of turf, and long dark shoots
Of ivy-plants, and fragrant hanging bells
Of hyacinths, and on late anemones,
That muffle its wet banks; but glade,
And stream, and sward, and chestnut-trees,
End here; Etna beyond, in the broad glare
Of the hot noon, without a shade,
Slope behind slope, up to the peak, lies bare, —·
The peak, round which the white clouds play.

In such a glen, on such a day,
On Pelion, on the grassy ground
Chiron, the aged Centaur, lay,
The young Achilles standing by.
The Centaur taught him to explore
The mountains; where the glens are dry,
And the tired Centaurs come to rest,
And where the soaking springs abound,
And the straight ashes grow for spears,
And where the hill-goats come to feed,
And the sea-eagles build their nest.
He showed him Phthia far away,
And said, "O boy, I taught this lore
To Peleus, in long-distant years!"
He told him of the gods, the stars,
The tides; and then of mortal wars,

And of the life which heroes lead
Before they reach the Elysian place,
And rest in the immortal mead;
And all the wisdom of his race.

The music below ceases, and EMPEDOCLES *speaks, accompanying
himself in a solemn manner on his harp.*

The out-spread world to span,
A cord the gods first slung,
And then the soul of man
There, like a mirror, hung,
And bade the winds through space impel the gusty
toy.

Hither and thither spins
The wind-borne, mirroring soul;
A thousand glimpses wins,
And never sees a whole;
Looks once, and drives elsewhere, and leaves its last
employ.

The gods laugh in their sleeve
To watch man doubt and fear,
Who knows not what to believe
Since he sees nothing clear,
And dares stamp nothing false where he finds nothing
sure.

Is this, Pausanias, so?
And can our souls not strive,
But with the winds must go,
And hurry where they drive?
Is Fate indeed so strong, man's strength indeed so
poor?

I will not judge.   That man,
Howbeit, I judge as lost,
Whose mind allows a plan,
Which would degrade it most;
And he treats doubt the best who tries to see least ill.

Be not, then, fear's blind slave!
Thou art my friend; to thee,
All knowledge that I have,
All skill I wield, are free.
Ask not the latest news of the last miracle, —

Ask not what days and nights
In trance Pantheia lay,
But ask how thou such sights
May'st see without dismay;
Ask what most helps when known, thou son of
    Anchitus!

What! hate, and awe, and shame
Fill thee to see our time;
Thou feelest thy soul's frame
Shaken and out of chime?
What! life and chance go hard with thee too, as
    with us;

Thy citizens, 'tis said,
Envy thee and oppress,
Thy goodness no men aid,
All strive to make it less;
Tyranny, pride, and lust fill Sicily's abodes;

Heaven is with earth at strife;
Signs make thy soul afraid, —
The dead return to life,
Rivers are dried, winds stayed;
Scarce can one think in calm, so threatening are the
    gods;

And we feel, day and night,
The burden of ourselves :
Well, then, the wiser wight
In his own bosom delves,
And asks what ails him so, and gets what cure he can.

The sophist sneers, " Fool, take
Thy pleasure, right or wrong."
The pious wail, " Forsake
A world these sophists throng."
Be neither saint- nor sophist-led, but be a man !

These hundred doctors try
To preach thee to their school.
"We have the truth !" they cry ;
And yet their oracle,
Trumpet it as they will, is but the same as thine.

Once read thy own breast right,
And thou hast done with fears ;
Man gets no other light,
Search he a thousand years.
Sink in thyself ! there ask what ails thee, at that shrine.

What makes thee struggle and rave ?
Why are men ill at ease ?
'Tis that the lot they have
Fails their own will to please ;
For man would make no murmuring, were his will
    obeyed.

And why is it, that still
Man with his lot thus fights ?
'Tis that he makes this *will*
The measure of his *rights*,
And believes nature outraged if his will's gainsaid.

Couldst thou, Pausanias, learn
How deep a fault is this;
Couldst thou but once discern
Thou hast no *right* to bliss,
No title from the gods to welfare and repose, —

Then thou wouldst look less mazed
Whene'er of bliss debarred,
Nor think the gods were crazed
When thy own lot went hard.
But we are all the same, — the fools of our own woes!

For, from the first faint morn
Of life, the thirst for bliss
Deep in man's heart is born;
And, sceptic as he is,
He fails not to judge clear if this be quenched or no.

Nor is that thirst to blame.
Man errs not that he deems
His welfare his true aim:
He errs because he dreams
The world does but exist that welfare to bestow.

We mortals are no kings
For each of whom to sway
A new-made world upsprings,
Meant merely for his play:
No, we are strangers here; the world is from of old.

In vain our pent wills fret,
And would the world subdue.
Limits we did not set
Condition all we do;
Born into life we are, and life must be our mould.

Born into life! man grows
Forth from his parents' stem,
And blends their bloods, as those
Of theirs are blent in them;
So each new man strikes root into a far fore-time.

Born into life! we bring
A bias with us here,
And, when here, each new thing
Affects us we come near;
To tunes we did not call, our being must keep chime.

Born into life! in vain,
Opinions, those or these,
Unaltered to retain,
The obstinate mind decrees:
Experience, like a sea, soaks all-effacing in.

Born into life! who lists
May what is false hold dear,
And for himself make mists
Through which to see less clear:
The world is what it is, for all our dust and din.

Born into life! 'tis we,
And not the world, are new;
Our cry for bliss, our plea,
Others have urged it too:
Our wants have all been felt, our errors made before.

No eye could be too sound
To observe a world so vast,
No patience too profound
To sort what's here amassed;
How man may here best live, no care too great to
explore.

But we, — as some rude guest
Would change, where'er he roam,
The manners there professed
To those he brings from home, —
We mark not the world's course, but would have *it*
    take *ours*.

The world's course proves the terms
On which man wins content;
Reason the proof confirms:
We spurn it, and invent
A false course for the world, and for ourselves false
    powers.

Riches we wish to get,
Yet remain spendthrifts still;
We would have health, and yet
Still use our bodies ill;
Bafflers of our own prayers, from youth to life's last
    scenes.

We would have inward peace,
Yet will not look within;
We would have misery cease,
Yet will not cease from sin;
We want all pleasant ends, but will use no harsh means;

We do not what we ought;
What we ought not, we do;
And lean upon the thought
That chance will bring us through:
But our own acts, for good or ill, are mightier powers.

Yet even when man forsakes
All sin, — is just, is pure,
Abandons all which makes
His welfare insecure, —
Other existences there are, that clash with ours.

Like us, the lightning-fires
Love to have scope and play;
The stream, like us, desires
An unimpeded way;
Like us, the Libyan wind delights to roam at large.

Streams will not curb their pride
The just man not to entomb,
Nor lightnings go aside
To give his virtues room;
Nor is that wind less rough which blows a good man's
barge.

Nature, with equal mind,
Sees all her sons at play;
Sees man control the wind,
The wind sweep man away;
Allows the proudly riding and the foundering bark.

And, lastly, though of ours
No weakness spoil our lot,
Though the non-human powers
Of nature harm us not,
The ill deeds of other men make often *our* life dark.

What were the wise man's plan?
Through this sharp, toil-set life,
To fight as best he can,
And win what's won by strife.
But we an easier way to cheat our pains have found.

Scratched by a fall, with moans
As children of weak age
Lend life to the dumb stones
Whereon to vent their rage,
And bend their little fists, and rate the senseless
ground;

So, loath to suffer mute,
We, peopling the void air,
Make gods to whom to impute
The ills we ought to bear ;
With God and fate to rail at, suffering easily.

Yet grant, — as sense long missed
Things that are now perceived,
And much may still exist
Which is not yet believed, —
Grant that the world were full of gods we cannot see ;

All things the world which fill
Of but one stuff are spun,
That we who rail are still,
With what we rail at, one ;
One with the o'er-labored Power that through the
    breadth and length

Of earth, and air, and sea,
In men, and plants, and stones,
Hath toil perpetually,
And travails, pants, and moans ;
Fain would do all things well, but sometimes fails in
    strength.

And patiently exact
This universal God
Alike to any act
Proceeds at any nod,
And quietly declaims the cursings of himself.

This is not what man hates,
Yet he can curse but this.
Harsh gods and hostile fates
Are dreams ! this only *is*, —
Is everywhere ; sustains the wise, the foolish elf.

Nor only, in the intent
To attach blame elsewhere,
Do we at will invent
Stern powers who make their care
To imbitter human life, malignant deities;

But, next, we would reverse
The scheme ourselves have spun,
And what we made to curse
We now would lean upon,
And feign kind gods who perfect what man vainly tries.

Look, the world tempts our eye,
And we would know it all!
We map the starry sky,
We mine this earthen ball,
We measure the sea-tides, we number the sea-sands;

We scrutinize the dates
Of long-past human things,
The bounds of effaced states,
The lines of deceased kings;
We search out dead men's words, and works of dead
men's hands;

We shut our eyes, and muse
How our own minds are made,
What springs of thought they use,
How rightened, how betrayed, —
And spend our wit to name what most employ unnamed.

But still, as we proceed,
The mass swells more and more
Of volumes yet to read,
Of secrets yet to explore.
Our hair grows gray, our eyes are dimmed, our heat
is tamed;

We rest our faculties,
And thus address the gods :
" True science if there is,
It stays in your abodes !
Man's measures cannot mete the immeasurable all.

" You only can take in
The world's immense design ;
Our desperate search was sin,
Which henceforth we resign,
Sure only that your mind sees all things which befall."

Fools ! That in man's brief term
He cannot all things view,
Affords no ground to affirm
That there are gods who do ;
Nor does being weary prove that he has where to rest.

Again : Our youthful blood
Claims rapture as its right ;
The world, a rolling flood
Of newness and delight,
Draws in the enamoured gazer to its shining breast ;

Pleasure, to our hot grasp,
Gives flowers after flowers ;
With passionate warmth we clasp
Hand after hand in ours ;
Now do we soon perceive how fast our youth is spent.

At once our eyes grow clear !
We see, in blank dismay,
Year posting after year,
Sense after sense decay ;
Our shivering heart is mined by secret discontent.

Yet still, in spite of truth,
In spite of hopes entombed,
That longing of our youth
Burns ever unconsumed,
Still hungrier for delight as delights grow more rare.

We pause ; we hush our heart,
And thus address the gods : —
" The world hath failed to impart
The joy our youth forebodes,
Failed to fill up the void which in our breasts we bear.

" Changeful till now, we still
Looked on to something new ;
Let us, with changeless will,
Henceforth look on to you,
To find with you the joy we in vain here require ! "

Fools ! That so often here
Happiness mocked our prayer,
I think, might make us fear
A like event elsewhere ;
Make us not fly to dreams, but moderate desire.

And yet, for those who know
Themselves, who wisely take
Their way through life, and bow
To what they cannot break,
Why should I say that life need yield but *moderate*
    bliss ?

Shall we, with temper spoiled,
Health sapped by living ill,
And judgment all embroiled
By sadness and self-will, —
Shall *we* judge what for man is not true bliss or is ?

Is it so small a thing
To have enjoyed the sun,
To have lived light in the spring,
To have loved, to have thought, to have done
To have advanced true friends, and beat down baffling
        foes, —

That we must feign a bliss
Of doubtful future date,
And. while we dream on this,
Lose all our present state,
And relegate to worlds yet distant our repose?

Not much, I know, you prize
What pleasures may be had,
Who look on life with eyes
Estranged, like mine, and sad ;
And yet the village-churl feels the truth more than you ;

Who's loath to leave this life
Which to him little yields, —
His hard-tasked sunburnt wife,
His often-labored fields,
The boors with whom he talked, the country-spots he
        knew.

But thou, because thou hear'st
Men scoff at heaven and fate,
Because the gods thou fear'st
Fail to make blest thy state,
Tremblest, and wilt not dare to trust the joys there are !

I say : Fear not !   Life still
Leaves human effort scope.
But, since life teems with ill,
Nurse no extravagant hope ;
Because thou must not dream, thou need'st not then
        despair !

A long pause. At the end of it the notes of a harp below are again heard, and CALLICLES *sings:—*

Far, far from here,
The Adriatic breaks in a warm bay
Among the green Illyrian hills; and there
The sunshine in the happy glens is fair,
And by the sea, and in the brakes.
The grass is cool, the sea-side air
Buoyant and fresh, the mountain flowers
More virginal and sweet than ours.

And there, they say, two bright and aged snakes,
Who once were Cadmus and Harmonia,
Bask in the glens or on the warm seashore,
In breathless quiet, after all their ills;
Nor do they see their country, nor the place
Where the Sphinx lived among the frowning hills,
Nor the unhappy palace of their race,
Nor Thebes, nor the Ismenus, any more.

There those two live, far in the Illyrian brakes!
They had stayed long enough to see,
In Thebes, the billow of calamity
Over their own dear children rolled,
Curse upon curse, pang upon pang,
For years, they sitting helpless in their home,
A gray old man and woman; yet of old
The gods had to their marriage come,
And at the banquet all the Muses sang.

Therefore they did not end their days
In sight of blood; but were rapt, far away,
To where the west-wind plays,
And murmurs of the Adriatic come
To those untrodden mountain lawns; and there
Placed safely in changed forms, the pair

Wholly forget their first sad life, and home,
And all that Theban woe, and stray
Forever through the glens, placid and dumb.

EMPEDOCLES.

That was my harp-player again ! Where is he?
Down by the stream?

PAUSANIAS.

Yes, master, in the wood.

EMPEDOCLES.

He ever loved the Theban story well !
But the day wears. Go now, Pausanias,
For I must be alone. Leave me one mule ;
Take down with thee the rest to Catana.
And for young Callicles, thank him from me ;
Tell him, I never failed to love his lyre ;
But he must follow me no more to-night.

PAUSANIAS.

Thou wilt return to-morrow to the city?

EMPEDOCLES.

Either to-morrow or some other day,
In the sure revolutions of the world,
Good friend, I shall revisit Catana.
I have seen many cities in my time,
Till mine eyes ache with the long spectacle,
And I shall doubtless see them all again ;
Thou know'st me for a wanderer from of old.
Meanwhile, stay me not now. Farewell, Pausanias !

He departs on his way up the mountain

PAUSANIAS (*alone*).

I dare not urge him further — he must go ;
But he is strangely wrought ! I will speed back,

And bring Peisianax to him from the city ;
His counsel could once soothe him.   But, Apollo !
How his brow lightened as the music rose !
Callicles must wait here, and play to him ;
I saw him through the chestnuts far below,
Just since, down at the stream. — Ho ! Callicles !

He descends, calling.

ACT II.

Evening.   The Summit of Etna.

EMPEDOCLES.

Alone !

On this charred, blackened, melancholy waste,
Crowned by the awful peak, Etna's great mouth,
Round which the sullen vapor rolls, — alone !
Pausanias is far hence, and that is well,
For I must henceforth speak no more with man.
He has his lesson too, and that debt's paid ;
And the good, learned, friendly, quiet man,
May bravelier front his life, and in himself
Find henceforth energy and heart.   But I, —
The weary man, the banished citizen,
Whose banishment is not his greatest ill,
Whose weariness no energy can reach,
And for whose hurt courage is not the cure, —
What should I do with life and living more?

No, thou art come too late, Empedocles !
And the world hath the day, and must break thee,
Not thou the world.   With men thou canst not live :
Their thoughts, their ways, their wishes, are not thine.
And being lonely thou art miserable ;

For something has impaired thy spirit's strength,
And dried its self-sufficing fount of joy.
Thou canst not live with men nor with thyself,
O sage! O sage! Take, then, the one way left;
And turn thee to the elements, thy friends,
Thy well-tried friends, thy willing ministers,
And say: Ye servants, hear Empedocles,
Who asks this final service at your hands!
Before the sophist-brood hath overlaid
The last spark of man's consciousness with words;
Ere quite the being of man, ere quite the world,
Be disarrayed of their divinity;
Before the soul lose all her solemn joys,
And awe be dead, and hope impossible,
And the soul's deep eternal night come on, —
Receive me, hide me, quench me, take me home!

*He advances to the edge of the crater. Smoke and fire
break forth with a loud noise, and* CALLICLES *is
heard below singing:* —

The lyre's voice is lovely everywhere;
In the court of gods, in the city of men,
And in the lonely rock-strewn mountain-glen,
In the still mountain air.

Only to Typho it sounds hatefully, —
To Typho only, the rebel o'erthrown,
Through whose heart Etna drives her roots of stone,
To embed them in the sea.
Wherefore dost thou groan so loud?
Wherefore do thy nostrils flash,
Through the dark night, suddenly,
Typho, such red jets of flame?
Is thy tortured heart still proud?
Is thy fire-scathed arm still rash?

Still alert thy stone-crushed frame?
Doth thy fierce soul still deplore
Thine ancient rout by the Cilician hills,
And that curst treachery on the Mount of Gore?[1]
Do thy bloodshot eyes still weep
The fight which crowned thine ills,
Thy last mischance on this Sicilian deep?
Hast thou sworn, in thy sad lair,
Where erst the strong sea-currents sucked thee down,
Never to cease to writhe, and try to rest,
Letting the sea-stream wander through thy hair?
That thy groans, like thunder prest,
Begin to roll, and almost drown
The sweet notes whose lulling spell
Gods and the race of mortals love so well,
When through thy caves thou hearest music swell?

But an awful pleasure bland
Spreading o'er the Thunderer's face,
When the sound climbs near his seat,
The Olympian council sees;
As he lets his lax right hand,
Which the lightnings doth embrace,
Sink upon his mighty knees.
And the eagle, at the beck
Of the appeasing, gracious harmony,
Droops all his sheeny, brown, deep-feathered neck,
Nestling nearer to Jove's feet;
While o'er his sovran eye
The curtains of the blue films slowly meet.
And the white Olympus-peaks
Rosily brighten, and the soothed gods smile
At one another from their golden chairs,
And no one round the charmed circle speaks.

---

[1] Mount Hæmus. See APOLLODORUS, *Bibliotheca*, book i. chapter 6.

Only the loved Hebe bears
The cup about, whose draughts beguile
Pain and care, with a dark store
Of fresh-pulled violets wreathed and nodding o'er;
And her flushed feet glow on the marble floor.

EMPEDOCLES.

He fables, yet speaks truth!
The brave impetuous heart yields everywhere
To the subtle, contriving head;
Great qualities are trodden down,
And littleness united
Is become invincible.

These rumblings are not Typho's groans, I know!
These angry smoke-bursts
Are not the passionate breath
Of the mountain-crushed, tortured, intractable Titan
    king;
But over all the world
What suffering is there not seen
Of plainness oppressed by cunning,
As the well-counselled Zeus oppressed
That self-helping son of earth!
What anguish of greatness,
Railed and hunted from the world,
Because its simplicity rebukes
This envious, miserable age!

I am weary of it.
— Lie there, ye ensigns
Of my unloved pre-eminence
In an age like this!
Among a people of children,
Who thronged me in their cities,

Who worshipped me in their houses,
And asked, not wisdom,
But drugs to charm with,
But spells to mutter
All the fool's-armory of magic !   Lie there,
My golden circlet,
My purple robe !

CALLICLES (*from below*).

As the sky-brightening south-wind clears the day,
And makes the massed clouds roll,
The music of the lyre blows away
The clouds which wrap the soul.

Oh that fate had let me see
That triumph of the sweet persuasive lyre,
That famous, final victory
When jealous Pan with Marsyas did conspire !

When, from far Parnassus' side,
Young Apollo, all the pride
Of the Phrygian flutes to tame,
To the Phrygian highlands came ;
Where the long green reed-beds sway
In the rippled waters gray
Of that solitary lake
Where Mæander's springs are born ;
Where the ridged pine-wooded roots
Of Messogis westward break,
Mounting westward, high and higher.
There was held the famous strife ;
There the Phrygian brought his flutes,
And Apollo brought his lyre ;
And, when now the westering sun
Touched the hills, the strife was done,

And the attentive muses said, —
" Marsyas, thou art vanquishèd ! "
Then Apollo's minister
Hanged upon a branching fir
Marsyas, that unhappy Faun,
And began to whet his knife.
But the Mænads, who were there,
Left their friend, and with robes flowing
In the wind, and loose dark hair
O'er their polished bosoms blowing,
Each her ribboned tambourine
Flinging on the mountain-sod,
With a lovely frightened mien
Came about the youthful god.
But he turned his beauteous face
Haughtily another way,
From the grassy sun-warmed place
Where in proud repose he lay,
With one arm over his head,
Watching how the whetting sped.

But aloof, on the lake-strand,
Did the young Olympus stand,
Weeping at his master's end ;
For the Faun had been his friend.
For he taught him how to sing,
And he taught him flute-playing.
Many a morning had they gone
To the glimmering mountain lakes,
And had torn up by the roots
The tall crested water-reeds
With long plumes and soft brown seeds,
And had carved them into flutes,
Sitting on a tabled stone

Where the shoreward ripple breaks.
And he taught him how to please
The red-snooded Phrygian girls,
Whom the summer evening sees
Flashing in the dance's whirls
Underneath the starlit trees
In the mountain villages.
Therefore now Olympus stands,
At his master's piteous cries
Pressing fast with both his hands
His white garment to his eyes,
Not to see Apollo's scorn. —
Ah, poor Faun, poor Faun! ah, poor Faun!

EMPEDOCLES.

And lie thou there,
My laurel bough!
Scornful Apollo's ensign, lie thou there!
Though thou hast been my shade in the world's heat,
Though I have loved thee, lived in honoring thee,
Yet lie thou there,
My laurel bough!

I am weary of thee.
I am weary of the solitude
Where he who bears thee must abide, —
Of the rocks of Parnassus,
Of the gorge of Delphi,
Of the moonlight peaks, and the caves.
Thou guardest them, Apollo!
Over the grave of the slain Pytho,
Though young, intolerably severe!
Thou keepest aloof the profane,
But the solitude oppresses thy votary.
The jars of men reach him not in thy valley,

But can life reach him?
Thou fencest him from the multitude:
Who will fence him from himself?
He hears nothing but the cry of the torrents,
And the beating of his own heart;
The air is thin, the veins swell,
The temples tighten and throb there —
Air! air!

Take thy bough, set me free from my solitude;
I have been enough alone!

Where shall thy votary fly, then? back to men?
But they will gladly welcome him once more,
And help him to unbend his too tense thought,
And rid him of the presence of himself,
And keep their friendly chatter at his ear,
And haunt him, till the absence from himself,
That other torment, grow unbearable;
And he will fly to solitude again,
And he will find its air too keen for him,
And so change back; and many thousand times
Be miserably bandied to and fro
Like a sea-wave, betwixt the world and thee,
Thou young, implacable god! and only death
Shall cut his oscillations short, and so
Bring him to poise.   There is no other way.

And yet what days were those, Parmenides!
When we were young, when we could number friends
In all the Italian cities like ourselves;
When with elated hearts we joined your train,
Ye Sun-born Virgins! on the road of truth.[16]
Then we could still enjoy, then neither thought
Nor outward things were closed and dead to us;
But we received the shock of mighty thoughts

On simple minds with a pure natural joy;
And if the sacred load oppressed our brain,
We had the power to feel the pressure eased,
The brow unbound, the thoughts flow free again,
In the delightful commerce of the world.
We had not lost our balance then, nor grown
Thought's slaves, and dead to every natural joy.
The smallest thing could give us pleasure then, —
The sports of the country-people,
A flute-note from the woods,
Sunset over the sea;
Seed-time and harvest,
The reapers in the corn,
The vinedresser in his vineyard,
The village-girl at her wheel.

Fulness of life and power of feeling, ye
Are for the happy, for the souls at ease,
Who dwell on a firm basis of content!
But he who has outlived his prosperous days;
But he whose youth fell on a different world
From that on which his exiled age is thrown, —
Whose mind was fed on other food, was trained
By other rules than are in vogue to-day;
Whose habit of thought is fixed, who will not change,
But, in a world he loves not, must subsist
In ceaseless opposition, be the guard
Of his own breast, fettered to what he guards,
That the world win no mastery over him;
Who has no friend, no fellow left, not one;
Who has no minute's breathing-space allowed
To nurse his dwindling faculty of joy, —
Joy and the outward world must die to him,
As they are dead to me.

A long pause, during which EMPEDOCLES *remains mo-*
tionless, plunged in thought. The night deepens.
He moves forward, and gazes around him, and pro-
ceeds: —

And you, ye stars,
Who slowly begin to marshal,
As of old, in the fields of heaven,
Your distant, melancholy lines !
Have you, too, survived yourselves?
Are you, too, what I fear to become?
You too once lived ;
You too moved joyfully,
Among august companions,
In an older world, peopled by gods,
In a mightier order,
The radiant, rejoicing, intelligent sons of heaven.
But now ye kindle
Your lonely, cold-shining lights,
Unwilling lingerers
In the heavenly wilderness,
For a younger, ignoble world ;
And renew, by necessity,
Night after night your courses,
In echoing, unneared silence,
Above a race you know not,
Uncaring and undelighted,
Without friend and without home ;
Weary like us, though not
Weary with our weariness.

No, no, ye stars ! there is no death with you,
No languor, no decay ! languor and death,
They are with me, not you ! ye are alive, —
Ye, and the pure dark ether where ye ride

Brilliant above me! And thou, fiery world,
That sapp'st the vitals of this terrible mount
Upon whose charred and quaking crust I stand, —
Thou, too, brimmest with life! the sea of cloud,
That heaves its white and billowy vapors up
To moat this isle of ashes from the world,
Lives; and that other fainter sea, far down,
O'er whose lit floor a road of moonbeams leads
To Etna's Lipareän sister-fires
And the long dusky line of Italy, —
That mild and luminous floor of waters lives,
With held-in joy swelling its heart: I only,
Whose spring of hope is dried, whose spirit has failed,
I, who have not, like these, in solitude
Maintained courage and force, and in myself
Nursed an immortal vigor, — I alone
Am dead to life and joy, therefore I read
In all things my own deadness.

A long silence. He continues: —

Oh that I could glow like this mountain!
Oh that my heart bounded with the swell of the sea!
Oh that my soul were full of light as the stars!
Oh that it brooded over the world like the air!

But no, this heart will glow no more; thou art
A living man no more, Empedocles!
Nothing but a devouring flame of thought, —
But a naked, eternally restless mind!

After a pause: —

To the elements it came from,
Every thing will return, —
Our bodies to earth,
Our blood to water,

Heat to fire,
Breath to air :
They were well born, they will be well entombed.
But mind? . . .

And we might gladly share the fruitful stir
Down in our mother earth's miraculous womb ;
Well would it be
With what rolled of us in the stormy main ;
We might have joy, blent with the all-bathing air,
Or with the nimble, radiant life of fire.

But mind, but thought,
If these have been the master part of us, —
Where will *they* find their parent element?
What will receive *them*, who will call *them* home?
But we shall still be in them, and they in us ;
And we shall be the strangers of the world ;
And they will be our lords, as they are now,
And keep us prisoners of our consciousness,
And never let us clasp and feel the All
But through their forms, and modes, and stifling veils.
And we shall be unsatisfied as now ;
And we shall feel the agony of thirst,
The ineffable longing for the life of life
Baffled forever ; and still thought and mind
Will hurry us with them on their homeless march
Over the unallied unopening earth,
Over the unrecognizing sea ; while air
Will blow us fiercely back to sea and earth,
And fire repel us from its living waves.
And then we shall unwillingly return
Back to this meadow of calamity,
This uncongenial place, this human life :

And in our individual human state
Go through the sad probation all again,
To see if we will poise our life at last,
To see if we will now at last be true
To our own only true, deep-buried selves,
Being one with which, we are one with the whole world;
Or whether we will once more fall away
Into the bondage of the flesh or mind,
Some slough of sense, or some fantastic maze
Forged by the imperious lonely thinking-power.
And each succeeding age in which we are born
Will have more peril for us than the last;
Will goad our senses with a sharper spur,
Will fret our minds to an intenser play,
Will make ourselves harder to be discerned.
And we shall struggle a while, gasp and rebel;
And we shall fly for refuge to past times,
Their soul of unworn youth, their breath of greatness;
And the reality will pluck us back,
Knead us in its hot hand, and change our nature.
And we shall feel our powers of effort flag,
And rally them for one last fight — and fail;
And we shall sink in the impossible strife,
And be astray forever.

Slave of sense

I have in no wise been; but slave of thought?
And who can say: I have been always free,
Lived ever in the light of my own soul?
I cannot; I have lived in wrath and gloom,
Fierce, disputatious, ever at war with man,
Far from my own soul, far from warmth and light;
But I have not grown easy in these bonds,
But I have not denied what bonds these were.
Yea, I take myself to witness,

That I have loved no darkness,
Sophisticated no truth,
Nursed no delusion,
Allowed no fear !

And therefore, O ye elements ! I know —
Ye know it too — it hath been granted me
Not to die wholly, not to be all enslaved.
I feel it in this hour.   The numbing cloud
Mounts off my soul ; I feel it, I breathe free.

Is it but for a moment?
— Ah, boil up, ye vapors !
Leap and roar, thou sea of fire !
My soul glows to meet you.
Ere it flag, ere the mists
Of despondency and gloom
Rush over it again,
Receive me, save me !

[*He plunges into the crater.*

CALLICLES (*from below*).

Through the black, rushing smoke-bursts,
Thick breaks the red flame ;
All Etna heaves fiercely
Her forest-clothed frame.

Not here, O Apollo !
Are haunts meet for thee ;
But where Helicon breaks down
In cliff to the sea, —

Where the moon-silvered inlets
Send far their light voice
Up the still vale of Thisbe, —
Oh, speed, and rejoice !

On the sward at the cliff-top
Lie strewn the white flocks :
On the cliff-side the pigeons
Roost deep in the rocks.

In the moonlight the shepherds,
Soft lulled by the rills,
Lie wrapped in their blankets
Asleep on the hills.

— What forms are these coming
So white through the gloom?
What garments out-glistening
The gold-flowered broom?

What sweet-breathing presence
Out-perfumes the thyme?
What voices enrapture
The night's balmy prime?

'Tis Apollo comes leading
His choir, the Nine.
The leader is fairest,
But all are divine.

They are lost in the hollows !
They stream up again !
What seeks on this mountain
The glorified train?

They bathe on this mountain,
In the spring by their road ;
Then on to Olympus,
Their endless abode.

—Whose praise do they mention?
Of what is it told?
What will be forever,
What was from of old.

First hymn they the Father
Of all things; and then,
The rest of immortals,
The action of men.

The day in his hotness,
The strife with the palm;
The night in her silence,
The stars in their calm.

BACCHANALIA; OR, THE NEW AGE.

I.

THE evening comes, the fields are still.
The tinkle of the thirsty rill,
Unheard all day, ascends again;
Deserted is the half-mown plain,
Silent the swaths; the ringing wain,
The mower's cry, the dog's alarms,
All housed within the sleeping farms.
The business of the day is done,
The last-left haymaker is gone.
And from the thyme upon the height,
And from the elder-blossom white
And pale dog-roses in the hedge,
And from the mint-plant in the sedge,
In puffs of balm the night-air blows
The perfume which the day foregoes.
And on the pure horizon far,
See, pulsing with the first-born star,
The liquid sky above the hill!
The evening comes, the fields are still.

Loitering and leaping,
With saunter, with bounds,
Flickering and circling
In files and in rounds,
Gayly their pine-staff green
Tossing in air,
Loose o'er their shoulders white
Showering their hair,
See ! the wild Mænads
Break from the wood,
Youth and Iacchus
Maddening their blood.
See ! through the quiet land
Rioting they pass,
Fling the fresh heaps about,
Trample the grass,
Tear from the rifled hedge
Garlands, their prize ;
Fill with their sports the field,
Fill with their cries.

Shepherd, what ails thee, then?
Shepherd, why mute?
Forth with thy joyous song !
Forth with thy flute !
Tempts not the revel blithe?
Lure not their cries?
Glow not their shoulders smooth?
Melt not their eyes?
Is not, on cheeks like those,
Lovely the flush?
— Ah! so the quiet was !
So was the hush !

II.

The epoch ends, the world is still.
The age has talked and worked its fill.
The famous orators have shone,
The famous poets sung and gone,
The famous men of war have fought,
The famous speculators thought,
The famous players, sculptors, wrought,
The famous painters filled their wall,
The famous critics judged it all.
The combatants are parted now ;
Uphung the spear, unbent the bow,
The puissant crowned, the weak laid low.
And in the after-silence sweet,
Now strifes are hushed, our ears doth meet,
Ascending pure, the bell-like fame
Of this or that down-trodden name,
Delicate spirits, pushed away
In the hot press of the noonday.
And o'er the plain, where the dead age
Did its now-silent warfare wage, —
O'er that wide plain, now wrapped in gloom,
Where many a splendor finds its tomb,
Many spent fames and fallen nights —
The one or two immortal lights
Rise slowly up into the sky,
To shine there everlastingly,
Like stars over the bounding hill.
The epoch ends, the world is still.

Thundering and bursting
In torrents, in waves,
Carolling and shouting

Over tombs, amid graves,
See ! on the cumbered plain
Clearing a stage,
Scattering the past about,
Comes the new age.
Bards make new poems,
Thinkers new schools,
Statesmen new systems,
Critics new rules.
All things begin again ;
Life is their prize ;
Earth with their deeds they fill,
Fill with their cries.

Poet, what ails thee, then ?
Say, why so mute ?
Forth with thy praising voice !
Forth with thy flute !
Loiterer ! why sittest thou
Sunk in thy dream ?
Tempts not the bright new age ?
Shines not its stream ?
Look, ah ! what genius,
Art, science, wit !
Soldiers like Cæsar,
Statesmen like Pitt !
Sculptors like Phidias,
Raphaels in shoals,
Poets like Shakspeare,—
Beautiful souls !
See, on their glowing cheeks
Heavenly the flush !
— *Ah ! so the silence was !*
So was the hush !

The world but feels the present's spell:
The poet feels the past as well;
Whatever men have done, might do,
Whatever thought, might think it too.

EPILOGUE TO LESSING'S LAOCOÖN.

ONE morn as through Hyde Park we walked,
My friend and I, by chance we talked
Of Lessing's famed Laocoön;
And after we a while had gone
In Lessing's track, and tried to see
What painting is, what poetry, —
Diverging to another thought,
"Ah!" cries my friend, "but who hath taught
Why music and the other arts
Oftener perform aright their parts
Than poetry? why she, than they,
Fewer fine successes can display?

"For 'tis so, surely! Even in Greece,
Where best the poet framed his piece,
Even in that Phœbus-guarded ground
Pausanias on his travels found
Good poems, if he looked, more rare
(Though many) than good statues were —
For these, in truth, were everywhere.
Of bards full many a stroke divine
In Dante's, Petrarch's, Tasso's line,
The land of Ariosto showed;
And yet, e'en there, the canvas glowed
With triumphs, a yet ampler brood,
Of Raphael and his brotherhood.

And nobly perfect, in our day
Of haste, half-work, and disarray,
Profound yet touching, sweet yet strong,
Hath risen Goethe's, Wordsworth's song;
Yet even I (and none will bow
Deeper to these) must needs allow,
They yield us not, to soothe our pains,
Such multitude of heavenly strains
As from the kings of sound are blown,—
Mozart, Beethoven, Mendelssohn."

While thus my friend discoursed, we pass
Out of the path, and take the grass.
The grass had still the green of May,
And still the unblackened elms were gay;
The kine were resting in the shade,
The flies a summer murmur made.
Bright was the morn, and south the air;
The soft-couched cattle were as fair
As those which pastured by the sea,
That old-world morn, in Sicily,
When on the beach the Cyclops lay,
And Galatea from the bay
Mocked her poor lovelorn giant's lay.
" Behold," I said, " the painter's sphere!
The limits of his art appear.
The passing group, the summer morn,
The grass, the elms, that blossomed thorn,—
Those cattle couched, or, as they rise,
Their shining flanks, their liquid eyes,—
These, or much greater things, but caught
Like these, and in one aspect brought!
In outward semblance he must give
A moment's life of things that live;

Then let him choose his moment well,
With power divine its story tell."

Still we walked on, in thoughtful mood,
And now upon the bridge we stood.
Full of sweet breathings was the air,
Of sudden stirs and pauses fair.
Down o'er the stately bridge the breeze
Came rustling from the garden-trees,
And on the sparkling waters played;
Light-plashing waves an answer made,
And mimic boats their haven neared.
Beyond, the abbey-towers appeared,
By mist and chimneys unconfined,
Free to the sweep of light and wind;
While through their earth-moored nave below,
Another breath of wind doth blow,
Sound as of wandering breeze — but sound
In laws by human artists bound.
"The world of music!" I exclaimed, —
"This breeze that rustles by, that famed
Abbey, recall it! what a sphere,
Large and profound, hath genius here!
The inspired musician, what a range,
What power of passion, wealth of change!
Some source of feeling he must choose,
And its locked fount of beauty use,
And through the stream of music tell
Its else unutterable spell;
To choose it rightly is his part,
And press into its inmost heart.

" *Miserere, Domine!*
The words are uttered, and they flee.

Deep is their penitential moan,
Mighty their pathos, but 'tis gone.
They have declared the spirit's sore,
Sore load, and words can do no more.
Beethoven takes them then, — those two
Poor, bounded words, — and makes them new;
Infinite makes them, makes them young;
Transplants them to another tongue,
Where they can now, without constraint,
Pour all the soul of their complaint,
And roll adown a channel large
The wealth divine they have in charge.
Page after page of music turn,
And still they live, and still they burn,
Eternal, passion-fraught, and free, —
Miserere, Domine!"

Onward we moved, and reached the ride
Where gayly flows the human tide.
Afar, in rest the cattle lay;
We heard, afar, faint music play;
But agitated, brisk, and near,
Men, with their stream of life, were here.
Some hang upon the rails, and some
On foot behind them go and come.
This through the ride upon his steed
Goes slowly by, and this at speed.
The young, the happy, and the fair,
The old, the sad, the worn, were there;
Some vacant and some musing went,
And some in talk and merriment.
Nods, smiles, and greetings, and farewells!
And now and then, perhaps, there swells
A sigh, a tear — but in the throng
All changes fast, and hies along.

Hies, ah ! from whence, what native ground?
And to what goal, what ending, bound?
"Behold at last the poet's sphere !
But who," I said, "suffices here?

"For, ah ! so much he has to do, —
Be painter and musician too !
The aspect of the moment show,
The feeling of the moment know !
The aspect not, I grant, express
Clear as the painter's art can dress ;
The feeling not, I grant, explore
So deep as the musician's lore :
But clear as words can make revealing,
And deep as words can follow feeling.
But, ah ! then comes his sorest spell
Of toil, — he must life's *movement* tell !
The thread which binds it all in one,
And not its separate parts alone.
The *movement* he must tell of life,
Its pain and pleasure, rest and strife ;
His eye must travel down, at full,
The long, unpausing spectacle ;
With faithful, unrelaxing force
Attend it from its primal source,
From change to change and year to year
Attend it of its mid-career,
Attend it to the last repose
And solemn silence of its close.

"The cattle rising from the grass,
His thought must follow where they pass ;
The penitent with anguish bowed,
His thought must follow through the crowd.

Yes ! all this eddying, motley throng
That sparkles in the sun along, —
Girl, statesman, merchant, soldier bold,
Master and servant, young and old,
Grave, gay, child, parent, husband, wife, —
He follows home, and lives their life.

"And many, many are the souls
Life's movement fascinates, controls.
It draws them on, they cannot save
Their feet from its alluring wave ;
They cannot leave it, they must go
With its unconquerable flow.
But ah ! how few, of all that try
This mighty march, do aught but die !
For ill-endowed for such a way,
Ill-stored in strength, in wits, are they.
They faint, they stagger to and fro,
And wandering from the stream they go ;
In pain, in terror, in distress,
They see, all round, a wilderness.
Sometimes a momentary gleam
They catch of the mysterious stream ;
Sometimes, a second's space, their ear
The murmur of its waves doth hear ;
That transient glimpse in song they say,
But not as painter can portray ;
That transient sound in song they tell,
But not as the musician well.
And when at last their snatches cease,
And they are silent and at peace,
The stream of life's majestic whole
Hath ne'er been mirrored on their soul.

" Only a few the life-stream's shore
With safe unwandering feet explore ;
Untired its movement bright attend,
Follow its windings to the end.
Then from its brimming waves their eye
Drinks up delighted ecstasy,
And its deep-toned, melodious voice
Forever makes their ear rejoice.
They speak ! the happiness divine
They feel runs o'er in every line ;
Its spell is round them like a shower ;
It gives them pathos, gives them power.
No painter yet hath such a way,
Nor no musician made, as they,
And gathered on immortal knolls
Such lovely flowers for cheering souls.
Beethoven, Raphael, cannot reach
The charm which Homer, Shakspeare, teach.
To these, to these, their thankful race
Gives, then, the first, the fairest place ;
And brightest is their glory's sheen,
For greatest hath their labor been."

PERSISTENCY OF POETRY.

THOUGH the Muse be gone away,
Though she move not earth to-day,
Souls, erewhile who caught her word,
Ah ! still harp on what they heard.

A CAUTION TO POETS.

WHAT poets feel not, when they make,
   A pleasure in creating,
The world, in *its* turn, will not take
   Pleasure in contemplating.

THE YOUTH OF NATURE.

RAISED are the dripping oars,
Silent the boat ! The lake,
Lovely and soft as a dream,
Swims in the sheen of the moon.
The mountains stand at its head
Clear in the pure June-night,
But the valleys are flooded with haze.
Rydal and Fairfield are there ;
In the shadow Wordsworth lies dead.
So it is, so it will be for aye.
Nature is fresh as of old,
Is lovely ; a mortal is dead.

The spots which recall him survive,
For he lent a new life to these hills.
The Pillar still broods o'er the fields
Which border Ennerdale Lake,
And Egremont sleeps by the sea.
The gleam of The Evening Star
Twinkles on Grasmere no more,
But ruined and solemn and gray
The sheepfold of Michael survives ;
And far to the south, the heath
Still blows in the Quantock coombs,
By the favorite waters of Ruth.
These survive ! Yet not without pain,
Pain and dejection to-night,
Can I feel that their poet is gone.

He grew old in an age he condemned.
He looked on the rushing decay
Of the times which had sheltered his youth ;
Felt the dissolving throes

Of a social order he loved ;
Outlived his brethren, his peers ;
And, like the Theban seer,
Died in his enemies' day.

Cold bubbled the spring of Tilphusa,
Copais lay bright in the moon,
Helicon glassed in the lake
Its firs, and afar rose the peaks
Of Parnassus, snowily clear ;
Thebes was behind him in flames,
And the clang of arms in his ear,
When his awe-struck captors led
The Theban seer to the spring.
Tiresias drank and died.
Nor did reviving Thebes
See such a prophet again.

Well may we mourn, when the head
Of a sacred poet lies low
In an age which can rear them no more !
The complaining millions of men
Darken in labor and pain ;
But he was a priest to us all
Of the wonder and bloom of the world,
Which we saw with his eyes, and were glad.
He is dead, and the fruit-bearing day
Of his race is past on the earth ;
And darkness returns to our eyes.

For, oh ! is it you, is it you,
Moonlight, and shadow, and lake,
And mountains, that fill us with joy,
Or the poet who sings you so well?
Is it you, O beauty, O grace,

O charm, O romance, that we feel,
Or the voice which reveals what you are?
Are ye, like daylight and sun,
Shared and rejoiced in by all?
Or are ye immersed in the mass
Of matter, and hard to extract,
Or sunk at the core of the world
Too deep for the most to discern?
Like stars in the deep of the sky,
Which arise on the glass of the sage,
But are lost when their watcher is gone.

"They are here," — I heard, as men heard
In Mysian Ida the voice
Of the mighty Mother, or Crete,
The murmur of Nature, reply, —
" Loveliness, magic, grace,
They are here ! they are set in the world,
They abide ; and the finest of souls
Hath not been thrilled by them all,
Nor the dullest been dead to them quite.
The poet who sings them may die,
But they are immortal and live,
For they are the life of the world.
Will ye not learn it, and know,
When ye mourn that a poet is dead,
That the singer was less than his themes,
Life, and emotion, and I?

" More than the singer are these.
Weak is the tremor of pain
That thrills in his mournfullest chord
To that which once ran through his soul.
Cold the elation of joy

In his gladdest, airiest song,
To that which of old in his youth
Filled him and made him divine.
Hardly his voice at its best
Gives us a sense of the awe,
The vastness, the grandeur, the gloom,
Of the unlit gulf of himself.

"Ye know not yourselves; and your bards —
The clearest, the best, who have read
Most in themselves — have beheld
Less than they left unrevealed.
Ye express not yourselves: can ye make
With marble, with color, with word,
What charmed you in others re-live?
Can thy pencil, O artist! restore
The figure, the bloom of thy love,
As she was in her morning of spring?
Canst thou paint the ineffable smile
Of her eyes as they rested on thine?
Can the image of life have the glow,
The motion of life itself?

"Yourselves and your fellows ye know not; and me,
The mateless, the one, will ye know?
Will ye scan me, and read me, and tell
Of the thoughts that ferment in my breast,
My longing, my sadness, my joy?
Will ye claim for your great ones the gift
To have rendered the gleam of my skies,
To have echoed the moan of my seas,
Uttered the voice of my hills?
When your great ones depart, will ye say, —
All things have suffered a loss,
Nature is hid in their grave?

" Race after race, man after man,
Have thought that my secret was theirs,
Have dreamed that I lived but for them,
That they were my glory and joy.
— They are dust, they are changed, they are gone !
I remain."

THE YOUTH OF MAN.

WE, O Nature, depart :
Thou survivest us !   This,
This, I know, is the law.
Yes ! but, more than this,
Thou who seest us die
Seest us change while we live ;
Seest our dreams, one by one,
Seest our errors depart ;
Watchest us, Nature ! throughout
Mild and inscrutably calm.

Well for us that we change !
Well for us that the power
Which in our morning prime
Saw the mistakes of our youth,
Sweet, and forgiving, and good,
Sees the contrition of age !

Behold, O Nature, this pair !
See them to-night where they stand,
Not with the halo of youth
Crowning their brows with its light,
Not with the sunshine of hope,
Not with the rapture of spring,

Which they had of old, when they stood
Years ago at my side
In this self-same garden, and said, —
"We are young, and the world is ours;
Man, man is king of the world!
Fools that these mystics are
Who prate of Nature! but she
Hath neither beauty, nor warmth,
Nor life, nor emotion, nor power.
But man has a thousand gifts,
And the generous dreamer invests
The senseless world with them all.
Nature is nothing; her charm
Lives in our eyes which can paint,
Lives in our hearts which can feel."

Thou, O Nature, wast mute,
Mute as of old! Days flew,
Days and years; and Time
With the ceaseless stroke of his wings
Brushed off the bloom from their soul.
Clouded and dim grew their eye,
Languid their heart — for youth
Quickened its pulses no more.
Slowly, within the walls
Of an ever-narrowing world,
They drooped, they grew blind, they grew old
Thee, and their youth in thee,
Nature! they saw no more.

Murmur of living,
Stir of existence,
Soul of the world!
Make, oh, make yourselves felt

To the dying spirit of youth !
Come, like the breath of the spring !
Leave not a human soul
To grow old in darkness and pain !
Only the living can feel you,
But leave us not while we live !

Here they stand to-night, —
Here, where this gray balustrade
Crowns the still valley ; behind
In the castled house with its woods
Which sheltered their childhood ; the sun
On its ivied windows ; a scent
From the gray-walled gardens, a breath
Of the fragrant stock and the pink,
Perfumes the evening air.
Their children play on the lawns.
They stand and listen ; they hear
The children's shouts, and at times,
Faintly, the bark of a dog
From a distant farm in the hills.
Nothing besides ! in front
The wide, wide valley outspreads
To the dim horizon, reposed
In the twilight, and bathed in dew,
Cornfield and hamlet and copse
Darkening fast ; but a light,
Far off, a glory of day,
Still plays on the city-spires ;
And there in the dusk by the walls,
With the gray mist marking its course
Through the silent, flowery land,
On, to the plains, to the sea,
Floats the imperial stream.

Well I know what they feel!
They gaze, and the evening wind
Plays on their faces; they gaze,—
Airs from the Eden of youth
Awake and stir in their soul;
The past returns: they feel
What they are, alas! what they were.
They, not Nature, are changed.
Well I know what they feel!

Hush, for tears
Begin to steal to their eyes!
Hush, for fruit
Grows from such sorrow as theirs!

And they remember,
With piercing, untold anguish,
The proud boasting of their youth.
And they feel how Nature was fair.
And the mists of delusion,
And the scales of habit,
Fall away from their eyes;
And they see, for a moment,
Stretching out like the desert
In its weary, unprofitable length,
Their faded, ignoble lives.

While the locks are yet brown on thy head,
While the soul still looks through thine eyes,
While the heart still pours
The mantling blood to thy cheek,
Sink, O youth, in thy soul!
Yearn to the greatness of Nature;
Rally the good in the depths of thyself!

PALLADIUM.

Set where the upper streams of Simois flow,
Was the Palladium, high 'mid rock and wood;
And Hector was in Ilium, far below,
And fought, and saw it not; but there it stood!

It stood, and sun and moonshine rained their light
On the pure columns of its glen-built hall.
Backward and forward rolled the waves of fight
Round Troy; but while this stood, Troy could not fall.

So, in its lovely moonlight, lives the soul.
Mountains surround it, and sweet virgin air;
Cold plashing, past it, crystal waters roll:
We visit it by moments, ah, too rare!

Men will renew the battle in the plain
To-morrow: red with blood will Xanthus be;
Hector and Ajax will be there again,
Helen will come upon the wall to see.

Then we shall rust in shade, or shine in strife,
And fluctuate 'twixt blind hopes and blind despairs,
And fancy that we put forth all our life,
And never know how with the soul it fares.

Still doth the soul, from its lone fastness high,
Upon our life a ruling effluence send;
And when it fails, fight as we will, we die;
And, while it lasts, we cannot wholly end.

PROGRESS.

The Master stood upon the mount, and taught.
He saw a fire in his disciples' eyes;
"The old law," they said, "is wholly come to naught:
  Behold the new world rise!"

"Was it," the Lord then said, "with scorn ye saw
The old law observed by scribes and Pharisees?
I say unto you, see *ye* keep that law
　　　More faithfully than these!

"Too hasty heads for ordering worlds, alas!
Think not that I to annul the law have willed:
No jot, no tittle, from the law shall pass
　　　Till all have been fulfilled."

So Christ said eighteen hundred years ago.
And what, then, shall be said to those to-day,
Who cry aloud to lay the old world low
　　　To clear the new world's way?

"Religious fervors! ardor misapplied!
Hence, hence!" they cry, "ye do but keep man blind!
But keep him self-immersed, pre-occupied,
　　　And lame the active mind."

Ah! from the old world let some one answer give:
"Scorn ye this world, their tears, their inward cares?
I say unto you, see that *your* souls live
　　　A deeper life than theirs!

"Say ye, 'The spirit of man has found new roads,
And we must leave the old faiths, and walk therein'?
Leave, then, the cross as ye have left carved gods,
　　　But guard the fire within!

"Bright, else, and fast the stream of life may roll,
And no man may the other's hurt behold;
Yet each will have one anguish, — his own soul
　　　Which perishes of cold."

Here let that voice make end; then let a strain
From a far lonelier distance, like the wind
Be heard, floating through heaven, and fill again
　　　These men's profoundest mind: —

" Children of men ! the unseen Power, whose eye
Forever doth accompany mankind,
Hath looked on no religion scornfully
    That men did ever find.

" Which has not taught weak wills how much they can ?
Which has not fallen on the dry heart like rain ?
Which has not cried to sunk, self-weary man, —
    Thou must be born again !

" Children of men ! not that your age excel
In pride of life the ages of your sires,
But that *ye* think clear, feel deep, bear fruit well,
    The Friend of man desires."

REVOLUTIONS.

BEFORE man parted for this earthly strand,
While yet upon the verge of heaven he stood,
God put a heap of letters in his hand,
And bade him make with them what word he could.

And man has turned them many times ; made Greece,
Rome, England, France ; yes, nor in vain essayed
Way after way, changes that never cease !
The letters have combined, something was made.

But ah ! an inextinguishable sense
Haunts him that he has not made what he should ;
That he has still, though old, to recommence,
Since he has not yet found the word God would.

And empire after empire, at their height
Of sway, have felt this boding sense come on ;
Have felt their huge frames not constructed right,
And drooped, and slowly died upon their throne.

One day, thou say'st, there will at last appear
The word, the order, which God meant should be.
—Ah ! we shall know *that* well when it comes near ;
The band will quit man's heart, he will breathe free.

SELF-DEPENDENCE.

WEARY of myself, and sick of asking
What I am, and what I ought to be,
At this vessel's prow I stand, which bears me
Forwards, forwards, o'er the starlit sea.

And a look of passionate desire
O'er the sea and to the stars I send :
" Ye who from my childhood up have calmed me,
Calm me, ah, compose me to the end !

Ah, once more," I cried, " ye stars, ye waters,
On my heart your mighty charm renew ;
Still, still let me, as I gaze upon you,
Feel my soul becoming vast like you ! "

From the intense, clear, star-sown vault of heaven,
Over the lit sea's unquiet way,
In the rustling night-air came the answer,—
" Wouldst thou *be* as these are ? *Live* as they.

" Unaffrighted by the silence round them,
Undistracted by the sights they see,
These demand not that the things without them
Yield them love, amusement, sympathy.

" And with joy the stars perform their shining,
And the sea its long moon-silvered roll ;
For self-poised they live, nor pine with noting
All the fever of some differing soul.

" Bounded by themselves, and unregardful
In what state God's other works may be,
In their own tasks all their powers pouring,
These attain the mighty life you see."

O air-born voice ! long since, severely clear,
A cry like thine in mine own heart I hear, —
" Resolve to be thyself ; and know, that he
Who finds himself loses his misery ! "

MORALITY.

WE cannot kindle when we will
The fire which in the heart resides ;
The spirit bloweth and is still,
In mystery our soul abides.
    But tasks in hours of insight willed
    Can be through hours of gloom fulfilled.

With aching hands and bleeding feet
We dig and heap, lay stone on stone ;
We bear the burden and the heat
Of the long day, and wish 'twere done.
    Not till the hours of light return,
    All we have built do we discern.

Then, when the clouds are off the soul,
When thou dost bask in Nature's eye,
Ask how *she* viewed thy self-control,
Thy struggling, tasked morality, —
    Nature, whose free, light, cheerful air,
    Oft made thee, in thy gloom, despair.

And she, whose censure thou dost dread,
Whose eye thou wast afraid to seek,

See, on her face a glow is spread,
A strong emotion on her cheek !
　"Ah, child ! " she cries, " that strife divine,
　Whence was it, for it is not mine?

" There is no effort on *my* brow ;
I do not strive, I do not weep :
I rush with the swift spheres, and glow
In joy, and when I will, I sleep.
　Yet that severe, that earnest air,
　I saw, I felt it once — but where?

" I knew not yet the gauge of time,
Nor wore the manacles of space ;
I felt it in some other clime,
I saw it in some other place.
　'Twas when the heavenly house I trod,
　And lay upon the breast of God."

A SUMMER NIGHT.

In the deserted, moon-blanched street,
How lonely rings the echo of my feet !
Those windows, which I gaze at, frown,
Silent and white, unopening down,
Repellent as the world ; but see,
A break between the housetops shows
The moon ! and lost behind her, fading dim
Into the dewy dark obscurity
Down at the far horizon's rim,
Doth a whole tract of heaven disclose !

And to my mind the thought
Is on a sudden brought
Of a past night, and a far different scene.

Headlands stood out into the moonlit deep
As clearly as at noon ;
The spring-tide's brimming flow
Heaved dazzlingly between ;
Houses, with long white sweep,
Girdled the glistening bay ;
Behind, through the soft air,
The blue haze-cradled mountains spread away.
That night was far more fair —
But the same restless pacings to and fro,
And the same vainly throbbing heart was there,
And the same bright, calm moon.

And the calm moonlight seems to say, —
Hast thou, then, still the old unquiet breast,
Which neither deadens into rest,
Nor ever feels the fiery glow
That whirls the spirit from itself away,
But fluctuates to and fro,
Never by passion quite possessed,
And never quite benumbed by the world's sway ?
And I, I know not if to pray
Still to be what I am, or yield, and be
Like all the other men I see.

For most men in a brazen prison live,
Where, in the sun's hot eye,
With heads bent o'er their toil, they languidly
Their lives to some unmeaning task-work give,
Dreaming of naught beyond their prison-wall.
And as, year after year,
Fresh products of their barren labor fall
From their tired hands, and rest
Never yet comes more near,
Gloom settles slowly down over their breast.

And while they try to stem
The waves of mournful thought by which they are prest,
Death in their prison reaches them,
Unfreed, having seen nothing, still unblest.

And the rest, a few,
Escape their prison, and depart
On the wide ocean of life anew.
There the freed prisoner, where'er his heart
Listeth, will sail ;
Nor doth he know how there prevail,
Despotic on that sea,
Trade-winds which cross it from eternity.
Awhile he holds some false way, undebarred
By thwarting signs, and braves
The freshening wind and blackening waves.
And then the tempest strikes him ; and between
The lightning-bursts is seen
Only a driving wreck,
And the pale master on his spar-strewn deck
With anguished face and flying hair,
Grasping the rudder hard,
Still bent to make some port, he knows not where,
Still standing for some false, impossible shore.
And sterner comes the roar
Of sea and wind ; and through the deepening gloom
Fainter and fainter wreck and helmsman loom,
And he too disappears, and comes no more.

Is there no life, but these alone?
Madman or slave, must man be one?

Plainness and clearness without shadow of stain !
Clearness divine !
Ye heavens, whose pure dark regions have no sign

Of languor, though so calm, and though so great
Are yet untroubled and unpassionate ;
Who, though so noble, share in the world's toil,
And, though so tasked, keep free from dust and soil !
I will not say that your mild deeps retain
A tinge, it may be, of their silent pain
Who have longed deeply once, and longed in vain ;
But I will rather say that you remain
A world above man's head, to let him see
How boundless might his soul's horizons be,
How vast, yet of what clear transparency !
How it were good to live there, and breathe free ;
How fair a lot to fill
Is left to each man still !

THE BURIED LIFE.

LIGHT flows our war of mocking words ; and yet,
Behold, with tears mine eyes are wet !
I feel a nameless sadness o'er me roll.
Yes, yes, we know that we can jest,
We know, we know that we can smile !
But there's a something in this breast,
To which thy light words bring no rest,
And thy gay smiles no anodyne ;
Give me thy hand, and hush awhile,
And turn those limpid eyes on mine,
And let me read there, love ! thy inmost soul.

Alas ! is even love too weak
To unlock the heart, and let it speak ?
Are even lovers powerless to reveal
To one another what indeed they feel ?

I knew the mass of men concealed
Their thoughts, for fear that if revealed
They would by other men be met
With blank indifference, or with blame reproved;
I knew they lived and moved
Tricked in disguises, alien to the rest
Of men, and alien to themselves — and yet
The same heart beats in every human breast!

But we, my love! doth a like spell benumb
Our hearts, our voices? must we too be dumb?

Ah! well for us, if even we,
Even for a moment, can get free
Our heart, and have our lips unchained;
For that which seals them hath been deep-ordained!

Fate, which foresaw
How frivolous a baby man would be, —
By what distractions he would be possessed,
How he would pour himself in every strife,
And well-nigh change his own identity, —
That it might keep from his capricious play
His genuine self, and force him to obey
Even in his own despite his being's law,
Bade through the deep recesses of our breast
The unregarded river of our life
Pursue with indiscernible flow its way;
And that we should not see
The buried stream, and seem to be
Eddying at large in blind uncertainty,
Though driving on with it eternally.

But often, in the world's most crowded streets,
But often, in the din of strife,

There rises an unspeakable desire
After the knowledge of our buried life;
A thirst to spend our fire and restless force
In tracking out our true, original course;
A longing to inquire
Into the mystery of this heart which beats
So wild, so deep in us,— to know
Whence our lives come, and where they go.
And many a man in his own breast then delves,
But deep enough, alas! none ever mines.
And we have been on many thousand lines,
And we have shown, on each, spirit and power;
But hardly have we, for one little hour,
Been on our own line, have we been ourselves,—
Hardly had skill to utter one of all
The nameless feelings that course through our breast,
But they course on forever unexpressed.
And long we try in vain to speak and act
Our hidden self, and what we say and do
Is eloquent, is well — but 'tis not true!
And then we will no more be racked
With inward striving, and demand
Of all the thousand nothings of the hour
Their stupefying power;
Ah, yes, and they benumb us at our call!
Yet still, from time to time, vague and forlorn,
From the soul's subterranean depth upborne
As from an infinitely distant land,
Come airs, and floating echoes, and convey
A melancholy into all our day.

Only — but this is rare —
When a belovèd hand is laid in ours,
When, jaded with the rush and glare

Of the interminable hours,
Our eyes can in another's eyes read clear,
When our world-deafened ear
Is by the tones of a loved voice caressed, —
A bolt is shot back somewhere in our breast,
And a lost pulse of feeling stirs again.
The eye sinks inward, and the heart lies plain,
And what we mean, we say, and what we would, we know.

A man becomes aware of his life's flow,
And hears its winding murmur, and he sees
The meadows where it glides, the sun, the breeze.

And there arrives a lull in the hot race
Wherein he doth forever chase
The flying and elusive shadow, rest.
An air of coolness plays upon his face,
And an unwonted calm pervades his breast;
And then he thinks he knows
The hills where his life rose,
And the sea where it goes.

LINES WRITTEN IN KENSINGTON GARDENS.

In this lone, open glade I lie,
Screened by deep boughs on either hand;
And at its end, to stay the eye,
Those black-crowned, red-boled pine-trees stand.

Birds here make song, each bird has his,
Across the girdling city's hum.
How green under the boughs it is!
How thick the tremulous sheep-cries come!

Sometimes a child will cross the glade
To take his nurse his broken toy ;
Sometimes a thrush flit overhead
Deep in her unknown day's employ.

Here at my feet what wonders pass !
What endless, active life is here !
What blowing daisies, fragrant grass !
An air-stirred forest, fresh and clear.

Scarce fresher is the mountain sod
Where the tired angler lies, stretched out,
And, eased of basket and of rod,
Counts his day's spoil, the spotted trout.

In the huge world which roars hard by,
Be others happy if they can !
But in my helpless cradle I
Was breathed on by the rural Pan.

I, on men's impious uproar hurled,
Think often, as I hear them rave,
That peace has left the upper world,
And now keeps only in the grave.

Yet here is peace forever new !
When I who watch them am away,
Still all things in this glade go through
The changes of their quiet day.

Then to their happy rest they pass ;
The flowers upclose, the birds are fed,
The night comes down upon the grass,
The child sleeps warmly in his bed.

Calm soul of all things ! make it mine
To feel, amid the city's jar,
That there abides a peace of thine,
Man did not make, and cannot mar.

The will to neither strive nor cry,
The power to feel with others, give !
Calm, calm me more ! nor let me die
Before I have begun to live.

A WISH.

I ASK not that my bed of death
From bands of greedy heirs be free ;
For these besiege the latest breath
Of fortune's favored sons, not me.

I ask not each kind soul to keep
Tearless, when of my death he hears.
Let those who will, if any, weep !
There are worse plagues on earth than tears.

I ask but that my death may find
The freedom to my life denied ;
Ask but the folly of mankind
Then, then at last, to quit my side.

Spare me the whispering, crowded room,
The friends who come, and gape, and go ;
The ceremonious air of gloom, —
All which makes death a hideous show !

Nor bring, to see me cease to live,
Some doctor full of phrase and fame,
To shake his sapient head, and give
The ill he cannot cure a name.

Nor fetch, to take the accustomed toll
Of the poor sinner bound for death,
His brother-doctor of the soul,
To canvass with official breath

The future and its viewless things, —
That undiscovered mystery
Which one who feels death's winnowing wings
Must needs read clearer, sure, than he !

Bring none of these ; but let me be,
While all around in silence lies,
Moved to the window near, and see
Once more, before my dying eyes, —

Bathed in the sacred dews of morn
The wide aërial landscape spread, —
The world which was ere I was born,
The world which lasts when I am dead ;

Which never was the friend of *one*,
Nor promised love it could not give,
But lit for all its generous sun,
And lived itself, and made us live.

There let me gaze, till I become
In soul, with what I gaze on, wed !
To feel the universe my home ;
To have before my mind — instead

Of the sick-room, the mortal strife,
The turmoil for a little breath —
The pure eternal course of life,
Not human combatings with death !

Thus feeling, gazing, might I grow
Composed, refreshed, ennobled, clear ;
Then willing let my spirit go
To work or wait elsewhere or here !

THE FUTURE.

A WANDERER is man from his birth.
He was born in a ship
On the breast of the river of Time;
Brimming with wonder and joy,
He spreads out his arms to the light,
Rivets his gaze on the banks of the stream.

As what he sees is, so have his thoughts been.
Whether he wakes
Where the snowy mountainous pass,
Echoing the screams of the eagles,
Hems in its gorges the bed
Of the new-born, clear-flowing stream;
Whether he first sees light
Where the river in gleaming rings
Sluggishly winds through the plain;
Whether in sound of the swallowing sea, —
As is the world on the banks,
So is the mind of the man.

Vainly does each, as he glides,
Fable and dream
Of the lands which the river of Time
Had left ere he woke on its breast,
Or shall reach when his eyes have been closed.
Only the tract where he sails
He wots of; only the thoughts,
Raised by the objects he passes, are his.

Who can see the green earth any more
As she was by the sources of Time?
Who imagines her fields as they lay
In the sunshine, unworn by the plough?

Who thinks as they thought,
The tribes who then roamed on her breast,
Her vigorous, primitive sons?

What girl
Now reads in her bosom as clear
As Rebekah read, when she sate
At eve by the palm-shaded well?
Who guards in her breast
As deep, as pellucid a spring
Of feeling, as tranquil, as sure?

What bard,
At the height of his vision, can deem
Of God, of the world, of the soul,
With a plainness as near,
As flashing, as Moses felt,
When he lay in the night by his flock
On the starlit Arabian waste?
Can rise and obey
The beck of the Spirit like him?

This tract which the river of Time
Now flows through with us, is the plain.
Gone is the calm of its earlier shore.
Bordered by cities, and hoarse
With a thousand cries is its stream.
And we on its breast, our minds
Are confused as the cries which we hear,
Changing and short as the sights which we see.

And we say that repose has fled
Forever the course of the river of Time.
That cities will crowd to its edge
In a blacker, incessanter line;
That the din will be more on its banks,

Denser the trade on its stream,
Flatter the plain where it flows,
Fiercer the sun overhead ;
That never will those on its breast
See an ennobling sight,
Drink of the feeling of quiet again.

But what was before us we know not,
And we know not what shall succeed.

Haply, the river of Time —
As it grows, as the towns on its marge
Fling their wavering lights
On a wider, statelier stream —
May acquire, if not the calm
Of its early mountainous shore,
Yet a solemn peace of its own.

And the width of the waters, the hush
Of the gray expanse where he floats,
Freshening its current, and spotted with foam
As it draws to the ocean, may strike
Peace to the soul of the man on its breast, —
As the pale waste widens around him,
As the banks fade dimmer away,
As the stars come out, and the night-wind
Brings up the stream
Murmurs and scents of the infinite sea.

NEW ROME.

LINES WRITTEN FOR MISS STORY'S ALBUM.

THE armless Vatican Cupid
   Hangs down his beautiful head ;
For the priests have got him in prison,
   And Psyche long has been dead.

But see, his shaven oppressors
   Begin to quake and disband !
And *The Times*, that bright Apollo,
   Proclaims salvation at hand.

" And what," cries Cupid, " will save us ? "
   Says Apollo : " *Modernise Rome!*
What inns !   Your streets, too, how narrow !
   Too much of palace and dome !

" O learn of London, whose paupers
   Are not pushed out by the swells !
Wide streets with fine double trottoirs ;
   And then — the London hotels ! "

The armless Vatican Cupid
   Hangs down his head as before.
Through centuries past it has hung so,
   And will through centuries more.

THE LORD'S MESSENGERS.

THUS saith the Lord to his own : —
  "See ye the trouble below?
    Warfare of man from his birth !
Too long let we them groan ;
  Haste, arise ye, and go,
    Carry my peace upon earth ! "

Gladly they rise at his call,
  Gladly obey his command,
    Gladly descend to the plain.
— Ah ! how few of them all,
  Those willing servants, shall stand
    In the Master's presence again !

Some in the tumult are lost ;
  Baffled, bewilder'd, they stray.
    Some, as prisoners, draw breath.
Some, unconquer'd, are cross'd
  (Not yet half through the day)
    By a pitiless arrow of Death.

Hardly, hardly shall one
  Come, with countenance bright,
    At the close of day, from the plain ;
His Master's errand well done,
  Safe through the smoke of the fight,
    Back to his Master again.

MEROPE.

A TRAGEDY.

STORY OF THE DRAMA.

APOLLODORUS says: — " Cresphontes had not reigned long in Messenia when he was murdered, together with two of his sons. And Polyphontes reigned in his stead, he, too, being of the family of Hercules; and he had for his wife, against her will, Merope, the widow of the murdered king. But Merope had borne to Cresphontes a third son, called Æpytus; him she gave to her own father to bring up. He, when he came to man's estate, returned secretly to Messenia, and slew Polyphontes and the other murderers of his father."

Hyginus says: — " Merope sent away and concealed her infant son. Polyphontes sought for him everywhere in vain. He, when he grew up, laid a plan to avenge the murder of his father and brothers. In pursuance of this plan he came to king Polyphontes and reported the death of the son of Cresphontes and Merope. The king ordered him to be hospitably entertained, intending to inquire further of him. He, being very tired, went to sleep, and an old man, who was the channel through whom the mother and son used to communicate, arrived at this moment in tears, bringing word to Merope that her son had disappeared from his protector's house, and was slain. Merope, believing that the sleeping stranger was the murderer of her son, came into the guest-chamber with an axe, not knowing that he whom she would slay was her son; the old man recognized him, and withheld Merope from slaying him. The king, Polyphontes, rejoicing at the supposed death of Æpytus, celebrated a sacrifice; his guest, pretending to strike the sacrificial victim, slew the king, and so got back his father's kingdom."

The events on which the action of the drama turns belong to the period of transition from the heroic and fabulous to the human and historic age of Greece. The doings of the hero Hercules, the ancestor of the Messenian Æpytus, belong to fable; but the invasion of Peloponnesus by the Dorians under chiefs claiming to be descended from Hercules, and their settlement in Argos, Lacedæmon, and Messenia, belong to history.

Æpytus is descended on the father's side from Hercules, Perseus, and the kings of Argos; on the mother's side from Pelasgus, and the aboriginal kings of Arcadia. Callisto, the daughter of the wicked Lyçaon, and the mother, by Zeus, of Arcas, from whom the Arcadians took their name, was the granddaughter of Pelasgus. The birth of Arcas brought upon Callisto the anger of the virgin-goddess Artemis, whose service she followed : she was changed into a she-bear, and in this form was chased by her own son, grown to manhood. Zeus interposed, and the mother and son were removed from the earth, and placed among the stars. Callisto became the famous constellation of the Great Bear; her son became Arcturus, Arctophylax, or Boötes. From this son of Callisto were descended Cypselus, the maternal grandfather of Æpytus, and the children of Cypselus, Laias and Merope.

The story of the life of Hercules, the paternal ancestor of Æpytus, is so well known that there is no need to record it. The reader will remember that, although entitled to the throne of Argos by right of descent from Perseus and Danaus, and to the thrones of Sparta and Messenia by right of conquest, Hercules yet passed his life in labors and wanderings, subjected by the decree of fate to the commands of his kinsman, the feeble and malignant Eurystheus. At his death he bequeathed to his offspring, the Heracleidæ, his own claims to the kingdoms of Peloponnesus, and to the persecution of Eurystheus. They at first sought shelter with Ceyx, king of Trachis; he was too weak to protect them, and they then took refuge at Athens. The Athenians refused to deliver them up at the demand of Eurystheus; he invaded Attica, and a battle was fought near Marathon, in which, after Macaria, a daughter of Hercules, had devoted herself for the preservation of her house, Eurystheus fell, and the Heracleidæ and their Athenian protectors were victorious. The memory of Macaria's self-sacrifices was perpetuated by the name of a spring of water on the plain of Marathon, the spring Macaria. The Heracleidæ then endeavored to effect their return to Peloponnesus. Hyllus, the eldest of them, inquired of the oracle at Delphi respecting their return; he was told to return by the *narrow passage* and in the *third harvest.* Accordingly, in the third year from that time Hyllus led an army to the Isthmus of Corinth; but there he was encountered by an army of Achaians and Arcadians, and fell in single combat with Echemus, king of Tegea. Upon this defeat the Heracleidæ retired to northern Greece; there, after much wandering, they finally took refuge with Ægimius, king of the Dorians, who appears to have been the fastest friend of their house, and whose Dorian warriors formed the army which at last achieved their return. But, for a hundred years from the date of their first attempt, the Heracleidæ were defeated in their successive invasions of Peloponnesus. Cleolaus and Aristomachus, the son and grandson of Hyllus, fell in unsuccessful expeditions. At length the sons of Aristomachus, Temenus, Cresphontes, and Aristodemus, when grown up, repaired to Delphi and taxed the oracle with the non-fulfilment of the promise made to their ancestor Hyllus. But Apollo replied that his oracle had been misunderstood; for that by the *third harvest* he had meant the third generation, and by the *narrow passage* he had meant the straits of the Corinthian Gulf. After this explanation the sons of Aristomachus built a fleet at Naupactus; and finally, in the hundredth year from the death of Hyllus and the eightieth from the fall of Troy, the invasion was again attempted and was this time successful. The son of Orestes, Tisamenus, who ruled both Argos and Lacedæmon, fell in battle; many of his vanquished subjects left their homes and took refuge in Achaia.

The spoil was now to be divided among the conquerors. Aristodemus, the youngest of the sons of Aristomachus, did not survive to enjoy his share. He was slain at Delphi by the sons of Pylades and Electra, the kinsmen, through their mother, of the house of Agamemnon, that house which the Heracleidæ with their Dorian army had dispossessed. The claims of Aristodemus descended to his two sons, Procles and Eurysthenes, children under the guardianship of their maternal uncle, Theras. Temenus, the eldest of the sons of Aristomachus, took the kingdom of Argos. For the two remaining kingdoms, that of Sparta and that of Messenia, his two nephews, who were to rule jointly, and their uncle Cresphontes, had to cast lots. Cresphontes wished to have the fertile Messenia, and induced his brother to acquiesce in a trick which secured it to him. The lot of Cresphontes and that of his two nephews were to be placed in a water-jar, and thrown out. Messenia was to belong to him whose lot came out first. With the connivance of Temenus, Cresphontes marked as his own lot a pellet composed of baked clay, as the lot of his nephews, a pellet of unbaked clay; the unbaked pellet was of course dissolved in the water, while the brick pellet fell out alone. Messenia, therefore, was assigned to Cresphontes.

Messenia was at this time ruled by Melanthus, a descendant of Neleus. This ancestor, a prince of the great house of Æolus, had come from Thessaly and succeeded to the Messenian throne on the failure of the previous dynasty. Melanthus and his race were thus foreigners in Messenia and were unpopular. His subjects offered little or no opposition to the invading Dorians; Melanthus abandoned his kingdom to Cresphontes, and retired to Athens.

Cresphontes married Merope, whose native country, Arcadia, was not affected by the Dorian invasion. This marriage, the issue of which was three sons, connected him with the native population of Peloponnesus. He built a new capital of Messenia, Stenyclaros, and transferred thither, from Pylos, the seat of government; he proposed, moreover, says Pausanias, to divide Messenia into five states, and to confer on the native Messenians equal privileges with their Dorian conquerors. The Dorians complained that his administration unduly favored the vanquished people; his chief magnates, headed by Polyphontes, himself a descendant of Hercules, formed a cabal against him, and he was slain with his two eldest sons. The youngest son of Cresphontes, Æpytus, then an infant, was saved by his mother, who sent him to her father, Cypselus, the king of Arcadia, under whose protection he was brought up.

The drama begins at the moment when Æpytus, grown to manhood, returns secretly to Messenia to take vengeance on his father's murderers. At this period Temenus was no longer reigning at Argos; he had been murdered by his sons, jealous of their brother-in-law, Deiphontes. The sons of Aristodemus, Procles and Eurysthenes, at variance with their uncle and exguardian, Theras, were reigning at Sparta.

PERSONS OF THE DRAMA.

LAIAS, *uncle of* ÆPYTUS, *brother of* MEROPE.
ÆPYTUS, *son of* MEROPE *and* CRESPHONTES.
POLYPHONTES, *king of* MESSENIA.
MEROPE, *widow of* CRESPHONTES, *the murdered king of* MESSENIA.
THE CHORUS, *of* MESSENIAN *maidens.*
ARCAS, *an old man of* MEROPE'S *household.*
MESSENGER.
GUARDS, ATTENDANTS, *etc.*

The Scene is before the royal palace in STENYCLAROS, *the capital of* MESSENIA. *In the foreground is the tomb of* CRESPHONTES. *The action commences at daybreak.*

MEROPE.

LAIAS.   ÆPYTUS.

LAIAS.

Son of Cresphontes, we have reach'd the goal
Of our night-journey, and thou seest thy home.
Behold thy heritage, thy father's realm !
This is that fruitful, famed Messenian land,
Wealthy in corn and flocks, which, when at last
The late-relenting Gods with victory brought
The Heracleidæ back to Pelops' isle,
Fell to thy father's lot, the second prize.
Before thy feet this recent city spreads
Of Stenyclaros, which he built, and made
Of his fresh-conquer'd realm the royal seat,
Degrading Pylos from its ancient rule.
There stands the temple of thine ancestor,
Great Heracles ; and, in that public place,
Zeus hath his altar, where thy father fell.
Southward and west, behold those snowy peaks,
Taygetus, Laconia's border-wall ;
And, on this side, those confluent streams which make
Pamisus watering the Messenian plain ;
Then to the north, Lycæus and the hills
Of pastoral Arcadia, where, a babe
Snatch'd from the slaughter of thy father's house,
Thy mother's kin received thee, and rear'd up. —
Our journey is well made, the work remains
Which to perform we made it ; means for that
Let us consult, before this palace sends
Its inmates on their daily tasks abroad.
Haste and advise, for day comes on apace.

ÆPYTUS.

O brother of my mother, guardian true,
And second father from that hour when first
My mother's faithful servant laid me down,
An infant, at the hearth of Cypselus,
My grandfather, the good Arcadian king —
Thy part it were to advise, and mine to obey.
But let us keep that purpose, which, at home,
We judged the best ; chance finds no better way.
Go thou into the city, and seek out
Whate'er in the Messenian people stirs
Of faithful fondness for their former king
Or hatred to their present ; in this last
Will lie, my grandsire said, our fairest chance.
For tyrants make man good beyond himself ;
Hate to their rule, which else would die away,
Their daily-practised chafings keep alive.
Seek this ! revive, unite it, give it hope ;
Bid it rise boldly at the signal given.
Meanwhile within my father's palace I,
An unknown guest, will enter, bringing word
Of my own death — but, Laias, well I hope
Through that pretended death to live and reign.

[THE CHORUS *comes forth.*

Softly, stand back ! — see, to these palace gates
What black procession slowly makes approach ? —
Sad-chanting maidens clad in mourning robes,
With pitchers in their hands, and fresh-pull'd flowers —
Doubtless, they bear them to my father's tomb.

[MEROPE *comes forth.*

And look, to meet them, that one, grief-plunged Form,
Severer, paler, statelier than they all,
A golden circlet on her queenly brow !

O Laias, Laias, let the heart speak here —
Shall I not greet her? shall I not leap forth?

> [POLYPHONTES *comes forth, following* MEROPE.

LAIAS.

Not so ! thy heart would pay its moment's speech
By silence ever after, for, behold !
The King (I know him, even through many years)
Follows the approaching Queen, who stops, as call'd.
No lingering now ! straight to the city I ;
Do thou, till for thine entrance to this house
The happy moment comes, lurk here unseen
Behind the shelter of thy father's tomb ;
Remove yet further off, if aught comes near.
But, here while harboring, on its margin lay,
Sole offering that thou hast, locks from thy head ;
And fill thy leisure with an earnest prayer
To his avenging Shade, and to the Gods
Who under earth watch guilty deeds of men,
To guide our vengeance to a prosperous close.

> [LAIAS *goes out.* POLYPHONTES, MEROPE, *and* THE CHORUS
> *come forward. As they advance,* ÆPYTUS, *who at first
> conceals himself behind the tomb, moves off the stage.*

POLYPHONTES. (*To* THE CHORUS.)

Set down your pitchers, maidens, and fall back !
Suspend your melancholy rites awhile ;
Shortly ye shall resume them with your Queen. —

(*To* MEROPE.)

I sought thee, Merope ; I find thee thus,
As I have ever found thee ; bent to keep,
By sad observances and public grief,
A mournful feud alive, which else would die.

I blame thee not, I do thy heart no wrong !
Thy deep seclusion, thine unyielding gloom,
Thine attitude of cold, estranged reproach,
These punctual funeral honors, year by year
Repeated, are in thee, I well believe,
Courageous, faithful actions, nobly dared.
But, Merope, the eyes of other men
Read in these actions, innocent in thee,
Perpetual promptings to rebellious hope,
War-cries to faction, year by year renew'd,
Beacons of vengeance, not to be let die.
And me, believe it, wise men gravely blame,
And ignorant men despise me, that I stand
Passive, permitting thee what course thou wilt.
Yes, the crowd mutters that remorseful fear
And paralyzing conscience stop my arm,
When it should pluck thee from thy hostile way.
All this I bear, for, what I seek, I know :
Peace, peace is what I seek, and public calm ;
Endless extinction of unhappy hates,
Union cemented for this nation's weal.
And even now, if to behold me here,
This day, amid these rites, this black-robed train,
Wakens, O Queen ! remembrance in thy heart
Too wide at variance with the peace I seek —
I will not violate thy noble grief,
The prayer I came to urge I will defer.

MEROPE.

This day, to-morrow, yesterday, alike
I am, I shall be, have been, in my mind
Tow'rd thee ; toward thy silence as thy speech.
Speak, therefore, or keep silence, which thou wilt.

POLYPHONTES.

Hear me, then, speak ; and let this mournful day,
The twentieth anniversary of strife,
Henceforth be honor'd as the date of peace.
Yes, twenty years ago this day beheld
The king Cresphontes, thy great husband, fall ;
It needs no yearly offerings at his tomb
To keep alive that memory in my heart —
It lives, and, while I see the light, will live.
For we were kinsmen — more than kinsmen — friends ;
Together we had grown, together lived ;
Together to this isle of Pelops came
To take the inheritance of Heracles,
Together won this fair Messenian land —
Alas, that, how to rule it, was our broil !
He had his counsel, party, friends — I mine ;
He stood by what he wish'd for — I the same ;
I smote him, when our wishes clash'd in arms —
He had smit me, had he been swift as I.
But while I smote him, Queen, I honor'd him ;
Me, too, had he prevail'd, he had not scorn'd.
Enough of this ! Since that, I have maintain'd
The sceptre — not remissly let it fall —
And I am seated on a prosperous throne ;
Yet still, for I conceal it not, ferments
In the Messenian people what remains
Of thy dead husband's faction — vigorous once,
Now crush'd but not quite lifeless by his fall.
And these men look to thee, and from thy grief —
Something too studiously, forgive me, shown —
Infer thee their accomplice ; and they say
That thou in secret nurturest up thy son,
Him whom thou hiddest when thy husband fell,

To avenge that fall, and bring them back to power.
Such are their hopes — I ask not if by thee
Willingly fed or no — their most vain hopes;
For I have kept conspiracy fast-chain'd
Till now, and I have strength to chain it still.
But, Merope, the years advance; — I stand
Upon the threshold of old age, alone,
Always in arms, always in face of foes.
The long repressive attitude of rule
Leaves me austerer, sterner, than I would;
Old age is more suspicious than the free
And valiant heart of youth, or manhood's firm
Unclouded reason; I would not decline
Into a jealous tyrant, scourged with fears,
Closing in blood and gloom his sullen reign.
The cares which might in me with time, I feel,
Beget a cruel temper, help me quell!
The breach between our parties help me close!
Assist me to rule mildly; let us join
Our hands in solemn union, making friends
Our factions with the friendship of their chiefs.
Let us in marriage, King and Queen, unite
Claims ever hostile else, and set thy son —
No more an exile fed on empty hopes,
And to an unsubstantial title heir,
But prince adopted by the will of power,
And future king — before this people's eyes.
Consider him! consider not old hates!
Consider, too, this people, who were dear
To their dead king, thy husband — yea, too dear,
For that destroy'd him. Give them peace! thou canst.
O Merope, how many noble thoughts,
How many precious feelings of man's heart,
How many loves, how many gratitudes,

Do twenty years wear out, and see expire !
Shall they not wear one hatred out as well?

MEROPE.

Thou hast forgot, then, who I am who hear,
And who thou art who speakest to me?   I
Am Merope, thy murder'd master's wife ;
And thou art Polyphontes, first his friend,
And then . . . his murderer.   These offending tears
That murder moves ; this breach that thou would'st
        close
Was by that murder open'd ; that one child
(If still, indeed, he lives) whom thou would'st seat
Upon a throne not thine to give, is heir,
Because thou slew'st his brothers with their father.
Who can patch union here ?   What can there be
But everlasting horror 'twixt us two,
Gulfs of estranging blood ?   Across that chasm
Who can extend their hands ? . . .   Maidens, take back
These offerings home ! our rites are spoil'd to-day.

POLYPHONTES.

Not so ; let these Messenian maidens mark
The fear'd and blacken'd ruler of their race,
Albeit with lips unapt to self-excuse,
Blow off the spot of murder from his name. —
Murder ! — but what *is* murder?   When a wretch
For private gain or hatred takes a life,
We call it murder, crush him, brand his name.
But when, for some great public cause, an arm
Is, without love or hate, austerely raised
Against a power exempt from common checks,
Dangerous to all, to be but thus annull'd —

Ranks any man with murder such an act?
With grievous deeds, perhaps; with murder, no!
Find then such cause, the charge of murder falls —
Be judge thyself if it abound not here.
All know how weak the eagle, Heracles,
Soaring from his death-pile on Œta, left
His puny, callow eaglets; and what trials —
Infirm protectors, dubious oracles
Construed awry, misplann'd invasions — wore
Three generations of his offspring out;
Hardly the fourth, with grievous loss, regain'd
Their fathers' realm, this isle, from Pelops named.
Who made that triumph, though deferr'd, secure?
Who, but the kinsmen of the royal brood
Of Heracles, scarce Heracleidæ less
Than they? these, and the Dorian lords, whose king
Ægimius gave our outcast house a home
When Thebes, when Athens dared not; who in arms
Thrice issued with us from their pastoral vales,
And shed their blood like water in our cause?
Such were the dispossessors; of what stamp
Were they we dispossessed? — of us I speak,
Who to Messenia with thy husband came;
I speak not now of Argos, where his brother,
Not now of Sparta, where his nephews reign'd. —
What we found here were tribes of fame obscure,
Much turbulence, and little constancy,
Precariously ruled by foreign lords
From the Æolian stock of Neleus sprung,
A house once great, now dwindling in its sons.
Such were the conquer'd, such the conquerors; who
Had most thy husband's confidence?   Consult
His acts! the wife he chose was — full of virtues —
But an Arcadian princess, more akin

To his new subjects than to us ; his friends
Were the Messenian chiefs ; the laws he framed
Were aim'd at their promotion, our decline.
And, finally, this land, then half-subdued,
Which from one central city's guarded seat
As from a fastness in the rocks our scant
Handful of Dorian conquerors might have curb'd,
He parcell'd out in five confederate states,
Sowing his victors thinly through them all,
Mere prisoners, meant or not, among our foes.
If this was fear of them, it shamed the king ;
If jealousy of us, it shamed the man.
Long we refrain'd ourselves, submitted long,
Construed his acts indulgently, revered,
Though found perverse, the blood of Heracles ;
Reluctantly the rest — but, against all,
One voice preach'd patience, and that voice was mine !
At last it reach'd us, that he, still mistrustful,
Deeming, as tyrants deem, our silence hate,
Unadulating grief conspiracy,
Had to this city, Stenyclaros, call'd
A general assemblage of the realm,
With compact in that concourse to deliver,
For death, his ancient to his new-made friends.
Patience was thenceforth self-destruction.   I,
I his chief kinsman, I his pioneer
And champion to the throne, I honoring most
Of men the line of Heracles, preferr'd
The many of that lineage to the one ;
What his foes dared not, I, his lover, dared ;
I at that altar, where mid shouting crowds
He sacrificed, our ruin in his heart,
To Zeus, before he struck his blow, struck mine —
Struck once, and awed his mob, and saved this realm.

Murder let others call this, if they will ;
I, self-defence and righteous execution.

MEROPE.

Alas, how fair a color can his tongue,
Who self-exculpates, lend to foulest deeds !
Thy trusting lord didst thou, his servant, slay ;
Kinsman, thou slew'st thy kinsman ; friend, thy friend—
This were enough ; but let me tell thee, too,
Thou hadst no cause, as feign'd, in his misrule.
For ask at Argos, asked in Lacedæmon,
Whose people, when the Heracleidæ came,
Were hunted out, and to Achaia fled,
Whether is better, to abide alone,
A wolfish band, in a dispeopled realm,
Or conquerors with conquer'd to unite
Into one puissant folk, as he design'd?
These sturdy and unworn Messenian tribes,
Who shook the fierce Neleidæ on their throne,
Who to the invading Dorians stretch'd a hand,
And half bestow'd, half yielded up their soil—
He would not let his savage chiefs alight,
A cloud of vultures, on this vigorous race,
Ravin a little while in spoil and blood,
Then, gorged and helpless, be assail'd and slain.
He would have saved you from your furious selves.
Not in abhorr'd estrangement let you stand ;
He would have mix'd you with your friendly foes,
Foes dazzled with your prowess, well inclined
To reverence your lineage, more, to obey ;
So would have built you, in a few short years,
A just, therefore a safe, supremacy.
For well he knew, what you, his chiefs, did not—
How of all human rules the over-tense

Are apt to snap ; the easy-stretch'd endure
O gentle wisdom, little understood !
O arts above the vulgar tyrant's reach !
O policy too subtle far for sense
Of heady, masterful, injurious men !
This good he meant you, and for this he died !
Yet not for this — else might thy crime in part
Be error deem'd — but that pretence is vain.
For, if ye slew him for supposed misrule,
Injustice to his kin and Dorian friends,
Why with the offending father did ye slay
Two unoffending babes, his innocent sons?
Why not on them have placed the forfeit crown,
Ruled in their name, and train'd them to your will?
Had *they* misruled? had *they* forgot their friends,
Forsworn their blood? ungratefully had *they*
Preferr'd Messenian serfs to Dorian lords?
No ! but to thy ambition their poor lives
Were bar — and this, too, was their father's crime.
That thou might'st reign he died, not for his fault
Even fancied ; and his death thou wroughtest chief !
For, if the other lords desired his fall
Hotlier than thou, and were by thee kept back,
Why dost thou only profit by his death?
Thy crown condemns thee, while thy tongue absolves.
And now to me thou tenderest friendly league,
And to my son reversion to thy throne !
Short answer is sufficient ; league with thee,
For me I deem such impious ; and for him
Exile abroad more safe than heirship here.

POLYPHONTES.

I ask thee not to approve thy husband's death,
No, nor expect thee to admit the grounds,

In reason good, which justified my deed.
With women the heart argues, not the mind.
But, for thy children's death, I stand assoil'd —
I saved them, meant them honor ; but thy friends
Rose, and with fire and sword assailed my house
By night ; in that blind tumult they were slain.
To chance impute their deaths, then, not to me.

MEROPE.

Such chance as kill'd the father, kill'd the sons.

POLYPHONTES.

One son at least I spared, for still he lives.

MEROPE.

Tyrants think him they murder not they spare.

POLYPHONTES.

Not much a tyrant thy free speech displays me.

MEROPE.

Thy shame secures my freedom, not thy will.

POLYPHONTES.

Shame rarely checks the genuine tyrant's will.

MEROPE.

One merit, then, thou hast ; exult in that.

POLYPHONTES.

Thou standest out, I see, repellest peace.

MEROPE.

Thy sword repell'd it long ago, not I.

POLYPHONTES.

Doubtless thou reckonest on the help of friends.

MEROPE.

Not help of men, although, perhaps, of Gods.

POLYPHONTES.

What Gods? the Gods of concord, civil weal?

MEROPE.

No! the avenging Gods, who punish crime.

POLYPHONTES.

Beware! from thee upbraidings I receive
With pity, nay, with reverence; yet, beware!
I know, I know how hard it is to think
That right, that conscience pointed to a deed,
Where interest seems to have enjoin'd it too.
Most men are led by interest; and the few
Who are not, expiate the general sin,
Involved in one suspicion with the base.
Dizzy the path and perilous the way
Which in a deed like mine a just man treads,
But it is sometimes trodden, oh! believe it.
Yet how *canst* thou believe it? therefore thou
Hast all impunity. Yet, lest thy friends,
Embolden'd by my lenience, think it fear,
And count on like impunity, and rise,
And have to thank thee for a fall, beware!
To rule this kingdom I intend; with sway
Clement, if may be, but to rule it — there
Expect no wavering, no retreat, no change.
And now I leave thee to these rites, esteem'd
Pious, but impious, surely, if their scope

Be to foment old memories of wrath.
Pray, as thou pour'st libations on this tomb,
To be deliver'd from thy foster'd hate,
Unjust suspicion, and erroneous fear.

[POLYPHONTES *goes into the palace.* THE CHORUS *and*
MEROPE *approach the tomb with their offerings.*

THE CHORUS.

Draw, draw near to the tomb!   *strophe.*
Lay honey-cakes on its marge,
Pour the libation of milk,
Deck it with garlands of flowers.
Tears fall thickly the while!
Behold, O King from the dark
House of the grave, what we do.

O Arcadian hills,   *antistrophe.*
Send us the Youth whom ye hide,
Girt with his coat for the chase,
With the low broad hat of the tann'd
Hunter o'ershadowing his brow ;
Grasping firm, in his hand
Advanced, two javelins, not now
Dangerous alone to the deer !

MEROPE.

What shall I bear, O lost   *str.* I.
Husband and King, to thy grave?—
Pure libations, and fresh
Flowers?   But thou, in the gloom,
Discontented, perhaps,
Demandest vengeance, not grief?
Sternly requirest a man,
Light to spring up to thy house?

THE CHORUS.

Vengeance, O Queen, is his due,   *str.* 2.
His most just prayer ; yet his house —
If that might soothe him below —
Prosperous, mighty, came back
In the third generation, the way
Order'd by Fate, to their home ;
And now, glorious, secure,
Fill the wealth-giving thrones
Of their heritage, Pelops' isle.

MEROPE.

Suffering sent them, Death   *ant.* 1.
March'd with them, Hatred and Strife
Met them entering their halls.
For from the day when the first
Heracleidæ received
That Delphic hest to return,
What hath involved them, but blind
Error on error, and blood ?

THE CHORUS.

Truly I hear of a Maid   *ant.* 2.
Of that stock born, who bestow'd
Her blood that so she might make
Victory sure to her race,
When the fight hung in doubt ! but she now,
Honor'd and sung of by all,
Far on Marathon plain,
Gives her name to the spring
Macaria, blessed Child.

MEROPE.

She led the way of death.   *str.* 3.
And the plain of Tegea,
And the grave of Orestes —
Where, in secret seclusion
Of his unreveal'd tomb,
Sleeps Agamemnon's unhappy,
Matricidal, world-famed,
Seven-cubit-statured son —
Sent forth Echemus, the victor, the king,
By whose hand, at the Isthmus,
At the fate-denied straits,
Fell the eldest of the sons of Heracles,
Hyllus, the chief of his house.
Brother follow'd sister
The all-wept way.

THE CHORUS.

Yes ; but his seed still, wiser-counsell'd,
Sail'd by the fate-meant Gulf to their conquest —
Slew their enemies' king, Tisamenus.
Wherefore accept that happier omen !
Yet shall restorer appear to the race.

MEROPE.

Three brothers won the field,   *ant.* 3.
And to two did Destiny
Give the thrones that they conquer'd.
But the third, what delays him
From his unattain'd crown? . . .
Ah Pylades and Electra,
Ever faithful, untired,
Jealous, blood-exacting friends !

Your sons leap upon the foe of your kin,
In the passes of Delphi,
In the temple-built gorge !
There the youngest of the band of conquerors
Perish'd, in sight of the goal.
Thrice son follow'd sire
The all-wept way.

THE CHORUS.

Thou tellest the fate of the last   *str.* 4.
Of the three Heracleidæ.
Not of him, of Cresphontes thou shared'st the lot !
A king, a king was he while he lived,
Swaying the sceptre with predestined hand ;
And now, minister loved,
Holds rule.

MEROPE.

Ah me . . . Ah . . .

THE CHORUS.

For the awful Monarchs below.

MEROPE.

Thou touchest the worst of my ills.   *str.* 5.
Oh had he fallen of old
At the Isthmus, in fight with his foes,
By Achaian, Arcadian spear !
Then had his sepulchre risen
On the high sea-bank, in the sight
Of either Gulf, and remain'd
All-regarded afar,
Noble memorial of worth
Of a valiant Chief, to his own.

THE CHORUS.

There rose up a cry in the streets *ant.* 4.
From the terrified people.
From the altar of Zeus, from the crowd, came a wail.
A blow, a blow was struck, and he fell,
Sullying his garment with dark-streaming blood ;
While stood o'er him a Form —
Some Form

MEROPE.

Ah me . . . Ah . . .

THE CHORUS.

Of a dreadful Presence of fear.

MEROPE.

More piercing the second cry rang, *ant.* 5.
Wail'd from the palace within,
From the Children. . . . The Fury to them,
Fresh from their father, draws near.
Ah bloody axe ! dizzy blows !
In these ears, they thunder, they ring,
These poor ears, still ! and these eyes
Night and day see them fall,
Fiery phantoms of death,
On the fair, curl'd heads of my sons.

THE CHORUS.

Not to thee only hath come *str.* 6.
Sorrow, O Queen, of mankind.
Had not Electra to haunt
A palace defiled by a death unavenged,

For years, in silence, devouring her heart?
But her nursling, her hope, came at last.
Thou, too, rearest in hope,
Far 'mid Arcadian hills,
Somewhere, for vengeance, a champion, a light.
Soon, soon shall Zeus bring him home !
Soon shall he dawn on this land !

MEROPE.

Him in secret, in tears,   *str.* 7.
Month after month, I await
Vainly.   For he, in the glens
Of Lycæus afar,
A gladsome hunter of deer,
Basks in his morning of youth,
Spares not a thought to his home.

THE CHORUS.

Give not thy heart to despair.   *ant.* 6.
No lamentation can loose
Prisoners of death from the grave ;
But Zeus, who accounteth thy quarrel his own,
Still rules, still watches, and numb'reth the hours
Till the sinner, the vengeance, be ripe.
Still, by Acheron stream,
Terrible Deities throned
Sit, and eye grimly the victim unscourged.
Still, still the Dorian boy,
Exiled, remembers his home.

MEROPE.

Him if high-ruling Zeus   *ant.* 7.
Bring to me safe, let the rest

Go as it will !   But if this
Clash with justice, the Gods
Forgive my folly, and work
Vengeance on sinner and sin —
Only to me give my child !

THE CHORUS.

Hear us and help us, Shade of our King !   *str.* 8.

MEROPE.

A return, O Father ! give to thy boy !   *str.* 9.

THE CHORUS.

Send an avenger, Gods of the dead !   *ant.* 8.

MEROPE.

An avenger I ask not — send me my son !   *ant.* 9.

THE CHORUS.

O Queen, for an avenger to appear,
Thinking that so I pray'd aright, I pray'd ;
If I pray'd wrongly, I revoke the prayer.

MEROPE.

Forgive me, maidens, if I seem too slack
In calling vengeance on a murderer's head.
Impious I deem the alliance which he asks,
Requite him words severe for seeming kind,
And righteous, if he falls, I count his fall.
With this, to those unbribed inquisitors
Who in man's inmost bosom sit and judge,
The true avengers these, I leave his deed,

By him shown fair, but, I believe, most foul.
If these condemn him, let them pass his doom!
That doom obtain effect, from Gods or men!
So be it; yet will that more solace bring
To the chafed heart of Justice than to mine.
To hear another tumult in these streets,
To have another murder in these halls,
To see another mighty victim bleed—
Small comfort offers for a woman there!
A woman, O my friends, has one desire:
To see secure, to live with, those she loves.
Can vengeance give me back the murdered? no!
Can it bring home my child? Ah, if it can,
I pray the Furies' ever-restless band,
And pray the Gods, and pray the all-seeing sun:
"Sun, who careerest through the height of Heaven,
When o'er the Arcadian forests thou art come,
And seest my stripling hunter there afield,
Put tightness in thy gold-embossed rein,
And check thy fiery steeds, and, leaning back,
Throw him a pealing word of summons down,
To come, a late avenger, to the aid
Of this poor soul who bare him, and his sire."
If this will bring him back, be this my prayer!
But Vengeance travels in a dangerous way,
Double of issue, full of pits and snares
For all who pass, pursuers and pursued—
That way is dubious for a mother's prayer.
Rather on thee I call, Husband beloved—
May Hermes, herald of the dead, convey
My words below to thee, and make thee hear—
Bring back our son! if may be, without blood!
Install him in thy throne, still without blood!
Grant him to reign there wise and just like thee,

More fortunate than thee, more fairly judged !
This for our son ; and for myself I pray,
Soon, having once beheld him, to descend
Into the quiet gloom, where thou art now.
These words to thine indulgent ear, thy wife,
I send, and these libations pour the while.

> [*They make their offerings at the tomb.* MEROPE *then
> turns to go towards the palace.*]

THE CHORUS.

The dead hath now his offerings duly paid.
But whither go'st thou hence, O Queen, away?

MEROPE.

To receive Arcas, who to-day should come,
Bringing me of my boy the annual news.

THE CHORUS.

No certain news if like the rest it run.

MEROPE.

Certain in this, that 'tis uncertain still.

THE CHORUS.

What keeps him in Arcadia from return?

MEROPE.

His grandsire and his uncles fear the risk.

THE CHORUS.

Of what? it lies with them to make risk none.

MEROPE.

Discovery of a visit made by stealth.

THE CHORUS.

With arms then they should send him, not by stealth.

MEROPE.

With arms they dare not, and by stealth they fear.

THE CHORUS.

I doubt their caution little suits their ward.

MEROPE.

The heart of youth I know; that most I fear.

THE CHORUS.

I augur thou wilt hear some bold resolve.

MEROPE.

I dare not wish it; but, at least, to hear
That my son still survives, in health, in bloom;
To hear that still he loves, still longs for, me,
Yet, with a light uncareworn spirit, turns
Quick from distressful thought, and floats in joy —
Thus much from Arcas, my old servant true,
Who saved him from these murderous halls a babe,
And since has fondly watch'd him night and day
Save for this annual charge, I hope to hear.
If this be all, I know not; but I know,
These many years I live for this alone.

[MEROPE *goes in.*

THE CHORUS.

Much is there which the sea   *str.* I.
Conceals from man, who cannot plumb its depths.
Air to his unwing'd form denies a way,
And keeps its liquid solitudes unscaled.
Even earth, whereon he treads,
So feeble is his march, so slow,
Holds countless tracts untrod.

But more than all unplumb'd,   *ant.* I.
Unscaled, untrodden, is the heart of man.
More than all secrets hid, the way it keeps.
Nor any of our organs so obtuse,
Inaccurate, and frail,
As those wherewith we try to test
Feelings and motives there.

Yea, and not only have we not explored   *str.* 2.
That wide and various world, the heart of others,
But even our own heart, that narrow world
Bounded in our own breast, we hardly know,
Of our own actions dimly trace the causes.
Whether a natural obscureness, hiding
That region in perpetual cloud,
Or our own want of effort, be the bar.

Therefore — while   acts   are   from   their   motives
            judged,   *ant.* 2.
And to one act many most unlike motives,
This pure, that guilty, may have each impell'd —
Power fails us to try clearly if that cause
Assign'd us by the actor be the true one ;
Power fails the man himself to fix distinctly
The cause which drew him to his deed,
And stamp himself, thereafter, bad or good.

The most are bad, wise men have said. *str.* 3.
Let the best rule, they say again.
The best, then, to dominion hath the right.
Rights unconceded and denied,
Surely, if rights, may be by force asserted —
May be, nay should, if for the general weal.
The best, then, to the throne may carve his way,
And strike opposers down,
Free from all guilt of lawlessness,
Or selfish lust of personal power ;
Bent only to serve virtue,
Bent to diminish wrong.

And truly, in this ill-ruled world, *ant.* 3.
Well sometimes may the good desire
To give to virtue her dominion due !
Well may he long to interrupt
The reign of folly, usurpation ever,
Though fenced by sanction of a thousand years !
Well thirst to drag the wrongful ruler down ;
Well purpose to pen back
Into the narrow path of right
The ignorant, headlong multitude,
Who blindly follow, ever,
Blind leaders, to their bane !

But who can say, without a fear : *str.* 4.
That best, who ought to rule, am I ;
The mob, who ought to obey, are these ;
I the one righteous, they the many bad ?
Who, without check of conscience, can aver
That he to power makes way by arms,
Sheds blood, imprisons, banishes, attaints,
Commits all deeds the guilty oftenest do,

Without a single guilty thought,
Arm'd for right only, and the general good?

Therefore, with censure unallay'd,   *ant.* 4.
Therefore, with unexcepting ban,
Zeus and pure-thoughted Justice brand
Imperious self-asserting violence;
Sternly condemn the too bold man, who dares
Elect himself Heaven's destined arm;
And, knowing well man's inmost heart infirm,
However noble the committer be,
His grounds however specious shown,
Turn with averted eyes from deeds of blood.

Thus, though a woman, I was school'd   *epode.*
By those whom I revere.
Whether I learnt their lessons well,
Or, having learnt them, well apply
To what hath in this house befall'n,
If in the event be any proof,
The event will quickly show.

[ÆPYTUS *comes in.*

ÆPYTUS.

Maidens, assure me if they told me true
Who told me that the royal house was here.

THE CHORUS.

Rightly they told thee, and thou art arrived.

ÆPYTUS.

Here, then, it is, where Polyphontes dwells?

THE CHORUS.

He doth; thou hast both house and master right.

ÆPYTUS.

Might some one straight inform him he is sought?

THE CHORUS.

Inform him that thyself, for here he comes.

[POLYPHONTES *comes forth, with* ATTENDANTS *and* GUARDS.

ÆPYTUS.

O King, all hail! I come with weighty news;
Most likely, grateful; but, in all case, sure.

POLYPHONTES.

Speak them, that I may judge their kind myself.

ÆPYTUS.

Accept them in one word, for good or bad:
Æpytus, the Messenian prince, is dead!

POLYPHONTES.

Dead!—and when died he? where? and by what
      hand?
And who art thou, who bringest me such news?

ÆPYTUS.

He perish'd in Arcadia, where he dwelt
With Cypselus; and two days since he died.
One of the train of Cypselus am I.

POLYPHONTES.

Instruct me of the manner of his death.

ÆPYTUS.

That will I do, and to this end I came.
For, being of like age, of birth not mean,

The son of an Arcadian noble, I
Was chosen his companion from a boy ;
And on the hunting-rambles which his heart,
Unquiet, drove him ever to pursue
Through all the lordships of the Arcadian dales,
From chief to chief, I wander'd at his side,
The captain of his squires, and his guard.
On such a hunting-journey, three morns since,
With beaters, hounds, and huntsmen, he and I
Set forth from Tegea, the royal town.
The prince at start seem'd sad, but his regard
Clear'd with blithe travel and the morning air.
We rode from Tegea, through the woods of oaks,
Past Arnê spring, where Rhea gave the babe
Poseidon to the shepherd-boys to hide
From Saturn's search among the new-yean'd lambs
To Mantineia, with its unbaked walls ;
Thence, by the Sea-God's Sanctuary and the tomb
Whither from wintry Mænalus were brought
The bones of Arcas, whence our race is named,
On, to the marshy Orchomenian plain,
And the Stone Coffins ; — then, by Caphyæ Cliffs,
To Pheneos with its craggy citadel.
There, with the chief of that hill-town, we lodged
One night ; and the next day at dawn fared on
By the Three Fountains and the Adder's Hill
To the Stymphalian Lake, our journey's end,
To draw the coverts on Cyllenê's side.
There, on a high green spur which bathes its point
Far in the liquid lake, we sate, and drew
Cates from our hunters' pouch, Arcadian fare,
Sweet chestnuts, barley-cakes, and boar's-flesh dried ;
And as we ate, and rested there, we talk'd
Of places we had pass'd, sport we had had,

Of beasts of chase that haunt the Arcadian hills,
Wild hog, and bear, and mountain-deer, and roe ;
Last, of our quarters with the Arcadian chiefs.
For courteous entertainment, welcome warm,
Sad, reverential homage, had our prince
From all, for his great lineage and his woes ;
All which he own'd, and praised with grateful mind.
But still over his speech a gloom there hung,
As of one shadow'd by impending death ;
And strangely, as we talk'd, he would apply
The story of spots mention'd to his own ;
Telling us, Arnê minded him, he too
Was saved a babe, but to a life obscure,
Which he, the seed of Heracles, dragg'd on
Inglorious, and should drop at last unknown,
Even as those dead unepitaph'd, who lie
In the stone coffins at Orchomenus.
And, then, he bade remember how we pass'd
The Mantineän Sanctuary, forbid
To foot of mortal, where his ancestor,
Named Æpytus like him, having gone in,
Was blinded by the outgushing springs of brine.
Then, turning westward to the Adder's Hill —
Another ancestor, named, too, like me,
Died of a snake-bite, said he, *on that brow ;*
Still at his mountain-tomb men marvel, built
Where, as life ebb'd, his bearers laid him down.
So he play'd on ; then ended, with a smile :
This region is not happy for my race.
We cheer'd him ; but, that moment, from the copse
By the lake-edge, broke the sharp cry of hounds ;
The prickers shouted that the stag was gone.
We sprang upon our feet, we snatch'd our spears,
We bounded down the swarded slope, we plunged

Through the dense ilex-thickets to the dogs.
Far in the woods ahead their music rang;
And many times that morn we coursed in ring
The forests round that belt Cyllenê's side;
Till I, thrown out and tired, came to halt
On that same spur where we had sate at morn.
And resting there to breathe, I watch'd the chase —
Rare, straggling hunters, foil'd by brake and crag,
And the prince, single, pressing on the rear
Of that unflagging quarry and the hounds.
Now in the woods far down I saw them cross
An open glade; now he was high aloft
On some tall scar fringed with dark feathery pines,
Peering to spy a goat-track down the cliff,
Cheering with hand, and voice, and horn his dogs.
At last the cry drew to the water's edge —
And through the brushwood, to the pebbly strand,
Broke, black with sweat, the antler'd mountain-stag,
And took the lake.   Two hounds alone pursued,
Then came the prince; he shouted and plunged in.
— There is a chasm rifted in the base
Of that unfooted precipice, whose rock
Walls on one side the deep Stymphalian Lake;
There the lake-waters, which in ages gone
Wash'd, as the marks upon the hills still show,
All the Stymphalian plain, are now suck'd down.
A headland, with one aged plane-tree crown'd,
Parts from this cave-pierced cliff the shelving bay
Where first the chase plunged in; the bay is
        smooth,
But round the headland's point a current sets,
Strong, black, tempestuous, to the cavern-mouth.
Stoutly, under the headland's lee, they swam;
But when they came abreast the point, the race

Caught them as wind takes feathers, whirl'd them
　　round
Struggling in vain to cross it, swept them on,
Stag, dogs, and hunter, to the yawning gulph.
All this, O King, not piecemeal, as to thee
Now told, but in one flashing instant pass'd.
While from the turf whereon I lay I sprang
And took three strides, quarry and dogs were gone;
A moment more — I saw the prince turn round
Once in the black and arrowy race, and cast
An arm aloft for help ; then sweep beneath
The low-brow'd cavern-arch, and disappear.
And what I could, I did — to call by cries
Some straggling hunters to my aid, to rouse
Fishers who live on the lake-side, to launch
Boats, and approach, near as we dared, the chasm.
But of the prince nothing remain'd, save this,
His boar-spear's broken shaft, back on the lake
Cast by the rumbling subterranean stream ;
And this, at landing spied by us and saved,
His broad-brimm'd hunter's hat, which, in the bay,
Where first the stag took water, floated still.
And I across the mountains brought with haste
To Cypselus, at Basilis, this news —
Basilis, his new city, which he now
Near Lycosura builds, Lycaon's town,
First city founded on the earth by men.
He to thee sends me on, in one thing glad,
While all else grieves him, that his grandchild's death
Extinguishes distrust 'twixt him and thee.
But I from our deplored mischance learn this :
The man who to untimely death is doom'd,
Vainly you hedge him from the assault of harm ;
He bears the seed of ruin in himself.

THE CHORUS.

So dies the last shoot of our royal tree !
Who shall tell Merope this heavy news?

POLYPHONTES.

Stranger, this news thou bringest is too great
For instant comment, having many sides
Of import, and in silence best received,
Whether it turn at last to joy or woe.
But thou, the zealous bearer, hast no part
In what it hath of painful, whether now,
First heard, or in its future issue shown.
Thou for thy labor hast deserved our best
Refreshment, needed by thee, as I judge,
With mountain-travel and night-watching spent. —
To the guest-chamber lead him, some one ! give
All entertainment which a traveller needs,
And such as fits a royal house to show ;
To friends, still more, and laborers in our cause.

[ATTENDANTS *conduct* ÆPYTUS *within the palace.*

THE CHORUS.

The youth is gone within ; alas ! he bears
A presence sad for some one through those doors.

POLYPHONTES.

Admire then, maidens, how in one short hour
The schemes, pursued in vain for twenty years,
Are — by a stroke, though undesired, complete —
Crown'd with success, not in my way, but Heaven's !
This at a moment, too, when I had urged
A last, long-cherish'd project, in my aim

Of peace, and been repulsed with hate and scorn.
Fair terms of reconcilement, equal rule,
I offer'd to my foes, and they refused ;
Worse terms than mine they have obtain'd from
      Heaven.
Dire is this blow for Merope ; and I
Wish'd, truly wish'd, solution to our broil
Other than by this death ; but it hath come !
I speak no word of boast, but this I say :
A private loss here founds a nation's peace.

              [POLYPHONTES *goes out.*

THE CHORUS.

Peace, who tarriest too long ;   *str.*
Peace, with delight in thy train ;
Come, come back to our prayer !
Then shall the revel again
Visit our streets, and the sound
Of the harp be heard with the pipe,
When the flashing torches appear
In the marriage-train coming on,
With dancing maidens and boys —
While the matrons come to the doors,
And the old men rise from their bench,
When the youths bring home the bride.

Not condemn'd by my voice   *ant.*
He who restores thee shall be,
Not unfavor'd by Heaven.
Surely no sinner the man,
Dread though his acts, to whose hand
Such a boon to bring hath been given.
Let her come, fair Peace ! let her come !
But the demons long nourish'd here,

Murder, Discord, and Hate,
In the stormy desolate waves
Of the Thracian Sea let her leave,
Or the howling outermost main !

> [MEROPE *comes forth.*

MEROPE.

A whisper through the palace flies of one
Arrived from Tegea with weighty news ;
And I came, thinking to find Arcas here.
Ye have not left this gate, which he must pass ;
Tell me — hath one not come ? or, worse mischance,
Come, but been intercepted by the King ?

THE CHORUS.

A messenger, sent from Arcadia here,
Arrived, and of the King had speech but now.

MEROPE.

Ah me ! the wrong expectant got his news.

THE CHORUS.

The message brought was for the King design'd.

MEROPE.

How so ? was Arcas not the messenger ?

THE CHORUS.

A younger man, and of a different name.

MEROPE.

And what Arcadian news had he to tell ?

THE CHORUS.

Learn that from other lips, O Queen, than mine.

MEROPE.

He kept his tale, then, for the King alone?

THE CHORUS.

His tale was meeter for that ear than thine.

MEROPE.

Why dost thou falter, and make half reply?

THE CHORUS.

O thrice unhappy, how I groan thy fate!

MEROPE.

Thou frightenest and confound'st me by thy words.
O were but Arcas come, all would be well!

THE CHORUS.

If so, all's well: for look, the old man speeds
Up from the city tow'rd this gated hill.

[ARCAS *comes in.*

MEROPE.

Not with the failing breath and foot of age
My faithful follower comes.   Welcome, old friend!

ARCAS.

Faithful, not welcome, when my tale is told.
O that my over-speed and bursting grief
Had on the journey choked my laboring breath,
And lock'd my speech for ever in my breast!

Yet then another man would bring this news,
Wherewith from end to end Arcadia rings. —
O honor'd Queen, thy son, my charge, is gone.

THE CHORUS.

Too suddenly thou tellest such a loss.
Look up, O Queen ! look up, O mistress dear !
Look up, and see thy friends who comfort thee.

MEROPE.

Ah . . . ah . . . ah me !

THE CHORUS.

And I, too, say, ah me !

ARCAS.

Forgive, forgive the bringer of such news !

MEROPE.

Better from thine than from an enemy's tongue.

THE CHORUS.

And yet no enemy did this, O Queen :
But the wit-baffling will and hand of Heaven.

ARCAS.

No enemy ! and what hast thou, then, heard ?
Swift as I came, hath falsehood been before ?

THE CHORUS.

A youth arrived but now — the son, he said,
Of an Arcadian lord — our prince's friend —
Jaded with travel, clad in hunter's garb.

He brought report that his own eyes had seen
The prince, in chase after a swimming stag,
Swept down a chasm rifted in the cliff
Which hangs o'er the Stymphalian Lake, and drown'd.

ARCAS.

Ah me ! with what a foot doth treason post,
While loyalty, with all her speed, is slow !
Another tale, I trow, thy messenger
For the King's private ear reserves, like this
In one thing only, that the prince is dead.

THE CHORUS.

And how then runs this true and private tale?

ARCAS.

As much to the King's wish, more to his shame,
This young Arcadian noble, guard and mate
To Æpytus, the king seduced with gold,
And had him at the prince's side in leash,
Ready to slip on his unconscious prey.
He on a hunting party two days since,
Among the forests on Cyllenê's side,
Perform'd good service for his bloody wage ;
Our prince, and the good Laias, whom his ward
Had in a father's place, he basely murder'd.
'Tis so, 'tis so, alas, for see the proof:
Uncle and nephew disappear ; their death
Is charged against this stripling ; agents, fee'd
To ply 'twixt the Messenian king and him,
Come forth, denounce the traffic and the traitor.
Seized, he escapes — and next I find him here.
Take this for true, the other tale for feign'd.

THE CHORUS.

The youth, thou say'st, we saw and heard but now —

ARCAS.

He comes to tell his prompter he hath sped.

THE CHORUS.

Still he repeats the drowning story here.

ARCAS.

To thee — that needs no Œdipus to explain.

THE CHORUS.

Interpret, then ; for we, it seems, are dull.

ARCAS.

Your King desired the profit of his death,
Not the black credit of his murderer.
That stern word *" murder "* had too dread a sound
For the Messenian hearts, who loved the prince.

THE CHORUS.

Suspicion grave I see, but no firm proof.

MEROPE.

Peace ! peace ! all's clear.—The wicked watch and work
While the good sleep ; the workers have the day.
Yes ! yes ! now I conceive the liberal grace
Of this far-scheming tyrant, and his boon
Of heirship to his kingdom for my son :
He had his murderer ready, and the sword
Lifted, and that unwish'd-for heirship void —

A tale, meanwhile, forged for his subjects' ears —
And me, henceforth sole rival with himself
In their allegiance, me, in my son's death-hour,
When all turn'd tow'rds me, me he would have shown
To my Messenians, duped, disarm'd, despised,
The willing sharer of his guilty rule,
All claim to succor forfeit, to myself
Hateful, by each Messenian heart abhorr'd.
His offers I repell'd — but what of that?
If with no rage, no fire of righteous hate,
Such as ere now hath spurr'd to fearful deeds
Weak women with a thousandth part my wrongs,
But calm, but unresentful, I endured
His offers, coldly heard them, cold repell'd?
How must men think me abject, void of heart,
While all this time I bear to linger on
In this blood-deluged palace, in whose halls
Either a vengeful Fury I should stalk,
Or else not live at all ! — but here I haunt,
A pale, unmeaning ghost, powerless to fright
Or harm, and nurse my longing for my son,
A helpless one, I know it — but the Gods
Have temper'd me e'en thus, and, in some souls,
Misery, which rouses others, breaks the spring.
And even now, my son, ah me ! my son,
Fain would I fade away, as I have lived,
Without a cry, a struggle, or a blow,
All vengeance unattempted, and descend
To the invisible plains, to roam with thee,
Fit denizen, the lampless under-world ——
But with what eyes should I encounter there
My husband, wandering with his stern compeers,
Amphiaraos, or Mycenæ's king,
Who led the Greeks to Ilium, Agamemnon,

Betray'd like him, but, not like him, avenged?
Or with what voice shall I the questions meet
Of my two elder sons, slain long ago,
Who sadly ask me, what, if not revenge,
Kept me, their mother, from their side so long?
Or how reply to thee, my child last-born,
Last-murder'd, who reproachfully wilt say:
Mother, I well believed thou lived'st on
In the detested palace of thy foe,
With patience on thy face, death in thy heart,
Counting, till I grew up, the laggard years,
That our joint hands might then together pay
To our unhappy house the debt we owe.
My death makes my debt void, and doubles thine —
But down thou fleest here, and leav'st our scourge
Triumphant, and condemnest all our race
To lie in gloom for ever unappeased.
What shall I have to answer to such words? —
No, something must be dared; and, great as erst
Our dastard patience, be our daring now!
Come, ye swift Furies, who to him ye haunt
Permit no peace till your behests are done;
Come Hermes, who dost friend the unjustly kill'd,
And canst teach simple ones to plot and feign;
Come, lightning Passion, that with foot of fire
Advancest to the middle of a deed
Almost before 'tis plann'd; come, glowing Hate;
Come, baneful Mischief, from thy murky den
Under the dripping black Tartarean cliff
Which Styx's awful waters trickle down —
Inspire this coward heart, this flagging arm!
How say ye, maidens, do ye know these prayers?
Are these words Merope's — is this voice mine?
Old man, old man, thou hadst my boy in charge,

And he is lost, and thou hast that to atone !
Fly, find me on the instant where confer
The murderer and his impious setter-on —
And ye, keep faithful silence, friends, and mark
What one weak woman can achieve alone.

ARCAS.

O mistress, by the Gods, do nothing rash !

MEROPE.

Unfaithful servant, dost thou, too, desert me?

ARCAS.

I go ! I go ! — The King holds council — there
Will I seek tidings.   Take, the while, this word:
Attempting deeds beyond thy power to do,
Thou nothing profitest thy friends, but mak'st
Our misery more, and thine own ruin sure.

[ARCAS *goes out.*

THE CHORUS.

I have heard, O Queen, how a **prince,**   *str.* I.
Agamemnon's son, in Mycenæ,
Orestes, died but in name,
Lived for the death of his foes.

MEROPE.

Peace !

THE CHORUS.

What is it?

MEROPE.

Alas,
Thou destroyest me !

THE CHORUS.

How?

MEROPE.

Whispering hope of a life
Which no stranger unknown,
But the faithful servant and nurse,
Whose tears warrant his truth,
Bears sad witness is lost.

THE CHORUS.

Wheresoe'er men are, there is grief.   *ant.* 1
In a thousand countries, a thousand
Homes, e'en now is there wail;
Mothers lamenting their sons.

MEROPE.

Yes ——

THE CHORUS.

Thou knowest it?

MEROPE.

This,
Who lives, witnesses.

THE CHORUS.

True.

MEROPE.

But is it only a fate
Sure, all-common, to lose
In a land of friends, by a friend,
One last, murder-saved child?

THE CHORUS.

Ah me !   *str.* 2.

MEROPE.

Thou confessest the prize
In the rushing, thundering, mad,
Cloud-enveloped, obscure,
Unapplauded, unsung
Race of calamity, mine?

THE CHORUS.

None can truly claim that
Mournful pre-eminence, not
Thou.

MEROPE.

Fate *gives* it, ah me !

THE CHORUS.

Not, above all, in the doubts,
Double and clashing, that hang——

MEROPE.

What then?   *ant.* 2.
Seems it lighter, my loss,
If, perhaps, unpierced by the sword,
My child lies in his jagg'd
Sunless prison of rock,
On the black wave borne to and fro?

THE CHORUS.

Worse, far worse, if his friend,
If the Arcadian within,
If——

MEROPE (*with a start*).

How say'st thou? within? . . .

THE CHORUS.

He in the guest-chamber now,
Faithlessly murder'd his friend.

MEROPE.

Ye, too, ye, too, join to betray, then
Your Queen!

THE CHORUS.

What is this?

MEROPE.

Ye knew,
O false friends! into what
Haven the murderer had dropp'd?
Ye kept silence?

THE CHORUS.

In fear,
O loved mistress! in fear,
Dreading thine over-wrought mood,
What I knew, I conceal'd.

MEROPE.

Swear by the Gods henceforth to obey me!

THE CHORUS.

Unhappy one, what deed
Purposes thy despair?
I promise; but I fear.

MEROPE.

From the altar, the unavenged tomb,
Fetch me the sacrifice-axe ! ——

> [THE CHORUS *goes towards the tomb of* CRESPHONTES,
> *and their leader brings back the axe.*

O Husband, O clothed
With the grave's everlasting,
All-covering darkness !   O King,
Well-mourn'd, but ill-avenged !
Approv'st thou thy wife now? ——
The axe ! — who brings it ?

THE CHORUS.

'Tis here !
But thy gesture, thy look,
Appall me, shake me with awe.

MEROPE.

Thrust back now the bolt of that door !

THE CHORUS.

Alas ! alas ! —
Behold the fastenings withdrawn
Of the guest-chamber door ! —
Ah ! I beseech thee — with tears ——

MEROPE.

Throw the door open !

THE CHORUS.

'Tis done ! . . .

> [*The door of the house is thrown open : the interior
> of the guest-chamber is discovered, with* ÆPYTUS
> *asleep on a couch.*

MEROPE.

He sleeps — sleeps calm.   O ye all-seeing Gods!
Thus peacefully do ye let sinners sleep,
While troubled innocents toss, and lie awake?
What sweeter sleep than this could I desire
For thee, my child, if thou wert yet alive?
How often have I dream'd of thee like this,
With thy soil'd hunting-coat, and sandals torn,
Asleep in the Arcadian glens at noon,
Thy head droop'd softly, and the golden curls
Clustering o'er thy white forehead, like a girl's;
The short proud lip showing thy race, thy cheeks
Brown'd with thine open-air, free, hunter's life.
Ah me!
And where dost thou sleep now, my innocent boy? —
In some dark fir-tree's shadow, amid rocks
Untrodden, on Cyllenê's desolate side;
Where travellers never pass, where only come
Wild beasts, and vultures sailing overhead.
There, there thou liest now, my hapless child!
Stretch'd among briers and stones, the slow, black gore
Oozing through thy soak'd hunting-shirt, with limbs
Yet stark from the death-struggle, tight-clench'd hands,
And eyeballs staring for revenge in vain.
Ah miserable!
And thou, thou fair-skinn'd Serpent! thou art laid
In a rich chamber, on a happy bed,
In a king's house, thy victim's heritage;
And drink'st untroubled slumber, to sleep off
The toils of thy foul service, till thou wake
Refresh'd, and claim thy master's thanks and gold. —
Wake up in hell from thine unhallow'd sleep,
Thou smiling Fiend, and claim thy guerdon there!

Wake amid gloom, and howling, and the noise
Of sinners pinion'd on the torturing wheel,
And the stanch Furies' never-silent scourge.
And bid the chief tormentors there provide
For a grand culprit shortly coming down.
Go thou the first, and usher in thy lord !
A more just stroke than that thou gav'st my son
Take ——

[MEROPE *advances towards the sleeping* ÆPYTUS, *with the axe uplifted. At the same moment* ARCAS *re-enters.*

ARCAS (*to* THE CHORUS).

   Not with him to council did the King
Carry his messenger, but left him here.

       [*Sees* MEROPE *and* ÆPYTUS.
O Gods ! . . .

MEROPE.

   Foolish old man, thou spoil'st my blow !

ARCAS.

What do I see ? . . .

MEROPE.

      A murderer at death's door.
Therefore no words !

ARCAS.

    A murderer ? . . .

MEROPE.

        And a captive
To the dear next-of-kin of him he murder'd.
Stand, and let vengeance pass !

ARCAS.

Hold, O Queen, hold !
Thou know'st not whom thou strik'st. . . .

MEROPE.

I know his crime.

ARCAS.

Unhappy one ! thou strik'st ——

MEROPE.

A most just blow.

ARCAS.

No, by the Gods, thou slay'st ——

MEROPE.

Stand off !

ARCAS.

Thy son !

MEROPE.

Ah !

[*She lets the axe drop, and falls insensible.*

ÆPYTUS (*awaking*).

Who are these ? What shrill, ear-piercing scream
Wakes me thus kindly from the perilous sleep
Wherewith fatigue and youth had bound mine eyes,
Even in the deadly palace of my foe ? —
Arcas ! Thou here ?

ARCAS (*embracing him*).

O my dear master ! O
My child, my charge beloved, welcome to life !
As dead we held thee, mourn'd for thee as dead.

ÆPYTUS.

In word I died, that I in deed might live.
But who are these?

ARCAS.

Messenian maidens, friends.

ÆPYTUS.

And, Arcas! — but I tremble!

ARCAS.

Boldly ask.

ÆPYTUS.

That black-robed, swooning figure? . . .

ARCAS.

Merope.

ÆPYTUS.

O mother! mother!

MEROPE.

Who upbraids me? Ah! . . .
[*seeing the axe.*

ÆPYTUS.

Upbraids thee? no one.

MEROPE.

Thou dost well: but take . . .

ÆPYTUS.

What wav'st thou off?

MEROPE.

That murderous axe away !

ÆPYTUS.

Thy son is here.

MEROPE.

One said so, sure, but now.

ÆPYTUS.

Here, here thou hast him !

MEROPE.

Slaughter'd by this hand ! . . .

ÆPYTUS.

No, by the Gods, alive and like to live !

MEROPE.

What, thou? — I dream ——

ÆPYTUS.

May'st thou dream ever so !

MEROPE (*advancing towards him*).

My child? unhurt? . . .

ÆPYTUS.

Only by over joy.

MEROPE.

Art thou, then, come? . . .

ÆPYTUS.

Never to part again.

[*They fall into one another's arms.   Then* MEROPE,
   holding ÆPYTUS *by the hand, turns to* THE CHORUS.

MEROPE.

O kind Messenian maidens, O my friends,
Bear witness, see, mark well, on what a head
My first stroke of revenge had nearly fallen !

THE CHORUS.

We see, dear mistress : and we say, the Gods,
As hitherto they kept him, keep him now.

MEROPE.   *str.*

O my son !
I have, I have thee . . . the years
Fly back, my child ! and thou seem'st
Ne'er to have gone from these eyes,
Never been torn from this breast.

ÆPYTUS.

Mother, my heart runs over ; but the time
Presses me, chides me, will not let me weep.

MEROPE.

Fearest thou now?

ÆPYTUS.

I fear not, but I think on my design.

MEROPE.

At the undried fount of this breast,
A babe, thou smilest again.
Thy brothers play at my feet,
Early-slain innocents ! near,
Thy kind-speaking father stands.

ÆPYTUS.

Remember, to avenge his death I come !

MEROPE.

Ah . . . revenge !   *ant.*
That word ! it kills me !   I see
Once more roll back on my house,
Never to ebb, the accurst
All-flooding ocean of blood.

ÆPYTUS.

Mother, sometimes the justice of the Gods
Appoints the way to peace through shedding blood.

MEROPE.

Sorrowful peace !

ÆPYTUS.

And yet the only peace to us allow'd.

MEROPE.

From the first-wrought vengeance is born
A long succession of crimes.
Fresh blood flows, calling for blood.
Fathers, sons, grandsons, are all
One death-dealing vengeful train.

ÆPYTUS.

Mother, thy fears are idle ; for I come
To close an old wound, not to open new.
In all else willing to be taught, in this
Instruct me not ; I have my lesson clear.
Arcas, seek out my uncle Laias, now
Conferring in the city with our friends ;
Here bring him, ere the King come back from council.
That, how to accomplish what the Gods enjoin,
And the slow-ripening time at last prepares,
We two with thee, my mother, may consult ;
For whose help dare I count on, if not thine?

MEROPE.

Approves my brother Laias this intent?

ÆPYTUS.

Yes, and alone is with me here to share.

MEROPE.

And what of thine Arcadian mate, who bears
Suspicion from thy grandsire of thy death,
For whom, as I suppose, thou passest here?

ÆPYTUS.

Sworn to our plot he is ; if false surmise
Fix him the author of my death, I know not.

MEROPE.

Proof, not surmise, shows him in commerce close ——

ÆPYTUS.

With this Messenian tyrant — that I know.

MEROPE.

And entertain'st thou, child, such dangerous friends?

ÆPYTUS.

This commerce for my best behoof he plies.

MEROPE.

That thou mayst read thine enemy's counsel plain?

ÆPYTUS.

Too dear his secret wiles have cost our house.

MEROPE.

And of his unsure agent what demands he?

ÆPYTUS.

News of my business, pastime, temper, friends.

MEROPE.

His messages, then, point not to thy murder?

ÆPYTUS.

Not yet, though such, no doubt, his final aim.

MEROPE.

And what Arcadian helpers bring'st thou here?

ÆPYTUS.

Laias alone; no errand mine for crowds.

MEROPE.

On what relying, to crush such a foe?

ÆPYTUS.

One sudden stroke, and the Messenians' love.

MEROPE.

O thou long-lost, long seen in dreams alone,
But now seen face to face, my only child!
Why wilt thou fly to lose as soon as found
My new-won treasure, thy belovéd life?
Or how expectest not to lose, who com'st
With such slight means to cope with such a foe?
Thine enemy thou know'st not, nor his strength.
The stroke thou purposest is desperate, rash —
Yet grant that it succeeds — thou hast behind
The stricken King a second enemy
Scarce dangerous less than him, the Dorian lords.
These are not now the savage band who erst
Follow'd thy father from their northern hills,
Mere ruthless and uncounsell'd wolves of war,
Good to obey, without a leader nought.
Their chief hath train'd them, made them like himself,
Sagacious, men of iron, watchful, firm,
Against surprise and sudden panic proof.
Their master fall'n, these will not flinch, but band
To keep their master's power; thou wilt find
Behind his corpse their hedge of serried spears.
But, to match these, thou hast the people's love?

On what a reed, my child, thou leanest there !
Knowest thou not how timorous, how unsure,
How useless an ally a people is
Against the one and certain arm of power?
Thy father perish'd in this people's cause,
Perish'd before their eyes, yet no man stirr'd !
For years, his widow, in their sight I stand,
A never-changing index to revenge —
What help, what vengeance, at their hands have I? —
At least, if thou wilt trust them, try them first.
Against the King himself array the host
Thou countest on to back thee 'gainst his lords ;
First rally the Messenians to thy cause,
Give them cohesion, purpose, and resolve,
Marshal them to an army — then advance,
Then try the issue ; and not, rushing on
Single and friendless, give to certain death
That dear-beloved, that young, that gracious head.
Be guided, O my son ! spurn counsel not !
For know thou this, a violent heart hath been
Fatal to all the race of Heracles.

THE CHORUS.

With sage experience she speaks ; and thou,
O Æpytus, weigh well her counsel given.

ÆPYTUS.

Ill counsel, in my judgment, gives she here,
Maidens, and reads experience much amiss ;
Discrediting the succor which our cause
Might from the people draw, if rightly used ;
Advising us a course which would, indeed,
If follow'd, make their succor slack and null.

A people is no army, train'd to fight,
A passive engine, at their general's will;
And, if so used, proves, as thou say'st, unsure.
A people, like a common man, is dull,
Is lifeless, while its heart remains untouch'd;
A fool can drive it, and a fly may scare.
When it admires and loves, its heart awakes:
Then irresistibly it lives, it works;
A people, then, is an ally indeed —
It is ten thousand fiery wills in one.
Now I, if I invite them to run risk
Of life for my advantage, and myself,
Who chiefly profit, run no more than they —
How shall I rouse their love, their ardor so?
But, if some signal, unassisted stroke,
Dealt at my own sole risk, before their eyes,
Announces me their rightful prince return'd —
The undegenerate blood of Heracles —
The daring claimant of a perilous throne —
How might not such a sight as this revive
Their loyal passion tow'rd my father's house,
Kindle their hearts, make them no more a mob,
A craven mob, but a devouring fire?
Then might I use them, then, for one who thus
Spares not himself, themselves they will not spare.
Haply, had but one daring soul stood forth
To rally them and lead them to revenge,
When my great father fell, they had replied!
Alas! our foe alone stood forward then.
And thou, my mother, hadst thou made a sign —
Hadst thou, from thy forlorn and captive state
Of widowhood in these polluted halls,
Thy prison-house, raised one imploring cry —
Who knows but that avengers thou hadst found?

But mute thou sat'st, and each Messenian heart
In thy despondency desponded too.
Enough of this ! — Though not a finger stir
To succor me in my extremest need ;
Though all free spirits in this land were dead,
And only slaves and tyrants left alive ;
Yet for me, mother, I had liefer die
On native ground, than drag the tedious hours
Of a protected exile any more.
Hate, duty, interest, passion call one way ;
Here stand I now, and the attempt shall be.

THE CHORUS.

Prudence is on the other side ; but deeds
Condemn'd by prudence have sometimes gone well.

MEROPE.

Not till the ways of prudence all are tried,
And tried in vain, the turn of rashness comes.
Thou leapest to thy deed, and hast not ask'd
Thy kinsfolk and thy father's friends for aid.

ÆPYTUS.

And to what friends should I for aid apply?

MEROPE.

The royal race of Temenus, in Argos ——

ÆPYTUS.

That house, like ours, intestine murder maims.

MEROPE.

Thy Spartan cousins, Procles and his brother ——

ÆPYTUS.

Love a won cause, but not a cause to win.

MEROPE.

My father, then, and his Arcadian chiefs ——

ÆPYTUS.

Mean still to keep aloof from Dorian broil.

MEROPE.

Wait, then, until sufficient help appears.

ÆPYTUS.

Orestes in Mycenæ had no more.

MEROPE.

He to fulfil an order raised his hand.

ÆPYTUS.

What order more precise had he than I?

MEROPE.

Apollo peal'd it from his Delphian cave.

ÆPYTUS.

A mother's murder needed hest divine.

MEROPE.

He had a hest, at least, and thou hast none.

ÆPYTUS.

The Gods command not where the heart speaks clear.

MEROPE.

Thou wilt destroy, I see, thyself and us.

ÆPYTUS.

O suffering ! O calamity ! how ten,
How twentyfold worse are ye, when your blows
Not only wound the sense, but kill the soul,
The noble thought, which is alone the man !
That I, to-day returning, find myself
Orphan'd of both my parents — by his foes
My father, by your strokes my mother slain !
For this is not my mother, who dissuades,
At the dread altar of her husband's tomb,
His son from vengeance on his murderer ;
And not alone dissuades him, but compares
His just revenge to an unnatural deed,
A deed so awful, that the general tongue
Fluent of horrors, falters to relate it —
Of darkness so tremendous, that its author,
Though to his act empower'd, nay, impell'd,
By the oracular sentence of the Gods,
Fled, for years after, o'er the face of earth,
A frenzied wanderer, a God-driven man,
And hardly yet, some say, hath found a grave —
With such a deed as *this* thou matchest mine,
Which Nature sanctions, which the innocent blood
Clamors to find fulfill'd, which good men praise,
And only bad men joy to see undone !
O honor'd father ! hide thee in thy grave
Deep as thou canst, for hence no succor comes ;
Since from thy faithful subjects what revenge
Canst thou expect, when thus thy widow fails ?
Alas ! an adamantine strength indeed,

Past expectation, hath thy murderer built ;
For this is the true strength of guilty kings,
When they corrupt the souls of those they rule.

THE CHORUS.

Zeal makes him most unjust ; but, in good time,
Here, as I guess, the noble Laias comes.

LAIAS.

Break off, break off your talking, and depart
Each to his post, where the occasion calls ;
Lest from the council-chamber presently
The King return, and find you prating here.
A time will come for greetings ; but to-day
The hour for words is gone, is come for deeds.

ÆPYTUS.

O princely Laias ! to what purpose calls
The occasion, if our chief confederate fails?
My mother stands aloof, and blames our deed.

LAIAS.

My royal sister? . . . but, without some cause,
I know, she honors not the dead so ill.

MEROPE.

Brother, it seems thy sister must present,
At this first meeting after absence long,
Not welcome, exculpation to her kin ;
Yet exculpation needs it, if I seek,
A woman and a mother, to avert
Risk from my new-restored, my only son?—

Sometimes, when he was gone, I wish'd him back,
Risk what he might ; now that I have him here,
Now that I feed mine eyes on that young face,
Hear that fresh voice, and clasp that gold-lock'd head,
I shudder, Laias, to commit my child
To murder's dread arena, where I saw
His father and his ill-starr'd brethren fall !
I loathe for him the slippery way of blood ;
I ask if bloodless means may gain his end.
In me the fever of revengeful hate,
Passion's first furious longing to imbrue
Our own right hand in the detested blood
Of enemies, and count their dying groans —
If in this feeble bosom such a fire
Did ever burn — is long by time allay'd,
And I would now have Justice strike, not me.
Besides — for from my brother and my son
.I hide not even this — the reverence deep,
Remorseful, tow'rd my hostile solitude,
By Polyphontes never fail'd-in once
Through twenty years ; his mournful anxious zeal
To efface in me the memory of his crime —
Though it efface not that, yet makes me wish
His death a public, not a personal act,
Treacherously plotted 'twixt my son and me ;
To whom this day he came to proffer peace,
Treaty, and to this kingdom for my son
Heirship, with fair intent, as I believe. —
For that he plots thy death, account it false ;

(*To* ÆPYTUS.)

Number it with the thousand rumors vain,
Figments of plots, wherewith intriguers fill
The enforcéd leisure of an exile's ear.

Immersed in serious state-craft is the King,
Bent above all to pacify, to rule,
Rigidly, yet in settled calm, this realm ;
Not prone, all say, averse to bloodshed now.—
So much is due to truth, even tow'rds our foe.

(*To* LAIAS.)

Do I, then, give to usurpation grace,
And from his natural rights my son debar?
Not so ! let him — and none shall be more prompt
Than I to help — raise his Messenian friends ;
Let him fetch succors from Arcadia, gain
His Argive or his Spartan cousins' aid ;
Let him do this, do aught but recommence
Murder's uncertain, secret, perilous game —
And I, when to his righteous standard down
Flies Victory wing'd, and Justice raises *then*
Her sword, will be the first to bid it fall.
If, haply, at this moment, such attempt
Promise not fair, let him a little while
Have faith, and trust the future and the Gods.
He may ; for never did the Gods allow
Fast permanence to an ill-gotten throne. —
These are but woman's words — yet, Laias, thou
Despise them not ! for, brother, thou and I
Were not among the feuds of warrior-chiefs,
Each sovereign for his dear-bought hour, born ;
But in the pastoral Arcadia rear'd,
With Cypselus our father, where we saw
The simple patriarchal state of kings,
Where sire to son transmits the unquestion'd crown,
Unhack'd, unsmirch'd, unbloodied, and have learnt
That spotless hands unshaken sceptres hold.
Having learnt this, then, use thy knowledge now.

THE CHORUS.

Which way to lean I know not : bloody strokes
Are never free from doubt, though sometimes due.

LAIAS.

O Merope, the common heart of man
Agrees to deem some deeds so dark in guilt,
That neither gratitude, nor tie of race,
Womanly pity, nor maternal fear,
Nor any pleader else, shall be indulged
To breathe a syllable to bar revenge.
All this, no doubt, thou to thyself hast urged —
Time presses, so that theme forbear I now ;
Direct to thy dissuasions I reply.
Blood-founded thrones, thou say'st, are insecure ;
Our father's kingdom, because pure, is safe.
True ; but what cause to our Arcadia gives
Its privileged immunity from blood,
But that, since first the black and fruitful Earth
In the primeval mountain-forests bore
Pelasgus, our forefather and mankind's,
Legitimately sire to son, with us,
Bequeaths the allegiance of our shepherd-tribes,
More loyal, as our line continues more ? —
How can your Heracleidan chiefs inspire
This awe which guards our earth-sprung, lineal kings ?
What permanence, what stability like ours,
Whether blood flows or no, can yet invest
The broken order of your Dorian thrones,
Fix'd yesterday, and ten times changed since then ? —
Two brothers, and their orphan nephews, strove
For the three conquer'd kingdoms of this isle ;
The eldest, mightiest brother, Temenus, took

Argos ; a juggle to Cresphontes gave
Messenia; to those helpless Boys, the lot
Worst of the three, the stony Sparta, fell.
August, indeed, was the foundation here !
What follow'd ? — His most trusted kinsman slew
Cresphontes in Messenia ; Temenus
Perish'd in Argos by his jealous sons ;
The Spartan Brothers with their guardian strive.
Can houses thus ill-seated, thus embroil'd,
Thus little founded in their subjects' love,
Practise the indulgent, bloodless policy
Of dynasties long-fix'd, and honor'd long ?
No ! Vigor and severity must chain
Popular reverence to these recent lines.
Be their first-founded order strict maintain'd —
Their murder'd rulers terribly avenged —
Ruthlessly their rebellious subjects crush'd !
Since policy bids thus, what fouler death
Than thine illustrious husband's to avenge
Shall we select ? than Polyphontes, what
More daring and more grand offender find ?
Justice, my sister, long demands this blow,
And Wisdom, now thou seest, demands it too.
To strike it, then, dissuade thy son no more ;
For to live disobedient to these two,
Justice and Wisdom, is no life at all.

THE CHORUS.

The Gods, O mistress dear ! the hard-soul'd man,
Who spared not others, bid not us to spare.

MEROPE.

Alas ! against my brother, son, and friends,
One, and a woman, how can I prevail ? —

O brother, thou hast conquer'd ; yet, I fear !
Son ! with a doubting heart thy mother yields ;
May it turn happier than my doubts portend !

LAIAS.

Meantime on thee the task of silence only
Shall be imposed ; to us shall be the deed.
Now, not another word, but to our act !
Nephew ! thy friends are sounded, and prove true.
Thy father's murderer, in the public place,
Performs, this noon, a solemn sacrifice ;
Be with him — choose the moment — strike thy blow !
If prudence counsels thee to go unarm'd,
The sacrificer's axe will serve thy turn.
To me and the Messenians leave the rest,
With the Gods' aid — and, if they give but aid
As our just cause deserves, I do not fear.

[ÆPYTUS, LAIAS, *and* ARCAS *go out.*

THE CHORUS.

O Son and Mother,   *str.* I.
Whom the Gods o'ershadow
In dangerous trial,
With certainty of favor !
As erst they shadow'd
Your race's founders
From irretrievable woe ;
When the seed of Lycaon
Lay forlorn, lay outcast,
Callisto and her Boy.

What deep-grass'd meadow   *ant.* I.
At the meeting valleys —
Where clear-flowing Ladon,

Most beautiful of waters,
Receives the river
Whose trout are vocal,
The Aroanian stream —
Without home, without mother,
Hid the babe, hid Arcas,
The nursling of the dells?

But the sweet-smelling myrtle,   *str.* 2.
And the pink-flower'd oleander,
And the green agnus-castus,
To the west-wind's murmur,
Rustled round his cradle ;
And Maia rear'd him.
Then, a boy, he startled,
In the snow-fill'd hollows
Of high Cyllenê,
The white mountain-birds ;
Or surprised, in the glens,
The basking tortoises,
Whose striped shell founded
In the hand of Hermes
The glory of the lyre.

But his mother, Callisto,   *ant.* 2.
In her hiding-place of the thickets
Of the lentisk and ilex
In her rough form, fearing
The hunter on the outlook,
Poor changeling ! trembled.
Or the children, plucking
In the thorn-choked gullies
Wild gooseberries, scared her,
The shy mountain-bear !

Or the shepherds, on slopes
With pale-spiked lavender
And crisp thyme tufted,
Came upon her, stealing
At day-break through the dew.

Once, 'mid those gorges,   *str.* 3.
Spray-drizzled, lonely,
Unclimb'd of man —
O'er whose cliffs the townsmen
Of crag-perch'd Nonacris
Behold in summer
The slender torrent
Of Styx come dancing,
A wind-blown thread —
By the precipices of Khelmos,
The fleet, desperate hunter,
The youthful Arcas, born of Zeus,
His fleeing mother,
Transform'd Callisto,
Unwitting follow'd —
And raised his spear.

Turning, with piteous,   *ant.* 3.
Distressful longing,
Sad, eager eyes,
Mutely she regarded
Her well-known enemy.
Low moans half utter'd
What speech refused her ;
Tears coursed, tears human,
Down those disfigured,
Once human cheeks.
With unutterable foreboding

Her son, heart-stricken, eyed her.
The Gods had pity, made them Stars.
Stars now they sparkle
In the northern Heaven —
The guard Arcturus,
The guard-watch'd Bear.

So, o'er thee and thy child,   *epode.*
Some God, Merope, now,
In dangerous hour, stretches his hand.
So, like a star, dawns thy son,
Radiant with fortune and joy.

[POLYPHONTES *comes in.*

POLYPHONTES.

O Merope, the trouble on thy face
Tells me enough thou know'st the news which all
Messenia speaks ! the prince, thy son, is dead.
Not from my lips should consolation fall ;
To offer that, I come not ; but to urge,
Even after news of this sad death, our league.
Yes, once again I come ; I will not take
This morning's angry answer for thy last.
To the Messenian kingdom thou and I
Are the sole claimants left ; what cause of strife
Lay in thy son is buried in his grave.
Most honorably I meant, I call the Gods
To witness, offering him return and power ;
Yet, had he lived, suspicion, jealousy,
Inevitably had surged up, perhaps,
'Twixt thee and me — suspicion, that I nursed
Some ill design against him ; jealousy,
That he enjoy'd but part, being heir to all.
And he himself, with the impetuous heart

Of youth, 'tis like, had never quite forgone
The thought of vengeance on me, never quite
Unclosed his itching fingers from his sword.
But thou, O Merope, though deeply wrong'd,
Though injured past forgiveness, as men deem,
Yet hast been long at school with thoughtful time,
And from that teacher mayst have learn'd, like me,
That all may be endured, and all forgiv'n —
Have learn'd, that we must sacrifice the bent
Of personal feeling to the public weal —
Have learn'd, that there are guilty deeds, which leave
The hand that does them guiltless ; in a word,
That kings live for their peoples, not themselves.
This having known, let us a union found
(For the last time I ask, ask earnestly)
Based on pure public welfare ; let us be
Not Merope and Polyphontes, foes
Blood-sever'd, but Messenia's King and Queen !
Let us forget ourselves for those we rule !
Speak !   I go hence to offer sacrifice
To the Preserver Zeus ; let me return
Thanks to him for our amity as well.

MEROPE.

Oh hadst thou, Polyphontes, still but kept
The silence thou hast kept for twenty years !

POLYPHONTES.

Henceforth, if what I urge displease, I may.
But fair proposal merits fair reply.

MEROPE.

And thou shalt have it !   Yes, because thou *hast*
For twenty years forborne to interrupt

The solitude of her whom thou hast wrong'd —
That scanty grace shall earn thee this reply. —
First, for our union.   Trust me, 'twixt us two
The brazen-footed Fury ever stalks,
Waving her hundred hands, a torch in each,
Aglow with angry fire, to keep us twain.
Now, for thyself.   Thou com'st with well-cloak'd joy,
To announce the ruin of my husband's house,
To sound thy triumph in his widow's ears,
To bid her share thine unendanger'd throne.
To this thou wouldst have answer.   Take it : Fly ! . . .
Cut short thy triumph, seeming at its height ;
Fling off thy crown, supposed at last secure ;
Forsake this ample, proud Messenian realm ;
To some small, humble, and unnoted strand,
Some rock more lonely than that Lemnian isle
Where Philoctetes pined, take ship and flee !
Some solitude more inaccessible
Than the ice-bastion'd Caucasian Mount
Chosen a prison for Prometheus, climb !
There in unvoiced oblivion sink thy name,
And bid the sun, thine only visitant,
Divulge not to the far-off world of men
What once-famed wretch he there did espy hid.
There nurse a late remorse, and thank the Gods,
And thank thy bitterest foe, that, having lost
All things but life, thou lose not life as well.

POLYPHONTES.

What mad bewilderment of grief is this?

MEROPE.

Thou art bewilder'd ; the sane head is mine.

POLYPHONTES.

I pity thee, and wish thee calmer mind.

MEROPE.

Pity thyself; none needs compassion more.

POLYPHONTES.

Yet, oh! couldst thou but act as reason bids!

MEROPE.

And in my turn I wish the same for thee.

POLYPHONTES.

All I could do to soothe thee has been tried.

MEROPE.

For that, in this my warning, thou art paid.

POLYPHONTES.

Know'st thou then aught, that thus thou sound'st the
alarm?

MEROPE.

Thy crime! that were enough to make one fear.

POLYPHONTES.

My deed is of old date, and long atoned.

MEROPE.

Atoned this very day, perhaps, it is.

POLYPHONTES.

My final victory proves the Gods appeased.

MEROPE.

O victor, victor, trip not at the goal!

POLYPHONTES.

Hatred and passionate envy blind thine eyes.

MEROPE.

O Heaven-abandon'd wretch, that envies thee!

POLYPHONTES.

Thou hold'st so cheap, then, the Messenian crown?

MEROPE.

I think on what the future hath in store.

POLYPHONTES.

To-day I reign; the rest I leave to Fate.

MEROPE.

For Fate thou wait'st not long; since, in this hour ——

POLYPHONTES.

What? for so far Fate hath not proved my foe ——

MEROPE.

Fate seals my lips, and drags to ruin thee.

POLYPHONTES.

Enough! enough! I will no longer hear
The ill-boding note which frantic hatred sounds
To affright a fortune which the Gods secure.
Once more my friendship thou rejectest; well!

More for this land's sake grieve I, than mine own.
I chafe not with thee, that thy hate endures,
Nor bend myself too low, to make it yield.
What I have done is done ; by my own deed,
Neither exulting nor ashamed, I stand.
Why should this heart of mine set mighty store
By the construction and report of men?
Not men's good word hath made me what I am.
Alone I master'd power ; and alone,
Since so thou wilt, I dare maintain it still.

[POLYPHONTES goes out.

THE CHORUS.

Did I then waver   *str.* I.
(O woman's judgment !)
Misled by seeming
Success of crime?
And ask, if sometimes
The Gods, perhaps, allow'd **you,**
O lawless daring of the strong,
O self-will recklessly indulged?

Not time, not lightning,   *ant.* I.
Not rain, not thunder,
Efface the endless
Decrees of Heaven —
Make Justice alter,
Revoke, assuage her sentence,
Which dooms dread ends to dreadful deeds,
And violent deaths to violent men.

But the signal example   *str.* 2.
Of invariableness of justice
Our glorious founder

Heracles gave us,
Son loved of Zeus his father — for he sinn'd,

And the strand of Eubœa,   *ant.* 2.
And the promontory of Cenæum,
His painful, solemn
Punishment witness'd,
Beheld his expiation — for he died.

O villages of Œta   *str.* 3.
With hedges of the wild rose !
O pastures of the mountain,
Of short grass, beaded with dew,
Between the pine-woods and the cliffs !
O cliffs, left by the eagles,
On that morn, when the smoke-cloud
From the oak-built, fiercely-burning pyre,
Up the precipices of Trachis,
Drove them screaming from their eyries !
A willing, a willing sacrifice on that day
Ye witness'd, ye mountain lawns,
When the shirt-wrapt, poison-blister'd Hero
Ascended, with undaunted heart,
Living, his own funeral-pile,
And stood, shouting for a fiery torch ;
And the kind, chance-arrived Wanderer,[1]
The inheritor of the bow,
Coming swiftly through the sad Trachinians,
Put the torch to the pile.
That the flame tower'd on high to the Heaven ;
Bearing with it, to Olympus,

---

[1] Poias, the father of Philoctetes. Passing near, he was attracted by the concourse round the pyre, and at the entreaty of Hercules set fire to it, receiving the bow and arrows of the hero as his reward.

To the side of Hebe,
To immortal delight,
The labor-released Hero.

O heritage of Neleus,   *ant.* 3.
Ill-kept by his infirm heirs !
O kingdom of Messenê,
Of rich soil, chosen by craft,
Possess'd in hatred, lost in blood !
O town, high Stenyclaros,
With new walls, which the victors
From the four-town'd, mountain-shadow'd Doris,
For their Heracles-issued princes
Built in strength against the vanquish'd !
Another, another sacrifice on this day
Ye witness, ye new-built towers !
When the white-robed, garland-crowned Monarch
Approaches, with undoubting heart,
Living, his own sacrifice-block,
And stands, shouting for a slaughterous axe ;
And the stern, destiny-brought Stranger,
The inheritor of the realm,
Coming swiftly through the jocund Dorians,
Drives the axe to its goal.
That the blood rushes in streams to the dust ;
Bearing with it, to Erinnys,
To the Gods of Hades,
To the dead unavenged,
The fiercely-required Victim.

Knowing he did it, unknowing pays for it.   [*epode.*
Unknowing, unknowing,
Thinking atoned-for
Deeds unatonable,

Thinking appeased
Gods unappeasable,
Lo, the ill-fated one,
Standing for harbor
Right at the harbor-mouth
Strikes with all sail set
Full on the sharp-pointed
Needle of ruin !

[*A* MESSENGER *comes in.*

MESSENGER.

O honor'd Queen, O faithful followers
Of your dead master's line, I bring you news
To make the gates of this long-mournful house
Leap, and fly open of themselves for joy !

[*noise and shouting heard.*

Hark how the shouting crowds tramp hitherward
With glad acclaim !   Ere they forestall my news,
Accept it : — Polyphontes is no more.

MEROPE.

Is my son safe ? that question bounds my care.

MESSENGER.

He is, and by the people hail'd for king.

MEROPE.

The rest to me is little ; yet, since that
Must from some mouth be heard, relate it thou.

MESSENGER.

Not little, if thou saw'st what love, what zeal,
At thy dead husband's name the people show.

For when this morning in the public square
I took my stand, and saw the unarm'd crowds
Of citizens in holiday attire,
Women and children intermix'd ; and then,
Group'd around Zeus's altar, all in arms,
Serried and grim, the ring of Dorian lords —
I trembled for our prince and his attempt.
Silence and expectation held us all ;
Till presently the King came forth, in robe
Of sacrifice, his guards clearing the way
Before him — at his side, the prince, thy son,
Unarm'd and travel-soil'd, just as he was.
With him conferring the King slowly reach'd
The altar in the middle of the square,
Where, by the sacrificing minister,
The flower-dress'd victim stood — a milk-white bull,
Swaying from side to side his massy head
With short impatient lowings.   There he stopp'd,
And seem'd to muse awhile, then raised his eyes
To heaven, and laid his hand upon the steer,
And cried : *O Zeus, let what blood-guiltiness*
Yet stains our land be by this blood wash'd out,
And grant henceforth to the Messenians peace !
That moment, while with upturn'd eyes he pray'd,
The prince snatch'd from the sacrificer's hand
The axe, and on the forehead of the King,
Where twines the chaplet, dealt a mighty blow
Which fell'd him to the earth, and o'er him stood
And shouted : *Since by thee defilement came,*
What blood so meet as thine to wash it out ?
What hand to strike thee meet as mine, the hand
Of Æpytus, thy murder'd master's son ? —
But, gazing at him from the ground, the King . . .
Is it, then, thou ? he murmur'd ; and with that,

He bow'd his head, and deeply groan'd, and died.
Till then we all seem'd stone, but then a cry
Broke from the Dorian lords; forward they rush'd
To circle the prince round — when suddenly
Laias in arms sprang to his nephew's side,
Crying: *O ye Messenians, will ye leave*
The son to perish as ye left the sire ?
And from that moment I saw nothing clear;
For from all sides a deluge, as it seem'd
Burst o'er the altar and the Dorian lords,
Of holiday-clad citizens transform'd
To armed warriors; — I heard vengeful cries,
I heard the clash of weapons; then I saw
The Dorians lying dead, thy son hail'd king.
And, truly, one who sees, what seem'd so strong,
The power of this tyrant and his lords,
Melt like a passing smoke, a nightly dream,
At one bold word, one enterprising blow —
Might ask, why we endured their yoke so long;
But that we know how every perilous feat
Of daring, easy as it seems when done,
Is easy at no moment but the right.

THE CHORUS.

Thou speakest well; but here, to give our eyes
Authentic proof of what thou tell'st our ears,
The conquerors, with the King's dead body, come.

> [*Æ*PYTUS, LAIAS, *and* ARCAS *come in with the dead
> body of* POLYPHONTES, *followed by a crowd of the*
> MESSENIANS.

LAIAS.

Sister, from this day forth thou art no more
The widow of a husband unavenged,

The anxious mother of an exiled son.
Thine enemy is slain, thy son is king!
Rejoice with us! and trust me, he who wish'd
Welfare to the Messenian state, and calm,
Could find no way to found them sure as this.

ÆPYTUS.

Mother, all these approve me ; but if thou
Approve not too, I have but half my joy.

MEROPE.

O Æpytus, my son, behold, behold
This iron man, my enemy and thine,
This politic sovereign, lying at our feet,
With blood-bespatter'd robes, and chaplet shorn !
Inscrutable as ever, see, it keeps
Its sombre aspect of majestic care,
Of solitary thought, unshared resolve,
Even in death, that countenance austere !
So look'd he, when to Stenyclaros first,
A new-made wife, I from Arcadia came,
And found him at my husband's side, his friend,
His kinsman, his right hand in peace and war,
Unsparing in his service of his toil,
His blood — to me, for I confess it, kind ;
So look'd he in that dreadful day of death ;
So, when he pleaded for our league but now.
What meantest thou, O Polyphontes, what
Desired'st thou, what truly spurr'd thee on?
Was policy of state, the ascendency
Of the Heracleidan conquerors, as thou said'st,
Indeed thy lifelong passion and sole aim?
Or didst thou but, as cautious schemers use,

Cloak thine ambition with these specious words?
I know not; just, in either case, the stroke
Which laid thee low, for blood requires blood;
But yet, not knowing this, I triumph not
Over thy corpse, — triumph not, neither mourn, —
For I find worth in thee, and badness too.
What mood of spirit, therefore, shall we call
The true one of a man — what way of life
His fix'd condition and perpetual walk?
None, since a twofold color reigns in all.
But thou, my son, study to make prevail
One color in thy life, the hue of truth;
That justice, that sage order, not alone
Natural vengeance, may maintain thine act,
And make it stand indeed the will of Heaven.
Thy father's passion was this people's ease,
This people's anarchy, thy foe's pretence.
As the chiefs rule, my son, the people are.
Unhappy people, where the chiefs themselves
Are, like the mob, vicious and ignorant!
So rule, that even thine enemies may fail
To find in thee a fault whereon to found,
Of tyrannous harshness, or remissness weak —
So rule, that as thy father thou be loved!
So rule, that as his foe thou be obey'd!
Take these, my son, over thine enemy's corpse
Thy mother's prayers! and this prayer last of all:
That even in thy victory thou show,
Mortal, the moderation of a man.

ÆPYTUS.

O mother, my best diligence shall be
In all by thy experience to be ruled
Where my own youth falls short!   But, Laias, now,

First work after such victory, let us go
To render to my true Messenians thanks,
To the Gods grateful sacrifice ; and then,
Assume the ensigns of my father's power.

THE CHORUS.

Son of Cresphontes, past what perils
Com'st thou, guided safe, to thy home !
What things daring ! what enduring !
And all this by the will of the Gods.

ELEGIAC POEMS.

———◆◇◆———

THE SCHOLAR–GYPSY.[17]

Go, for they call you, shepherd, from the hill;
  Go, shepherd, and untie the wattled cotes!
    No longer leave thy wistful flock unfed,
  Nor let thy bawling fellows rack their throats,
    Nor the cropped grasses shoot another head;
      But when the fields are still,
  And the tired men and dogs all gone to rest,
    And only the white sheep are sometimes seen
    Cross and recross the strips of moon-blanched
      green,
  Come, shepherd, and again renew the quest!

Here, where the reaper was at work of late, —
  In this high field's dark corner, where he leaves
    His coat, his basket, and his earthen cruse,
  And in the sun all morning binds the sheaves,
    Then here at noon comes back his stores to use, —
      Here will I sit and wait,
  While to my ear from uplands far away
    The bleating of the folded flocks is borne,
    With distant cries of reapers in the corn, —
  All the live murmur of a summer's day.

381

Screened is this nook o'er the high, half-reaped field,
    And here till sundown, shepherd ! will I be.
        Through the thick corn the scarlet poppies peep,
    And round green roots and yellowing stalks I see
        Pale blue convolvulus in tendrils creep ;
            And air-swept lindens yield
        Their scent, and rustle down their perfumed
            showers
        Of bloom on the bent grass where I am laid,
        And bower me from the August-sun with shade ;
    And the eye travels down to Oxford's towers.

And near me on the grass lies Glanvil's book.
    Come, let me read the oft-read tale again !
        The story of that Oxford scholar poor,
    Of shining parts and quick inventive brain,
        Who, tired of knocking at preferment's door,
            One summer-morn forsook
        His friends, and went to learn the gypsy-lore,
        And roamed the world with that wild brother-
            hood,
        And came, as most men deemed, to little good,
    But came to Oxford and his friends no more.

But once, years after, in the country-lanes,
    Two scholars, whom at college erst he knew,
        Met him, and of his way of life inquired ;
    Whereat he answered, that the gypsy-crew,
        His mates, had arts to rule as they desired
            The workings of men's brains,
        And they can bind them to what thoughts they will.
        " And I," he said, " the secret of their art,
        When fully learned, will to the world impart ;
    But it needs Heaven-sent moments for this skill."

This said, he left them, and returned no more.
But rumors hung about the country-side,
That the lost Scholar long was seen to stray,
Seen by rare glimpses, pensive and tongue-tied,
In hat of antique shape, and cloak of gray,
The same the gypsies wore.
Shepherds had met him on the Hurst in spring;
At some lone alehouse in the Berkshire moors,
On the warm ingle-bench, the smock-frocked boors
Had found him seated at their entering;

But, 'mid their drink and clatter, he would fly.
And I myself seem half to know thy looks,
And put the shepherds, wanderer! on thy trace;
And boys who in lone wheat-fields scare the rooks
I ask if thou hast passed their quiet place;
Or in my boat I lie
Moored to the cool bank in the summer-heats,
'Mid wide grass meadows which the sunshine fills,
And watch the warm, green-muffled Cumner hills,
And wonder if thou haunt'st their shy retreats.

For most, I know, thou lov'st retired ground!
Thee at the ferry Oxford riders blithe,
Returning home on summer-nights, have met
Crossing the stripling Thames at Bab-lock-hithe,
Trailing in the cool stream thy fingers wet,
As the punt's rope chops round;
And leaning backward in a pensive dream,
And fostering in thy lap a heap of flowers
Plucked in shy fields and distant Wychwood bowers,
And thine eyes resting on the moonlit stream.

And then they land, and thou art seen no more !
  Maidens, who from the distant hamlets come
    To dance around the Fyfield elm in May,
  Oft through the darkening fields have seen thee
      roam,
      Or cross a stile into the public way ;
        Oft thou hast given them store
  Of flowers, — the frail-leafed, white anemone,
    Dark bluebells drenched with dews of summer eves,
    And purple orchises with spotted leaves, —
  But none hath words she can report of thee !

And, above Godstow Bridge, when hay-time's here
  In June, and many a scythe in sunshine flames,
    Men who through those wide fields of breezy grass,
  Where black-winged swallows haunt the glittering
      Thames,
      To bathe in the abandoned lasher pass,
        Have often passed thee near
  Sitting upon the river-bank o'ergrown ;
    Marked thine outlandish garb, thy figure spare,
    Thy dark vague eyes, and soft abstracted air :
  But, when they came from bathing, thou wast gone !

At some lone homestead in the Cumner hills,
  Where at her open door the housewife darns,
    Thou hast been seen, or hanging on a gate
  To watch the threshers in the mossy barns.
      Children, who early range these slopes and late
        For cresses from the rills,
  Have known thee eying, all an April day,
    The springing pastures and the feeding kine ;
      And marked thee, when the stars come out and
        shine,
  Through the long dewy grass move slow away.

In autumn, on the skirts of Bagley Wood, —
  Where most the gypsies by the turf-edged way
    Pitch their smoked tents, and every bush you
      see
  With scarlet patches tagged and shreds of gray,
    Above the forest ground called Thessaly, —
      The blackbird picking food
  Sees thee, nor stops his meal, nor fears at all ;
    So often has he known thee past him stray,
    Rapt, twirling in thy hand a withered spray,
  And waiting for the spark from heaven to fall.

And once, in winter, on the causeway chill
  Where home through flooded fields foot-travellers go,
    Have I not passed thee on the wooden bridge
  Wrapped in thy cloak and battling with the snow,
    Thy face toward Hinksey and its wintry ridge ?
      And thou hast climbed the hill,
  And gained the white brow of the Cumner range ;
    Turned once to watch, while thick the snow-
      flakes fall,
  The line of festal light in Christ-church hall :
  Then sought thy straw in some sequestered grange.

But what — I dream ! Two hundred years are flown
  Since first thy story ran through Oxford halls,
    And the grave Glanvil did the tale inscribe
  That thou wert wandered from the studious walls
    To learn strange arts, and join a gypsy-tribe.
      And thou from earth art gone
  Long since, and in some quiet churchyard laid, —
    Some country-nook, where o'er thy unknown
      grave
  Tall grasses and white flowering nettles wave,
  Under a dark, red-fruited yew-tree's shade.

— No, no, thou hast not felt the lapse of hours!
. For what wears out the life of mortal men?
　　'Tis that from change to change their being rolls;
　'Tis that repeated shocks, again, again,
　　Exhaust the energy of strongest souls,
　　　And numb the elastic powers,
　Till having used our nerves with bliss and teen,
　　And tired upon a thousand schemes our wit,
　　To the just-pausing Genius we remit
　Our well-worn life, and are — what we have been.

Thou hast not lived, why shouldst thou perish, so?
　Thou hadst *one* aim, *one* business, *one* desire;
　　Else wert thou long since numbered with the
　　　dead!
　Else hadst thou spent, like other men, thy fire!
　　The generations of thy peers are fled,
　　　And we ourselves shall go;
　But thou possessest an immortal lot,
　　And we imagine thee exempt from age,
　　And living as thou liv'st on Glanvil's page,
　Because thou hadst — what we, alas! have not.

For early didst thou leave the world, with powers
　Fresh, undiverted to the world without,
　　Firm to their mark, not spent on other things;
　Free from the sick fatigue, the languid doubt,
　　Which much to have tried, in much been baffled,
　　　brings.
　　　O life unlike to ours!
　Who fluctuate idly without term or scope,
　　Of whom each strives, nor knows for what he
　　　strives,
　　And each half lives a hundred different lives;
　Who wait like thee, but not, like thee, in hope.

Thou waitest for the spark from heaven ! and we,
   Light half-believers of our casual creeds,
     Who never deeply felt, nor clearly willed,
   Whose insight never has borne fruit in deeds,
     Whose vague resolves never have been fulfilled ;
       For whom each year we see
   Breeds new beginnings, disappointments new ;
     Who hesitate and falter life away,
     And lose to-morrow the ground won to-day —
Ah ! do not we, wanderer ! await it too ?

Yes, we await it ! but it still delays,
   And then we suffer ! and amongst us one,
     Who most has suffered, takes dejectedly
His seat upon the intellectual throne ;
     And all his store of sad experience he
       Lays bare of wretched days ;
   Tells us his misery's birth and growth and signs,
     And how the dying spark of hope was fed,
     And how the breast was soothed, and how the
       head,
And all his hourly varied anodynes.

This for our wisest ! and we others pine,
   And wish the long unhappy dream would end,
     And waive all claim to bliss, and try to bear ;
   With close-lipped patience for our only friend, —
     Sad patience, too near neighbor to despair, —
       But none has hope like thine !
   Thou through the fields and through the woods
       dost stray,
     Roaming the country-side, a truant boy,
     Nursing thy project in unclouded joy,
And every doubt long blown by time away.

Oh, born in days when wits were fresh and clear,
   And life ran gayly as the sparkling Thames ;
      Before this strange disease of modern life,
    With its sick hurry, its divided aims,
        Its heads o'ertaxed, its palsied hearts, was rife, —
          Fly hence, our contact fear !
   Still fly, plunge deeper in the bowering wood !
      Averse, as Dido did with gesture stern
      From her false friend's approach in Hades turn,
  Wave us away, and keep thy solitude !

Still nursing the unconquerable hope,
   Still clutching the inviolable shade,
      With a free, onward impulse brushing through,
    By night, the silvered branches of the glade, —
        Far on the forest-skirts, where none pursue,
          On some mild pastoral slope
   Emerge, and resting on the moonlit pales
      Freshen thy flowers as in former years
      With dew, or listen with enchanted ears,
  From the dark dingles, to the nightingales !

But fly our paths, our feverish contact fly !
   For strong the infection of our mental strife,
      Which, though it gives no bliss, yet spoils for rest ;
   And we should win thee from thy own fair life,
    Like us distracted, and like us unblest.
        Soon, soon thy cheer would die,
   Thy hopes grow timorous, and unfixed thy powers,
      And thy clear aims be cross and shifting made :
      And then thy glad perennial youth would fade,
  Fade, and grow old at last, and die like ours.

Then fly our greetings, fly our speech and smiles !
   — As some grave Tyrian trader, from the sea,

Descried at sunrise an emerging prow
 Lifting the cool-haired creepers stealthily,
  The fringes of a southward-facing brow
   Among the Ægean isles ;
And saw the merry Grecian coaster come,
 Freighted with amber grapes, and Chian wine,
 Green bursting figs, and tunnies steeped in
  brine,
And knew the intruders on his ancient home, —

The young light-hearted masters of the waves, —
 And snatched his rudder, and shook out more sail,
 And day and night held on indignantly
  O'er the blue Midland waters with the gale,
   Betwixt the Syrtes and soft Sicily,
    To where the Atlantic raves
 Outside the western straits, and unbent sails
  There where down cloudy cliffs, through sheets
   of foam,
  Shy traffickers, the dark Iberians come ;
And on the beach undid his corded bales.

THYRSIS.[18]

A MONODY, *to commemorate the author's friend*,
ARTHUR HUGH CLOUGH, *who died at Florence*, 1861.

How changed is here each spot man makes or fills !
 In the two Hinkseys nothing keeps the same ;
  The village street its haunted mansion lacks,
 And from the sign is gone Sibylla's name,
  And from the roofs the twisted chimney-stacks. —
   Are ye too changed, ye hills?

See, 'tis no foot of unfamiliar men
　　To-night from Oxford up your pathway strays !
　　Here came I often, often, in old days, —
Thyrsis and I : we still had Thyrsis then.

Runs it not here, the track by Childsworth Farm,
　　Past the high wood, to where the elm-tree crowns
　　The hill behind whose ridge the sunset flames?
The single-elm, that looks on Ilsley Downs,
　　　　The Vale, the three lone wears, the youthful
　　　　　Thames?
　　　This winter-eve is warm ;
Humid the air ; leafless, yet soft as spring,
　　The tender purple spray on copse and briers ;
　　And that sweet city with her dreaming spires,
She needs not June for beauty's heightening.

Lovely all times she lies, lovely to-night ! —
　　Only, methinks, some loss of habit's power
　　Befalls me wandering through this upland dim.
Once passed I blindfold here, at any hour ;
　　Now seldom come I, since I came with him.
　　　That single elm-tree bright
Against the west — I miss it ! is it gone?
　　We prized it dearly ; while it stood, we said,
　　Our friend the Gypsy-Scholar was not dead ;
While the tree lived, he in these fields lived on.

Too rare, too rare, grow now my visits here,
　　But once I knew each field, each flower, each stick ;
　　And with the country-folk acquaintance made
By barn in threshing-time, by new-built rick.
　　Here, too, our shepherd-pipes we first assayed.
　　　Ah me ! this many a year
My pipe is lost, my shepherd's-holiday !

Needs must I lose them, needs with heavy heart
   Into the world and wave of men depart,
But Thyrsis of his own will went away.

It irked him to be here, he could not rest.
   He loved each simple joy the country yields,
      He loved his mates; but yet he could not keep,
   For that a shadow lowered on the fields,
      Here with the shepherds and the silly sheep.
         Some life of men unblest
   He knew, which made him droop, and filled his
            head.
      He went; his piping took a troubled sound
      Of storms that rage outside our happy ground;
   He could not wait their passing; he is dead.

So, some tempestuous morn in early June,
   When the year's primal burst of bloom is o'er,
      Before the roses and the longest day,—
   When garden-walks, and all the grassy floor,
      With blossoms red and white of fallen May,
         And chestnut-flowers, are strewn,—
   So have I heard the cuckoo's parting cry,
      From the wet field, through the vexed garden-trees,
      Come with the volleying rain and tossing breeze:
   The bloom is gone, and with the bloom go I!

Too quick despairer, wherefore wilt thou go?
   Soon will the high midsummer pomps come on,
      Soon will the musk carnations break and swell,
   Soon shall we have gold-dusted snapdragon,
      Sweet-william with his homely cottage-smell,
         And stocks in fragrant blow;
   Roses that down the alleys shine afar,
      And open, jasmine-muffled lattices,

And groups under the dreaming garden-trees,
And the full moon, and the white evening-star.

He hearkens not! light comer, he is flown!
    What matters it? next year he will return,
        And we shall have him in the sweet spring-days,
    With whitening hedges, and uncrumpling fern,
        And bluebells trembling by the forest-ways,
            And scent of hay new-mown.
    But Thyrsis never more we swains shall see, —
        See him come back, and cut a smoother reed,
        And blow a strain the world at last shall heed;
    For Time, not Corydon, hath conquered thee!

Alack, for Corydon no rival now! —
    But when Sicilian shepherds lost a mate,
        Some good survivor with his flute would go,
    Piping a ditty sad for Bion's fate;
        And cross the unpermitted ferry's flow,
            And relax Pluto's brow,
    And make leap up with joy the beauteous head
        Of Proserpine, among whose crownèd hair
        Are flowers first opened on Sicilian air,
    And flute his friend, like Orpheus, from the dead.

Oh, easy access to the hearer's grace
    When Dorian shepherds sang to Proserpine!
        For she herself had trod Sicilian fields,
    She knew the Dorian water's gush divine,
        She knew each lily white which Enna yields,
            Each rose with blushing face;
    She loved the Dorian pipe, the Dorian strain.
        But ah! of our poor Thames she never heard;
        Her foot the Cumner cowslips never stirred;
    And we should tease her with our plaint in vain.

Well ! wind-dispersed and vain the words will be ;
  Yet, Thyrsis, let me give my grief its hour
    In the old haunt, and find our tree-topped hill !
  Who, if not I, for questing here hath power?
    I know the wood which hides the daffodil ;
      I know the Fyfield tree ;
    I know what white, what purple fritillaries
      The grassy harvest of the river-fields,
      Above by Ensham, down by Sandford, yields ;
    And what sedged brooks are Thames's tributaries ;

I know these slopes : who knows them if not I?
  But many a dingle on the loved hillside,
    With thorns once studded, old white-blossomed
      trees,
  Where thick the cowslips grew, and far descried
    High towered the spikes of purple orchises,
      Hath since our day put by
    The coronals of that forgotten time ;
      Down each green bank hath gone the plough-
        boy's team,
      And only in the hidden brookside gleam
    Primroses, orphans of the flowery prime.

Where is the girl who by the boatman's door,
  Above the locks, above the boating throng,
    Unmoored our skiff when through the Wytham
      flats,
  Red loosestrife and blond meadow-sweet among,
    And darting swallows and light water-gnats,
      We tracked the shy Thames shore?
  Where are the mowers, who, as the tiny swell
    Of our boat passing heaved the river-grass,
    Stood with suspended scythe to see us pass? —
  They all are gone, and thou art gone as well !

Yes, thou art gone ! and round me too the night
　In ever-nearing circle weaves her shade.
　　I see her veil draw soft across the day,
　I feel her slowly chilling breath invade
　　　The cheek grown thin, the brown hair sprent
　　　　　with gray ;
　　　　I feel her finger light
　Laid pausefully upon life's headlong train, —
　　The foot less prompt to meet the morning dew,
　　The heart less bounding at emotion new,
　And hope, once crushed, less quick to spring again.

And long the way appears, which seemed so short
　To the less-practised eye of sanguine youth ;
　　And high the mountain tops, in cloudy air, —
　The mountain tops where is the throne of Truth,
　　　Tops in life's morning-sun so bright and bare !
　　　　Unbreachable the fort
　Of the long-battered world uplifts its wall ;
　　And strange and vain the earthly turmoil grows,
　-　And near and real the charm of thy repose,
　And night as welcome as a friend would fall.

But hush ! the upland hath a sudden loss
　Of quiet !　Look, adown the dusk hillside,
　　A troop of Oxford hunters going home,
　As in old days, jovial and talking, ride !
　　　From hunting with the Berkshire hounds they
　　　　　come.
　　　　Quick ! let me fly, and cross
　Into yon farther field !　'Tis done ; and see,
　　Backed by the sunset, which doth glorify
　　The orange and pale violet evening-sky,
　Bare on its lonely ridge, the Tree ! the Tree !

I take the omen !   Eve lets down her veil,
   The white fog creeps from bush to bush about,
     The west unflushes, the high stars grow bright,
  And in the scattered farms the lights come out.
   I cannot reach the signal-tree to-night,
      Yet, happy omen, hail !
  Hear it from thy broad lucent Arno-vale
   (For there thine earth-forgetting eyelids keep
   The morningless and unawakening sleep
  Under the flowery oleanders pale) ;

Hear it, O Thyrsis, still our tree is there !—
  Ah, vain !   These English fields, this upland dim,
   These brambles pale with mist engarlanded,
  That lone, sky-pointing tree, are not for him :
   To a boon southern country he is fled,
     And now in happier air,
  Wandering with the great Mother's train divine
   (And purer or more subtile soul than thee,
   I trow the mighty Mother doth not see)
  Within a folding of the Apennine, —

Thou hearest the immortal chants of old !
  Putting his sickle to the perilous grain
   In the hot cornfield of the Phrygian king,
  For thee the Lityerses-song again
   Young Daphnis with his silver voice doth
      sing ; [19]
     Sings his Sicilian fold,
  His sheep, his hapless love, his blinded eyes ;
   And how a call celestial round him rang,
   And heavenward from the fountain-brink he
     sprang,
  And all the marvel of the golden skies.

There thou art gone, and me thou leavest here
  Sole in these fields ! yet will I not despair.
    Despair I will not, while I yet descry
    'Neath the soft canopy of English air
      That lonely tree against the western sky.
        Still, still these slopes, 'tis clear,
  Our Gypsy-Scholar haunts, outliving thee !
    Fields where soft sheep from cages pull the hay,
    Woods with anemones in flower till May,
Know him a wanderer still ; then why not me?

A fugitive and gracious light he seeks,
  Shy to illumine ; and I seek it too.
    This does not come with houses or with gold,
  With place, with honor, and a flattering crew ;
      'Tis not in the world's market bought and sold :
        But the smooth-slipping weeks
  Drop by, and leave its seeker still untired ;
    Out of the heed of mortals he is gone,
    He wends unfollowed, he must house alone ;
Yet on he fares, by his own heart inspired.

Thou too, O Thyrsis, on like quest wast bound !
  Thou wanderedst with me for a little hour.
    Men gave thee nothing ; but this happy quest,
  If men esteemed thee feeble, gave thee power,
      If men procured thee trouble, gave thee rest.
        And this rude Cumner ground,
  Its fir-topped Hurst, its farms, its quiet fields,
    Here cam'st thou in thy jocund youthful time,
    Here was thine height of strength, thy golden
        prime !
And still the haunt beloved a virtue yields.

What though the music of thy rustic flute
 Kept not for long its happy, country tone ;
  Lost it too soon, and learnt a stormy note
Of men contention-tost, of men who groan,
  Which tasked thy pipe too sore, and tired thy
   throat —
   It failed, and thou wast mute !
Yet hadst thou alway visions of our light,
  And long with men of care thou couldst not stay,
  And soon thy foot resumed its wandering way,
Left human haunt, and on alone till night.

Too rare, too rare, grow now my visits here !
 'Mid city-noise, not, as with thee of yore,
  Thyrsis ! in reach of sheep-bells is my home.
— Then through the great town's harsh, heart-
   wearying roar,
  Let in thy voice a whisper often come,
   To chase fatigue and fear :
 Why faintest thou ? I wandered till I died.
 Roam on ! The light we sought is shining still.
 Dost thou ask proof ? Our tree yet crowns the hill,
Our Scholar travels yet the loved hillside.

MEMORIAL VERSES.

APRIL, 1850.

Goethe in Weimar sleeps ; and Greece,
Long since, saw Byron's struggle cease.
But one such death remained to come :
The last poetic voice is dumb, —
We stand to-day by Wordsworth's tomb.

When Byron's eyes were shut in death,
We bowed our head, and held our breath.
He taught us little, but our soul
Had *felt* him like the thunder's roll.
With shivering heart the strife we saw
Of passion with eternal law;
And yet with reverential awe
We watched the fount of fiery life
Which served for that Titanic strife.

When Goethe's death was told, we said, —
Sunk, then, is Europe's sagest head.
Physician of the iron age,
Goethe has done his pilgrimage.
He took the suffering human race,
He read each wound, each weakness clear;
And struck his finger on the place,
And said, *Thou ailest here, and here!*
He looked on Europe's dying hour
Of fitful dream and feverish power;
His eye plunged down the weltering strife,
The turmoil of expiring life:
He said, *The end is everywhere,*
Art still has truth, take refuge there!
And he was happy, if to know
Causes of things, and far below
His feet to see the lurid flow
Of terror, and insane distress,
And headlong fate, be happiness.

And Wordsworth!   Ah, pale ghosts, rejoice!
For never has such soothing voice
Been to your shadowy world conveyed,
Since erst, at morn, some wandering shade

Heard the clear song of Orpheus come
Through Hades and the mournful gloom.
Wordsworth has gone from us ; and ye,
Ah, may ye feel his voice as we !
He too upon a wintry clime
Had fallen, — on this iron time
Of doubts, disputes, distractions, fears.
He found us when the age had bound
Our souls in its benumbing round ;
He spoke, and loosed our heart in tears.
He laid us as we lay at birth
On the cool flowery lap of earth :
Smiles broke from us, and we had ease ;
The hills were round us, and the breeze
Went o'er the sunlit fields again ;
Our foreheads felt the wind and rain.
Our youth returned ; for there was shed
On spirits that had long been dead,
Spirits dried up and closely furled,
The freshness of the early world.

Ah ! since dark days still bring to light
Man's prudence and man's fiery might,
Time may restore us in his course
Goethe's sage mind and Byron's force ;
But where will Europe's latter hour
Again find Wordsworth's healing power?
Others will teach us how to dare,
And against fear our breast to steel :
Others will strengthen us to bear —
But who, ah ! who will make us feel?
The cloud of mortal destiny,
Others will front it fearlessly ;
But who, like him, will put it by?

Keep fresh the grass upon his grave,
O Rotha, with thy living wave !
Sing him thy best ! for few or none
Hear thy voice right, now he is gone.

STANZAS.

In Memory of Edward Quillinan.

I saw him sensitive in frame,
  I knew his spirits low ;
And wished him health, success, and fame —
  I do not wish it now.

For these are all their own reward,
  And leave no good behind ;
They try us, oftenest make us hard,
  Less modest, pure, and kind.

Alas ! yet to the suffering man,
  In this his mortal state,
Friends could not give what fortune can, —
  Health, ease, a heart elate.

But he is now by fortune foiled
  No more ; and we retain
The memory of a man unspoiled,
  Sweet, generous, and humane ;

With all the fortunate have not,
  With gentle voice and brow.
— Alive, we would have changed his lot :
  We would not change it now.

STANZAS FROM CARNAC.

FAR on its rocky knoll descried,
Saint Michael's chapel cuts the sky.
I climbed ; beneath me, bright and wide,
Lay the lone coast of Brittany.

Bright in the sunset, weird and still,
It lay beside the Atlantic wave,
As though the wizard Merlin's will
Yet charmed it from his forest-grave.

Behind me on their grassy sweep,
Bearded with lichen, scrawled and gray,
The giant stones of Carnac sleep,
In the mild evening of the May.

No priestly stern procession now
Streams through their rows of pillars old :
No victims bleed, no Druids bow :
Sheep make the daisied aisles their fold.

From bush to bush the cuckoo flies,
The orchis red gleams everywhere ;
Gold furze with broom in blossom vies,
The bluebells perfume all the air.

And o'er the glistening, lonely land,
Rise up, all round, the Christian spires ;
The church of Carnac, by the strand,
Catches the westering sun's last fires.

And there, across the watery way,
See, low above the tide at flood,
The sickle-sweep of Quiberon Bay,
Whose beach once ran with loyal blood !

And beyond that, the Atlantic wide !—
All round, no soul, no boat, no hail ;
But, on the horizon's verge descried,
Hangs, touched with light, one snowy sail.

Ah ! where is he who should have come [20]
Where that far sail is passing now,
Past the Loire's mouth, and by the foam
Of Finistère's unquiet brow,—

Home, round into the English wave?—
He tarries where the Rock of Spain
Mediterranean waters lave ;
He enters not the Atlantic main.

Oh, could he once have reached this air
Freshened by plunging tides, by showers !
Have felt this breath he loved, of fair
Cool Northern fields, and grass, and flowers !

He longed for it—pressed on. In vain !
At the Straits failed that spirit brave.
The South was parent of his pain,
The South is mistress of his grave.

A SOUTHERN NIGHT.

THE sandy spits, the shore-locked lakes,
   Melt into open, moonlit sea ;
The soft Mediterranean breaks
   At my feet, free.

Dotting the fields of corn and vine,
   Like ghosts, the huge gnarled olives stand ;
Behind, that lovely mountain line !
   While, by the strand,—

Cette, with its glistening houses white,
  Curves with the curving beach away
To where the light-house beacons bright
    Far in the bay.

Ah ! such a night, so soft, so lone,
  So moonlit, saw me once of yore [21]
Wander unquiet, and my own
    Vexed heart deplore.

But now that trouble is forgot :
  Thy memory, thy pain, to-night,
My brother ! and thine early lot, [22]
    Possess me quite.

The murmur of this Midland deep
  Is heard to-night around thy grave,
There, where Gibraltar's cannoned steep
    O'erfrowns the wave.

For there, with bodily anguish keen,
  With Indian heats at last foredone,
With public toil and private teen, —
    Thou sank'st alone.

Slow to a stop, at morning gray,
  I see the smoke-crowned vessel come :
Slow round her paddles dies away
    The seething foam.

A boat is lowered from her side ;
  Ah, gently place him on the bench !
That spirit — if all have not yet died —
    A breath might quench.

Is this the eye, the footstep fast,
  The mien of youth, we used to see ?
Poor, gallant boy ! for such thou wast,
    Still art, to me.

The limbs their wonted tasks refuse;
    The eyes are glazed, thou canst not speak;
And whiter than thy white burnous
      That wasted cheek!

Enough! The boat, with quiet shock,
    Unto its haven coming nigh,
Touches, and on Gibraltar's rock
      Lands thee, to die.

Ah me! Gibraltar's strand is far;
    But farther yet across the brine
Thy dear wife's ashes buried are,
      Remote from thine.

For there, where morning's sacred fount
    Its golden rain on earth confers,
The snowy Himalayan Mount
      O'ershadows hers.

Strange irony of fate, alas!
    Which, for two jaded English, saves,
When from their dusty life they pass,
      Such peaceful graves!

In cities should we English lie,
    Where cries are rising ever new,
And men's incessant stream goes by, —
      We who pursue

Our business with unslackening stride,
    Traverse in troops, with care-filled breast,
The soft Mediterranean side,
      The Nile, the East, —

And see all sights from pole to pole,
    And glance, and nod, and bustle by;
And never once possess our soul
      Before we die.

Not by those hoary Indian hills,
　Not by this gracious Midland sea
Whose floor to-night sweet moonshine fills,
　　Should our graves be.

Some sage, to whom the world was dead,
　And men were specks, and life a play;
Who made the roots of trees his bed,
　　And once a day

With staff and gourd his way did bend
　To villages and homes of man,
For food to keep him till he end
　　His mortal span, —

And the pure goal of being reach;
　Gray-headed, wrinkled, clad in white;
Without companion, without speech,
　　By day and night

Pondering God's mysteries untold,
　And tranquil as the glacier-snows, —
He by those Indian mountains old
　　Might well repose.

Some gray crusading knight austere,
　Who bore Saint Louis company,
And came home hurt to death, and here
　　Landed to die;

Some youthful troubadour, whose tongue
　Filled Europe once with his love-pain,
Who here outworn had sunk, and sung
　　His dying strain;

Some girl, who here from castle-bower,
　With furtive step and cheek of flame,
'Twixt myrtle-hedges all in flower
　　By moonlight came

To meet her pirate-lover's ship,
     And from the wave-kissed marble stair
Beckoned him on with quivering lip
          And floating hair,

And lived some moons in happy trance,
     Then learnt his death, and pined away, —
Such by these waters of romance
          'Twas meet to lay.

But you — a grave for knight or sage,
     Romantic, solitary, still,
O spent ones of a work-day age !
          Befits you ill.

So sang I ; but the midnight breeze,
     Down to the brimmed, moon-charmèd main,
Comes softly through the olive-trees,
          And checks my strain.

I think of her whose gentle tongue
     All plaint in her own cause controlled ;
Of thee I think, my brother ! young
          In heart, high-souled ;

That comely face, that clustered brow,
     That cordial hand, that bearing free, —
I see them still, I see them now,
          Shall always see !

And what but gentleness untired,
     And what but noble feeling warm,
Wherever shown, howe'er inspired,
          Is grace, is charm ?

What else is all these waters are,
     What else is steeped in lucid sheen,
What else is bright, what else is fair,
          What else serene ?

Mild o'er her grave, ye mountains, shine !
   Gently by his, ye waters, glide !
To that in you which is divine
     They were allied.

HAWORTH CHURCHYARD.

APRIL, 1855.

WHERE, under Loughrigg, the stream
Of Rotha sparkles through fields
Vested forever with green,
Four years since, in the house
Of a gentle spirit now dead,
Wordsworth's son-in-law, friend, —
I saw the meeting of two
Gifted women.[23] The one,
Brilliant with recent renown,
Young, unpractised, had told
With a master's accent her feigned
Story of passionate life ;
The other, maturer in fame,
Earning, she too, her praise
First in fiction, had since
Widened her sweep, and surveyed
History, politics, mind.

The two held converse ; they wrote
In a book which of world-famous souls
Kept the memorial : bard,
Warrior, statesman, had signed
Their names : chief glory of all,
Scott had bestowed there his last

Breathings of song, with a pen
Tottering, a death-stricken hand.

Hope at that meeting smiled fair.
Years in number, it seemed,
Lay before both, and a fame
Heightened, and multiplied power. —
Behold ! The elder, to-day,
Lies expecting from death,
In mortal weakness, a last
Summons ! the younger is dead !

First to the living we pay
Mournful homage : the Muse
Gains not an earth-deafened ear.

Hail to the steadfast soul,
Which, unflinching and keen,
Wrought to erase from its depth
Mist and illusion and fear !
Hail to the spirit which dared
Trust its own thoughts, before yet
Echoed her back by the crowd !
Hail to the courage which gave
Voice to its creed, ere the creed
Won consecration from time !

Turn we next to the dead. —
How shall we honor the young,
The ardent, the gifted ? how mourn ?
Console we cannot, her ear
Is deaf. Far northward from here,
In a churchyard high 'mid the moors
Of Yorkshire, a little earth
Stops it forever to praise.

Where behind Keighley the road
Up to the heart of the moors
Between heath-clad showery hills
Runs, and colliers' carts
Poach the deep ways coming down,
And a rough, grimed race have their homes, —
There on its slope is built
The moorland town.   But the church
Stands on the crest of the hill,
Lonely and bleak ; at its side
The parsonage-house and the graves.

Strew with laurel the grave
Of the early-dying !   Alas !
Early she goes on the path
To the silent country, and leaves
Half her laurels unwon,
Dying too soon ; yet green
Laurels she had, and a course
Short, but redoubled by fame.

And not friendless, and not
Only with strangers to meet,
Faces ungreeting and cold,
Thou, O mourned one, to-day
Enterest the house of the grave !
Those of thy blood, whom thou lovedst,
Have preceded thee, — young,
Loving, a sisterly band ;
Some in art, some in gift
Inferior — all in fame.
They, like friends, shall receive
This comer, greet her with joy ;
Welcome the sister, the friend ;
Hear with delight of thy fame !

Round thee they lie ; the grass
Blows from their graves to thy own !
She whose genius, though not
Puissant like thine, was yet
Sweet and graceful ; and she
(How shall I sing her?) whose soul
Knew no fellow for might,
Passion, vehemence, grief,
Daring, since Byron died, —
The world-famed son of fire, — she who sank
Baffled, unknown, self-consumed ;
Whose too bold dying song [24]
Shook, like a clarion-blast, my soul.

Of one, too, I have heard,
A brother : sleeps he here?
Of all that gifted race
Not the least gifted ; young,
Unhappy, eloquent ; the child
Of many hopes, of many tears.
O boy, if here thou sleep'st, sleep well !
On thee too did the Muse
Bright in thy cradle smile ;
But some dark shadow came
(I know not what) and interposed.

Sleep, O cluster of friends,
Sleep ! or only when May,
Brought by the west-wind, returns
Back to your native heaths,
And the plover is heard on the moors,
Yearly awake to behold
The opening summer, the sky,
The shining moorland ; to hear
The drowsy bee, as of old,

Hum o'er the thyme, the grouse
Call from the heather in bloom!
Sleep, or only for this
Break your united repose!

EPILOGUE.

So I sang; but the Muse,
Shaking her head, took the harp —
Stern interrupted my strain,
Angrily smote on the chords.

April showers
Rush o'er the Yorkshire moors.
Stormy, through driving mist,
Loom the blurred hills; the rain
Lashes the newly-made grave.

Unquiet souls!
— In the dark fermentation of earth,
In the never-idle workshop of nature,
In the eternal movement,
Ye shall find yourselves again!

RUGBY CHAPEL.

NOVEMBER, 1857.

COLDLY, sadly descends
The autumn evening. The field
Strewn with its dank yellow drifts
Of withered leaves, and the elms,
Fade into dimness apace,
Silent; hardly a shout

From a few boys late at their play !
The lights come out in the street,
In the schoolroom windows ; but cold,
Solemn, unlighted, austere,
Through the gathering darkness, arise
The chapel-walls, in whose bound
Thou, my father ! art laid.

There thou dost lie, in the gloom
Of the autumn evening.   But ah !
That word *gloom* to my mind
Brings thee back in the light
Of thy radiant vigor again.
In the gloom of November we passed
Days not dark at thy side ;
Seasons impaired not the ray
Of thy buoyant cheerfulness clear.
Such thou wast ! and I stand
In the autumn evening, and think
Of bygone autumns with thee.

Fifteen years have gone round
Since thou arosest to tread,
In the summer-morning, the road
Of death, at a call unforeseen,
Sudden.   For fifteen years,
We who till then in thy shade
Rested as under the boughs
Of a mighty oak, have endured
Sunshine and rain as we might,
Bare, unshaded, alone,
Lacking the shelter of thee.

O strong soul, by what shore
Tarriest thou now?   For that force,

Surely, has not been left vain !
Somewhere, surely, afar,
In the sounding labor-house vast
Of being, is practised that strength,
Zealous, beneficent, firm !

Yes, in some far-shining sphere,
Conscious or not of the past,
Still thou performest the word
Of the Spirit in whom thou dost live,
Prompt, unwearied, as here.
Still thou upraisest with zeal
The humble good from the ground,
Sternly repressest the bad ;
Still, like a trumpet, dost rouse
Those who with half-open eyes
Tread the border-land dim
'Twixt vice and virtue ; reviv'st,
Succorest. This was thy work,
This was thy life upon earth.

What is the course of the life
Of mortal men on the earth?
Most men eddy about
Here and there, eat and drink,
Chatter and love and hate,
Gather and squander, are raised
Aloft, are hurled in the dust,
Striving blindly, achieving
Nothing ; and then they die, —
Perish ; and no one asks
Who or what they have been,
More than he asks what waves,
In the moonlit solitudes mild

Of the midmost ocean, have swelled,
Foamed for a moment, and gone.

And there are some whom a thirst
Ardent, unquenchable, fires,
Not with the crowd to be spent,
Not without aim to go round
In an eddy of purposeless dust,
Effort unmeaning and vain.
Ah yes ! some of us strive
Not without action to die
Fruitless, but something to snatch
From dull oblivion, nor all
Glut the devouring grave.
We, we have chosen our path, —
Path to a clear-purposed goal,
Path of advance ; but it leads
A long, steep journey, through sunk
Gorges, o'er mountains in snow.
Cheerful, with friends, we set forth :
Then, on the height, comes the storm.
Thunder crashes from rock
To rock ; the cataracts reply ;
Lightnings dazzle our eyes ;
Roaring torrents have breached
The track ; the stream-bed descends
In the place where the wayfarer once
Planted his footstep ; the spray
Boils o'er its borders ; aloft,
The unseen snow-beds dislodge
Their hanging ruin. Alas !
Havoc is made in our train !
Friends who set forth at our side
Falter, are lost in the storm.

We, we only are left!
With frowning foreheads, with lips
Sternly compressed, we strain on,
On; and at nightfall at last
Come to the end of our way,
To the lonely inn 'mid the rocks;
Where the gaunt and taciturn host
Stands on the threshold, the wind
Shaking his thin white hairs,
Holds his lantern to scan
Our storm-beat figures, and asks, —
Whom in our party we bring?
Whom we have left in the snow?

Sadly we answer, We bring
Only ourselves! we lost
Sight of the rest in the storm.
Hardly ourselves we fought through,
Stripped, without friends, as we are.
Friends, companions, and train,
The avalanche swept from our side.

But thou wouldst not *alone*
Be saved, my father! *alone*
Conquer and come to thy goal,
Leaving the rest in the wild.
We were weary, and we
Fearful, and we in our march
Fain to drop down and to die.
Still thou turnedst, and still
Beckonedst the trembler, and still
Gavest the weary thy hand.
If, in the paths of the world,
Stones might have wounded thy feet,

Toil or dejection have tried
Thy spirit, of that we saw
Nothing : to us thou wast still
Cheerful, and helpful, and firm !
Therefore to thee it was given
Many to save with thyself;
And, at the end of thy day,
O faithful shepherd ! to come,
Bringing thy sheep in thy hand.

And through thee I believe
In the noble and great who are gone ;
Pure souls honored and blest
By former ages, who else —
Such, so soulless, so poor,
Is the race of men whom I see —
Seemed but a dream of the heart,
Seemed but a cry of desire.
Yes ! I believe that there lived
Others like thee in the past,
Not like the men of the crowd
Who all round me to-day
Bluster or cringe, and make life
Hideous and arid and vile ;
But souls tempered with fire,
Fervent, heroic, and good,
Helpers and friends of mankind.

Servants of God ! — or sons
Shall I not call you? because
Not as servants ye knew
Your Father's innermost mind,
His who unwillingly sees
One of his little ones lost, —
Yours is the praise, if mankind

Hath not as yet in its march
Fainted and fallen and died.

See !   In the rocks of the world
Marches the host of mankind,
A feeble, wavering line.
Where are they tending ?   A God
Marshalled them, gave them their goal.
Ah, but the way is so long !

Years they have been in the wild :
Sore thirst plagues them ; the rocks,
Rising all round, overawe ;
Factions divide them ; their host
Threatens to break, to dissolve.
Ah ! keep, keep them combined !
Else, of the myriads who fill
That army, not one shall arrive ;
Sole they shall stray ; on the rocks
Batter forever in vain,
Die one by one in the waste.

Then, in such hour of need
Of your fainting, dispirited race,
Ye like angels appear,
Radiant with ardor divine.
Beacons of hope, ye appear !
Languor is not in your heart,
Weakness is not in your word,
Weariness not on your brow.
Ye alight in our van ! at your voice,
Panic, despair, flee away.
Ye move through the ranks, recall
The stragglers, refresh the outworn,
Praise, re-inspire the brave.

Order, courage, return ;
Eyes rekindling, and prayers,
Follow your steps as ye go.
Ye fill up the gaps in our files,
Strengthen the wavering line,
Stablish, contiï ïe our march,
On, to the bound of the waste,
On, to the City of God.

HEINE'S GRAVE.

" *Henri Heine* " — 'tis here !
The black tombstone, the name
Carved there — no more ; and the smooth,
Swarded alleys, the limes
Touched with yellow by hot
Summer, but under them still,
In September's bright afternoon,
Shadow, and verdure, and cool.
Trim Montmartre ! the faint
Murmur of Paris outside ;
Crisp everlasting-flowers,
Yellow and black, on the graves.

Half blind, palsied, in pain,
Hither to come, from the streets'
Uproar, surely not loath
Wast thou, Heine ! to lie
Quiet, to ask for closed
Shutters, and darkened room,
And cool drinks, and an eased
Posture, and opium, no more ;
Hither to come, and to sleep
Under the wings of Renown.

Ah ! not little, when pain
Is most quelling, and man
Easily quelled, and the fine
Temper of genius so soon
Thrills at each smart, is the praise,
Not to have yielded to pain !
No small boast, for a weak
Son of mankind, to the earth
Pinned by the thunder, to rear
His bolt-scathed front to the stars ;
And, undaunted, retort
'Gainst thick-crashing, insane,
Tyrannous tempests of bale,
Arrowy lightnings of soul.

Hark ! through the alley resounds
Mocking laughter !   A film
Creeps o'er the sunshine ; a breeze
Ruffles the warm afternoon,
Saddens my soul with its chill.
Gibing of spirits in scorn
Shakes every leaf of the grove,
Mars the benignant repose
Of this amiable home of the dead.

Bitter spirits, ye claim
Heine?   Alas, he is yours !
Only a moment I longed
Here in the quiet to snatch
From such mates the outworn
Poet, and steep him in calm.
Only a moment ! I knew
Whose he was who is here
Buried : I knew he was yours !
Ah ! I knew that I saw

Here no sepulchre built
In the laurelled rock, o'er the blue
Naples bay, for a sweet
Tender Virgil ; no tomb
On Ravenna sands, in the shade
Of Ravenna pines, for a high
Austere Dante ; no grave
By the Avon side, in the bright
Stratford meadows, for thee,
Shakspeare, loveliest of souls,
Peerless in radiance, in joy !

What, then, so harsh and malign,
Heine ! distils from thy life?
Poisons the peace of thy grave?

I chide with thee not, that thy sharp
Upbraidings often assailed
England, my country ; for we,
Heavy and sad, for her sons,
Long since, deep in our hearts,
Echo the blame of her foes.
We too sigh that she flags ;
We too say that she now —
Scarce comprehending the voice
Of her greatest, golden-mouthed sons
Of a former age any more —
Stupidly travels her round
Of mechanic business, and lets
Slow die out of her life
Glory, and genius, and joy.

So thou arraign'st her, her foe ;
So we arraign her, her sons.

Yes, we arraign her ! but she,
The weary Titan, with deaf
Ears, and labor-dimmed eyes,
Regarding neither to right
Nor left, goes passively by,
Staggering on to her goal ;
Bearing on shoulders immense,
Atlanteän, the load,
Well-nigh not to be borne,
Of the too vast orb of her fate.

But was it thou — I think
Surely it was ! — that bard
Unnamed, who, Goethe said,
Had every other gift, but wanted love —
Love, without which the tongue
Even of angels sounds amiss?

Charm is the glory which makes
Song of the poet divine.
Love is the fountain of charm.
How without charm wilt thou draw,
Poet ! the world to thy way?
Not by the lightnings of wit,
Not by the thunder of scorn.
These to the world too are given ;
Wit it possesses, and scorn :
Charm is the poet's alone.
Hollow and dull are the great,
And artists envious, and the mob profane.
We know all this, we know !
Cam'st thou from heaven, O child
Of light ! but this to declare?
Alas ! to help us forget

Such barren knowledge a while,
God gave the poet his song.

Therefore a secret unrest
Tortured thee, brilliant and bold ;
Therefore triumph itself
Tasted amiss to thy soul.
Therefore, with blood of thy foes,
Trickled in silence thine own.
Therefore the victor's heart
Broke on the field of his fame.

Ah ! as of old, from the pomp
Of Italian Milan, the fair
Flower of marble of white
Southern palaces, — steps
Bordered by statues, and walks
Terraced, and orange bowers
Heavy with fragrance, — the blond
German Kaiser full oft
Longed himself back to the fields,
Rivers, and high-roofed towns
Of his native Germany ; so,
So, how often ! from hot
Paris drawing-rooms, and lamps
Blazing, and brilliant crowds,
Starred and jewelled, of men
Famous, of women the queens
Of dazzling converse ; from fumes
Of praise, hot, heady fumes, to the poor brain
That mount, that madden, — how oft
Heine's spirit outworn
Longed itself out of the din,
Back to the tranquil, the cool
Far German home of his youth !

See ! in the May afternoon,
O'er the fresh short turf of the **Hartz**,
A youth, with the foot of youth,
Heine ! thou climbest again :
Up through the tall dark firs
Warming their heads in the sun,
Checkering the grass with their shade ;
Up by the stream, with its huge
Moss-hung bowlders, and thin
Musical water half-hid ;
Up o'er the rock-strewn slope,
With the sinking sun, and the air
Chill, and the shadows now
Long on the gray hillside, —
To the stone-roofed hut at the top !

Or, yet later, in watch
On the roof of the Brocken-tower
Thou standest, gazing ! — to see
The broad red sun over field,
Forest, and city, and spire,
And mist-tracked steam of the wide,
Wide German land, going down
In a bank of vapors, — again
Standest, at nightfall, alone !

Or, next morning, with limbs
Rested by slumber, and heart
Freshened and light with the May,
O'er the gracious spurs coming down
Of the Lower Hartz, among oaks
And beechen coverts, and copse
Of hazels green, in whose depth
Ilse, the fairy transformed,
In a thousand water-breaks light

Pours her petulant youth ;
Climbing the rock which juts
O'er the valley, — the dizzily perched
Rock, — to its iron cross
Once more thou cling'st ; to the cross
Clingest ! with smiles, with a sigh !

Goethe too had been there.[25]
In the long-past winter he came
To the frozen Hartz, with his soul
Passionate, eager ; his youth
All in ferment.   But he,
Destined to work and to live,
Left it, and thou, alas !
Only to laugh and to die.

But something prompts me : Not thus
Take leave of Heine ! not thus
Speak the last word at his grave !
Not in pity, and not
With half censure : with awe
Hail, as it passes from earth
Scattering lightnings, that soul !

The Spirit of the world,
Beholding the absurdity of men, —
Their vaunts, their feats, — let a sardonic smile,
For one short moment, wander o'er his lips.
That smile was Heine !   For its earthly hour
The strange guest sparkled ; now 'tis passed away.

That was Heine ! and we,
Myriads who live, who have lived,
What are we all, but a mood,
A single mood, of the life

Of the Spirit in whom we exist,
Who alone is all things in one?

Spirit, who fillest us all!
Spirit, who utterest in each
New-coming son of mankind
Such of thy thoughts as thou wilt!
O thou, one of whose moods,
Bitter and strange, was the life
Of Heine, — his strange, alas!
His bitter life, — may a life
Other and milder be mine!
May'st thou a mood more serene,
Happier, have uttered in mine!
May'st thou the rapture of peace
Deep have imbreathed at its core;
Made it a ray of thy thought,
Made it a beat of thy joy!

STANZAS FROM
THE GRANDE CHARTREUSE.

THROUGH Alpine meadows soft-suffused
With rain, where thick the crocus blows,
Past the dark forges long disused,
The mule-track from Saint Laurent goes.
The bridge is crossed, and slow we ride,
Through forest, up the mountain side.

The autumnal evening darkens round,
The wind is up, and drives the rain;
While, hark! far down, with strangled sound
Doth the Dead Guier's stream complain,

Where that wet smoke, among the woods,
Over his boiling caldron broods.

Swift rush the spectral vapors white
Past limestone scars with ragged pines,
Showing — then blotting from our sight ! —
Halt — through the cloud-drift something shines !
High in the valley, wet and drear,
The huts of Courrerie appear.

Strike leftward ! cries our guide ; and higher
Mounts up the stony forest way.
At last the encircling trees retire ;
Look ! through the showery twilight gray,
What pointed roofs are these advance ?
A palace of the kings of France ?

Approach, for what we seek is here !
Alight, and sparely sup, and wait
For rest in this outbuilding near ;
Then cross the sward, and reach that gate ;
Knock ; pass the wicket.   Thou art come
To the Carthusians' world-famed home.

The silent courts, where night and day
Into their stone-carved basins cold
The splashing icy fountains play,
The humid corridors behold,
Where, ghost-like in the deepening night,
Cowled forms brush by in gleaming white !

The chapel, where no organ's peal
Invests the stern and naked prayer !
With penitential cries they kneel
And wrestle ; rising then, with bare
And white uplifted faces stand,
Passing the Host from hand to hand ;

Each takes, and then his visage wan
Is buried in his cowl once more.
The cells ! — the suffering Son of man
Upon the wall ; the knee-worn floor ;
And where they sleep, that wooden bed,
Which shall their coffin be when dead !

The library, where tract and tome
Not to feed priestly pride are there,
To hymn the conquering march of Rome,
Nor yet to amuse, as ours are :
They paint of souls the inner strife,
Their drops of blood, their death in life.

The garden, overgrown — yet mild,
See, fragrant herbs are flowering there :
Strong children of the Alpine wild
Whose culture is the brethren's care ;
Of human tasks their only one,
And cheerful works beneath the sun.

Those halls, too, destined to contain
Each its own pilgrim-host of old,
From England, Germany, or Spain, —
All are before me ! I behold
The house, the brotherhood austere.
And what am I, that I am here ?

For rigorous teachers seized my youth,
And purged its faith, and trimmed its fire,
Showed me the high, white star of Truth,
There bade me gaze, and there aspire.
Even now their whispers pierce the gloom :
What dost thou in this living tomb ?

Forgive me, masters of the mind !
At whose behest I long ago

So much unlearned, so much resigned :
I come not here to be your foe !
I seek these anchorites, not in ruth,
To curse and to deny your truth ;

Not as their friend, or child, I speak !
But as, on some far northern strand,
Thinking of his own gods, a Greek
In pity and mournful awe might stand
Before some fallen Runic stone ;
For both were faiths, and both are gone.

Wandering between two worlds, one dead,
The other powerless to be born,
With nowhere yet to rest my head,
Like these, on earth I wait forlorn.
Their faith, my tears, the world deride :
I come to shed them at their side.

Oh, hide me in your gloom profound,
Ye solemn seats of holy pain !
Take me, cowled forms, and fence me round,
Till I possess my soul again ;
Till free my thoughts before me roll,
Not chafed by hourly false control !

For the world cries, your faith is now
But a dead time's exploded dream ;
My melancholy, sciolists say,
Is a passed mode, an outworn theme. —
As if the world had ever had
A faith, or sciolists been sad !

Ah ! if it *be* passed, take away,
At least, the restlessness, the pain !
Be man henceforth no more a prey
To these out-dated stings again !

The nobleness of grief is gone :
Ah, leave us not the fret alone !

But, — if you cannot give us ease, —
Last of the race of them who grieve,
Here leave us to die out with these
Last of the people who believe !
Silent, while years engrave the brow ;
Silent — the best are silent now.

Achilles ponders in his tent,
The kings of modern thought are dumb ;
Silent they are, though not content,
And wait to see the future come.
They have the grief men had of yore,
But they contend and cry no more.

Our fathers watered with their tears
This sea of time whereon we sail ;
Their voices were in all men's ears
Who passed within their puissant hail.
Still the same ocean round us raves,
But we stand mute, and watch the waves.

For what availed it, all the noise
And outcry of the former men ?
Say, have their sons achieved more joys ?
Say, is life lighter now than then ?
The sufferers died, they left their pain ;
The pangs which tortured them remain.

What helps it now, that Byron bore,
With haughty scorn which mocked the smart,
Through Europe to the Ætolian shore
The pageant of his bleeding heart ?
That thousands counted every groan,
And Europe made his woe her own ?

What boots it, Shelley! that the breeze
Carried thy lovely wail away,
Musical through Italian trees
Which fringe thy soft blue Spezzian bay?
Inheritors of thy distress,
Have restless hearts one throb the less?

Or are we easier, to have read,
O Obermann! the sad, stern page,
Which tells us how thou hidd'st thy head
From the fierce tempest of thine age
In the lone brakes of Fontainebleau,
Or chalets near the Alpine snow?

Ye slumber in your silent grave! —
The world, which for an idle day
Grace to your mood of sadness gave,
Long since hath flung her weeds away.
The eternal trifler breaks your spell;
But we — we learnt your lore too well!

Years hence, perhaps, may dawn an age,
More fortunate, alas! than we,
Which without hardness will be sage,
And gay without frivolity.
Sons of the world, oh! speed those years;
But, while we wait, allow our tears!

Allow them! We admire with awe
The exulting thunder of your race;
You give the universe your law,
You triumph over time and space:
Your pride of life, your tireless powers,
We praise them, but they are not ours.

We are like children reared in shade
Beneath some old-world abbey wall,

Forgotten in a forest-glade,
And secret from the eyes of all.
Deep, deep the greenwood round them waves,
Their abbey, and its close of graves !

But, where the road runs near the stream,
Oft through the trees they catch a glance
Of passing troops in the sun's beam, —
Pennon, and plume, and flashing lance ;
Forth to the world those soldiers fare,
To life, to cities, and to war.

And through the woods, another way,
Faint bugle-notes from far are borne,
Where hunters gather, staghounds bay,
Round some old forest-lodge at morn.
Gay dames are there, in sylvan green ;
Laughter and cries — those notes between !

The banners flashing through the trees
Make their blood dance, and chain their eyes ;
That bugle-music on the breeze
Arrests them with a charmed surprise.
Banner by turns and bugle woo :
Ye shy recluses, follow too !

O children, what do ye reply ?
" Action and pleasure, will ye roam
Through these secluded dells to cry
And call us ? but too late ye come !
Too late for us your call ye blow,
Whose bent was taken long ago.

" Long since we pace this shadowed nave ;
We watch those yellow tapers shine,
Emblems of hope over the grave,
In the high altar's depth divine.

The organ carries to our ear
Its accents of another sphere.

" Fenced early in this cloistral round
Of revery, of shade, of prayer,
How should we grow in other ground?
How can we flower in foreign air?
— Pass, banners, pass, and bugles, cease ;
And leave our desert to its peace ! "

STANZAS

IN MEMORY OF THE AUTHOR OF OBERMANN.[26]

NOVEMBER, 1849.

IN front the awful Alpine track
Crawls up its rocky stair ;
The autumn storm-winds drive the rack,
Close o'er it, in the air.

Behind are the abandoned baths [27]
Mute in their meadows lone ;
The leaves are on the valley-paths,
The mists are on the Rhone, —

The white mists rolling like a sea ;
I hear the torrents roar.
— Yes, Obermann, all speaks of thee ;
I feel thee near once more.

I turn thy leaves ; I feel their breath
Once more upon me roll ;
That air of languor, cold, and death,
Which brooded o'er thy soul.

Fly hence, poor wretch, whoe'er thou art,
Condemned to cast about,
All shipwreck in thy own weak heart,
For comfort from without !

A fever in these pages burns
Beneath the calm they feign ;
A wounded human spirit turns,
Here, on its bed of pain.

Yes, though the virgin mountain air
Fresh through these pages blows ;
Though to these leaves the glaciers spare
The soul of their mute snows ;

Though here a mountain murmur swells
Of many a dark-boughed pine ;
Though, as you read, you hear the bells
Of the high-pasturing kine, —

Yet through the hum of torrent lone,
And brooding mountain bee,
There sobs I know not what ground-tone
Of human agony.

Is it for this, because the sound
Is fraught too deep with pain,
That, Obermann ! the world around
So little loves thy strain ?

Some secrets may the poet tell,
For the world loves new ways :
To tell too deep ones is not well, —
It knows not what he says.

Yet, of the spirits who have reigned
In this our troubled day,

I know but two who have attained,
Save thee, to see their way.

By England's lakes, in gray old age,
His quiet home one keeps ;
And one, the strong much-toiling sage,
In German Weimar sleeps.

But Wordsworth's eyes avert their ken
From half of human fate ;
And Goethe's course few sons of men
May think to emulate.

For he pursued a lonely road,
His eyes on Nature's plan ;
Neither made man too much a god,
Nor God too much a man.

Strong was he, with a spirit free
From mists, and sane and clear ;
Clearer, how much ! than ours — yet we
Have a worse course to steer.

For, though his manhood bore the blast
Of a tremendous time,
Yet in a tranquil world was passed
His tenderer youthful prime.

But we, brought forth and reared in hours
Of change, alarm, surprise, —
What shelter to grow ripe is ours?
What leisure to grow wise?

Like children bathing on the shore,
Buried a wave beneath,
The second wave succeeds before
We have had time to breathe.

Too fast we live, too much are tried,
Too harassed, to attain
Wordsworth's sweet calm, or Goethe's wide
And luminous view to gain.

And then we turn, thou sadder sage,
To thee ! we feel thy spell !
— The hopeless tangle of our age,
Thou too hast scanned it well.

Immovable thou sittest, still
As death, composed to bear ;
Thy head is clear, thy feeling chill,
And icy thy despair.

Yes, as the son of Thetis said,
I hear thee saying now :
Greater by far than thou are dead;
Strive not ! die also thou !

Ah ! two desires toss about
The poet's feverish blood ;
One drives him to the world without,
And one to solitude.

The glow, he cries, *the thrill of life,*
Where, where do these abound ?
Not in the world, not in the strife
Of men, shall they be found.

He who hath watched, not shared, the strife,
Knows how the day hath gone :
He only lives with the world's life,
Who hath renounced his own.

To thee we come, then ! Clouds are rolled
Where thou, O seer ! art set ;

Thy realm of thought is drear and cold —
The world is colder yet.

And thou hast pleasures, too, to share
With those who come to thee, —
Balms floating on thy mountain air,
And healing sights to see.

How often, where the slopes are green
On Jaman, hast thou sate
By some high chalet-door, and seen
The summer day grow late;

And darkness steal o'er the wet grass
With the pale crocus starred,
And reach that glimmering sheet of glass
Beneath the piny sward, —

Lake Leman's waters, far below;
And watched the rosy light
Fade from the distant peaks of snow;
And on the air of night

Heard accents of the eternal tongue
Through the pine branches play, —
Listened, and felt thyself grow young!
Listened, and wept — Away!

Away the dreams that but deceive!
And thou, sad guide, adieu!
I go, fate drives me; but I leave
Half of my life with you.

We, in some unknown Power's employ,
Move on a rigorous line;
Can neither, when we will, enjoy,
Nor, when we will, resign.

I in the world must live ; but thou,
Thou melancholy shade !
Wilt not, if thou canst see' me now,
Condemn me, nor upbraid.

For thou art gone away from earth,
And place with those dost claim,
The children of the second birth,
Whom the world could not tame ;

And with that small transfigured band,
Whom many a different way
Conducted to their common land,
Thou learn'st to think as they

Christian and Pagan, king and slave,
Soldier and anchorite,
Distinctions we esteem so grave,
Are nothing in their sight.

They do not ask, who pined unseen,
Who was on action hurled,
Whose one bond is, that all have been
Unspotted by the world.

There without anger thou wilt see
Him who obeys thy spell
No more, so he but rest, like thee,
Unsoiled ; and so, farewell !

Farewell !   Whether thou now liest near
That much-loved inland sea,
The ripples of whose blue waves cheer
Vevey and Meillerie ;

And in that gracious region bland,
Where with clear-rustling wave

The scented pines of Switzerland
Stand dark round thy green grave,—

Between the dusty vineyard-walls
Issuing on that green place,
The early peasant still recalls
The pensive stranger's face,—

And stoops to clear thy moss-grown date
Ere he plods on again;
Or whether, by maligner fate,
Among the swarms of men,—

Where between granite terraces
The blue Seine rolls her wave,
The Capital of Pleasure sees
Thy hardly-heard-of grave,—

Farewell!   Under the sky we part,
In this stern Alpine dell.
O unstrung will! O broken heart!
A last, a last farewell!

OBERMANN ONCE MORE.

(COMPOSED MANY YEARS AFTER THE PRECEDING.)

Savez-vous quelque bien qui console du regret d'un monde?
                                        OBERMANN.

GLION?   Ah! twenty years, it cuts [28]
All meaning from a name!
White houses prank where once were huts;
Glion, but not the same!

And yet I know not!   All unchanged
The turf, the pines, the sky!

The hills in their old order ranged;
The lake, with Chillon by;

And 'neath those chestnut-trees, where stiff
And stony mounts the way,
The crackling husk-heaps burn, as if
I left them yesterday.

Across the valley, on that slope,
The huts of Avant shine;
Its pines, under their branches, ope
Ways for the pasturing kine.

Full-foaming milk-pails, Alpine fare,
Sweet heaps of fresh-cut grass,
Invite to rest the traveller there
Before he climb the pass, —

The gentian-flowered pass, its crown [29]
With yellow spires aflame;
Whence drops the path to Allière down,
And walls where Byron came; [30]

By their green river, who doth change
His birth-name just below,
Orchard and croft and full-stored grange
Nursed by his pastoral flow.

But stop! to fetch back thoughts that stray
Beyond this gracious bound,
The cone of Jaman, pale and gray,
See, in the blue profound!

Ah, Jaman! delicately tall
Above his sun-warmed firs, —
What thoughts to me his rocks recall,
What memories he stirs!

And who but thou must be, in truth,
Obermann ! with me here ?
Thou master of my wandering youth,
But left this many a year !

Yes, I forget the world's work wrought,
Its warfare waged with pain :
An eremite with thee, in thought
Once more I slip my chain, —

And to thy mountain chalet come,
And lie beside its door,
And hear the wild bee's Alpine hum,
And thy sad, tranquil lore.

Again I feel the words inspire
Their mournful calm ; serene,
Yet tinged with infinite desire
For all that *might* have been, —

The harmony from which man swerved
Made his life's rule once more ;
The universal order served,
Earth happier than before.

— While thus I mused, night gently ran
Down over hill and wood.
Then, still and sudden, Obermann
On the grass near me stood.

Those pensive features well I knew, —
On my mind, years before,
Imaged so oft, imaged so true !
— A shepherd's garb he wore ;

A mountain flower was in his hand,
A book was in his breast.

Bent on my face, with gaze which scanned
My soul, his eyes did rest.

"And is it thou," he cried, "so long
Held by the world which we
Loved not, who turnest from the throng
Back to thy youth and me?

"And from thy world, with heart opprest,
Choosest thou *now* to turn?
Ah me! we anchorites read things best,
Clearest their course discern!

"Thou fled'st me when the ungenial earth,
Man's work-place, lay in gloom:
Return'st thou in her hour of birth,
Of hopes and hearts in bloom?

"Perceiv'st thou not the change of day?
Ah! Carry back thy ken,
What, some two thousand years! Survey
The world as it was then.

"Like ours it looked in outward air.
Its head was clear and true,
Sumptuous its clothing, rich its fare,
No pause its action knew;

"Stout was its arm, each thew and bone
Seemed puissant and alive:
But, ah! its heart, its heart was stone,
And so it could not thrive!

"On that hard Pagan world, disgust
And secret loathing fell;
Deep weariness and sated lust
Made human life a hell.

" In his cool hall, with haggard eyes,
The Roman noble lay ;
He drove abroad, in furious guise,
Along the Appian Way.

" He made a feast, drank fierce and fast,
And crowned his hair with flowers ;
No easier nor no quicker passed
The impracticable hours.

" The brooding East with awe beheld
Her impious younger world.
The Roman tempest swelled and swelled,
And on her head was hurled.

" The East bowed low before the blast
In patient, deep disdain ;
She let the legions thunder past,
And plunged in thought again.

" So well she mused, a morning broke
Across her spirit gray ;
A conquering, new-born joy awoke,
And filled her life with day.

" ' Poor world !' she cried, 'so deep accurst,
That runn'st from pole to pole
To seek a draught to slake thy thirst.—
Go, seek it in thy soul !'

" She heard it, the victorious West,
In crown and sword arrayed ;
She felt the void which mined her breast,
She shivered and obeyed.

" She vailed her eagles, snapped her sword,
And laid her sceptre down ;

Her stately purple she abhorred,
And her imperial crown.

"She broke her flutes, she stopped her sports,
Her artists could not please.
She tore her books, she shut her courts,
She fled her palaces.

"Lust of the eye, and pride of life,
She left it all behind,
And hurried, torn with inward strife,
The wilderness to find.

"Tears washed the trouble from her face;
She changed into a child;
'Mid weeds and wrecks she stood,— a place
Of ruin,— but she smiled!

"Oh, had I lived in that great day,
How had its glory new
Filled earth and heaven, and caught away
My ravished spirit too!

"No thoughts that to the world belong
Had stood against the wave
Of love which set so deep and strong
From Christ's then open grave.

"No cloister-floor of humid stone
Had been too cold for me;
For me no Eastern desert lone
Had been too far to flee.

"No lonely life had passed too slow,
When I could hourly scan
Upon his cross, with head sunk low,
That nailed, thorn-crownèd Man;

"Could see the Mother with the Child
Whose tender winning arts
Have to his little arms beguiled
So many wounded hearts !

"And centuries came, and ran their course ;
And, unspent all that time,
Still, still went forth that Child's dear force,
And still was at its prime.

"Ay, ages long endured his span
Of life, — 'tis true received, —
That gracious Child, that thorn-crowned Man !
— He lived while we believed.

"While we believed, on earth he went,
And open stood his grave ;
Men called from chamber, church, and tent,
And Christ was by to save.

"Now he is dead !   Far hence he lies
In the lorn Syrian town ;
And on his grave, with shining eyes,
The Syrian stars look down.

"In vain men still, with hoping new,
Regard his death-place dumb,
And say the stone is not yet to,
And wait for words to come.

"Ah ! from that silent sacred land
Of sun, and arid stone,
And crumbling wall, and sultry sand,
Comes now one word alone !

• From David's lips that word did roll ;
'Tis true and living yet, —

No man can save his brother's soul,
Nor pay his brother's debt.

"Alone, self-poised, henceforward man
Must labor ; must resign
His all too human creeds, and scan
Simply the way divine ;

"But slow that tide of common thought,
Which bathed our life, retired ;
Slow, slow the old world wore to naught,
And pulse by pulse expired.

"Its frame yet stood without a breach,
When blood and warmth were fled ;
And still it spake its wonted speech,
But every word was dead.

"And oh ! we cried, that on this corse
Might fall a freshening storm !
Rive its dry bones, and with new force
A new-sprung world inform !

" — Down came the storm ! O'er France it passed
In sheets of scathing fire.
All Europe felt that fiery blast,
And shook as it rushed by her.

"Down came the storm !   In ruins fell
The worn-out world we knew.
It passed, that elemental swell :
Again appeared the blue ;

"The sun shone in the new-washed sky.
— And what from heaven saw he ?
Blocks of the past, like icebergs high,
Float on a rolling sea !

"Upon them plies the race of man
All it before endeavored :
'Ye live,' I cried, 'ye work and plan,
And know not ye are severed !

" 'Poor fragments of a broken world,
Whereon men pitch their tent !
Why were ye too to death not hurled
When your world's day was spent?

" 'That glow of central fire is done
Which with its fusing flame
Knit all your parts, and kept you one ;
But ye, ye are the same !

" 'The past, its mask of union on,
Had ceased to live and thrive :
The past, its mask of union gone,
Say, is it more alive?

" 'Your creeds are dead, your rites are dead,
Your social order too.
Where tarries he, the Power who said, —
See, I make all things new ?

" 'The millions suffer still, and grieve.
And what can helpers heal
With old-world cures men half believe
For woes they wholly feel?

" 'And yet men have such need of joy !
But joy whose grounds are true,
And joy that should all hearts employ
As when the past was new.

" 'Ah ! not the emotion of that past,
Its common hope, were vain !

Some new such hope must dawn at last,
Or man must toss in pain.

" ' But now the old is out of date,
The new is not yet born.
And who can be *alone* elate,
While the world lies forlorn? '

" Then to the wilderness I fled.
There among Alpine snows
And pastoral huts I hid my head,
And sought and found repose.

" It was not yet the appointed hour.
Sad, patient, and resigned,
I watched the crocus fade and flower,
I felt the sun and wind.

" The day I lived in was not mine :
Man gets no second day.
In dreams I saw the future shine,
But ah ! I could not stay !

" Action I had not, followers, fame.
I passed obscure, alone.
The after-world forgets my name,
Nor do I wish it known.

" Composed to bear, I lived and died,
And knew my life was vain.
With fate I murmur not, nor chide.
At Sèvres by the Seine

" (If Paris that brief flight allow)
My humble tomb explore !
It bears : *Eternity, be thou
My refuge !* and no more.

" But thou, whom fellowship of mood
Did make from haunts of strife
Come to my mountain solitude,
And learn my frustrate life ;

" O thou, who, ere thy flying span
Was past of cheerful youth,
Didst find the solitary man,
And love his cheerless truth, —

" Despair not thou as I despaired,
Nor be cold gloom thy prison !
Forward the gracious hours have fared,
And see ! the sun is risen !

" He breaks the winter of the past ;
A green, new earth appears.
Millions, whose life in ice lay fast,
Have thoughts and smiles and tears.

" What though there still need effort, strife ?
Though much be still unwon ?
Yet warm it mounts, the hour of life ;
Death's frozen hour is done.

" The world's great order dawns in sheen
After long darkness rude,
Divinelier imaged, clearer seen,
With happier zeal pursued.

" With hope extinct, and brow composed,
I marked the present die ;
Its term of life was nearly closed,
Yet it had more than I.

" But thou, though to the world's new hour
Thou come with aspect marred,

Shorn of the joy, the bloom, the power,
Which best befits its bard ;

" Though more than half thy years be past,
And spent thy youthful prime ;
Though, round thy firmer manhood cast,
Hang weeds of our sad time

" Whereof thy youth felt all the spell,
And traversed all the shade, —
Though late, though dimmed, though weak, yet tell
Hope to a world new-made !

" Help it to fill that deep desire,
The want which crazed our brain,
Consumed our soul with thirst like fire,
Immedicable pain ;

" Which to the wilderness drove out
Our life, to Alpine snow,
And palsied all our word with doubt,
And all our work with woe.

" What still of strength is left, employ,
This end to help attain :
One common wave of thought and joy
Lifting mankind again ! "

— The vision ended.   I awoke
As out of sleep, and no
Voice moved : only the torrent broke
The silence, far below.

Soft darkness on the turf did lie ;
Solemn, o'er hut and wood,
In the yet star-sown nightly sky,
The peak of Jaman stood.

Still in my soul the voice I heard
Of Obermann ! Away
I turned ; by some vague impulse stirred,
Along the rocks of Naye, —

Past Sonchaud's piny flanks I gaze,
And the blanched summit bare
Of Malatrait, to where in haze
The Valais opens fair,

And the domed Velan, with his snows,
Behind the upcrowding hills,
Doth all the heavenly opening close
Which the Rhone's murmur fills ;

And glorious there, without a sound,
Across the glimmering lake,
High in the Valais-depth profound,
I saw the morning break.

LATER POEMS.

><small>◆◆◆</small>

WESTMINSTER ABBEY.

JULY 25, 1881.

(*The Day of Burial, in the Abbey, of* ARTHUR PENRHYN
STANLEY, *Dean of Westminster.*)

> WHAT ! for a term so scant
>   Our shining visitant
> Cheer'd us, and now is pass'd into the night?
>   Couldst thou no better keep, O Abbey old,
>   The boon thy dedication-sign foretold,[31]
> The presence of that gracious inmate, light?—
>   A child of light appear'd;
> Hither he came, late-born and long-desired,
>   And to men's hearts this ancient place endear'd;
> What, is the happy glow so soon expired?
>
>   — Rough was the winter eve;
>   Their craft the fishers leave,
> And down over the Thames the darkness drew.
>   One still lags last, and turns, and eyes the Pile
>   Huge in the gloom, across in Thorney Isle,
> King Sebert's work, the wondrous Minster new.
>   —'Tis Lambeth now, where then
> They moor'd their boats among the bulrush stems;
>   And that new Minster in the matted fen
> The world-famed Abbey by the westering Thames.

His mates are gone, and he
For mist can scarcely see
A strange wayfarer coming to his side —
Who bade him loose his boat, and fix his oar,
And row him straightway to the further shore,
And wait while he did there a space abide.
The fisher awed obeys,
That voice had note so clear of sweet command ;
Through pouring tide he pulls, and drizzling haze,
And sets his freight ashore on Thorney strand.

The Minster's outlined mass
Rose dim from the morass,
And thitherward the stranger took his way.
Lo, on a sudden all the Pile is bright !
Nave, choir and transept glorified with light,
While tongues of fire on coign and carving play !
And heavenly odors fair
Come streaming with the floods of glory in,
And carols float along the happy air,
As if the reign of joy did now begin.

Then all again is dark ;
And by the fisher's bark
The unknown passenger returning stands.
O Saxon fisher ! thou hast had with thee
The fisher from the Lake of Galilee —
So saith he, blessing him with outspread hands ;
Then fades, but speaks the while :
At dawn thou to King Sebert shalt relate
How his St. Peter's Church in Thorney Isle
Peter, his friend, with light did consecrate.

Twelve hundred years and more
Along the holy floor
Pageants have pass'd, and tombs of mighty kings
Efface the humbler graves of Sebert's line,
And, as years sped, the minster-aisles divine
Grew used to the approach of Glory's wings.
Arts came, and arms, and law,
And majesty, and sacred form and fear ;
Only that primal guest the fisher saw,
Light, only light, was slow to reappear.

The Saviour's happy light,
Wherein at first was dight
His boon of life and immortality,
In desert ice of subtleties was spent
Or drown'd in mists of childish wonderment,
Fond fancies here, there false philosophy !
And harsh the temper grew
Of men with mind thus darken'd and astray ;
And scarce the boon of life could struggle
through,
For want of light which should the boon convey.

Yet in this latter time
The promise of the prime
Seem'd to come true at last, O Abbey old !
It seem'd, a child of light did bring the dower
Foreshown thee in thy consecration-hour,
And in thy courts his shining freight unroll'd :
Bright wits, and instincts sure,
And goodness warm, and truth without alloy,
And temper sweet, and love of all things pure,
And joy in light, and power to spread the joy.

And on that countenance bright
    Shone oft so high a light,
That to my mind there came how, long ago,
    Lay on the hearth, amid a fiery ring,
    The charm'd babe of the Eleusinian king —[32]
His nurse, the Mighty Mother, will'd it so.
    Warm in her breast, by day,
He slumber'd, and ambrosia balm'd the child ;
    But all night long amid the flames he lay,
Upon the hearth, and play'd with them, and smiled.

    But once, at midnight deep,
    His mother woke from sleep,
And saw her babe amidst the fire, and scream'd.
    A sigh the Goddess gave, and with a frown
    Pluck'd from the fire the child, and laid him down ;
Then raised her face, and glory round her stream'd.
    The mourning-stole no more
Mantled her form, no more her head was bow'd ;
    But raiment of celestial sheen she wore,
And beauty fill'd her, and she spake aloud : —

    " O ignorant race of man !
    Achieve your good who can
If your own hands the good begun undo ?
    Had human cry not marr'd the work divine,
    Immortal had I made this boy of mine ;
But now his head to death again is due
    And I have now no power
Unto this pious household to repay
    Their kindness shown me in my wandering hour."
— She spake, and from the portal pass'd away.

The Boy his nurse forgot,
And bore a mortal lot.
Long since, his name is heard on earth no more.
In some chance battle on Cithæron-side
The nursling of the Mighty Mother died,
And went where all his fathers went before.
—On thee too, in thy day
Of childhood, Arthur ! did some check have power,
That, radiant though thou wert, thou couldst but
stay,
Bringer of heavenly light, a human hour?

Therefore our happy guest
Knew care, and knew unrest,
And weakness warn'd him, and he fear'd decline.
And in the grave he laid a cherish'd wife,
And men ignoble harass'd him with strife,
And deadly airs his strength did undermine.
Then from his Abbey fades
The sound beloved of his victorious breath ;
And light's fair nursling stupor first invades,
And next the crowning impotence of death.

But hush ! This mournful strain,
Which would of death complain,
The oracle forbade, not ill-inspired. —
That Pair, whose head did plan, whose hands did
forge
The Temple in the pure Parnassian gorge,[33]
Finish'd their work, and then a meéd required.
" Seven days," the God replied,
" Live happy, then expect your perfect meed ! "
Quiet in sleep, the seventh night, they died.
Death, death was judged the boon supreme indeed.

And truly he who here
Hath run his bright career,
And served men nobly, and acceptance found,
And borne to light and right his witness high,
What could he better wish than then to die,
And wait the issue, sleeping underground?
Why should he pray to range
Down the long age of truth that ripens slow;
And break his heart with all the baffling change,
And all the tedious tossing to and fro?

For this and that way swings
The flux of mortal things,
Though moving inly to one far-set goal. —
What had our Arthur gain'd, to stop and see,
After light's term, a term of cecity,
A Church once large and then grown strait in soul?
To live, and see arise,
Alternating with wisdom's too short reign,
Folly revived, re-furbish'd sophistries,
And pullulating rites externe and vain?

Ay me! 'Tis deaf, that ear
Which joy'd my voice to hear;
Yet would I not disturb thee from thy tomb,
Thus sleeping in thine Abbey's friendly shade,
And the rough waves of life for ever laid!
I would not break thy rest, nor change thy doom.
Even as my father, thou —
Even as that loved, that well-recorded friend —
Hast thy commission done; ye both may now
Wait for the leaven to work, the let to end.

And thou, O Abbey gray !
Predestined to the ray
By this dear guest over thy precinct shed —
　　Fear not but that thy light once more shall burn,
　　Once more thine immemorial gleam return,
Though sunk be now this bright, this gracious head !
　　Let but the light appear
And thy transfigured walls be touch'd with flame —
　　Our Arthur will again be present here,
Again from lip to lip will pass his name.

GEIST'S GRAVE.

FOUR years ! — and didst thou stay above
The ground, which hides thee now, but four?
And all that life, and all that love,
Were crowded, Geist ! into no more?

Only four years those winning ways,
Which make me for thy presence yearn,
Call'd us to pet thee or to praise,
Dear little friend ! at every turn?

That loving heart, that patient soul,
Had they indeed no longer span,
To run their course, and reach their goal,
And read their homily to man?

That liquid, melancholy eye,
From whose pathetic, soul-fed springs
Seem'd surging the Virgilian cry,[1]
The sense of tears in mortal things —

---

[1] *Sunt lacrimæ rerum!*

That steadfast, mournful strain, consoled
By spirits gloriously gay,
And temper of heroic mould —
What, was four years their whole short day?

Yes, only four! — and not the course
Of all the centuries yet to come,
And not the infinite resource
Of Nature, with her countless sum

Of figures, with her fulness vast
Of new creation evermore,
Can ever quite repeat the past,
Or just thy little self restore.

Stern law of every mortal lot!
Which man, proud man, finds hard to bear,
And builds himself I know not what
Of second life I know not where.

But thou, when struck thine hour to go,
On us, who stood despondent by,
A meek last glance of love didst throw,
And humbly lay thee down to die.

Yet would we keep thee in our heart —
Would fix our favorite on the scene,
Nor let thee utterly depart
And be as if thou ne'er hadst been.

And so there rise these lines of verse
On lips that rarely form them now;
While to each other we rehearse:
Such ways, such arts, such looks hadst thou!

We stroke thy broad brown paws again,
We bid thee to thy vacant chair,
We greet thee by the window-pane,
We hear thy scuffle on the stair.

We see the flaps of thy large ears
Quick raised to ask which way we go ;
Crossing the frozen lake, appears
Thy small black figure on the snow !

Nor to us only art thou dear
Who mourn thee in thine English home ;
Thou hast thine absent master's tear,
Dropt by the far Australian foam.

Thy memory lasts both here and there,
And thou shalt live as long as we.
And after that — thou dost not care !
In us was all the world to thee.

Yet, fondly zealous for thy fame,
Even to a date beyond our own
We strive to carry down thy name,
By mounded turf, and graven stone.

We lay thee, close within our reach,
Here, where the grass is smooth and warm,
Between the holly and the beech,
Where oft we watch'd thy couchant form,

Asleep, yet lending half an ear
To travellers on the Portsmouth road ; —
There build we thee, O guardian dear,
Mark'd with a stone, thy last abode !

Then some, who through this garden pass,
When we too, like thyself, are clay,
Shall see thy grave upon the grass,
And stop before the stone, and say :

People who lived here long ago
Did by this stone, it seems, intend
To name for future times to know
The dachs-hound, Geist, their little friend.

POOR MATTHIAS.

POOR MATTHIAS ! — Found him lying
Fall'n beneath his perch and dying?
Found him stiff, you say, though warm —
All convulsed his little form?
Poor canary ! many a year
Well he knew his mistress dear ;
Now in vain you call his name,
Vainly raise his rigid frame,
Vainly warm him in your breast,
Vainly kiss his golden crest,
Smooth his ruffled plumage fine,
Touch his trembling beak with wine.
One more gasp — it is the end !
Dead and mute our tiny friend !
— Songster thou of many a year,
Now thy mistress brings thee here,
Says, it fits that I rehearse,
Tribute due to thee, a verse,
Meed for daily song of yore
Silent now for evermore.

Poor Matthias ! Wouldst thou have
More than pity? claim'st a stave?
— Friends more near us than a bird
We dismiss'd without a word.
Rover, with the good brown head,
Great Atossa, they are dead ;
Dead, and neither prose nor rhyme
Tells the praises of their prime.
Thou didst know them old and gray,
Know them in their sad decay.
Thou hast seen Atossa sage
Sit for hours beside thy cage ;
Thou wouldst chirp, thou foolish bird,
Flutter, chirp — she never stirr'd !
What were now these toys to her?
Down she sank amid her fur ;
Eyed thee with a soul resign'd —
And thou deemedst cats were kind !
— Cruel, but composed and bland,
Dumb, inscrutable and grand,
So Tiberius might have sat,
Had Tiberius been a cat.

Rover died — Atossa too.
Less than they to us are you !
Nearer human were their powers,
Closer knit their life with ours.
Hands had stroked them, which are cold,
Now for years, in churchyard mould ;
Comrades of our past were they,
Of that unreturning day.
Changed and aging, they and we
Dwelt, it seem'd, in sympathy.
Alway from their presence broke

Somewhat which remembrance woke
Of the loved, the lost, the young —
Yet they died, and died unsung.

Geist came next, our little friend;
Geist had verse to mourn his end.
Yes, but that enforcement strong
Which compell'd for Geist a song —
All that gay oouragrous cheer,
All that human pathos dear;
Soul-fed eyes with suffering worn,
Pain heroically borne,
Faithful love in depth divine —
Poor Matthias, were they thine?

Max and Kaiser we to-day
Greet upon the lawn at play;
Max a dachs-hound without blot —
Kaiser should be, but is not.
Max, with shining yellow coat,
Prinking ears and dewlap throat —
Kaiser, with his collie face,
Penitent for want of race.
— Which may be the first to die,
Vain to augur, they or I!
But, as age comes on, I know,
Poet's fire gets faint and low;
If so be that travel they
First the inevitable way,
Much I doubt if they shall have
Dirge from me to crown their grave.

Yet, poor bird, thy tiny corse
Moves me, somehow, to remorse;

Something haunts my conscience, brings
Sad, compunctious visitings.
Other favorites, dwelling here,
Open lived to us, and near ;
Well we knew when they were glad,
Plain we saw if they were sad,
Joy'd with them when they were gay,
Soothed them in their last decay;
Sympathy could feel and show
Both in weal of theirs and woe.

Birds, companions more unknown,
Live beside us, but alone ;
Finding not, do all they can,
Passage from their souls to man.
Kindness we bestow, and praise,
Laud their plumage, greet their lays ;
Still, beneath their feather'd breast,
Stirs a history unexpress'd.
Wishes there, and feelings strong,
Incommunicably throng ;
What they want, we cannot guess,
Fail to track their deep distress —
Dull look on when death is nigh,
Note no change, and let them die.
Poor Matthias ! couldst thou speak,
What a tale of thy last week !
Every morning did we pay
Stupid salutations gay,
Suited well to health, but how
Mocking, how incongruous now !
Cake we offer'd, sugar, seed,
Never doubtful of thy need ;
Praised, perhaps, thy courteous eye,

Praised thy golden livery.
Gravely thou the while, poor dear !
Sat'st upon thy perch to hear,
Fixing with a mute regard
Us, thy human keepers hard,
Troubling, with our chatter vain,
Ebb of life, and mortal pain —
Us, unable to divine
Our companion's dying sign,
Or o'erpass the severing sea
Set betwixt ourselves and thee,
Till the sand thy feathers smirch
Fallen dying off thy perch !

Was it, as the Grecian sings,
Birds were born the first of things,
Before the sun, before the wind,
Before the gods, before mankind,
Airy, ante-mundane throng —
Witness their unworldly song !
Proof they give, too, primal powers,
Of a prescience more than ours —
Teach us, while they come and go,
When to sail, and when to sow.
Cuckoo calling from the hill,
Swallow skimming by the mill,
Swallows trooping in the sedge,
Starlings swirling from the hedge,
Mark the seasons, map our year,
As they show and disappear.
But, with all this travail sage
Brought from that anterior age,
Goes an unreversed decree
Whereby strange are they and we ;

Making want of theirs, and plan,
Indiscernible by man.

No, away with tales like these
Stol'n from Aristophanes ! [34]
Does it, if we miss your mind,
Prove us so remote in kind?
Birds ! we but repeat on you
What amongst ourselves we do.
Somewhat more or somewhat less,
'Tis the same unskilfulness.
What you feel, escapes our ken —
Know we more our fellow men?
Human suffering at our side,
Ah, like yours is undescried !
Human longings, human fears,
Miss our eyes and miss our ears.
Little helping, wounding much,
Dull of heart, and hard of touch,
Brother man's despairing sign
Who may trust us to divine?
Who assure us, sundering powers
Stand not 'twixt his soul and ours?

Poor Matthias ! See, thy end
What a lesson doth it lend !
For that lesson thou shalt have,
Dead canary bird, a stave !
Telling how, one stormy day,
Stress of gale and showers of spray
Drove my daughter small and me
Inland from the rocks and sea.
Driv'n inshore, we follow down
Ancient streets of Hastings town —

Slowly thread them — when behold,
French canary-merchant old
Shepherding his flock of gold
In a low dim-lighted pen
Scann'd of tramps and fishermen !
There a bird, high-colorèd, fat,
Proud of port, though something squat —
Pursy, play'd-out Philistine —
Dazzled Nelly's youthful eyne,
But, far in, obscure, there stirr'd
On his perch a sprightlier bird,
Courteous-eyed, erect and slim ;
And I whisper'd : " Fix on *him!* "
Home we brought him, young and fair,
Songs to trill in Surrey air.
Here Matthias sang his fill,
Saw the cedars of Pains Hill ;
Here he pour'd his little soul,
Heard the murmur of the Mole.
Eight in number now the years
He hath pleased our eyes and ears ;
Other favorites he hath known
Go, and now himself is gone.
— Fare thee well, companion dear !
Fare for ever well, nor fear,
Tiny though thou art, to stray
Down the uncompanion'd way !
We without thee, little friend,
Many years have not to spend ;
What are left, will hardly be
Better than we spent with thee.

KAISER DEAD.

April 6, 1887.

WHAT, Kaiser dead?   The heavy news
Post-haste to Cobham calls the Muse,
From where in Farringford she brews
   The ode sublime,
Or with Pen-bryn's bold bard pursues
   A rival rhyme.

Kai's bracelet tail, Kai's busy feet,
Were known to all the village-street.
"What, poor Kai dead?" say all I meet;
   "A loss indeed!"
O for the croon pathetic, sweet,
   Of Robin's reed![35]

Six years ago I brought him down,
A baby dog, from London town;
Round his small throat of black and brown
   A ribbon blue,
And vouch'd by glorious renown
   A dachs-hound true.

His mother, most majestic dame,
Of blood-unmix'd, from Potsdam came;
And Kaiser's race we deem'd the same —
   No lineage higher.
And so he bore the imperial name.
   But ah, his sire!

Soon, soon the days conviction bring.
The collie hair, the collie swing,
The tail's indomitable ring,
   The eye's unrest —
The case was clear ; a mongrel thing
   Kai stood confest.

But all those virtues, which commend
The humbler suit who serve and tend,
Were thine in store, thou faithful friend.
   What sense, what cheer !
To us, declining tow'rds our end,
   A mate how dear !

For Max, thy brother-dog, began
To flag, and feel his narrowing span.
And cold, besides, his blue blood ran,
   Since, 'gainst the classes,
He heard, of late, the Grand Old Man
   Incite the masses.

Yes, Max and we grew slow and sad ;
But Kai, a tireless shepherd-lad,
Teeming with plans, alert, and glad
   In work or play,
Like sunshine went and came, and bade
   Live out the day !

Still, still I see the figure smart —
Trophy in mouth, agog to start,
Then, home return'd, once more depart ;
   Or prest together
Against thy mistress, loving heart,
   In winter weather.

I see the tail, like bracelet twirl'd,
In moments of disgrace uncurl'd,
Then at a pardoning word re-furl'd,
    A conquering sign ;
Crying, " Come on, and range the world,
    And never pine."

Thine eye was bright, thy coat it shone ;
Thou hadst thine errands, off and on ;
In joy thy last morn flew ; anon,
    A fit !   All's over ;
And thou art gone where Geist hath gone,
    And Toss, and Rover.

Poor Max, with downcast, reverent head,
Regards his brother's form outspread ;
Full well Max knows the friend is dead
    Whose cordial talk,
And jokes in doggish language said,
    Beguiled his walk.

And Glory, stretch'd at Burwood gate,
Thy passing by doth vainly wait ;
And jealous Jock, thy only hate,
    The chiel from Skye,
Lets from his shaggy Highland pate
    Thy memory die.

Well, fetch his graven collar fine,
And rub the steel, and make it shine,
And leave it round thy neck to twine,
    Kai, in thy grave.
There of thy master keep that sign,
    And this plain stave.

S. S. "LUSITANIA."

NINETEENTH CENTURY, No. XXIII., JANUARY, 1879.

I READ in Dante how that horned light,
Which hid Ulysses, waved itself and said :
" Following the sun, we set our vessel's head
To the great main ; pass'd Seville on the right

" And Ceuta on the left ; then southward sped.
And last in air, far off, dim rose a Height.
We cheer'd ; but from it rush'd a blast of might,
And struck — and o'er us the sea-waters spread."

I dropp'd the book, and of my child I thought
In his long black ship speeding night and day
O'er those same seas ; dark Teneriffe rose, fraught

With omen ; " Oh ! were that Mount pass'd," I say.
Then the door opens and this card is brought :
" Reach'd Cape Verde Islands, ' Lusitania.' "

ADDITIONAL EARLY POEMS.

ALARIC AT ROME.

A PRIZE POEM RECITED IN RUGBY SCHOOL, JUNE 12, 1840.

Admire, exult, despise, laugh, weep, for here
There is such matter for all feeling.

CHILDE HAROLD.

I.

UNWELCOME shroud of the forgotten dead,
Oblivion's dreary fountain, where art thou :
Why speed'st thou not thy deathlike wave to shed
O'er humbled pride, and self-reproaching woe :
Or time's stern hand, why blots it not away
The saddening tale that tells of sorrow and decay?

II.

There are, whose glory passeth not away —
Even in the grave their fragrance cannot fade :
Others there are as deathless full as they,
Who for themselves a monument have made
By their own crimes — a lesson to all eyes —
Of wonder to the fool — of warning to the wise.

471

III.

Yes, there are stories registered on high,
Yes, there are stains time's fingers cannot blot,
Deeds that shall live when they who did them, die ;
Things that may cease, but never be forgot :
Yet some there are, their very lives would give
To be remembered thus, and yet they cannot live.

IV.

But thou, imperial City ! that hast stood
In greatness once, in sackcloth now and tears,
A mighty name, for evil or for good,
Even in the loneness of thy widowed years :
Thou that hast gazed, as the world hurried by,
Upon its headlong course with sad prophetic eye.

V.

Is thine the laurel-crown that greatness wreathes
Round the wan temples of the hallowed dead —
Is it the blighting taint dishonor breathes
In fires undying o'er the guilty head,
Or the brief splendor of that meteor light
That for a moment gleams, and all again is night?

VI.

Fain would we deem that thou hast risen so high
Thy dazzling light an eagle's gaze should tire ;
No meteor brightness to be seen and die,
No passing pageant, born but to expire,
But full and deathless as the deep dark hue
Of ocean's sleeping face, or heaven's unbroken blue.

VII.

Yet stains there are to blot thy brightest page,
And wither half the laurels on thy tomb;
A glorious manhood, yet a dim old age,
And years of crime, and nothingness, and gloom:
And then that mightiest crash, that giant fall,
Ambition's boldest dream might sober and appal.

VIII.

Thou wondrous chaos, where together dwell
Present and past, the living and the dead,
Thou shattered mass, whose glorious ruins tell
The vanisht might of that discrownëd head:
Where all we see, or do, or hear, or say,
Seems strangely echoed back by tones of yesterday:

IX.

Thou solemn grave, where every step we tread
Treads on the slumbering dust of other years;
The while there sleeps within thy precincts dread
What once had human passions, hopes, and fears;
And memory's gushing tide swells deep and full
And makes thy very ruin fresh and beautiful.

X.

Alas, no common sepulchre art thou,
No habitation for the nameless dead,
Green turf above, and crumbling dust below,
Perchance some mute memorial at their head,
But one vast fane where all unconscious sleep
Earth's old heroic forms in peaceful slumbers deep.

XI.

Thy dead are kings, thy dust are palaces,
Relics of nations thy memorial-stones :
And the dim glories of departed days
Fold like a shroud around thy withered bones :
And o'er thy towers the wind's half-uttered sigh
Whispers, in mournful tones, thy silent elegy.

XII.

Yes, in such eloquent silence didst thou lie
When the Goth stooped upon his stricken prey,
And the deep hues of an Italian sky
Flasht on the rude barbarian's wild array :
While full and ceaseless as the ocean roll,
Horde after horde streamed up thy frowning Capitol.

XIII.

Twice, ere that day of shame, the embattled foe
Had gazed in wonder on that glorious sight ;
Twice had the eternal city bowed her low
In sullen homage to the invader's might :
Twice had the pageant of that vast array
Swept, from thy walls, O Rome, on its triumphant way.

XIV.

Twice, from without thy bulwarks, hath the din
Of Gothic clarion smote thy startled ear ;
Anger, and strife, and sickness are within,
Famine and sorrow are no strangers here :
Twice hath the cloud hung o'er thee, twice been
        stayed
Even in the act to burst, twice threatened, twice delayed.

XV.

Yet once again, stern Chief, yet once again,
Pour forth the foaming vials of thy wrath :
There lies thy goal, to miss or to attain,
Gird thee, and on upon thy fateful path,
The world hath bowed to Rome, oh ! cold were he
Who would not burst his bonds, and in his turn be free.

XVI.

Therefore arise and arm thee ! lo, the world
Looks on in fear ! and when the seal is set,
The doom pronounced, the battle-flag unfurled,
Scourge of the nations, wouldest thou linger yet?
Arise and arm thee ! spread thy banners forth,
Pour from a thousand hills thy warriors of the north !

XVII.

Hast thou not marked on a wild autumn day
When the wind slumbereth in a sudden lull,
What deathlike stillness o'er the landscape lay,
How calmly sad, how sadly beautiful;
How each bright tint of tree, and flower, and heath
Were mingling with the sere and withered hues of death.

XVIII.

And thus, beneath the clear, calm vault of heaven
In mournful loveliness that city lay,
And thus, amid the glorious hues of even
That city told of languor and decay :
Till what at morning's hour lookt warm and bright
Was cold and sad beneath that breathless, voiceless
night.

XIX.

Soon was that stillness broken : like the cry
Of the hoarse onset of the surging wave,
Or louder rush of whirlwinds sweeping by
Was the wild shout those Gothic myriads gave,
As towered on high, above their moonlit road,
Scenes where a Cæsar triumpht, or a Scipio trod.

XX.

Think ye it strikes too slow, the sword of fate,
Think ye the avenger loiters on his way,
That your own hands must open wide the gate,
And your own voice must guide him to his prey;
Alas, it needs not ; is it hard to know
Fate's threat'nings are not vain, the spoiler comes not
slow.

XXI.

And were there none, to stand and weep alone,
And as the pageant swept before their eyes
To hear a dim and long-forgotten tone
Tell of old times, and holiest memories,
Till fanciful regret and dreamy woe
Peopled night's voiceless shades with forms of long Ago.

XXII.

Oh yes ! if fancy feels, beyond to-day,
Thoughts of the past and of the future time,
How should that mightiest city pass away
And not bethink her of her glorious prime,
Whilst every chord that thrills at thoughts of home
Jarr'd with the bursting shout, "they come, the Goth,
they come !"

XXIII.

The trumpet swells yet louder : they are here !
Yea, on your fathers' bones the avengers tread,
Not this the time to weep upon the bier
That holds the ashes of your hero-dead,
If wreaths may twine for you, or laurels wave,
They shall not deck your life, but sanctify your grave.

XXIV.

Alas ! no wreaths are here.   Despair may teach
Cowards to conquer and the weak to die ;
Nor tongue of man, nor fear, nor shame can preach
So stern a lesson as necessity,
Yet here it speaks not.   Yea, though all around
Unhallowed feet are trampling on this haunted ground,

XXV.

Though every holiest feeling, every tie
That binds the heart of man with mightiest power,
All natural love, all human sympathy
Be crusht, and outraged in this bitter hour,
Here is no echo to the sound of home,
No shame that suns should rise to light a conquer'd
    Rome.

XXVI.

That troublous night is over : on the brow
Of thy stern hill, thou mighty Capitol,
One form stands gazing : silently below
The morning mists from tower and temple roll,
And lo ! the eternal city, as they rise,
Bursts, in majestic beauty, on her conqueror's eyes.

XXVII.

Yes, there he stood, upon that silent hill,
  And there beneath his feet his conquest lay :
Unlike that ocean-city, gazing still
  Smilingly forth upon her sunny bay,
  But o'er her vanisht might and humbled pride
Mourning, as widowed Venice o'er her Adrian tide.

XXVIII.

Breathe there not spirits on the peopled air?
  Float there not voices on the murmuring wind?
 Oh ! sound there not some strains of sadness there,
  To touch with sorrow even a victor's mind,
  And wrest one tear from joy !   Oh ! who shall pen
The thoughts that toucht thy breast, thou lonely
    conqueror, then?

XXIX.

Perchance his wandering heart was far away,
  Lost in dim memories of his early home,
And his young dreams of conquest ; how to-day
  Beheld him master of Imperial Rome,
  Crowning his wildest hopes : perchance his eyes
As they looked sternly on, beheld new victories,

XXX.

New dreams of wide dominion, mightier, higher,
  Come floating up from the abyss of years ;
 Perchance that solemn sight might quench the fire
  Even of that ardent spirit ; hopes and fears
  Might well be mingling at that murmured sigh,
Whispering from all around, " All earthly things must
    die."

XXXI.

Perchance that wondrous city was to him
But as one voiceless blank ; a place of graves,
And recollections indistinct and dim,
Whose sons were conquerors once, and now were
    slaves :
It may be in that desolate sight his eye
Saw but another step to climb to victory !

XXXII.

Alas ! that fiery spirit little knew
The change of life, the nothingness of power,
How both were hastening, as they flowered and grew,
Nearer and nearer to their closing hour :
How every birth of time's miraculous womb
Swept off the withered leaves that hide the naked tomb.

XXXIII.

One little year ; that restless soul shall rest,
That frame of vigor shall be crumbling clay,
And tranquilly, above that troubled breast,
The sunny waters hold their joyous way :
And gently shall the murmuring ripples flow,
Nor wake the weary soul that slumbers on below.

XXXIV.

Alas ! far other thoughts might well be ours
And dash our holiest raptures while we gaze :
Energies wasted, unimproved hours,
The saddening visions of departed days :
And while they rise here might we stand alone,
And mingle with thy ruins somewhat of our own.

XXXV.

Beautiful city !   If departed things
Ever again put earthly likeness on,
Here should a thousand forms on fancy's wings
Float up to tell of ages that are gone :
Yea though hand touch thee not, nor eye should see,
Still should the spirit hold communion, Rome, with
      thee !

XXXVI.

Oh ! it is bitter, that each fairest dream
Should fleet before us but to melt away ;
That wildest visions still should loveliest seem
And soonest fade in the broad glare of day :
That while we feel the world is dull and low,
Gazing on thee, we wake to find it is not so.

XXXVII.

A little while, alas ! a little while,
And the same world has tongue, and ear, and eye,
The careless glance, the cold unmeaning smile,
The thoughtless word, the lack of sympathy !
Who would not turn him from the barren sea
And rest his weary eyes on the green land and thee !

XXXVIII.

So pass we on.   But oh ! to harp aright
The vanisht glories of thine early day,
There needs a minstrel of diviner might,
A holier incense than this feeble lay ;
To chant thy requiem with more passionate breath,
And twine with bolder hand thy last memorial wreath !

CROMWELL.

A Prize Poem recited in the Theatre, Oxford, June 28, 1843.

*Schrecklich ist es, deiner Wahrheit
Sterbliches Gefäss zu seyn.*

SCHILLER.

High fate is theirs, ye sleepless waves, whose ear
Learns Freedom's lesson from your voice of fear ;
Whose spell-bound sense from childhood's hour hath
    known
Familiar meanings in your mystic tone :
Sounds of deep import — voices that beguile
Age of its tears and childhood of its smile,
To yearn with speechless impulse to the free
And gladsome greetings of the buoyant sea !
High fate is theirs, who where the silent sky
Stoops to the soaring mountains, live and die ;
Who scale the cloud-capt height, or sink to rest
In the deep stillness of its shelt'ring breast ;—
Around whose feet the exulting waves have sung,
The eternal hills their giant shadows flung.

No wonders nurs'd thy childhood ; not for thee
Did the waves chant their song of liberty !
Thine was no mountain home, where Freedom's form
Abides enthron'd amid the mist and storm,
And whispers to the listening winds, that swell
With solemn cadence round her citadel !
These had no sound for thee : that cold calm eye
Lit with no rapture as the storm swept by,
To mark with shiver'd crest the reeling wave

Hide his torn head beneath his sunless cave ;
Or hear 'mid circling crags, the impatient cry
Of the pent winds, that scream in agony !
Yet all high sounds that mountain children hear
Flash'd from thy soul upon thine inward ear ;
All Freedom's mystic language — storms that roar
By hill or wave, the mountain or the shore, —
All these had stirr'd thy spirit, and thine eye
In common sights read secret sympathy ;
Till all bright thoughts that hills or waves can yield
Deck'd the dull waste, and the familiar field ;
Or wondrous sounds from tranquil skies were borne
Far o'er the glistening sheets of windy corn :
Skies — that, unbound by clasp of mountain chain,
Slope stately down, and melt into the plain ;
Sounds — such as erst the lone wayfaring man
Caught, as he journeyed, from the lips of Pan ;
Or that mysterious cry, that smote with fear,
Like sounds from other worlds, the Spartan's ear,
While o'er the dusty plain, the murmurous throng
Of Heaven's embattled myriads swept along.

Say not such dreams are idle : for the man
Still toils to perfect what the child began ;
And thoughts, that were but outlines, time engraves
Deep on his life ; and childhood's baby waves,
Made rough with care, become the changeful sea,
Stemm'd by the strength of manhood fearlessly ;
And fleeting thoughts, that on the lonely wild
Swept o'er the fancy of that heedless child,
Perchance had quicken'd with a living truth
The cold dull soil of his unfruitful youth ;
Till with his daily life, a life that threw
Its shadows o'er the future flower'd and grew,

With common cares unmingling, and apart,
Haunting the shrouded chambers of his heart;
Till life unstirr'd by action, life became
Threaded and lighten'd by a track of flame;
An inward light, that, with its streaming ray
On the dark current of his changeless day,
Bound all his being with a silver chain —
Like a swift river through a silent plain!

High thoughts were his, when by the gleaming flood,
With heart new strung, and stern resolve, he stood;
Where rode the tall dark ships, whose loosen'd sail
All idly flutter'd in the eastern gale;
High thoughts were his; but Memory's glance the
    while
Fell on the cherish'd past with tearful smile;
And peaceful joys and gentler thoughts swept by,
Like summer lightnings o'er a darken'd sky.
The peace of childhood, and the thoughts that roam,
Like loving shadows, round that childhood's home;
Joys that had come and vanish'd, half unknown,
Then slowly brighten'd, as the days had flown;
Years that were sweet or sad, becalm'd or toss'd
On life's wild waves — the living and the lost.
Youth stain'd with follies: and the thoughts of ill
Crush'd, as they rose, by manhood's sterner will.
Repentant prayers, that had been strong to save;
And the first sorrow, which is childhood's grave!
All shapes that haunt remembrance — soft and fair,
Like a green land at sunset, all were there!
Eyes that he knew, old faces unforgot,
Gaz'd sadly down on his unrestful lot,
And Memory's calm clear voice, and mournful eye,
Chill'd every buoyant hope that floated by;

Like frozen winds on southern vales that blow
From a far land — the children of the snow —
O'er flowering plain and blossom'd meadow fling
The cold dull shadow of their icy wing.

Then Fancy's roving visions, bold and free,
A moment dispossess'd reality.
All airy hopes that idle hearts can frame,
Like dreams between two sorrows, went and came :
Fond hearts that fain would clothe the unwelcome truth
Of toilsome manhood in the dreams of youth,
To bend in rapture at some idle throne,
Some lifeless soulless phantom of their own ;
Some shadowy vision of a tranquil life,
Of joys unclouded, years unstirr'd by strife ;
Of sleep unshadow'd by a dream of woe ;
Of many a lawny hill, and streams with silver flow ;
Of giant mountains by the western main,
The sunless forest, and the sealike plain ;
Those lingering hopes of coward hearts, that still
Would play the traitor to the steadfast will,
One moment's space, perchance, might charm his eye
From the stern future, and the years gone by.
One moment's space might waft him far away
To western shores — the death-place of the day !
Might paint the calm, sweet peace — the rest of home,
Far o'er the pathless waste of laboring foam —
Peace, that recall'd his childish hours anew,
More calm, more deep, than childhood ever knew !
Green happy places, like a flowery lea
Between the barren mountains and the stormy sea.

O pleasant rest, if once the race were run !
O happy slumber, if the day were done !

Dreams that were sweet at eve, at morn were sin ;
With cares to conquer, and a goal to win !
His were no tranquil years — no languid sleep —
No life of dreams — no home beyond the deep —
No softening ray — no visions false and wild —
No glittering hopes on life's gray distance smiled —
Like isles of sunlight on a mountain's brow,
Lit by a wandering gleam, we know not how,
Far on the dim horizon, when the sky
With glooming clouds broods dark and heavily.

Then his eye slumber'd, and the chain was broke
That bound his spirit, and his heart awoke ;
Then, like a kingly river swift and strong,
The future roll'd its gathering tides along !
The shout of onset and the shriek of fear
Smote, like the rush of waters, on his ear ;
And his eye kindled with the kindling fray,
The surging battle and the mail'd array !
All wondrous deeds the coming days should see,
And the long Vision of the years to be.
Pale phantom hosts, like shadows, faint and far,
Councils, and armies, and the pomp of war !
And one sway'd all, who wore a kingly crown,
Until another rose and smote him down :
A form that tower'd above his brother men ;
A form he knew — but it was shrouded then !
With stern, slow steps, unseen yet still the same,
By leaguer'd tower and tented field it came ;
By Naseby's hill, o'er Marston's heathy waste,
By Worcester's field, the warrior-vision pass'd !
From their deep base, thy beetling cliffs, Dunbar,
Rang, as he trode them, with the voice of war !
The soldier kindled at his words of fire ;

The statesman quail'd before his glance of ire !
Worn was his brow with cares no thought could scan,
His step was loftier than the steps of man ;
And the winds told his glory, and the wave
Sonorous witness to his empire gave !

What forms are these, that with complaining sound,
And slow reluctant steps are gathering round ?
Forms that with him shall tread life's changing stage,
Cross his lone path, or share his pilgrimage.
There, as he gazed, a wond'rous band — they came,
Pym's look of hate, and Strafford's glance of flame :
There Laud, with noiseless steps and glittering eye,
In priestly garb, a frail old man, went by ;
His drooping head bowed meekly on his breast ;
His hands were folded, like a saint at rest !
There Hampden bent him o'er his saddle bow,
And death's cold dews bedimm'd his earnest brow ;
Still turn'd to watch the battle — still forgot
Himself, his sufferings, in his country's lot !
There Falkland eyed the strife that would not cease,
Shook back his tangled locks, and murmur'd " Peace ! "
With feet that spurn'd the ground, lo ! Milton there
Stood like a statue ; and his face was fair —
Fair beyond human beauty ; and his eye,
That knew not earth, soar'd upwards to the sky !

He, too, was there — it was the princely boy,
The child-companion of his childish joy !
But oh ! how chang'd ! those deathlike features wore
Childhood's bright glance and sunny smile no more !
That brow so sad, so pale, so full of care —
What trace of careless childhood linger'd there ?
What spring of youth in that majestic mien,

So sadly calm, so kingly, so serene?
No — all was chang'd! the monarch wept alone,
Between a ruin'd church and shatter'd throne!
Friendless and hopeless — like a lonely tree,
On some bare headland straining mournfully,
That all night long its weary moan doth make
To the vex'd waters of a mountain lake!
Still, as he gaz'd, the phantom's mournful glance
Shook the deep slumber of his deathlike trance;
Like some forgotten strain that haunts us still,
That calm eye follow'd, turn him where he will;
Till the pale monarch, and the long array,
Pass'd like a morning mist, in tears away!

Then all his dream was troubled, and his soul
Thrill'd with a dread no slumber could control;
On that dark form his eyes had gaz'd before,
Nor known it then; — but it was veil'd no more!
In broad clear light the ghastly vision shone, —
That form was his, — those features were his own!
The night of terrors, and the day of care,
The years of toil — all, all were written there!
Sad faces watch'd around him, and his breath
Came faint and feeble in the embrace of death.
The gathering tempest, with its voice of fear,
His latest loftiest music smote his ear!
That day of boundless hope and promise high,
That day that hail'd his triumphs, saw him die!
Then from those whitening lips, as death drew near,
The imprisoning chains fell off, and all was clear!
Like lowering clouds, that at the close of day,
Bath'd in a blaze of sunset, melt away;
And with its clear calm tones, that dying prayer
Cheer'd all the failing hearts that sorrow'd there!

A life — whose ways no human thought could scan ;
A life — that was not as the life of man ;
A life — that wrote its purpose with a sword,
Moulding itself into action, not in word !
Rent with tumultuous thoughts, whose conflict rung
Deep through his soul, and chok'd his faltering tongue ;
A heart that reck'd not of the countless dead,
That strew'd the blood-stain'd path where Empire led ;
A daring hand, that shrunk not to fulfil
The thought that spurr'd it ; and a dauntless will,
Bold action's parent ; and a piercing ken
Through the dark chambers of the hearts of men,
To read each thought, and teach that master-mind
The fears and hopes and passions of mankind ;
All these were thine — oh thought of fear ! — and thou,
Stretch'd on that bed of death, art nothing now.

———————

Then all his vision faded, and his soul
Sprang from its sleep ! and lo ! the waters roll
Once more beneath him ; and the fluttering sail,
Where the dark ships rode proudly, woo'd the gale ;
And the wind murmur'd round him, and he stood
Once more alone beside the gleaming flood.

———————

THE HAYSWATER BOAT.

A REGION desolate and wild.
Black, chafing water : and afloat,
And lonely as a truant child
In a waste wood, a single boat :
No mast, no sails are set thereon :
It moves, but never moveth on :
And welters like a human thing
Amid the wild waves weltering.

Behind, a buried vale doth sleep,
Far down the torrent cleaves its way:
In front the dumb rock rises steep,
A fretted wall of blue and gray;
Of shooting cliff and crumbled stone
With many a wild weed overgrown:
All else, black water: and afloat,
One rood from shore, that single boat.

Last night the wind was up and strong;
The gray-streak'd waters labor still:
The strong blast brought a pigmy throng
From that mild hollow in the hill;
From those twin brooks, that beached strand
So featly strewn with drifted sand;
From those weird domes of mounded green
That spot the solitary scene.

This boat they found against the shore:
The glossy rushes nodded by.
One rood from land they push'd, no more;
Then rested, listening silently.
The loud rains lash'd the mountain's crown,
The grating shingle straggled down:
All night they sate; then stole away,
And left it rocking in the bay.

Last night? — I look'd, the sky was clear.
The boat was old, a batter'd boat.
In sooth, it seems a hundred year
Since that strange crew did ride afloat.
The boat hath drifted in the bay —
The oars have moulder'd as they lay —
The rudder swings — yet none doth steer.
   What living hand hath brought it here?

SONNET TO THE HUNGARIAN NATION.

EXAMINER, JULY 21, 1849.

NOT in sunk Spain's prolong'd death agony;
Not in rich England, bent but to make pour
The flood of the world's commerce on her shore;
Not in that madhouse, France, from whence the cry
Afflicts grave Heaven with its long senseless roar;
Not in American vulgarity,
Nor wordy German imbecility —
Lies any hope of heroism more.
Hungarians! Save the world! Renew the stories
Of men who against hope repell'd the chain,
And make the world's dead spirit leap again!
On land renew that Greek exploit, whose glories
Hallow the Salaminian promontories,
And the Armada flung to the fierce main.

DESTINY.

WHY each is striving, from of old,
To love more deeply than he can?
Still would be true, yet still grows cold?
— Ask of the Powers that sport with man!

They yok'd in him, for endless strife,
A heart of ice, a soul of fire;
And hurl'd him on the Field of Life,
An aimless unallay'd Desire.

COURAGE.

TRUE, we must tame our rebel will:
True, we must bow to Nature's law:
Must bear in silence many an ill;
Must learn to wail, renounce, withdraw.

Yet now, when boldest wills give place,
When Fate and Circumstance are strong,
And in their rush the human race
Are swept, like huddling sheep, along:

Those sterner spirits let me prize,
Who, though the tendence of the whole
They less than us might recognize,
Kept, more than us, their strength of soul.

Yes, be the second Cato prais'd!
Not that he took the course to die —
But that, when 'gainst himself he rais'd
His arm, he rais'd it dauntlessly.

And, Byron! let us dare admire
If not thy fierce and turbid song,
Yet that, in anguish, doubt, desire,
Thy fiery courage still was strong.

The sun that on thy tossing pain
Did with such cold derision shine,
He crush'd thee not with his disdain —
He had his glow, and thou hadst thine.

Our bane, disguise it as we may,
Is weakness, is a faltering course.
Oh that past times could give our day,
Join'd to its clearness, of their force !

THEKLA'S ANSWER.

From SCHILLER.

WHERE I am, thou ask'st, and where I wended
  When my fleeting shadow pass'd from thee ? —
Am I not concluded now, and ended ?
  Have not life and love been granted me ?

Ask, where now those nightingales are singing,
  Who, of late, on the soft nights of May,
Set thine ears with soul-fraught music ringing —
  Only, while their love liv'd, lasted they.

Find I him, for whom I had to sever ? —
  Doubt it not, we met, and we are one.
There, where what is join'd, is join'd for ever,
  There, where tears are never more to run.

There thou too shalt live with us together,
  When thou too hast borne the love we bore :
There, from sin deliver'd, dwells my Father,
  Track'd by Murder's bloody sword no more.

There he feels, it was no dream deceiving
  Lur'd him starwards to uplift his eye :
God doth match his gifts to man's believing ;
  Believe, and thou shalt find the Holy nigh.

All thou augurest here of lovely seeming
  There shall find fulfilment in its day :
Dare, O Friend, be wandering, dare be dreaming ;
  Lofty thought lies oft in childish play.

NOTES.

NOTE 1, PAGE 2.

Saw The Wide Prospect, and the Asian Fen.

The name Europe (Εὐρώπη, *the wide prospect*) probably describes the appearance of the European coast to the Greeks on the coast of Asia Minor opposite. The name Asia, again, comes, it has been thought, from the muddy fens of the rivers of Asia Minor, such as the Cayster or Mæander, which struck the imagination of the Greeks living near them.

NOTE 2, PAGE 8.

Mycerinus.

"After Chephren, Mycerinus, son of Cheops, reigned over Egypt. He abhorred his father's courses, and judged his subjects more justly than any of their kings had done. To him there came an oracle from the city of Buto, to the effect that he was to live but six years longer, and to die in the seventh year from that time." — HERODOTUS.

NOTE 3, PAGE 37.

Stagirius.

Stagirius was a young monk to whom St. Chrysostom addressed three books, and of whom those books give an account. They will be found in the first volume of the Benedictine edition of St. Chrysostom's works.

NOTE 4, PAGE 51.

That wayside inn we left to-day.

Those who have been long familiar with the English Lake Country will find no difficulty in recalling, from the description

493

in the text, the roadside inn at Wythburn, on the descent from
Dunmail Raise towards Keswick; its sedentary landlord of
thirty years ago; and the passage over the Wythburn Fells to
Watendlath.

NOTE 5, PAGE 61.

Sohrab and Rustum.

The story of Sohrab and Rustum is told in Sir John
Malcolm's " History of Persia," as follows : —

"The young Sohrab was the fruit of one of Rustum's early
amours. He had left his mother, and sought fame under the
banners of Afrasiab, whose armies he commanded; and soon
obtained a renown beyond that of all contemporary heroes but
his father. He had carried death and dismay into the ranks
of the Persians, and had terrified the boldest warriors of that
country, before Rustum encountered him, which at last that
hero resolved to do under a feigned name. They met three
times. The first time, they parted by mutual consent, though
Sohrab had the advantage; the second, the youth obtained a
victory, but granted life to his unknown father; the third was
fatal to Sohrab, who, when writhing in the pangs of death,
warned his conqueror to shun the vengeance that is inspired
by parental woes, and bade him dread the rage of the mighty
Rustum, who must soon learn that he had slain his son Sohrab.
These words, we are told, were as death to the aged hero ; and
when he recovered from a trance, he called in despair for
proofs of what Sohrab had said. The afflicted and dying
youth tore open his mail, and showed his father a seal which
his mother had placed on his arm when she discovered to him
the secret of his birth, and bade him seek his father. The
sight of his own signet rendered Rustum quite frantic: he
cursed himself, attempting to put an end to his existence, and
was only prevented by the efforts of his expiring son. After
Sohrab's death, he burned his tents and all his goods, and carried the corpse to Seistan, where it was interred; the army of
Turan was, agreeably to the last request of Sohrab, permitted
to cross the Oxus unmolested. To reconcile us to the improb-
ability of this tale, we are informed that Rustum could have
no idea his son was in existence. The mother of Sohrab had
written to him her child was a daughter, fearing to lose her

darling infant if she revealed the truth; and Rustum, as before stated, fought under a feigned name, an usage not uncommon in the chivalrous combats of those days."

NOTE 6, PAGE 96.

Balder Dead.

"Balder the Good having been tormented with terrible dreams, indicating that his life was in great peril, communicated them to the assembled Æsir, who resolved to conjure all things to avert from him the threatened danger. Then Frigga exacted an oath from fire and water, from iron and all other metals, as well as from stones, earths, diseases, beasts, birds, poisons, and creeping things, that none of them would do any harm to Balder. When this was done, it became a favorite pastime of the Æsir, at their meetings, to get Balder to stand up and serve them as a mark, some hurling darts at him, some stones, while others hewed at him with their swords and battle-axes; for, do they what they would, none of them could harm him, and this was regarded by all as a great honor shown to Balder. But when Loki beheld the scene, he was sorely vexed that Balder was not hurt. Assuming, therefore, the shape of a woman, he went to Fensalir, the mansion of Frigga. That goddess, when she saw the pretended woman, inquired of her if she knew what the Æsir were doing at their meetings. She replied, that they were throwing darts and stones at Balder without being able to hurt him.

"'Ay,' said Frigga, 'neither metal nor wood can hurt Balder, for I have exacted an oath from all of them.'

"'What!' exclaimed the woman, 'have all things sworn to spare Balder?'

"'All things,' replied Frigga, 'except one little shrub that grows on the eastern side of Valhalla, and is called Mistletoe, and which I thought too young and feeble to crave an oath from.'

"As soon as Loki heard this, he went away, and, resuming his natural shape, cut off the mistletoe, and repaired to the place where the gods were assembled. There he found Hödur standing apart, without partaking of the sports, on account of his blindness; and going up to him said, 'Why dost thou not also throw something at Balder?'

" 'Because I am blind,' answered Hödur, 'and see not where Balder is, and have, moreover, nothing to throw with.'

" 'Come, then,' said Loki, 'do like the rest, and show honor to Balder by throwing this twig at him, and I will direct thy arm toward the place where he stands.'

" Hödur then took the mistletoe, and, under the guidance of Loki, darted it at Balder, who, pierced through and through, fell down lifeless." — *Edda.*

NOTE 7, PAGE 133.

Tristram and Iseult.

" In the court of his uncle King Marc, the king of Cornwall, who at this time resided at the castle of Tyntagel, Tristram became expert in all knightly exercises. The king of Ireland, at Tristram's solicitations, promised to bestow his daughter Iseult in marriage on King Marc. The mother of Iseult gave to her daughter's confidante a philtre, or love-potion, to be administered on the night of her nuptials. Of this beverage Tristram and Iseult, on their voyage to Cornwall, unfortunately partook. Its influence, during the remainder of their lives, regulated the affections and destiny of the lovers.

" After the arrival of Tristram and Iseult in Cornwall, and the nuptials of the latter with King Marc, a great part of the romance is occupied with their contrivances to procure secret interviews. — Tristram, being forced to leave Cornwall on account of the displeasure of his uncle, repaired to Brittany, where lived Iseult with the White Hands. He married her, more out of gratitude than love. Afterwards he proceeded to the dominions of Arthur, which became the theatre of unnumbered exploits.

" Tristram, subsequent to these events, returned to Brittany, and to his long-neglected wife. There, being wounded and sick, he was soon reduced to the lowest ebb. In this situation, he dispatched a confidant to the queen of Cornwall, to try if he could induce her to accompany him to Brittany," etc. — DUNLOP's *History of Fiction.*

NOTE 8, PAGE 169.

That son of Italy who tried to blow.

Giacopone di Todi.

NOTE 9, PAGE 174.

Recalls the obscure opposer he outweighed.

Gilbert de la Porrée, at the Council of Rheims in 1148.

NOTE 10, PAGE 175.

Of that unpitying Phrygian sect which cried.

The Montanists.

NOTE 11, PAGE 176.

Monica.

See St. Augustine's "Confessions," book ix. chapter 11.

NOTE 12, PAGE 177.

My Marguerite smiles upon the strand.

See, among "Early Poems," the poem called "A Memory-Picture," p. 23.

NOTE 13, PAGE 201.

The Hunter of the Tanagræan Field.

Orion, the Wild Huntsman of Greek legend, and in this capacity appearing in both earth and sky.

NOTE 14, PAGE 202.

O'er the sun-reddened western straits.

Erytheia, the legendary region around the Pillars of Hercules, probably took its name from the redness of the west, under which the Greeks saw it.

NOTE 15, PAGE 224.

Of the sun-loving gentian, in the heat.

The *gentiana lutea.*

NOTE 16, PAGE 248.

Ye Sun-born Virgins! on the road of truth.

See the Fragments of Parmenides: —

. . . κοῦραι δ' ὁδὸν ἡγεμόνευον,
ἡλιάδες κοῦραι, προλιποῦσαι δώματα νυκτός,
εἰς φάος. . . . .

Note 17, Page 381.

The Scholar-Gypsy.

"There was very lately a lad in the University of Oxford, who was by his poverty forced to leave his studies there; and at last to join himself to a company of vagabond gypsies. Among these extravagant people, by the insinuating subtilty of his carriage, he quickly got so much of their love and esteem as that they discovered to him their mystery. After he had been a pretty while exercised in the trade, there chanced to ride by a couple of scholars, who had formerly been of his acquaintance. They quickly spied out their old friend among the gypsies; and he gave them an account of the necessity which drove him to that kind of life, and told them that the people he went with were not such impostors as they were taken for, but that they had a traditional kind of learning among them, and could do wonders by the power of imagination, their fancy binding that of others; that himself had learned much of their art, and when he had compassed the whole secret, he intended, he said, to leave their company, and give the world an account of what he had learned." — GLANVIL'S *Vanity of Dogmatizing*, 1661.

Note 18, Page 389.

Thyrsis.

Throughout this poem there is reference to the preceding piece, "The Scholar-Gypsy."

Note 19, Page 395.

Young Daphnis with his silver voice doth sing.

Daphnis, the ideal Sicilian shepherd of Greek pastoral poetry, was said to have followed into Phrygia his mistress Piplea, who had been carried off by robbers, and to have found her in the power of the king of Phrygia, Lityerses. Lityerses used to make strangers try a contest with him in reaping corn, and to put them to death if he overcame them. Hercules arrived in time to save Daphnis, took upon himself the reaping-contest with Lityerses, overcame him, and slew him. The Lityerses-song connected with this tradition was, like the

Linus-song, one of the early plaintive strains of Greek popular poetry, and used to be sung by corn-reapers. Other traditions represented Daphnis as beloved by a nymph who exacted from him an oath to love no one else. He fell in love with a princess, and was struck blind by the jealous nymph. Mercury, who was his father, raised him to heaven, and made a fountain spring up in the place from which he ascended. At this fountain the Sicilians offered yearly sacrifices. See SERVIUS, *Comment. in Virgil. Bucol.*, v. 20 and viii. 68.

NOTE 20, PAGE 402.

Ah! where is he, who should have come.

The author's brother, William Delafield Arnold, Director of Public Instruction in the Punjab, and author of "Oakfield, or Fellowship in the East," died at Gibraltar, on his way home from India, April the 9th, 1859.

NOTE 21, PAGE 403.

So moonlit, saw me once of yore.

See the poem, "A Summer Night," p. 280.

NOTE 22, PAGE 403.

My brother! and thine early lot.

See Note 20.

NOTE 23, PAGE 407.

*I saw the meeting of two
Gifted women.*

Charlotte Brontë and Harriet Martineau.

NOTE 24, PAGE 410.

Whose too bold dying song.

See the last lines written by Emily Brontë, in "Poems by Currer, Ellis, and Acton Bell."

NOTE 25, PAGE 424.

Goethe too had been there.

See *Harzreise im Winter*, in Goethe's *Gedichte*.

Note 26, Page 432.

The author of *Obermann*, Étienne Pivert de Senancour, has little celebrity in France, his own country; and out of France he is almost unknown. But the profound inwardness, the austere sincerity, of his principal work, *Obermann*, the delicate feeling for nature which it exhibits, and the melancholy eloquence of many passages of it, have attracted and charmed some of the most remarkable spirits of this century, such as George Sand and Sainte-Beuve, and will probably always find a certain number of spirits whom they touch and interest.

Senancour was born in 1770. He was educated for the priesthood, and passed some time in the Seminary of St. Sulpice; broke away from the seminary and from France itself, and passed some years in Switzerland, where he married; returned to France in middle life, and followed thenceforward the career of a man of letters, but with hardly any fame or success. He died an old man in 1846, desiring that on his grave might be placed these words only : *Éternité, deviens mon asile !*

The influence of Rousseau, and certain affinities with more famous and fortunate authors of his own day, — Chateaubriand and Madame de Staël, — are everywhere visible in Senancour. But though, like these eminent personages, he may be called a sentimental writer, and though *Obermann*, a collection of letters from Switzerland treating almost entirely of nature and of the human soul, may be called a work of sentiment, Senancour has a gravity and severity which distinguish him from all other writers of the sentimental school. The world is with him in his solitude far less than it is with them ; of all writers he is the most perfectly isolated and the least attitudinizing. His chief work, too, has a value and power of its own, apart from these merits of its author. The stir of all the main forces by which modern life is and has been impelled lives in the letters of *Obermann ;* the dissolving agencies of the eighteenth century, the fiery storm of the French Revolution, the first faint promise and dawn of that new world which our own time is but now fully bringing to light, — all these are to be felt, almost to be touched, there. To me, indeed, it will always seem that the impressiveness of this production can hardly be rated too high.

Besides *Obermann*, there is one other of Senancour's works

which, for those spirits who feel his attraction, is very interesting : its title is *Libres Méditations d'un Solitaire Inconnu.*

NOTE 27, PAGE 432.

Behind are the abandoned baths.

The Baths of Leuk. This poem was conceived, and partly composed, in the valley going down from the foot of the Gemmi Pass towards the Rhone.

NOTE 28, PAGE 438.

Glion? Ah'! twenty years, it cuts.

Probably all who know the Vevey end of the Lake of Geneva will recollect Glion, the mountain village above the Castle of Chillon. Glion now has hotels, *pensions*, and villas; but twenty years ago it was hardly more than the huts of Avant opposite to it, — huts through which goes that beautiful path over the Col de Jaman, followed by so many foot-travellers on their way from Vevey to the Simmenthal and Thun.

NOTE 29, PAGE 439.

The gentian-flowered pass, its crown.

See Note 15.

NOTE 30, PAGE 439.

And walls where Byron came.

Montbovon. See Byron's Journal, in his "Works," vol. iii. p. 258. The river Saane becomes the Sarine below Montbovon.

NOTE 31, PAGE 451.

Couldst thou no better keep, O Abbey old,
The boon thy dedication-sign foretold.

"Ailred of Rievaulx, and several other writers, assert that Sebert, king of the East Saxons and nephew of Ethelbert, founded the Abbey of Westminster very early in the seventh century.

"Sulcardus, who lived in the time of William the Conqueror, gives a minute account of the miracle supposed to have been worked at the consecration of the Abbey.

"The church had been prepared against the next day for dedication. On the night preceding, St. Peter appeared on the opposite side of the water to a fisherman, desiring to be conveyed to the farther shore. Having left the boat, St. Peter ordered the fisherman to wait, promising him a reward on his return. An innumerable host from heaven accompanied the apostle, singing choral hymns, while everything was illuminated with a supernatural light. The dedication having been completed, St. Peter returned to the fisherman, quieted his alarm at what had passed, and announced himself as the apostle. He directed the fisherman to go as soon as it was day to the authorities, to state what he had seen and heard, and to inform them that, in corroboration of his testimony, they would find the marks of consecration on the walls of the church. In obedience to the apostle's direction, the fisherman waited on Mellitus, Bishop of London, who, going to the church, found not only marks of the chrism, but of the tapers with which the church had been illuminated. Mellitus, therefore, desisted from proceeding to a new consecration, and contented himself with the celebration of the mass." — DUGDALE, *Monasticon Anglicanum* (edition of 1817), vol. i. pp. 265, 266. See also MONTALEMBERT, *Les Moines d' Occident*, vol. iii. pp. 428–432.

NOTE 32, PAGE 454.

The charm'd babe of the Eleusinian king.

Demophoön, son of Celeus, king of Eleusis. See, in the *Homeric Hymns*, the *Hymn to Demeter*, 184–298.

NOTE 33, PAGE 455.

That Pair, whose head did plan, whose hands did forge
The Temple in the pure Parnassian gorge.

Agamedes and Trophonius, the builders of the temple of Apollo at Delphi. See PLUTARCH, *Consolatio ad Apollonium*, c. 14.

NOTE 34, PAGE 465.

Stol'n from Aristophanes.

See *The Birds* of Aristophanes, 465–485.

NOTE 35, PAGE 467.

Of Robin's reed.

"Come, join the melancholious croon
O' Robin's reed." — BURNS, *Poor Mailie's Elegy.*